MW00355354

Colonial Kinship

Colonial Kinship

Guaraní, Spaniards, and Africans in Paraguay

SHAWN MICHAEL AUSTIN

University of New Mexico Press | Albuquerque

Library of Congress Cataloging-in-Publication Data
Names: Austin, Shawn Michael, author.
Title: Colonial kinship: Guaraní, Spaniards, and Africans in Paraguay /
    Shawn Michael Austin.
Description: Albuquerque: University of New Mexico Press, 2020. |
    Includes bibliographical references and index.
Identifiers: LCCN 2020016908 (print) | LCCN 2020016909 (e-book) |
    ISBN 9780826361967 (cloth) | ISBN 9780826361974 (e-book)
Subjects: LCSH: Franciscans—Missions—Paraguay. | Guarani Indians—History. |
    Guarani Indians—Social conditions. | Kinship—Paraguay—History. | Encomiendas
    (Latin America)—History. | Cultural fusion—Paraguay. | Guarani Indians—Missions—
    Paraguay—History. | Slavery—Paraguay—History.
Classification: LCC F2230.2. G72 A87 2020 (print) | LCC F2230.2. G72 (e-book) |
    DDC 305.898/3822—dc23
LC record available at https://lccn.loc.gov/2020016908
LC e-book record available at https://lccn.loc.gov/2020016909

Cover illustration courtesy of Vecteezy.com
Designed by Felica Cedillos

Composed in Minion Pro 10.25/14.25

For Patrice and Mark Austin
&
for Camille—
with love and gratitude

CONTENTS

ILLUSTRATIONS

Figures

Maps

Tables

ACKNOWLEDGMENTS

My kin have been the greatest champions of this book. The person deserving of my deepest gratitude is Camille, whose love and encouragement made the process joyful and rich. My children Annie, Ethan, Richard, and Lucas have also been a source inspiration. Over the years, each child has innocently asked "when daddy is going to finish his book," and those queries kept me going when the going was tough. My parents, Patrice and Mark Austin, encouraged me to pursue lofty and exciting goals and I will be forever indebted to them for their support during graduate school and beyond. My in-laws, Christine and Robert Heywood, cheered me on at every turn. Thank you.

I began work on this book as a graduate student at the University of New Mexico nearly a decade ago and have accumulated many debts over the years. Core ideas in this book had their genesis in Judy Bieber's graduate seminar, and her support at the outset was crucial. My dissertation chair, Kimberly Gauderman, has been an intellectual anchor and a source of resolve. Kymm patiently and graciously took me on as a student after I transitioned out of a project on modern Paraguay and gave unflagging support for my research, despite its "fringe" status! Elizabeth Hutchison has been an honest mentor from the beginning and provided crucial support at key moments in my career. Les Field helped me build competency in ethnohistory and his graduate seminar, "Theory in Ethnology," was instrumental in shaping my approaches to writing about indigenous peoples. Timothy Graham and Mike Ryan provided critical training and support in paleography at the earliest stages of my research. The Mellon Foundation and the Newberry Library further propelled my paleography skills through the Summer Institute, led by the wonderful Carla Rahn Phillips. A special thanks to the

Latin American & Iberian Institute at UNM and the Tinker Foundation for their financial support.

Colleagues and funding committees at the University of Arkansas were generous supporters. Laurence Hare commented on several iterations of my work and patiently helped me refine ideas in across-the-hall conversations. Two different departmental chairs, Calvin White and Jim Gigantino, were wonderful mentors, and I could always count on administrative specialists Brenda Foster and Melinda Adams to process travel and funding requests. My Latin Americanist colleagues, especially Kirstin Erickson and Kathryn Sloan, were frequent sources of encouragement and positivity. The E. Mitchell and Barbara Singleton Endowed Faculty Award and the Robert C. and Sandra Connor Endowed Faculty Fellowship provided much-needed financial support.

Colleagues in the United States, South America, and Europe provided expert commentary on chapters and ideas. Kris Lane served on my dissertation committee and his suggestions were always spot on. During the initial phase of this project, Suzanne Oakdale helped me work through Tupí-Guaraní kinship, and as ideas evolved she was a reliable sounding board. After stumbling across a number of Guaraní-language passages in civil and criminal records, Carlos Fausto, the late Bartomeu Melià, Leonardo Cerno, Michael Huner, and Mickaël Orantin all generously lent their language expertise. Argentine scholars Guillermo Wilde, Ignacio Telesca, and María Laura Salinas each read iterations of my work or responded to my queries over the years. Julia Sarreal has been a good friend and provided expert advice between conference sessions. Thanks to Zeb Tortorici for offering feedback on the book's title. Participants of the Indigenous Borderlands of the Americas Symposium at Texas State University in 2018, the Southwest Seminar: Consortium on Colonial Latin America in 2017, and the Río de la Plata Working Group in 2017 and 2014 gave crucial feedback. Other scholars who have had a direct impact on my work over the years include Barbara Ganson, Brian Owensby, Kittiya Lee, Thom Whigham, Pedro Miguel Omar Svriz Wucherer, Laura Fahrenkrog, Capucine Boidin, Thomas Brignon, Laura Matthews, and Guillaume Candela. Thank you all.

I conducted research for this book at archives in Paraguay, Argentina,

Bolivia, Spain, and the United States, and the archivists and staff at each of these locales patiently guided me into the sources. Vicente Arrúa Ávalos at the Archivo Nacional de Asunción offered archival guidance and research tools without which this project would have failed. I also thank the archivists and staff at the Archivo General de Indias, the Archivo y Biblioteca Nacional de Bolivia, the Archivo General de la Nación in Buenos Aires, the Newberry Library in Chicago, and the Benson Latin American Library at the University of Texas at Austin. Suzanne Schadl at UNM Libraries was an incredible ally, facilitating the purchase of microfilm copies of civil documentation from Paraguay. A special thanks to my friend Marcos José Marmol and his family, who provided me with a home away from home while I conducted research in Asunción.

Thanks to Aaron Taylor, who provided transcription services for several censuses, and Gabe Moss, who produced the maps for this book. Chapters 2 and 3 are adaptations of previously published pieces, and I thank *Colonial Latin American Review* and the University of Arizona Press for permission to republish them. I thank the professionals at UNM Press, especially Sonia Dickey, for their patience with me and their careful handling of my manuscript. Finally, I'm grateful to the two anonymous reviewers for their candid and invaluable feedback on my manuscript.

GLOSSARY

bandeira: Slaving expedition from São Paulo
cacique: A term of Caribbean origins meaning "indigenous leader"
corregidor: Top *indio* official in a *reducción*
criada/o: Servant
guará: A group of *teko'a*
karaí: Spiritual specialist who is renowned and mobile
mandamiento: Governor-mandated infrastructure projects that rely on *indio* labor
mburuvichá: Supravillage leader
mita: Rotational labor draft
mitayo/a: *Indio* who pays the mita
monteses: A Spanish term for unconquered Natives who live in the forests
originario: A term that replaced *yanacona* and described an encomienda *indio/a* who resided permanently with *españoles*
pajé: Spiritual specialist
teko'a: Grouping of villages or a single village will multiple *teyÿ*
teyÿ: Extended kin group or lineage
tovajá: Originally "brother-in-law," but in the colonial context came to imply all male-male, *español*-Guaraní affinal kinship relationships
tuvichá: Leader of a village or lineage
yanacona: A term of Andean origins that in Paraguay describes an encomienda *india/o* who resides permanently with *españoles*

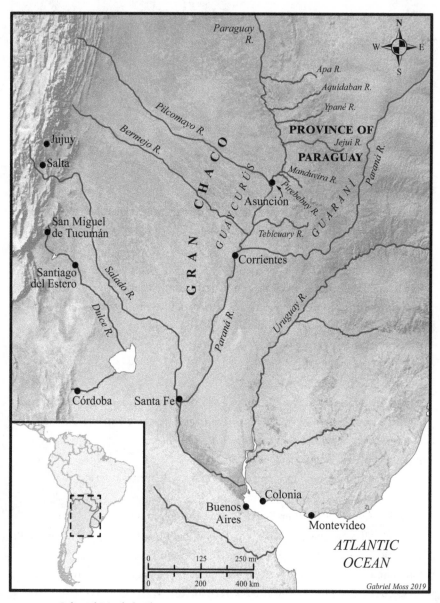

MAP 1. Colonial Río de la Plata

Introduction

A little more than kin, and less than kind.

—SHAKESPEARE, *HAMLET*, 1.2.67

"HE IS OUR kin."[1] Nearly a century after Spaniards had established a colonial presence in Paraguay, a Guaraní Indian speaking through a translator said this about his Spanish encomendero (a grantee of Indian tribute), but according to Western notions of kinship, this encomendero was not a relative to his Indians. What is more, encomenderos unequivocally exploited Guaraní for their labor and sometimes physically abused them, behaviors we would not expect from family. Nonetheless, this Guaraní, as well as other Guaraní throughout the colonial period, regularly described their encomenderos as relatives. Even more surprising is the fact that encomenderos frequently used Guaraní kinship terminology to describe the Guaraní who served them. *Colonial Kinship* makes sense of the ways that kinship and colonialism intertwined in Paraguay. It explores the nuances of colonialism and the multidirectional nature of cultural change and describes the early evolution of Guaraní ethnic communities in the Spanish city of Asunción and in Indian mission towns or *reducciones* from the 1530s to the turn of the eighteenth century. While disease, Catholic evangelization, and Spanish labor demands collectively precipitated transformative social and cultural changes among Guaraní, Guaraní forever changed Spaniards and their colonial institutions. When conquistadors arrived in Paraguay in 1537, Guaraní adopted them as brothers-in-law. Conquistadors drew on these brothers-in-law networks to acquire female "wives" who labored for them and who became their sexual partners and victims. In this confluence of coercion and cooperation, Guaraní transformed the newcomers into polygamous conquistadors.

The scholarship on Guaraní peoples subject to the Spanish encomienda has characterized their experiences as slave-like, but this assumes that the experience of servitude was universal and ignores the ways that indigenous patterns informed colonial practice. All forms of servitude and coerced service must be understood in its local context. In treating indigenous slavery in colonial New Mexico, James Brooks outlines a "borderland kinship" in which slaves moved in and out of New Mexican and Native households within networks of violent capture, trade, godparentage, or inheritance.[2] In the case of Guaraní, colonial tribute was a continuum that embraced degrees of coercion and nuanced gradations of "relatedness" borrowed from several cultural contexts.[3] The paradigm of exchange in Paraguay, therefore, is not an example of what James Lockhart calls double mistaken identity, "in which each side of the cultural exchange presumes that a given form or concept is functioning in the way familiar within its own tradition and is unaware of or unimpressed by the other side's interpretation."[4] Even if they were anxious about it, most conquistadors knew what they were doing when they became kin to Guaraní communities. Moreover, the conquistador society's rapid adoption of the Guaraní language precluded it from remaining ignorant of the cultural meanings of these exchanges. In this way, colonials willingly transposed the Guaraní social meanings of polygamy, or what Spaniards saw as a kind of concubinage, onto a colonial institution for tribute extraction, the encomienda. But even as encomenderos relied on polygamous Guaraní social organization to channel women to affinal kin, priests labored to eradicate it and enforce monogamy. The result was that by the 1640s, an encomienda system emerged that phased out direct kinship between conquistadors and Guaraní but was nonetheless bound together by an ideology of relatedness.

This book tells a story of how kinship became enmeshed with colonial governance. The Guaraní man cited at the opening of this chapter who identified his encomendero as his kin is an important example for it is a snapshot of Spanish-Guaraní relations within the encomienda after the institution had matured. The Guaraní's statement was recorded on March 11, 1652, during a *visita* or inspection of encomienda Indians in the small city of Villa

Rica del Espíritu Santo, on Paraguay's eastern borderland with Portuguese Brazil. On that day, the town bustled with activity and anticipation as encomenderos and Guaraní servant-tributaries entered the plaza and waited to see the official, Juan de Ibarra Velasco, inside the church. Once the visita got underway, an encomendero named Juan Cristaldo and the four Guaraní of his encomienda were called up. Ibarra Velasco instructed the encomendero to step outside in order to take the Indians' true account of his behavior, without fear of retribution. The official spoke over the sound of the notary's incessant scribbling to encourage the Guaraní to speak the truth and not withhold any information that might be seen as damaging to their encomendero. After these assurances, the official proceeded to ask the Guaraní men if Cristaldo paid them sufficiently and gave them Sundays and feast days to rest or if he physically abused them. If there was ever a chance to complain about maltreatment under the Spanish labor regime this was the moment—many Guaraní who had been mistreated did not hesitate to voice their grievances. But on this day, the four Guaraní had nothing negative to report about their encomendero. In their native tongue and with the help of a translator they explained that they were "very content" with their encomendero for "he is our kin, [and] treats us like brothers-in-law."[5] They further explained that their encomendero "divides what he has with us," suggesting that material benefits were important to the tributary-kinship relationship.

The brother-in-law (*tovajá*) relationship in Guaraní society was important because it was the primary way of incorporating outsiders into a kinship group and it implied reciprocal benefits. During the colonial period, *tovajá* acquired new meaning. In one of the first Spanish histories about Paraguay, Ruy Díaz de Guzmán (of Spanish and Guaraní descent), writing around 1612, noted that since the conquest era, conquistadors and their descendants used the word *tovajá* to refer to the Indians of their encomiendas.[6] Spaniards' use of Guaraní kinship terminology was just the tip of the iceberg and represented a long historical experience whereby transliterated Guaraní modes of kinship were applied to colonial systems of tribute. Around the same time that de Guzmán composed his history, a Jesuit priest, writing anonymously to his superiors about the peculiar arrangement between Guaraní and Spaniards, concluded that "the founding [of Asunción] was completed more by means of *cuñadasgo* than by conquest."

The neologism *cuñadasgo* is an elaboration on the word *cuñado* (brother-in-law) and meant something like "brother-in-law-ship."[7] All of this suggests that in order to understand colonial relations in Paraguay, kinship must be redefined.

Historians and anthropologists have theorized kinship in a variety of contexts and their work suggests that universal binaries of social versus biological constructions of kinship are arbitrary.[8] For example, many people use the term *fictive kinship* when describing any nonbiological relationship that is kinship-like, but the term is misleading, for there is nothing imaginary about the relationship—the relational sinews are real. Helen Lambert explains that there are indeed "social connections between persons that are collectively recognized and regarded as enduring, as extending beyond individual interpersonal relationships, and as carrying rights and responsibilities associated with being related."[9] In lieu of *fictive kinship,* Janet Carsten recommends the term *relatedness* to describe these kinds of associations. The term *relatedness* certainly describes some kinship dynamics among Iñupiat peoples of Northern Alaska, where anthropologist Barbara Bodenhorn shows individuals move in and out of kinship relationships depending on the care with which they maintain those relationships, either by virtue of material offerings or emotional investment—kinship requires work.[10] Relatedness also can be applied to the colonial world. Jane Mangan notes for colonial Peru that the family could be defined as any combination of a family tree, bloodlines, kinship ties, god-parentage, and households.[11] Extended family networks in large households included not only blood relatives but servants, tributaries, and slaves.

Bringing these insights to bear on colonial Paraguay, *Colonial Kinship* explains how Guaraní and Spanish modes of relatedness were transposed onto colonial sociality. Guaraní kinship combined with early-modern Spanish notions of the expansive family to inform a communal valuation of relatedness, or what the anonymous Jesuit called "cuñadasgo." Exploring the construction of these categories and the processes by which they came into being requires seeing colonialism in a new light. Conquistadors are often remembered as agents of violence and afflictions on indigenous communities, and this they were. But colonials also fostered relationships with subjugated groups.[12] This book asks how it was possible for Spaniards and Guaraní to call each other tovajá or brothers-in-law while simultaneously operating within a colonial paradigm of coercion.

Beyond the Missions

Historians and ethnohistorians have generally studied Guaraní in colonial Paraguay from the perspective of either the Jesuit or the Franciscan religious orders, with far greater emphasis on the former. This book takes a different methodological tack. Rather than studying Guaraní under a specific religious umbrella (a paradigm that certainly has its merits) and solely within mission towns, *Colonial Kinship* focuses on Guaraní in contexts of contact and exchange with *españoles*, Africans, and people of mixed descent in reducciones and in Spanish cities, especially the provincial capital of Asunción. Many Guaraní moved "in between" the reducciones: residing with their encomenderos during periods of labor service, deciding on their own to leave and reside elsewhere, changing reducciones, or relocating because of frontier violence. Centering on Guaraní outside and in between the Jesuit missions demonstrates that colonial Guaraní culture was not a phenomenon unique to the reducciones.

This does not mean that reducciones were unimportant; rather, it means that many reducciones were permeable and imbricated with cuñadasgo. William Hanks shows that the noun *reducción* and the verb *reducir(se)* reflected a colonial vision of cultural change. To *reducir(se)* was to be convinced, converted, or put in better order. The meaning of *reducción* as a colonial practice, then, was more than simply settling Indians into communities but involved changing their characters, their societies, and even their languages to adhere to Catholic-Spanish values.[13] In the minds of many colonial administrators and priests, reducciones were more than Indian towns; they were carefully planned "republic-utopias" that would generate Indian-Christian civilization.[14] The crown promoted the reducción as the privileged site of Indian sociocultural identity and feared that Guaraní outside the reducción would degenerate, lose their Indian tribute status, and fail to cultivate Catholic virtues. To deflect criticism from crown officials, encomenderos and Guaraní alike applied "reducción" to the encomienda and cuñadasgo.

This methodology hinges on an incredible body of historical work. It is no wonder that scholars have focused on the Jesuit mission enterprise: at their apogee in 1732, the Jesuits oversaw thirty reducciones totaling 141,182 Indians, compared with Franciscan and secular reducciones from a similar period, which totaled eighteen with around 20,000 individuals.[15] The demographic strength of the Guaraní-Jesuit reducciones especially was evidence that reducción was a success. Demographically, the Jesuit missions are compelling, but a kind of institutional "tunnel vision" characterizes early studies, which draw primarily on Jesuit sources and channel Jesuit perspectives.[16] These works provide accounts of Jesuit political and economic prowess in the Río de la Plata but rarely consider how Guaraní were agents in the construction of the missions.[17] More recently, scholars have paid greater attention to indigenous perspectives, focusing on Guaraní cultural change.[18] Emphasizing the power of Guaraní in their interethnic encounters, others demonstrate that priests deployed Guaraní modes of spiritual and political authority in order to attract adherents. The reducciones inhabited a liminal space in which Guaraní religion and Christianity mirrored each other: priests became shamans, shamans became priests.[19] Linguists and anthropologists have examined Guaraní-language records to understand Guaraní expressions of power and political identity.[20] Others find indigenous actors at the center of the mission economies and reveal that the Jesuits were not effective in creating communistic paradises but that Guaraní worked out their own rhythms of daily life in the missions.[21] Scholars' attention to indigenous leadership in the reducciones has revealed the interplay between imperial imperatives and ethnogenesis. Under the influence of Jesuits and Spanish officials, an indigenous leadership structure developed that only partially paralleled the cultural practice of leadership. Thus, there was plenty of disagreement among Guaraní populations over how to manage the reducción communities and differing levels of dedication to mission work and life.[22] Historical work on the period after the Jesuit expulsion in 1767 up to independence has revealed the many ways Guaraní responded to Bourbon liberal policies and sweeping political changes, which included degrees of cooperation, resistance, and migration.[23]

A much smaller body of work describes the Guaraní-Franciscan reducciones in the region of Asunción. Similar to the Jesuit literature, much of the scholarship on the Guaraní-Franciscan reducciones is written from an institutional perspective.[24] Breaking from this trend, Luis Necker's *Indios Guaraníes y chamanes franciscanos* (1990) provides an anthropological perspective, arguing that Guaraní were converted to the power of the priest, not to Christianity, and therefore maintained many of their beliefs.[25] Necker contends that Franciscans were successful where conquistadors failed because Guaraní saw them as legitimate religious and political authorities. Only a handful of scholars have analyzed the Guaraní-Franciscan reducciones from an economic and/or comparative perspective, leaving much to be understood about the productive activities of individual pueblos.[26] While a study of Franciscans and the reducciones they supported is a worthy goal, the dearth of institutional records severely limits historical scholarship. Not only is gaining access to Franciscan archives difficult, Franciscans in the colonial period were neglectful archivists.[27] For example, baptismal and marriage records from the Franciscan reducciones are not extant and priestly communications, reports, and chronicles are few.

Scholarship that treats the Guaraní outside institutional frameworks is generally anthropological but typically charts a narrative of indigenous declension.[28] Working from a structuralist paradigm, a large body of scholarship explores Tupí-Guaraní cultural change, putting modern anthropologies of Tupí-Guaraní in communication with both Spanish and Portuguese colonial sources.[29] Focusing on the regional economy, Juan Carlos Garavaglia's *Mercado interno y economía colonial* is a landmark in the historiography and provides a richly documented account of the effects of the encomienda and the yerba maté (a local tea) economy on Guaraní.[30] Still other scholars have revisited the conquest period, drawing on the anthropological literature to consider Guaraní perspectives on the early colonial system as well as transcultural modes of colonization.[31]

This book examines Guaraní in a variety of contexts at different times, but it is anchored in a study of Guaraní subject to encomenderos in Asunción. Until 1617, the Río de la Plata had been one large province subject to the Audiencia of Charcas, but in that year it was divided into three provinces: Paraguay, the Río de la Plata, and Tucumán, each with a governor and officers of the royal treasury. Asunción was the "mother city" of the Río de la Plata, providing a platform from which conquests were launched in the "relay" fashion.[32] Its geographic position and history as the first conquistador city make Asunción an ideal location for studying Guaraní. As the hub for the legal and juridical management of the region, the city and its society generated litigation, wills, censuses, sales, registers, petitions, and official correspondence, providing rich descriptions of interethnic relations in the region. The most underutilized of these records in the scholarship is litigation. This book draws on nearly 350 heretofore unexamined litigation files from Asunción and Villa Rica as well as hundreds of other sociohistorical records to provide an account of social relations and cultural change. Whereas previous narratives have emphasized Spanish violence, litigation reveals Guaraní actively negotiating, contesting, and cooperating with Spaniards. Importantly, litigation also uncovers Guaraní voices in the form of complaints, defenses, and depositions.

In this rich body of documentation, we hear individuals who have remained relatively silent in the priestly sources: women. As the link between Guaraní and Spanish sociopolitical worlds, crucial laborers, and mothers to the second generation of mestizo conquistadors, Guaraní women played a vital role in the history of Paraguay. Like Ross Hassig's study of Aztec marriages, *Colonial Kinship* asserts that Guaraní women were the "dark matter" of Guaraní colonial history.[33] The dearth of research on Guaraní women is largely a result of the emphasis on male authority in the ecclesiastical records, for when priests commented on women they often did so with great moral anxiety.[34] Fixated on eliminating the practice of polygyny and creating a male leadership structure in the reducciones, priests rarely commented on women.[35] By contrast, Spaniards were constantly in contact with women as sexual partners, personal servants, and political allies. Litigation reveals that encomenderos fought among each other for access to Guaraní women and demonstrates that they were the linchpin of the labor regime until the mid-seventeenth century. As Guaraní societies experienced changes in the reducciones, men replaced women as the primary agriculturalists. Even so, women continued to be counted in censuses and were, by all accounts, tributaries, serving in Spanish households as domestics or as producers of cotton. The transformation of labor norms among Guaraní was a gendered process influenced by both Spanish and Guaraní cultural logics.

Apart from constituting a crucial source for the construction of a social history of Guaraní, litigation records provide insights into colonial

Paraguay's linguistic dynamics. Most Spaniards learned Guaraní and Spanish while very few Guaraní learned Spanish. The Guaraní and Tupí languages were similar enough that Jesuits concluded it was an indigenous lingua franca. Priests seized on this and promoted Guaraní above any other indigenous language they encountered in the region; therefore, the reducciones helped to produce a colonial Guaraní language. Of the Guaraní language spoken in the missions, Bartomeu Melià notes that it stopped being an indigenous language but continued being the language of the Indians. The Guaraní language that evolved in Asunción, spoken by Spaniards, also changed. Writing disparagingly of Spaniards, one Jesuit claimed that the Guaraní spoken by españoles was "gobbledygook" while the Guaraní spoken in the missions was more refined.[36] Albeit modified and regionally diverse, Guaraní became the lingua franca among Natives in the reducciones as well as among creole españoles, mestizos, and even blacks. The dominance of the modified Guaraní language created more common cultural ground between españoles and Guaraní and ironically created a situation in which españoles became the most important cultural intermediaries.[37] Thus, cuñadasgo cannot be separated from Paraguay's bilingualism. It was through the Guaraní language that encomenderos forged tovajá relationships with Guaraní chieftains. Their fluency in Guaraní led many Spaniards to coordinate directly with Guaraní instead of relying on intermediaries. When Spaniards did employ intermediaries, these were usually Guaraní-speaking españoles. With so much Guaraní being spoken, there was also a significant amount of ink spilled in the Guaraní language, but much of this writing was produced under the auspices of the Jesuits or by Jesuits themselves.[38] This book, therefore, does not provide in-depth analysis of Guaraní-language sources, though there are exceptions to this rule. The Jesuit dictionaries and lexicons provide invaluable ethnohistorical insights into Guaraní cultural concepts such as love, vengeance, and kinship. Moreover, litigation records reveal rare and precious snippets of the Guaraní language before it took on modified forms in the reducciones.

Drawing on heretofore unused sources, this book shines a light on Guaraní who resided in Asunción and in reducciones that became subject to the encomienda and were in frequent contact with Spanish society. These Guaraní have not been as attractive in the historiography perhaps because their indigeneity has been suspect. Garavaglia, for example, argues that to be "indio" was to be tied to an español through labor obligations.[39] This was true in many ways, but "indio" was also a corporate category created by Spanish law that provided Natives with special privileges and protections. Thanks to the work of Garavaglia and others, we have a good sense of the labor demands on "indios," but this book asks how *indios* were also Guaraní. The result is a portrait of Guaraní cultural change over nearly two centuries that takes account of the dramatic changes Guaraní experienced and how they actively pursued or mitigated that change.

Ethnogenesis

Natives in Paraguay acquired a new corporate-legal status as indios under Spanish law, but they also experienced ethnogenesis and became "Guaraní." Karen Powers describes ethnogenesis, the process by which distinct ethnic cultures are continually recreated over time, as a constellation of various factors and forces brought on by colonialism but also as acts of indigenous agency and survival strategies.[40] Guaraní ethnogenesis was not simply determined by Spanish colonialism but was an expression of Guaraní cultural agency. The binaries of cultural continuity versus cultural loss do not work here. Drawing on Lucas Bessire's ethnography of Ayoreo peoples in Paraguay and Bolivia, this book seeks to avoid fetishizing "traditional" Guaraní culture and to instead understand the ways that Guaraní charted new lifeways in a context of colonialism. Guaraní chieftains' embrace of Spaniards as kin, prompted voluntarily through trade or coercively through violence, set in motion patterns of interactions that favored Guaraní social norms.

To a greater degree than their counterparts in the Jesuit reducciones who received exemptions from the encomienda, Guaraní in the political orbit of Asunción were embedded in a thick array of social networks and experienced much more intimate encounters with Spaniards. Because of this long and intimate encounter with Spaniards, Guaraní in Asunción have been considered "hispanized." For decades now, scholars have been working against the assertion that when Spanish and Indian societies mixed, Indian societies always experienced cultural loss, but recent work convincingly shows that cultural mixing, sometimes called hybridity, was unremarkable for contemporaries living the experience. After all, "cultures are collective, they are inherently heterogeneous."[41] The anthropological and ethnohistorical literature on Tupí-Guaraní culture offers useful paradigms for analyzing Guaraní in a context of cultural exchange. Tupí-Guaraní culture tended to extend outside of itself, what Brazilian anthropologist Eduardo Batalha Viveiros de Castro calls a "centripetal dynamism."[42] Guillermo Wilde documents this dynamic in his analysis of Guaraní-Christian leaders in the Jesuit reducciones: "Indian receptivity towards objects, concepts, and Christian practices can be understood in terms of an 'opening towards the outside.'"[43] In this way, Guaraní use of European or Christian ceremonies, symbols, objects, and behaviors was less a function of colonial acculturation than a reflection of Guaraní attitudes toward what they perceived to be external forces. This "plastic capacity of the Tupi-Guarani matrix" is especially manifest in Guaraní kinship relations with Spaniards.[44] But this structuralist view of Guaraní culture runs the risk of flattening the Guaraní experience, a problem that Kittiya Lee addresses in her work on sixteenth- and seventeenth-century Tupian peoples in Brazil. She demonstrates that while Tupinambá's avid adoption of Christian rites and symbols may reflect a "centrifugal tendency" toward what is foreign, there are other explanatory factors that provide historical nuance. For example, Jesuits actively tried to make Christianity attractive to Tupí-Guaraní through modified Catholic rituals, like offering the eucharist in the form of cassava cakes and corn beer.[45] This book similarly describes Guaraní attitudes toward colonialism as part of complex "dialogues" between colonials and Natives of diverse goals and motivations.[46]

Colonial Kinship is anchored in ethnohistory and by extension it engages the ethnogenesis of groups in contact with Guaraní. Recent studies of ethnogenesis in the Atlantic world have highlighted indigenous or Afro-American agency under the pressure of colonialism but rarely reflect on the transformations at work on colonials.[47] Reflecting on these trends, Barbara L. Voss notes that "acts of colonization cause profound ruptures in the cultures of both colonizer and colonized. Though the indigenous populations displaced by or entangled with colonial institutions are the most severely affected, the colonists themselves are irrevocably transformed by their own displacement and by their encounters with local indigenous people."[48] Voss was not the first to argue that colonials were changed through their own colonial experience. Earlier literature made similar arguments but filtered cultural change through a national prism. Beginning in the 1940s, anthropologists began exploring colonials' cultural changes. Fernando Ortiz's profoundly influential *Cuban Counterpoint* seeks to find the origins of a Cuban national culture by analyzing the relationship between environment and cultural mixing.[49] Ortiz's "transculturation" describes the process whereby new cultural types are created, as opposed to "acculturation," which for Ortiz meant moving from one culture to another, implying cultural loss. Elman R. Service's classic account of the Paraguayan encomienda inserts colonial history into a national teleology: "the true Paraguayan was, and is, a mestizo with a distinctive national language and culture, the basis of which was formed before the end of the sixteenth century."[50] Solange Alberro's *Del gachupín al criollo* similarly operates around a national teleology.[51]

Other scholars address indigenous influence on new colonial societies in British North America.[52] More recently, Rebecca Earle contends that Spaniards perceived of conquest and colonization as an anxiety-ridden experience in which foreign foods, hot or cold air, and even the constellations could transform their bodies.[53] There was plenty of anxiety over cultural exchange in colonial Paraguay, but a bottom-up view suggests rapid adoption and familiarity: while outsiders were disturbed, local Spaniards had no qualms about preferring cassava over wheat bread. The ethnogenesis described here did not produced "Paraguayans" in the nationalist sense of the term.[54] Instead, the processes examined here produced local "españoles," "indios," "Guaraní," "negros," etc. For the first generation of creoles (locally born españoles), being español implied speaking Guaraní and Spanish, regularly eating manioc, fish, and tapir, and creating kinship with Guaraní communities in order to maintain a labor force, among other things. In this way, "español" was a term that could be ascribed to those of mixed ancestry or mestizos and could be invoked as corporate, fiscal, social, and cultural categories. Similarly, "indio" indicates a fiscal and corporate identity applied to those who possessed the right to partially govern themselves in Indian towns and who were subject to tribute. "Mestizo" is a relevant category for this study, but it was rarely invoked. While outsiders frequently called Paraguayans mestizos, locals rarely used "mestizo" as a way of snubbing another because nearly everyone was of mixed descent. All of this point toward the fluidity of categories of difference; race was situational.[55] By analyzing various ethnogenic transformations, this book avoids inventing a homogenizing narrative of ethnogenesis and portraying "colonizers" and "colonized" as static groupings.[56]

Afro-Guaraní Relations

An understanding of Guaraní experiences within a paradigm of cuñadasgo requires analyzing African slaves and their descendants. Afro-Guaraní relations were characterized by close social contact on Spanish farmsteads that led to Africans' adoption of the Guaraní language and the application of cuñadasgo to Africans slaves and free blacks.

In 1682, Afro-descendants represented 11 percent of Asunción's population. A century later, that number rose to around 54 percent.[57] Slaveholding in Paraguay was variegated with individual encomenderos and traders owning relatively few slaves when compared to the religious orders, especially the Jesuit college in Asunción, which was the largest slaveholder in the region. The significant populations of Africans in Paraguay is surprising given the poverty of the region; however, in the light of recent scholarship it is becoming increasingly clear that slavery was "a fundamental feature of colonial practice."[58] The lack of scholarship on African slaves and their descendants in Paraguay is not for lack of sources but is instead a result of modern Paraguayan nationalism and its erasure of "blackness" from the "Paraguayan race."[59] A generation of Paraguayan nationalist historians who sought to rebuild a shattered Paraguay following the War of the Triple Alliance—a war that pitted Paraguay against Brazil, Argentina, and Uruguay (1864–1870)—posited that blacks were nowhere to be found in Paraguay.[60] These historians produced two main ideas that persist, despite attempts to unseat them. The first was that *mestizaje* was a purely peaceful union of hidalgo conquistadors and noble Guaraní women. The second was a strong racism generated through anti-Brazilian (read as black or African) propaganda during the war. These ideas, expressed in generations of historical production, have served to de-Africanize Paraguay.[61]

Building on the insights of recent studies, this book demonstrates that

Africans must be viewed within the broader indigenous social context.[62] Matthew Restall argues that blacks found themselves in the "middle" of the colonial social order, awkwardly fixed as intermediaries between the Republic of Spaniards and the Republic of Indians. The paradigm that emerges in Paraguay is that blacks were more closely associated with the Indian sphere and had fewer opportunities to function as overseers. The culturally charged paradigm of cuñadasgo was applied to the practice of slavery and the treatment of free blacks. Along with recent scholarship, this book demonstrates that in order to understand African slavery in Paraguay, one must understand Indian tribute and vice versa.[63] Slavery and tribute, as two distinct systems of "race governance," were nonetheless connected through the lived reality of labor, the social closeness of blacks and Guaraní, and the paradigm of cuñadasgo as it was applied to personal service.

Organization

This book is organized into eight chapters, divided into three parts: Beginnings, Challenges, and Communities. The first part treats moments of encounter and the creation of colonial institutions. Chapter 1 traces the genesis of cuñadasgo from contact in the 1530s to 1556 when official encomiendas were created. Drawing on official reports and litigation records, chapter 2 explains how Spanish encomenderos modified Guaraní kinship relations as they increased their demands for labor on Guaraní communities and as priests worked to transform Guaraní social practice in reducciones. During this period, Guaraní leaders asserted their rights to control the movement of women out of their kin units and thereby sustained the practice of cuñadasgo, albeit in modified form. Shifting from the Asunción region to the eastern region of Guairá and from Franciscan to Jesuit jurisdictions, chapter 3 examines the rise and decline of the Spanish colonial presence on Paraguay's borderland with Portuguese Brazil. The period from 1570 to 1628 was marked by a tenuous colonial expansion to the east and ended with the devastating attacks of Portuguese slavers or *bandeirantes* on Guaraní-Jesuit reducciones.

Chapters 4 and 5 take up the direct challenges to colonial rule and constitute part 2. Chapter 4 analyzes two Guaraní rebellions. The first was spearheaded by a baptized shaman named Juan Cuaraçí and the second was a violent uprising in 1660 in the relatively young reducción of Arecayá. These resistance movements reflect Guaraní awareness of the risks involved in becoming Guaraní-Christians. In response to each of the resistance movements examined in chapter 4, officials deployed Guaraní soldiers to defend Spanish colonial hegemony. The subject of chapter 5 is the emergence of Guaraní militias in Franciscan and secular reducciones as a response to the dominance of Guaicurú Indians of the Gran Chaco. The existence of Indian militias in Paraguay highlights the weak power of colonials in the region. This service yielded important social capital for Guaraní, including tribute exemptions or direct payments. Moreover, unsegregated military service contributed to a sense of solidarity between Spaniards and Indians and thereby strengthened the institution of cuñadasgo.

Part 3 describes the tensions that bound society together. Chapter 6 examines mainly secular and Franciscan reducciones and their connections to español society and the regional economy. The reducciones were fluid spaces and cuñadasgo was an important factor in drawing Guaraní out of their communities to live with Spanish encomenderos as personal servants. Chapter 7 deepens the analysis of the relationship between Asunción and the pueblos and examines the city of Asunción as an indigenous space, an unusual reducción. Given the proliferation of Indian encomiendas in Asunción, the relative humility of the encomendero class, and the lack of a traditional urban structure, Asunción is best understood as a rural-urban space. The final chapter turns to Africans and free blacks and shows that Afro-Guaraní relations were marked more by cooperation than conflict. Blacks and Guaraní interacted on many levels: sexual partners, laborers on farms and ranches, and even as bandits. The Guaraní contributions of kinship to the encomienda system influenced the practice of slavery in Paraguay. Specifically, freedmen and Spaniards forged relationships similar to those between Guaraní and encomenderos, using a language of kinship to define their reliance on one another.

Part 1.

Beginnings

CHAPTER 1

Cuñadasgo and Conquistador Polygamists, 1530s–1550s

IN THE YEAR 1537 when Spanish conquistadors disembarked at a bend in the Paraguay River that would become the city of Asunción and began trading iron tools for food and female servants with local Guaraní villages, patterns of reciprocal exchange emerged that would transform all involved. It was not exclusively the violence of the "conquest" that changed the peoples of Paraguay but rather the movement of goods and women along transcultural fields of exchange. Early trades or *trueques* may appear to have been innocent, but by giving women to conquistadors, Guaraní were making conquistadors their kindred. Guaraní transformed potential enemies into affines, brothers-in-law and sons-in-law with whom a political bond was expected. But instead of relocating to Guaraní villages and serving their new in-laws—a typical pattern among Guaraní—conquistadors took these women back to their own homes where they sowed fields, weaved textiles and hammocks, tended to children, and were subject to the sexual demands of their new "husbands."[1] The earliest reports suggest that conquistadors were able to acquire many Guaraní female servants: three, ten, thirty, even seventy Guaraní women—this last figure likely an exaggeration.[2] Similar to the ways that Guaraní chieftains exercised power, a conquistador's status in the young colonial society was tied to the number of Guaraní kin at his behest. The newcomers had become polygamist conquistadors.[3]

When in 1620 a Jesuit asserted that the Spanish colony in Paraguay was created "by means of *cuñadasgo*," he provided a rather rich analytical term."[4] The brother-in-law relationship in Guaraní society was a strong one and therefore became associated with the conquistador-chieftain alliance. Writing in the first half of the twentieth century about modern Tupí-Guaraní peoples of Western Mato Grosso Brazil called the Nambikuara, Claude

Lévi-Strauss noted that the brother-in-law relationships can be "regarded as an actual institution."[5] It would seem that the same held true in the sixteenth century. This chapter explains the emergence of the dominant system of exchange between Guaraní and conquistadors. It demonstrates that cuñadasgo was not a direct copy of Guaraní kinship patterns but that it borrowed from both Spanish and Guaraní cultural priorities. It simultaneously generated reciprocal expectations while producing a supply of servants for conquistadors.

As we have already seen, the Guaraní word for brother-in-law was *tovajá*. Many Spaniards used the term to refer to chieftains that provided them with their Guaraní kin. Cuñadasgo, therefore, serves as an accurate reference to the male-to-male relationships that resulted in the exchange of women. Cuñadasgo's analytical richness runs even deeper. The Guaraní word for woman was *kuña* and cuñadasgo was, at least initially, about the exchange of women between men.[6] Finally, to initiate and sustain the kinship relationships of cuñadasgo, conquistadors provided Guaraní leaders with *cuñas* (Castilian for axes), as well as other objects like knives, fishhooks, and clothing. Thus, on economic, social, and cultural levels, cuñadasgo summarizes a new colonial institution that borrowed from both Spanish and Guaraní cultural logics.

While the sources overwhelmingly refer to female servants, there were also male Guaraní servants in Spanish households.[7] Besides the men and boys taken as captives after violent encounters, sometimes Guaraní women's male relatives were obliged to serve a new leader.[8] When a conquistador took a Guaraní woman, he was subject to the influence of his father- or brother-in-law. As the junior affine, the conquistador was expected to serve a kind of "bride debt." But most conquistadors entered these relationships with important gifts, thereby reversing the bride debt and channeling their new wives' male relatives to themselves.[9] In this way, conquistadors were able to acquire male servants through the networks of cuñadasgo.

Sixteenth- and early seventeenth-century chronicles, letters to crown authorities, and a handful of social records contain a bewildering tangle of events, episodes, and literary flourishes, but a basic narrative of Spanish contact and early colonization in Paraguay emerges.[10] In 1535, don Pedro de Mendoza led an expedition to the Río de la Plata that would result in a lasting colonial presence in the region. Mendoza founded a fort at Buenos Aires in 1536 but was frustrated by neighboring indigenous groups who resisted the newcomers. Mendoza took ill, departed for Spain, and died en route, leaving the expedition with an unclear and splintered leadership. Before he left the Río de la Plata, Mendoza put Juan de Ayolas in charge of a scouting party, which in August 1537 founded the city of Asunción along the banks of the Paraguay River. Ayolas met an unhappy fate when he was killed by Payaguá (also called Agaz) allies while on an expedition to find a route to the Andes in the north. Ayolas's death in 1538 left a minor lieutenant, Domingo Martínez de Irala, as the de facto commander. From 1538 to Irala's death in 1556—minus the brief rule of don Álvar Núñez Cabeza de Vaca from 1542 to 1544—Irala was the consistent ruler in Paraguay. What marks the conquistadors' activities during the period from the founding of Asunción in 1537 to the creation of the encomienda in 1556 is their tenuous colonial presence. It was not until 1555 that Irala was forced to begin organizing the encomienda, which would formally regulate the rights of conquest or Indian tribute. Until then, many conquistadors hoped to lay claim to Andean populations and gain access to mineral wealth. The result was that conquistadors were frequently on expeditions or entradas to the Northern Chaco. Domingo de Irala led entradas in November 1539, 1547–1549, and 1553. During his short rule, Cabeza de Vaca led a large expedition from September 1543 to March 1544. Once the conquistadors discovered that much of Peru had already been claimed in the 1550s, they began establishing the institutions of a permanent colonial presence—namely, the encomienda. During this period, from contact to the creation of the encomienda, the patterns of cuñadasgo were established. But understanding cuñadasgo requires understanding the Guaraní social patterns that could embrace conquistadors as brothers-in-law.

Guaraní Social Organization

Early observers of Guaraní were somewhat dismayed by the ease with which women could be exchanged. Mercenary-conquistador and early chronicler Ulrich Schmidl (1510–1579) noted that "the father sells his daughter, the husband his wife, and the brother his sister when the women do not please them."[11] In his 1639 account, the Jesuit Antonio Ruíz de Montoya remarked that the Guaraní, "being people without contracts of any sort, they never had any thought of the burdensome contract of permanent marriage."[12] What these observers perceived to be fickleness or a lack of commitment was in fact a core aspect of inter- and intravillage politics and the foundation of Guaraní leaders' political economy.

At the time of contact, there was no political organization uniting the various Tupí-Guaraní groups across the La Plata basin. The basic unit of social and economic organization was the *teyÿ*, which constituted an extended kin group or lineage, headed by a male patriarch, the *teyÿ-ru* (father of the teyÿ).[13] A teyÿ might have contained anywhere from 10 to 60 nuclear families or between 40 and 240 individuals. Each family occupied a space delineated by the pillars that sustained the *oga* or longhouse.[14] The next social unit was the *amundá* or a village of several teyÿ.[15] A grouping of villages was called a *teko'a*, but a teko'a could also be a single village. A tuvichá or chieftain led these villages or village groupings. The highest level of political organization was the *guará* or a group of teko'a, which could be organized temporarily for war or festivals and was headed by a *mburuvichá*. Branislava Susnik argues that at the time of contact there were fourteen guará and their mburuvichá possessed considerable political power.[16] Several scholars challenge this interpretation, noting the tendency toward fragmentation among political units above the teyÿ.[17]

The earliest sources indicate that among Guaraní groups in the Asunción region, endogamy was the norm. The priest Francisco de Andrada noted that "they have for [concubines/wives] their relatives." The marriage pattern that Andrada observed was common in lowland South America and is called Dravidian kinship.[18] In a Dravidian kinship system, children of same-sex siblings are considered children while children of opposite-sex siblings are preferred marriage partners. In sum, cross-cousin marriages are normal and sometimes expected. Among contact-era Guaraní, men possessed strong authority over their sisters, nieces, and cousins, granting the former authority to marry the latter to potential suitors. This control over multiple women increased among men who practiced polygyny, which was generally limited to tuvichá or mburuvichá. A leader's status in a community was not based on lineage but instead on generosity, eloquence, warrior prowess, and charisma.[19] On the social status of Guaraní leaders, the Jesuit Antonio Ruíz de Montoya observed:

> By their eloquence they gather followers and vassals, thus ennobling themselves and their descendants. The common folk serve them; they clear their ground and sow and reap their crops; they build their houses and give them their daughters when they crave them. In this matter they behave with pagan freedom: we met some with fifteen, twenty, or thirty wives.[20]

Women helped sustain a tuvichá's status because they increased his productive capacity and therefore his ability to share and give gifts. Women could be acquired through exchanges or war. If acquired through exchange, the chieftain provided the giving party exotic items or foodstuffs. A successful warrior who took women in war could invert what might be called a spouse debt by gifting women taken in captivity, thereby redirecting to himself tribute, service, and prestige. If he had enough power and materials, a tuvichá could acquire wives through gifting instead of the spouse debt.[21]

According to Ruíz de Montoya, women were expected to labor in all kinds of domestic and agricultural activities. Coming of age rituals for girls emphasized hard toil.[22] Women were the primary agriculturalists in Guaraní society; women planted and tended to crops after men cleared the garden plots of trees and shrubs. Moreover, women were weavers, gatherers, cooks, and mothers and therefore played an important role in the ability of a lineage to sustain and regenerate itself. Multiple women meant that the tuvichá had more opportunities to create brothers-in-law or sons-in-law and therefore political allies. The children of the junior affine, nephews especially, were also expected to serve their father's brother-in-law and/or father-in-law. In short, women were at the nexus of political status and production.

As Guaraní social practices—especially polygyny—were threatened under Spanish colonialism, many Guaraní leaders turned against colonial agents, especially priests. Abandoning polygyny became the crucible of colonialism for Guaraní leaders. Ruíz de Montoya observed just as much in the reducción of San Ignacio where a Guaraní leader voiced his opposition to monogamy:

For with new teachings they want to take away from us the good old way
of life of our ancestors, who had many wives and servant women and
were free to choose them at will. Now they want us to tie ourselves to a
single woman. It is not right for this to go any further.[23]

Many other tuvichá expressed similar sentiments. The phrase "good old way
of life" may have been rendered in Guaraní as "teko katu" or "good life" and
implied social reproduction and the liberty (*jepe*) to choose one or many
wives.[24] In other words, tuvichás did not cling to a status derived from economic dominance but instead recognized that polygyny was the key to sustaining the teyÿ or teko'a.

This social sketch of Guaraní at the time of contact is not meant to suggest
that tuvichás were a well-defined social elite who only sought to enrich themselves and increase their productive capacity. This would be to impose on
historical subjects Western notions of economy and gain that did not inform
their lives.[25] Instead, this survey of Guaraní kinship patterns demonstrates
the porousness of family. Anthropologists have shown that modern Guaraní
groups used kinship to incorporate people outside their immediate lineage
groups, especially by becoming brothers-in-law with outsiders through marriages.[26] Similar patterns can be observed during the early years of the Spanish conquest.

The First *Tovajá*

Cuñadasgo developed as conquistadors and Guaraní communities created
and sustained reciprocal relations. The context for such relationships
emerged at different times during moments of contact and conquest. Even
before the Pedro de Mendoza expedition arrived in the Río de la Plata, European go-betweens had already forged cuñadasgo, providing an example to
the newly arrived conquistadors. By the time conquistadors arrived among
the Darío-Guaraní in the upper Paraguay River region, the former had
become reliant on indigenous provisions and service.

There were several expeditions to the Río de la Plata in the sixteenth century, and the earliest to result in permanent settlements in Paraguay were the
Pedro de Mendoza expedition (1535) and the Álvar Núñez Cabeza de Vaca

expedition (1541). Before these two expeditions set sail, other European ventures to the Río de la Plata created bridges for engagement by generating translators as well as early geographic and ethnographic knowledge. For example, after Sebastian Cabot's expedition (1526–1530) explored the Río de la Plata region, it left behind a number of mariners on an island named Santa Catalina off the southern coast of Brazil. Depositing common sailors on unknown lands was a common tactic among Atlantic pilots, although the sailors left behind may have considered "abandoned" a more appropriate term for this activity. Portuguese pilots in Africa, Brazil, and India left behind *degredados* or penal exiles, hoping that they would become cultural intermediaries for future expeditions. Early colonists, degredados or otherwise, who remained behind or mingled with Native societies in *tierra incógnita* were know by the Portuguese as *lançados*, from the verb *lançar* (to throw). These lançados became the crucial "go-betweens" who mediated between Native societies and Europeans, providing translations, cultural knowledge, and the potential for political alliances.[27]

The don Pedro de Mendoza expedition to the Río de la Plata was huge, consisting of eleven ships and 1,200 conquistadors—not including women, servants, and slaves—and without local cultural mediation, it was listless and vulnerable to disaster.[28] In 1536 Mendoza founded the fort of Buenos Aires, but conditions quickly deteriorated as supplies ran low. To salvage the expedition, Mendoza sent one of his captains up the coast to locate lançados who could serve as interpreters and help secure provisions. On Santa Catalina island, Mendoza's men found a lançado named Hernando Ribera. Ribera was originally from the Cabot expedition and had been on Santa Catalina for eight years where he resided among a Tupí-Guaraní group called the Carijó. In a letter addressed to the crown in 1545, Ribera recounts his experience in the hopes of convincing his royal audience that he was a willing servant and powerful go-between. Ribera relates that during the eight years he (and an unknown number of other lançados) remained on Santa Catalina, he dutifully prepared for the next Spanish expedition by securing provisions. More importantly, while on Santa Catalina, Ribera had established and maintained relations with Carijós by becoming their kin. When Ribera made contact with the Mendoza expedition in 1536, he had a Carijó "wife" and children. Ribera left Santa Catalina to accompany the expedition, and he brought his wife and children as well as "slaves, servants, relatives (*deudos*) and friends."[29] Ribera and his Carijó retinue possessed utilitarian and symbolic significance. When this group arrived in Buenos Aires, they provided much-needed supplies to a group of conquistadors who had risen to new heights of desperation after cannibalizing their dead.[30] Like other cultural intermediaries—indigenous servants, mestizos, castaways, and other lançados—Ribera provided crucial cultural knowledge and was valued in the conquest. In a few short years, Ribera went from a Portuguese mariner-gone-native to a prominent player in the conquest: during the Cabeza de Vaca expedition to the Chaco in 1543, Ribera led a reconnaissance mission and served as translator.[31]

Apart from his cultural knowledge, Ribera and others like him influenced his conquistador peers through his example of interethnic kinship. Observant conquistadors would not have failed to notice that Ribera enjoyed relatives and servants through marriage to a Carijó wife. They likely recognized that indigenous kinship provided tremendous benefits: female companionship and service, a following of indigenous retainers, and political options through cultural brokerage. So while Ribera and his retinue served as what Alida Metcalf calls a "transactional go-between," or someone who provided direct cultural mediation, and as a "biological go-between" because of his mestizo children, Ribera was also a "representational go-between." Metcalf defines "representational go-betweens" as those who through their writing produce and shape "on a grand scale how Europeans and Native Americans viewed each other."[32] Ribera's single letter may qualify him for this category, as Metcalf defines it, but on a more local and immediate level, Ribera was a powerful representational go-between for the conquistadors. He provided an example of interethnic kinship for the conquistadors as they established themselves in the Río de la Plata and vied for status in the inchoate conquest society.

Of course, there is no direct causal relationship between Ribera's kinship and the widespread adoption of Guaraní kinship among conquistadors. Spanish-Guaraní relations in the Asunción area evolved over months and years amid tumultuous circumstances. From Buenos Aires, the *adelantado* (expeditionary commander) don Pedro de Mendoza sent an advance company, led by Juan de Ayolas with Domingo de Irala as the lieutenant, up the Paraguay River in search of information about the route north and the peoples who resided there. The group reached a bend in the river where there were many Guaraní peoples who Spaniards called Carío. The Carío were of interest to the conquistadors because of what we might call a "starch bias." The conquistadors spoke enthusiastically about groups who produced mandioca (cassava) and maize as opposed to those who relied only on fish and wild game.[33] This enthusiasm for Native agriculturalists did not necessarily ensue from a European "taste" for specific kinds of food but instead a Spanish-Christian notion of civilization. Many early moderns believed that agricultural production or, more broadly, the appropriate management of the land represented a degree of civility.[34] The conquistadors saw in Carío peoples a consistent supply of provisions and potential allies.

In August of 1537, the conquistadors founded the city of Asunción in order to use the authority the city granted them to pursue conquests in the Gran Chaco and the Andes.[35] But Carío groups did not passively accept the Spanish presence. Initial reactions were mixed as individual groups negotiated relationships of commerce, kinship, and political alliance. In his chronicle, Schmidl relates that after a quick exchange of supplies from their canoes, Carío leaders asked the conquistadors to move along and continue their journey upriver. The conquistadors were determined to remain among the Carío and so they forced their acceptance with violence. After defeating the valiant chieftain named Lambaré, Schmidl related, the Caríos offered their political alliance through a kinship exchange. The defeated Guaraní chieftains handed over six girls to Ayolas and two women apiece to the rest of the conquistadors.[36] For Schmidl, conquistador-Guaraní relations began in violence but ended in political alliance and exchange of women. Schmidl's account has appealed to chroniclers and nationalists alike. In his 1602 poem about the genesis of colonial society in Paraguay, Martín Barco de Centenera describes the Battle of Lambaré on a hill named after the valiant but defeated chieftain.[37] Lambaré inhabits an important place in nationalist histories: he was the first Guaraní to offer peace and women to the Spaniards, thereby inaugurating the Paraguayan mestizo race.[38] Today, a monument on Cerro Lambaré depicts a resolute but friendly-looking Lambaré making a sign of peace and holding a gift in his hand. Schmidl's account has been attractive because of its simplicity: conquistadors' use of violence quickly yielded a pliant and harmonious relationship with Guaraní. Many early twentieth-century nationalist historians emphasized the peaceful and voluntary sexual unions that occurred between the daughters of Guaraní chieftains and the conquistadors as producing an offspring that brought together the romantic exoticism of the Guaraní race with the virile and civilized Spaniard. The problems with these interpretations are many and outside the bounds of this investigation. Suffice it to say that Schmidl probably invented or "misremembered" the initial encounter, for no other account remembers it in this way. Florencia Roulet convincingly demonstrates that the earliest encounters between Carío and conquistadors were cautious but peaceful: in exchange for iron tools and other goods, Spaniards received provisions.[39]

Even though violence did not mark the first encounter between Spaniards and Guaraní, by 1538 the relationships were straining, especially because of a devastating locust plague that destroyed most of the Carío's crops. The lack of food resulted in the deaths of a significant number of both Christians and Guaraní.[40] Desperation led conquistadors to launch raids (often called *rancheadas* in the documentation) on Guaraní villages for food and female servants. The plague and the subsequent raids turned Guaraní opinion against the conquistadors, and many Guaraní took up arms or simply fled from Spaniards who demanded provisions or service. Irala responded with violence, which resulted in some Guaraní's recognition of the military prowess of the conquistadors and resignation to Spanish demands for trade and servants.[41]

Despite the tensions of 1538, conquistadors rapidly adopted Guaraní polygyny. Conquistadors of all stripes, from the lowliest lançados to the adelantado himself, participated in cuñadasgo. Extending kinship to the conquistadors seemed to be the Natives' de facto method for receiving the Spaniards as they moved through new territories. For example, several Carío chieftains gave Juan de Ayolas their female kin and called him a tovajá or brother-in-law.[42] During the 1543 entrada to Puerto de los Reyes, Cabeza de Vaca was offered daughters of principal Indians.[43] This practice of giving women or daughters was common throughout South America and was a primary way of initiating relationships among political leaders. Conquistadors observed the new social paradigms of the conquest and associated women with a life relatively free from manual labor. Luxury is contextual and for conquistadors engaged in lengthy and life-threatening entradas to the Chaco, "luxury" meant having access to people who served them so they did not have to produce their own provisions. Gerónimo Ochoa de Eizaguirre wrote in 1545 that during the 1543 entrada, the conquistadors without female servants faired worst. Nearly fifty "Christians," he claimed, died of illness during the entrada because "they did not have an india who could carry their food, nor did they have a hammock to sleep in" and so they slept on the swampy ground. By contrast, the "captains" had ten or sometimes twenty indias serving them and consequently suffered less on the expedition.[44]

After Ayolas died in 1538, Domingo de Irala assumed power in Asunción. In an effort to bolster his new position and prepare for further expeditions, Irala ordered the conquistadors to abandon the fort at Buenos Aires and relocate to Asunción. To orient and inform future arrivals, Irala left a note at the abandoned fort that was discovered by a later expedition. His optimistic message was that Asunción was a much better location because the 400 conquistadors there had "700 women that serve them in their houses and gardens" providing an "abundance of support." He further promised that if 3,000 more men arrived there would be enough women to support them.[45] Irala's letter reflected a widespread enthusiasm among the conquistadors for possessing Guaraní wives and the freedoms they could provide. An anonymous *relación* written in 1545 by a partisan of Irala noted that because of Irala's leadership and support for cuñadasgo, common conquistadors were freed from relations of subjectivity to hidalgos. Before Irala, the account contended, regular expeditionary members were treated like "slaves."[46] The opportunity to be freed from onerous demands of a social superior and to become a superior with "gente de servicio" or servants was a boon for conquistadors. Conquistadors may have dreamed of finding fabulous mineral wealth, but most were content to be free of a social superior's direct authority and to assume the role of "master."[47]

This alliance or friendship hinged on kinship and joint military raids. Dorothy Tuer argues that Irala's initial military victories over Carío transformed him in their eyes into a powerful leader with warrior prowess. Many Carío made the strategic decision to leverage their relationship with Irala and his conquistadors to attack their enemies the Agaces, a nonsedentary group of the Chaco. The conquistadors, although successful in quelling Guaraní resistance, did not act as though they were the lords of the land. In raids against Carío enemies, Spanish and Carío military cultures operated side by side with some unsettling results. During a 1539 joint Spanish-Carío attack on the Agaces, Carío warriors returned with enemy captives who were later cannibalized. Tuer argues that conquistadors' inability to prohibit these cannibal rites as part of joint military activities reflects the transcultural nature of the conquest and the tenuous position of the conquistadors.[48] The continuation of anthropophagy among Christians became a major accusation among competing conquistadors. When the newly appointed adelantado don Álvar Núñez Cabeza de Vaca arrived in Asunción in March of 1541, he prohibited cannibal activities during joint raids or any other time. This crackdown on anthropophagy contributed to Cabeza de Vaca's failures during his important 1543 expedition to Puerto de los Reyes in the Northern Chaco.[49] Besides disrupting the warrior norms that helped to sustain the Spanish-Carío alliance, Cabeza de Vaca overturned Irala's policy of going to war against Carío enemies and even made new alliances with Yaperús, Huemes, and Guatatas, all Carío enemies. Cabeza de Vaca likely intended to increase the conquistadors' access to supplies and reduce their reliance on Carío, but he also recognized that these alliances added tension to the conquistador-Carío relationship and cautioned his lieutenants to tread extra carefully with the Carío.[50]

Cabeza de Vaca also sought to severely restrict conquistadors' direct access to Guaraní communities and thereby regulate kinship relationships. Pero Hernández, a scribe and secretary to Cabeza de Vaca, noted that when Cabeza de Vaca arrived in Asunción and observed the colonists' "bad customs," he removed all of their "relatives."[51] In his *ordenanzas* (ordinances) regulating conquistador behavior in Asunción, the new adelantado prohibited conquistadors from keeping mothers, daughters, sisters, or first cousins in their homes.[52] Anyone caught trading with Guaraní communities without a license from the adelantado was threatened with severe punishment. Moreover, conquistadors were ordered to cease disassembling their swords and firearms to make trade objects. Cabeza de Vaca recognized that kinship was the key to social and political power and sought to regulate and manage these relationships of cuñadasgo, thereby solidifying his control.

In the aftermath of Cabeza de Vaca's new regulations restricting access to Guaraní kinship and his failures in the 1543 entrada to Puerto de los Reyes, the stage was set for an uprising. Days after Cabeza de Vaca returned from the expedition in March 1544, Irala and his partisans imprisoned the adelantado. They eventually convicted Cabeza de Vaca of treason and abuse and shipped him downriver in a craft named *The Comunero* (the name given to the Castilian rebellion against Charles V from 1520 to 1521). With Cabeza de Vaca out of the way, Irala solidified his position as governor of Paraguay. These conflicts emerged out of fractured political allegiances among the conquistadors as well as divergent attitudes toward indios. In his *Comentarios*, a lengthy defense of his actions as adelantado, Cabeza de Vaca accused Irala of ruining the colony, especially after he allowed conquistadors to have access to Guaraní villages and kinship.

By the 1540s, access to Guaraní communities was crucial for conquistadors. Relationships of cuñadasgo emerged out of conquistador reliance on Guaraní foodstuffs, labor, and military power. The way to acquire a degree of social status in the conquest was through the acquisition of female servants via kinship. From a certain point of view, Guaraní women in Spanish homes provided only social and economic benefits to the conquistadors, but these relationships could not be simply stripped of Guaraní social meanings.

Polygamist Conquistadors

In the early years, both Guaraní and conquistadors stepped into new social patterns. A select few Guaraní adopted monogamous Catholic marriages while conquistadors accepted multiple Guaraní "wives" from chieftains. Priests were initially very cautious when it came to instructing Guaraní and offering them Catholic rites. After the cleric Francisco de Andrada married a Guaraní man to one of his wives, other Guaraní desired marriage, but Andrada hesitated to begin marrying indios en masse when polygyny was still alive and well. Andrada and other priests moved forward with caution, unsure about how the conceptual gaps would affect the new faith.[53] These priests were justified in being cautious, for the road toward Guaraní acceptance of monogamy was slow and meandering. Monogamy would not become a norm among Guaraní until reducciones were established decades later (discussed in subsequent chapters).

If certain Guaraní men saw utility in Catholic marriages, conquistadors saw benefits in polygyny. Conquistadors knew that female service was not separate from the Guaraní social context. Writing to the Council of the Indies in 1545, Francisco de Andrada observed that Spaniards needed Guaraní women because of the gendered division of labor: "we find in this land the bad custom that the women are the ones who plant and collect the provisions." But conquistadors did not simply take Guaraní women because they were agriculturalists. Indian service did not come without kinship. The sources are replete with references to female indias' "relatives" who expected reciprocity. Andrada stated that conquistadors acquired Guaraní women via trade (*rescates*) with "their relatives" and that trade was required to "keep them happy."[54] The Guaraní women who came into conquistadors' homes experienced new forms of power relations defined by European notions of servitude and domestic service. Even so, these women were not completely divorced from their home villages. As conquistadors fostered cuñadasgo, their households became embedded in Guaraní social networks. In a way, conquistadors carved out a space for themselves in the region that was analogous to other Guaraní tuvichá who practiced polygyny, insofar as they drew on their wives for labor and requested that their relatives serve them in times of extra labor needs or war.[55] The bulk of the labor, as well as military power, for conquest activities in Paraguay were provided by Guaraní through bonds of kinship. Thus, the conquest was realized through affinal bonds with Guaraní communities.

But how did Spaniards understand their relationships with Guaraní women and their relatives? It is possible that Spaniards took Guaraní women as concubine-servants without possessing any understanding of the Guaraní social context and the obligations this kinship entailed. If this was the case, then James Lockhart's "double mistaken identity" could apply to Paraguay. Double mistaken identity is a situation "in which each side of the cultural exchange presumes that a given form or concept is functioning in the way familiar within its own tradition and is unaware of or unimpressed by the other side's interpretation."[56] This would explain why Guaraní-conquistador relations broke down when Spaniards treated them like conquered subjects who owed taxes and why Guaraní were willing to offer conquistadors their women: they assumed that Spaniards would treat them like kin and reciprocate. This paradigm functions to a degree, but in light of other evidence it is incompatible with the Paraguayan case. In fact, most conquistadors were at least partially aware of the differences between concubinage, tribute, and Guaraní polygynous cuñadasgo. The most important indicator that conquistadors were aware of the Guaraní meanings associated with cuñadasgo was that conquistadors used the indigenous terms of kinship to describe their relationships with Guaraní communities in common parlance even when officials obscured these terms in government records. Officials and scribes used *cacique* (a term from the Caribbean that Spaniards applied to all Amerindian leaders) or *principal* to refer to Guaraní chieftains with whom they possessed affinity. When referring to the Guaraní females in encomenderos' service, scribes used the terms *india, criadas,* or *gente de servicio,* which could all be glossed as domestic servants. If taken in war, women and children might be called *piezas,* a term commonly used to describe a slave.[57] But beyond the official records, Guaraní kinship terminology was commonly employed. In his 1612 history of the region, Ruy Díaz de Guzmán wrote that after giving their daughters and wives to Spaniards, Guaraní caciques and Spaniards referred to each other as "tovajá" or brother-in-law.[58] Around the same time (ca. 1602), the poet-historian Barco de Centenera made the same observation:

> The Guaraní are greatly pleased
> To be found related to the Christians:
> To each is given his companion
> The fathers and closest relatives
> What a shame to see so pitiable,
> That of these concubines their brothers,
> Of all those who are cohabiting,
> They call them today their brothers-in-law.[59]

The mutual use of Guaraní kinship terminology among Guaraní and Spaniards suggests the latter understood that the brother-in-law (or father-in-law) relationship was the nexus of political, economic, and military power between Spaniards and Guaraní social units.

The sources do not specify what terms conquistadors used to describe their Guaraní "wives." However, if they spoke Guaraní to their servants, they most likely would have called them *kuña*. Montoya translates *kuña* as "india woman, female, relative, true woman."[60] When describing marriage relationships Montoya used the word *mujer* instead of *wife* because there was no easy counterpart in the Guaraní language—this is born out in modern studies of Tupí-Guaraní kinship.[61] *Kuña mbuku* or *kuñataĩ*, according to Montoya, meant *moza* (young girl or servant) and is another possible name applied to the indigenous women in conquistadors' homes.[62] The linguistics surrounding the practice of cuñadasgo hint at the ways Spaniards were embedded in a network of Guaraní and colonial power dynamics and that a woman's relocation from Guaraní village to Spanish homestead did not imply a Guaraní "social death."[63]

Even if they called Guaraní chieftains "tovajá," Spaniards applied different expectations to the women entering their households than their Guaraní counterparts. Perhaps the most potentially abusive aspect of this new institution related to coerced sex. When a tuvichá gave away a female relative to another tuvichá, a sexual relationship was expected, but Guaraní sexual unions were rather fluid. There was no formal separation or divorce ceremony and individuals suffered little shame when changing sexual partners. This attitude toward sexuality likely provided women with greater freedom and a way to escape from an unwanted partner.[64] So when a Guaraní woman entered a conquistador's household she most likely expected him to make sexual advances, but she was surely surprised by the conquistador's use of force and the expectations surrounding the sexual double standard.[65] Ann Stoler points out that the field of sexuality as a site for the production of power was highly unstable. Colonial power was simultaneously reinforced and destabilized as the subjugation produced through coerced sex also resulted in ties of intimacy, especially when it came to mestizo children. By identifying colonial sexual contact as a bundle of "tense and tender ties," Stoler seeks to complicate the colonial counter without effacing the violence implicit in the dynamics of colonial sexuality.[66] Similarly, Nancy van Deusen examines "intimacies of bondage" among colonials and Indian servants/slaves in the first half of the sixteenth century by placing violence and intimacy side by side. A nuanced examination of intimacy in a colonial context, she argues, is more than parsing out the coercive or consensual sexual dimensions of conquistador-india relations. "Intimacy also involved other forms of bodily, material, and emotional attachments which were varied and complex."[67]

Such attachments are on display in conquistadors' bequests to their indias and their offspring. The bequests made by conquistadors to the children of indigenous partners reveal what van Deusen calls the "'thin blue lines' of affective ties' which are often difficult to detect because scholars have been intent on seeing the thick red lines of 'family' based upon Castilian aristocratic prescriptions."[68] In other words, the position of indigenous women and their progeny in conquistadors' bequests suggests that these women were not merely "property" but members of conquistadors' households. Bequests reveal how ties of relatedness were maintained, created, or dissolved. Governor Domingo Martínez de Irala's family is a rich example. A crown official observed that Irala "had many . . . sisters and first cousins and other relatives, having carnal access to them, watching over them as if they were his legitimate women."[69] What did it mean for Irala to treat Guaraní women like "legitimate women"? One possibility is that Irala closely guarded their sexual lives and arranged marriages for them with other tuvichá. In his last will and testament, dated March 13, 1556, Irala betrothed seven mestiza daughters, all born of different india mothers, to españoles. Irala's deployment of sexuality and sexual labor was not so different than other conquistadors in the Americas who took elite indigenous concubines and then used their offspring to create patronage networks.[70] One of these mestiza's mothers, named María, was daughter of the powerful chieftain the conquistadors called Pedro de Mendoza (after the deceased adelantado). By giving away these daughters to other Spaniards, Irala extended kinship between other conquistadors and Guaraní tuvichá via Spanish family strategy.[71]

Other conquistadors—including at least one priest—arranged marriages and financial security for their mestiza children. Virtually all of these children were born out of wedlock and therefore would have been considered "hijos naturales." In 1547, father Martín González provided a significant sum of money to his Guaraní servants' children: "to María, child-daughter of María, my servant (*mi criada*), and Petrolina, child-daughter of Francisca, my servant, to each be given one thousand gold pesos. God be served that when the time arrives they marry and assume another condition and manner of living."[72] The size of these girls' dowries strongly suggests that this cleric was their father. By offering such a large dowry, González tried to ensure that these girls would be brought up among Spanish-Christian society. Unlike the conquistadors in Cuzco who created the convent of Santa Clara to house their mestiza daughters, the conquistadors in Paraguay did not have the means to create a convent for their mixed-race children. Only by 1603 was an orphanage and casa de recogidas officially established by a laywoman named doña Francisca de Bocanegra, but it was a poor institution, dependent on daily charities in the form of basic provisions.[73] Even though the Paraguayan conquistadors were not able to place their daughters in a convent, they shared with their Peruvian counterparts what Kathryn Burns calls a "gendered double vision of their own progeny."[74] To wit, conquistadors rarely bequeathed property or arranged marriages for their male mestizo children, who were often considered politically and culturally dangerous. Mestizos were feared and neglected; mestizas were protected and used to solidify patronage networks.

At first glance, conquistadors' attitudes in their testaments toward their criadas, many of the mothers of their mestizo children, is similar to those of a master to his or her slaves. However, many of these criadas came from Guaraní communities with which the conquistadors hoped to maintain relationships of peace and reciprocity. Most conquistadors ensured that criadas remain in networks of friends and relatives—they were not sold off to the highest bidder or to Brazilian slavers. These women inhabited an ambiguous legal identity: they were neither slaves nor encomienda tributaries. Luís de Hernández ordered that the "Christian indias" in his service "remain in the company and union of the Christians, that they be indoctrinated and taught in our holy Catholic faith."[75] Hernández's language suggests that he was concerned with the Christian tutelage of his criadas. Pedro Arias had come by several indigenous "piezas" taken in war and he ordered that these remain with his other servants, Elena and Juana, under a relative's control.[76]

So while conquistadors treated Guaraní women as concubines and servants, their own households were situated within Guaraní social contexts. In fact, some conquistadors' mestizo children were included in interteyÿ kinship bonds. In a 1556 letter, conquistador Diego Tellez de Escobar summarizes why Guaraní served Spaniards and suggests that mestizo/a children figured in cuñadasgo's reciprocal dynamics:

> It was the custom of the Indians of the land to serve the Christians and to give [the Christians] their daughters and sisters and to come to [the Christians'] houses by way of kinship and friendship and thus were the Christians served *because the Christians had many children with the Indians* of the land and for this reason did the Indians come to serve like to the house of relatives and nephews.[77]

Tellez de Escobar observed that Guaraní leaders gave to Spaniards their "daughters and sisters" through ties of kinship but added that another reason for this mutual exchange of kin/servants was related to the Spanish-Guaraní offspring: "because the Christians had many children with the Indians." This passage suggests that some of the conquistadors' mestizo progeny were part of the kinship systems between a polygynous conquistador's household and his Guaraní brother-in-law's village. These mestizos were potential marriage partners to Guaraní leaders or their kin. In the next breath (and again with puzzling syntax) Tellez de Escobar mentions "relatives and nephews."[78] In Tupí-Guaraní societies nephews were the most junior affines and potential marriages partners in avuncular or cross-cousin unions. If you were a male tuvichá, male nephews were potential sons-in-laws or brothers-in-law and therefore the kinds of people who served you. Thus, for the polygynous conquistador, the exchange of kin was not simply through affinal networks (i.e., taking Guaraní concubines) but through the propagation of children—especially male children.[79]

Relationships of cuñadasgo were informed by both Guaraní and Spanish cultural logics and priorities. Guaraní indios, and especially indias, affected the inchoate colonial society as physical manifestations of the real social bonds that bound conquistadors and Guaraní chieftains in reciprocal relationships. At the same time, cuñadasgo was bound up with colonial domination, warfare, captivity, and motivations of economic gain for Spaniards to put Guaraní servants to work in their fields, construction projects, hammock making, and other menial tasks.[80] The next section will address these practices before concluding with an analysis of the material costs of kinship.

Servants, Kin, or Slaves?

Guaraní and other Natives were channeled into conquistadors' homes via three methods: peaceful cuñadasgo exchanges, rancheadas or raids, and as the result of war on groups deemed "enemies."[81] When dealing with Guaraní groups, either through peaceful exchanges or rancheadas, cuñadasgo was nearly always created. This was because Spaniards deemed most Guaraní groups their allies and therefore sought to maintain peace while simultaneously benefiting from Guaraní communities. Peace was best achieved through cuñadasgo. Even when conquistadors violently raided a Guaraní village, they would sustain the relationship with trade and kinship. This interpretation has not been the norm in the scholarship, which has depicted Indian personal service as a kind of informal slavery.[82]

That conquistadors and settlers rented, sold, and bequeathed indio/a servants throughout the sixteenth century has contributed to this slavery model.[83] As conquistadors recognized that Guaraní women were the primary means to get ahead in the tenuous colonial society, women's values increased dramatically.[84] The priest Martín González lamented that women had been transformed into a "currency," being traded for horses, clothing, and other necessary things.[85] Pero Hernández remembered that Domingo de Irala sold a "free Carío" woman to another Spaniard for a few items of clothing.[86] González was particularly scandalized by conquistadors' use of Guaraní servants as currency in games of chance. Other accounts indicate that in exchange for iron trade goods, Irala gave permission to traders from Brazil to take Corocotoquies and Carío from Paraguay to Brazil and sell them into slavery.[87] Gerónimo Ochoa de Eizaguirre observed the sale of Indian women in Asunción for excessive prices "as if they were slaves."[88] To many contemporaries, these kinds of exchanges stripped Guaraní of their status as Spanish allies and citizens.

Despite the abundant evidence that women were exchanged in trades and sales, given the cultural networks within which women were exchanged, the term *slave* is problematic. *Slave* connotes a fixed legal framework while Guaraní indias inhabited an inchoate legal framework and an evolving social and cultural matrix of relationships.[89] Moreover, indias were not universally deracinated but maintained associations with their communities. Once conquistadors took an india to his homestead, he became a tovajá to a Guaraní leader and was expected to maintain a relationship of reciprocity. This becomes evident in the very sources that make the strongest accusations of unjust enslavement. For example, Ochoa de Eizaguirre was concerned that women were sold "as if they were slaves" specifically because "the indias are given to us by their parents and relatives."[90] Trading or selling women who were freely given by their kin, Ochoa de Eizaguirre argued, unjustly abused the reciprocity implicit in cuñadasgo. Others similarly recognized that selling and trading Guaraní women "as if they were slaves" would upset relations between the conquistadors and Guaraní villages. After describing the sale of a Darío woman between Irala and a conquistador, Pero Hernández noted that the india's "relatives were very angry."[91] Even when conquistadors traded a woman, they recognized that she remained embedded in political networks of cuñadasgo and that their actions toward her could upset relations with Guaraní tuvichás. By contrast, owners of African slaves were not concerned with how their treatment of slaves would affect their relations with the slaves' native communities. Spaniards generally did not sever their relationships with indias' communities. In fact, many indias maintained social networks with their home villages even after relocating to conquistadors' households. After the purported murder of a Guaraní man in 1545, a member of "Ytacumbu's house" (a nearby teyÿ or teko'a identified by its principal cacique) came to gather the dead man's sister so that she could mourn with her community.[92] For many Guaraní criadas, the bonds of family with the original Guaraní village remained intact after entering into the service of a Spaniard. The existence of these networks suggests that many Guaraní women serving in Spanish homes did not experience deracination.

One of the reasons that Guaraní servants in Spaniards' homes maintained contact with their home villages was that their chieftains and/or male relatives initiated exchanges with Spaniards. Guaraní leaders would do this to acquire new allies and tools. Contemporaries who observed Guaraní men actively pursuing the exchange of their female kin saw it as an evil omen for the Guaraní's future. Paniagua was alarmed that Guaraní women's "brothers" would publicly "announce in the streets and plazas" their intent to "trade" their women with conquistadors, suggesting that these Guaraní men

were opportunists hoping to turn a quick profit by selling their female relatives. Ulrich Schmidl took a similarly pessimistic position when he noted
how easily Guaraní men transferred women from their own households to
other teyÿ: "the father sells his daughter, the husband his wife, and the
brother his sister when the women do not please them."[93] Schmidl's and
Paniagua's assertions that Guaraní men sold their female kin because of avarice, opportunism, or caprice is reflective of colonial depictions of Indians as
morally depraved and easily swayed by the worst of the conquistadors' mor-
als. Regardless of the ways that colonials characterized these exchanges,
many Guaraní enthusiastically exchanged their female kin.

Even so, not all Guaraní leaders willingly exchanged their female kin with
conquistadors. Rancheadas or raids were a frequent means of acquiring
Guaraní servants, especially when Guaraní responded with violence to
Spaniards or attempted to abandon their villages. Individual conquistadors
sowed havoc in many Guaraní villages, taking women and provisions without consent and without license from the governor.[94] Historians have teased
out of the sources the political contexts surrounding periods of intense rancheadas. As previously noted, there was increased violence following the 1538
locust plague that destroyed much of the Guaraní's crops. Moreover, Roulet
suggests that after the arrival of Cabeza de Vaca, more aggressive attitudes
toward Guaraní led many Guaraní to flee from Spaniards. Others chose to
fight and organized serious attacks on Spaniards, resulting in bloody coun-
teractions between 1544 and 1545. Spaniards wanted the benefits of a tuvichá
without reciprocating, resulting in a breakdown of peaceful relations.[95] Dorothy Tuer notes that rancheadas increased in the 1550s as Spaniards encountered Guaraní at greater distances from Asunción to the south in the Paraná
region and east of Asunción.[96] One of the few extant registers of indigenous
captives taken by Asunceños is from an expedition against the naciónes
Ñungüaras, Cumunyhán, and Cutaguays, circa 1595.[97] Over a dozen Spaniards registered women and children as their captives, averaging four individuals per Spaniard. Many had not been baptized and, therefore, appeared
nameless. For example, Juan de Rojas registered "an yndia, two girls and one
boy."[98] The erasure of identity is even more pronounced in the following
entry: Agustín Cantero took "four piezas . . . and because they are not baptized they have no names."[99] The violent reality of these expeditions is

evident in Juan de Roças's declaration: "an *yndia* with a child and two [other] children, their mother died."[100]

But even when conquistadors took Guaraní women by force, kinship norms grew back around these relationships as long as the social integrity of the village survived. This is supported by the abundant references to the cost of service: gifts. When Cabeza de Vaca came to power, he ordered that conquistadors gave Indians "gifts" or payment for their work.[101] The gifting and exchange of material goods within cuñadasgo is a final characteristic that distinguishes it from slavery.

Cuña-dasgo: Gifts, Iron, and Exchange

In his *Discourse on the Origin and Basis of Inequality among Men* (1754), Jean-Jacques Rousseau famously argues that it was not gold or silver that "ruined humanity" but "iron and corn."[102] The Genevan philosophe argues that objects typically associated with the rise of "civilization"—agriculture and technology—led to the social relationships that produced avarice and political power. Rousseau thought that humanity's best moments were in a "state of nature" without the greed and competition of complex societies. Philosophers and historians generally find Rousseau's theory unconvincing. Even so, had Rousseau been able to observe the effects of iron tools on Guaraní, he would have had more grist for the mill. While the Guaraní's enthusiastic adoption of iron tools could fit neatly into a "Columbian exchange" narrative that describes the transformative effect of a European import on an indigenous group, the results were much more complicated.[103] The outcome of Guaraní adoption of iron tools was never a given and is still poorly understood. A comprehensive treatment of the role that iron played among Guaraní is beyond the scope of this work, but it will suffice to point out the multidimensional effects of gifting on Guaraní and Spaniards, for not only did Guaraní adopt transformative new tools but Spaniards also accepted new forms of exchange.

Trade items became so scarce that conquistadors disassembled their swords and firearms to fashion their own knives, fishhooks, and axes.[104] Conquistador Domingo Martínez (not the governor) was the colony's first smithy and he remembered in 1556 that in the earliest days he was tasked with making fishhooks (*anzuelos*) and that the molds for these were incredibly useful, for without them the conquistadors would not have had "dealings with the indios," not to mention the ability to fish. Martínez made many other metal tools besides fishhooks, including "cuchillos de rescate" ("trade knives"), for "trade with the indios."[105] If metal tools were the primary currency, then Domingo Martínez ran the first mint of Paraguay. Even though priests did not enter into relationships of cuñadasgo with Guaraní, they did not hesitate to use gifts. Reflecting on the importance of iron tools for interethnic relations in the eastern territory of Guairá, the Jesuit father Diego González noted in 1611 that "one can win a lineage of Indians with an ax head," implying that a priest or conquistador could gain the alliance of a cacique and his village by gifting metal tools.[106] So while contemporaries described women as a kind of currency, iron tools literally became monetized. The first attempt to standardize the *moneda de la tierra* or local currency was in 1544 when the cabildo (city council) moved to fix the prices of commodities on metal exchange items: "two hens for three knives, eight eggs for one knife, three sets of fishing line for one knife, and two sets of fishing line for one knife."[107] In legal proceedings, penalties and legal costs were meted out in axes (*cuñas*). For example, in a suit from 1577 in Guairá, the notary was rewarded 324 cuñas for the performance of his duties.[108] Spanish officials monetized iron tools to provide stability to the system of cuñadasgo. Gifts and commodities intertwined.

The exchange of axes, trade knives, and other goods for Guaraní women must be examined as the intermingling of two different kinds of exchange systems. David Murray argues that European-Native exchanges in North America "need to be seen as operating within a set of interlocking economies, which include the realms of the discursive and religious as well as the material." This does not mean that we should ascribe to Euro-Native economies an ahistorical binary between acquisitive capitalism and reciprocal gifting, for this would flatten Natives and Europeans onto the same plane.[109] When individuals today exchange commodities in a marketplace, the commodities themselves are privileged, not necessarily the relationship between those making the exchanges. In gift economies, the relationship between exchanging parties acquired a higher priority. C. A. Gregory holds that "what a gift transactor desires is the personal relationships that the exchange of gifts creates, and not the things themselves." This may oversimplify the matter. The objects still possess incredible weight, but the importance of the exchange networks add a layer of social significance to the exchange that may in fact strengthen the desire for the "things" changing hands.[110] For Guaraní, iron tools did not just possess powerful utilitarian value; they also were part of the equation of kinship and political peace with Spaniards.[111] The *cuña* (ax) and *kuña* (woman) were not easily separated in the early exchanges.

Guaraní-conquistador exchanges in Paraguay were not only shaped by a gift economy; they also acquired meaning from the related concept of vengeance. Reciprocity was the principle that undergirded the practice of trade and vengeance. In fact, the word for trade was related to the word for vengeance.[112] Antonio Ruíz de Montoya's *Tesoro*, the earliest lexicon of the Guaraní language, affirms that the word *tepy* could signify either "payment" or "vengeance."[113] Payment is a response to a gift, while vengeance is a response to violence. The homograph *tepy* underscores the centrality of reciprocity in Guaraní culture. An exchange of any kind, albeit violent, always required a response from the receiving party. The payment/vengeance paradigm has conceptual cousins in the relationship between social reproduction and violence. For example, a close variant of the word *tovajá* (brother-in-law) is *tovajára*, signifying "competitor."[114] This concept can be seen in Hans Staden's account of his captivity among Tupinambá (cultural cousins of Guaraní) of coastal Brazil from 1554 to 1555. As a captive and enemy, Hans Staden was destined to be consumed. But before he was to be killed, he was given a woman, a hammock, and treated well by the community.[115] Tupí-Guaraní also imagined the captive as a pet in the community, signaling a kind of "adoptive filiation."[116] Carlos Fausto observes that the "master-pet dialectic is a version of the master-slave relation in societies in which the production of immaterial and/or symbolic goods—virtualities of existence, names, songs, ritual objects, emblems—encompass the production of material goods and utilities."[117] In other words, the treatment of the material captive (Staden) as a kind of adopted relative signaled his potential to regenerate immaterialities in society. While Staden escaped death at the hands of his captors, he did witness the killing of another captive and noted that the killer and the women who dealt blows on the corpse were given new names.[118] Materiality and immateriality, vengeance and exchange, violence and reproduction, kinship and enmity—these concepts mingled and coalesced in Guaraní culture. When conquistadors and Guaraní chieftains traded axes for servants, these transactions transcended simple material or utilitarian exchanges.

These symbolic aspects of exchange must be seen alongside the profound impact of the material items on Guaraní communities. There is a consensus among historians and archaeologists that at the time of contact Guaraní groups used stone technology. The time required to chop down a tree to clear a field for cultivation or for building materials with stone tools is staggering when compared to the completion of the same tasks with a steel or iron ax.[119] It is no wonder that Guaraní took to iron and steel tools so quickly. What remains unanswered is the effect the adoption of these tools had on Guaraní society. Complicating the matter is that adoption of new tools cannot be viewed apart from the myriad factors accompanying colonization. Some scholars argue that the introduction of metal tools in Amazonia stimulated swidden agriculture.[120] This was not the case among Guaraní, who practiced swidden agricultural at the time of contact. Even so, it is possible that iron tools contributed to increased cultivation and sedentariness. A 1620 Jesuit report provides one of the clearest descriptions of Guaraní cultivation practices in the Asunción region: Guaraní are "very agricultural (labradora) always sowing in the forests and every three years, at least, they move gardens."[121] This source has been interpreted as a statement on the pre-Columbian Guaraní, but it may also reflect enhanced swidden activities thanks to iron tools. A Jesuit in Guairá clearly identified the ax as the favorite tool for clearing land for cultivation. Beyond their application to cultivation, metal tools were applied to all kinds of activities, especially the construction of longhouses (oga) and palisades.[122] Even though Guaraní used new steel and iron tools for cultivation and construction, this does not necessarily mean that all Guaraní produced more food or houses simply because they could. Carlos Fausto found that when a twentieth-century band of Parakanã gained access to greater numbers of axes and machetes, this actually reinforced their turn away from agriculture and toward hunting, gathering, and warfare. For example, with axes and machetes, this group found it much easier to open the extremely hard babassu coconut.[123] Guaraní adoption of European metal contributed to decreased time in clearing land for gardens, building dwellings, and increased potential for gathering, hunting, trade, and warfare. These developments may have led to increased sedentariness *or* to increased mobility.

Aside from their potential to affect efficiency and social organization, new objects in Guaraní hands likely acquired transcendental meaning. In a structuralist reading of Tupí-Guaraní desire for European objects, anthropologist Eduardo Viveiros de Castro notes that "European implements . . . were also signs of the powers of exteriority, which it was necessary to capture, to incorporate, and to make circulate, exactly like the writing, the clothes, the ritual bowing gestures of the missionaries, the bizarre cosmology that they disseminated."[124] The visions of a Guaraní shaman named Juan Cuaraçí, who opposed the reducciones and Spanish power in the 1620s, provide a concrete example of the "powers of exteriority." (I provide detailed analysis of Cuaraçí in chapter 4.) In a yerba-induced vision, Cuaraçí, who was born into a world with conquistadors and priests, saw a variety of heavenly beings (*diablos*) and one of them bore a trumpet made of iron. This may reflect the perception that iron was a powerful metal. While the word for iron as recorded in Montoya's lexicon does not suggest this connection, an iron mine in Guairá does. Sometime in the sixteenth century, Spaniards discovered raw iron ore in Guairá and began mining it with indigenous laborers. It was named Coraçy Berá, which may have meant "resplendent sun." In the context of cuñadasgo exchanges, it is possible that iron cuñas were associated with otherworldly strength.[125]

Women, metal tools, and clothing or cloth circulated with frequency in Paraguay, and these exchanges acquired meanings derived from divergent notions of exchange. While women appear to have been commodified as essential servants, they also represented the political alliance between conquistadors and tuvichá. Material objects or even human beings can easily be stripped down to their utilitarian purposes, but to more fully appreciate their importance in the landscape of contact and transculturation they must be understood within a complex of meanings revolving around reciprocity and social reproduction.

Conclusion

Conquistadors' reliance on Guaraní kinship caused cognitive dissonance among early settlers. At the least, it caused the perhaps uncomfortable realization that something beyond concubinage was occurring. The conquistador Ochoa de Eizaguirre pointed out the ironies of Christians taking on multiple Guaraní wives, considering Spaniards' long history of *reconquista* in Muslim Iberia:

> There is so much shamelessness and so little fear of God among us. We cohabit with the indias and there is not a Koran of Mohammad (*alcoran de maoma*) that permits such shamelessness. . . . There are men so depraved that they think of nothing else; you couldn't give them anything to return to Spain. . . . This vice is deeply rooted in us.[126]

Ochoa de Eizaguirre was further discomforted by the fact that while priests were teaching Guaraní monogamy as required by the Christian gospel, the conquistadors were taking "ten" or "twenty" "relatives and sisters" and having sexual relations with these ("echandonos con todas"). (Despite his strong condemnation of conquistadors taking on multiple Guaraní wives, Ochoa de Eizaguirre himself likely had his own Guaraní concubines, for he switches from first person to third person throughout his letter.) By indexing Christian behaviors as going beyond what Muslim law deemed appropriate—the Koran limited Muslim men to four wives—Ochoa de Eizaguirre suggested that the conquistadors were becoming even worse than heretics: they were becoming Guaraní.[127] He worried that if the political divisions among the conquistadors were not resolved "the Christians [would] be worse than the indios (*infieles*)."[128] Juan de Salazar reported to the Council of the Indies in 1556 that if the conquistadors were all to die, their children (mostly mestizos) would "remain as Indians in their customs, not having dealings with Christians."[129]

Other observers found Spaniards' adoption of cuñadasgo to be morally reprehensible. The friar Francisco González Paniagua declared in 1545 that Paraguay was a "Mohammed's Paradise."[130] He was further scandalized by the fact that Christians did not call the relatives of their Guaraní servants "brothers of my servants" but instead "brother of my women" (*mujeres*) and "my brothers-in-law" (*cuñados*), "fathers-in-law" (*suegros*), and "mothers-in-law (*suegras*) with such shamelessness as if they were united in legitimate marriage to the daughters of these indios and indias." Conquistadors did not make "legitimate" wives of their Guaraní criadas, either in the Spanish-Christian context or in the Guaraní social context. What Guaraní and conquistadors forged together was a new system of exchange that, while ultimately unequally beneficial to the conquistadors, provided a cultural and social landscape of interaction and reciprocity that Guaraní could patch into their social framework. This pattern of cuñadasgo emerged because there were few other viable options. Elman Service notes that in the case of Paraguay, "control had to be immediate and specific, reaching the individual Indian, in contrast to the situation in . . . Mexico" where greater institutional overlay between Spanish and Nahua institutions existed.[131] In other words, the indirect rule common in other regions was not possible in Paraguay because of the diffuse and fluid nature of Guaraní political power. But "control" may overstate conquistadors' presence, at least in the first fifty years, for kinship and alliance was costly.[132] The emergence of iron tools as a currency is a strong reminder of the ways in which cuñadasgo and economy were intertwining in the early years. Cuñadasgo continued to change as colonial priorities changed and as Guaraní became more integrated in the colonial political system. The next chapter will explain how cuñadasgo became institutionalized as a formal system of colonial exploitation while simultaneously promoting kinship and reciprocity.

CHAPTER 2

Institutionalizing Kinship

The Encomienda and Franciscan Reducciones, *1550s–1640s*

WRITING TO THE crown in 1573, the veteran conquistador Martín de Orué detailed the ecological potential of the Paraguayan province: fertile soils, vast pasture lands, and rich natural resources. But according to Orué, this abundance had been wasted during the first three decades of colonial presence: "instead of populating the land, [the conquistadors] have destroyed it by searching for the Lake of El Dorado and the New Atahualpa."[1] By "New Atahualpa" Orué implied that the conquistadors had chased the dream of finding a wealthy political empire they could topple, loot, and extract surplus from tributaries. Populated with politically autonomous groups of semisedentary Guaraní and nonsedentary peoples of the Chaco, Paraguay provided no indigenous political framework for exploitation. Orué reveals a truth about the Spanish conquest: conquistadors sought out indigenous political empires with the assumption that these would provide easier access to labor and precious metals.[2] Conquistadors in Paraguay persisted in seeking out greener colonial pastures for nearly two decades after founding Asunción in 1537. In fact, until encomiendas were distributed in 1556, many of the settlers in Paraguay still considered the region to be a "conquest" or a region where conquistadors held tenuous political authority over Natives and sought to establish their own authority.[3] Spaniards could not claim any general "conquest" of the Guaraní; only a handful of villages were subject to Spanish political power, and even then it was generally through the bonds of cuñadasgo.

By the mid-1550s, however, things began to change. Royal officials and settlers pressured Governor Irala to institutionalize a tributary system with the assignment of repartimientos or encomienda units, which he did in 1556. This abrupt shift from relationships forged through Guaraní norms of kinship to a formalized institution of colonial tribute has led several scholars to suggest that 1556 marked the beginning of a rapid slide toward Guaraní cultural loss.[4] Louis Necker's conclusions on the topic are representative of the consensus: "Spaniards transformed themselves from kin and allies of the Indians to masters and oppressors, exercising domination within the encomienda, an institution totally foreign to the indigenous culture."[5] More recent histories address the transition from a system based on Guaraní kinship to colonial tribute with greater nuance.[6] It is indisputable that the formalization of the encomienda ultimately contributed to the transformation of Guaraní social organization over the long term; nonetheless, Guaraní cultural norms informed the function and practice of encomienda. As in other regions of Spanish America, the encomienda took on a transcultural dynamic. So whereas *coatiquitl* correlated to the encomienda in central Mexico and *mit'a* corresponded to repartimiento in the Andes, Guaraní tovajá-polygyny informed the encomienda in Paraguay.[7] As central actors in cuñadasgo, Guaraní chieftains actively contributed to the development of the encomienda.

In the period between 1556 and the 1570s, there are few sources with indigenous perspectives, limiting our ability to evaluate encomienda relations; therefore, measuring the effect the encomienda had on Guaraní social organization requires examining Guaraní responses to colonial conditions across a wider span of time. The period from 1556 to 1640, a period in which the encomienda was created and Franciscans actively founded the majority of Guaraní reducciones, is a useful periodization because these activities produced more sources that contain Guaraní voices. The encomienda as a colonial institution evolved alongside the reducciones, the latter serving as population bases for the former. It was during this critical period of transition, transformation, and disruption that encomenderos solidified their claims on formal encomienda units and a more consistent form of tribute payment emerged. Yet, even as encomenderos gained a more formalized grip on laborers, Guaraní infused the encomienda with the cultural logic of kinship.

The tribute Guaraní gave to Spaniards within the encomienda was considered *servicio personal* (personal service) and was frowned upon by officials and many priests because of its affinity to legal servitude. The accusations of illegal enslavement that contemporaries made against encomenderos moved easily into modern scholarship.[8] But historical work across the Atlantic world has critiqued the idea that slavery had universal sociocultural meaning and that to better understand slavery or coerced labor in the colonial context, historians need to understand the meaning of those institutions locally.[9] Across sixteenth-century Spanish America, the experiences of indigenous servants varied widely.[10] After the creation of Indian reducciones in Paraguay, two kinds of tributary categories emerged. After the first distribution of encomiendas, indios who lived permanently among Spaniards were often called *yanaconas*, an Andean term that means personal retainer or servant. This terminology persisted to around the first quarter of the seventeenth century when it was replaced by the terms *indio de servicio* or just *indio*. By the late seventeenth century, yanaconas were described as *indios originarios*, a term implying that their origin or birth was the city of Asunción. This terminology is confusing, since *originario* in Tucumán and other regions in the Andes meant communities or villages of Indians tied to their own lands. Encomenderos' and officials' use of the term *originario* to describe indio populations living permanently in Asunción was likely an attempt to apply a sense of fixity to a transplanted population and thereby rhetorically create an air of legality around an illegal practice. *Originario* also reflected Spaniards' attempts to legally construct the city as a reducción, or a place where indios could realize crown-approved forms of Christian life. These ideas shine through in the career of governor Juan de Garay (r. 1578–1581), who admonished Spaniards to keep Guaraní on their ranches, farms, and homes. Garay hoped that Guaraní would remain on Spanish estates for longer than ten years and thereby become "natural" yanaconas of the city—a Spanish law of Roman origins stipulated that ten-year residency produced citizenship. In this case, the ten-year rule allowed encomenderos to claim that indios belonged on their chacras and not in their original villages. Garay noted that the Indians would live "congregados" in the city and receive instruction on how to be good Christians from their Spanish masters, thereby fulfilling the requirements for encomenderos in the New Laws of 1542.[11] The second category of tributaries in Paraguay were *mitayos* or indios from reducciones who served the mita, another Andean term that came to mean rotational labor draft. Unlike yanaconas/originarios, mitayos served for months at a time before returning to their reducciones.

Unlike other regions in Spanish America where personal service was largely extinguished in the sixteenth century, in Paraguay personal service was the primary means by which Guaraní fulfilled tribute obligations under the encomienda system. Despite crown officials' multiple attempts to eradicate personal service in Paraguay, it remained the primary form of tribute throughout the colonial period. But the persistence of personal service was not wholly the result of Spanish stubbornness; rather, it can be attributed to the choices of countless Guaraní to integrate their evolving social practices with colonial society. While disruptive to many Guaraní communities, the encomienda did not constitute a rupture with the practice of cuñadasgo; instead, it resulted in its institutionalization.

Cuñadasgo, as practiced within the encomienda, evolved as Guaraní joined reducciones spearheaded by Franciscan and secular priests between the 1580s and the 1640s. The pueblos created a more stable (i.e., sedentary) labor pool for encomenderos and promoted a streamlined indigenous leadership structure. Whereas before the encomienda Spaniards engaged with autonomous Guaraní tuvichá independently, in the reducciones they negotiated with caciques whose status was officially recognized within the reducciones. During this transformative period for Guaraní, the shift from village to reducción and from Guaraní tovajá exchanges to encomienda cuñadasgo, personal connection between cacique and encomendero remained—even the kinship terms—but these relationships were inherited or meted out by the governor as encomiendas.

Occurring over the course of two or three generations, these gradual transformations had a profound impact on Guaraní in the orbit of cuñadasgo and the encomienda. Having made conquistadors into polygamists, Guaraní who congregated into the reducciones gradually adopted monogamy, and the power of the tuvichá became increasingly detached from his ability to control female kin. These changes contributed to a formalized system of tribute that congealed in the 1640s and served encomenderos until after independence in the nineteenth century.[12]

Institutionalizing Kinship

Governor Irala launched two final expeditions for the Andes in 1547 and in 1553, both fraught with desertion and internal rivalries among conquistadors and Guaraní warriors. One outcome of these expeditions was that Irala learned that highland Bolivia had already been claimed by conquistadors from Peru.[13] This development led officials to treat Paraguay more like a permanent settlement, not merely a platform for expeditions. In 1551, officials made the first census or padrón of surrounding Guaraní villages. Four years later, royal provisions arrived instructing Irala to distribute Indian communities in encomiendas, and in 1555 and early 1556 Native communities were finally assigned encomenderos.[14] Irala noted that he allocated nearly 20,000 Guaraní to 320 Spaniards (out of around 650 Spaniards), thus making over half of the Spanish population encomenderos.[15] Before examining what these allocations meant for Guaraní, it is important to consider why it took so long to create encomiendas in Paraguay.

The pressure to congregate and "encomendar" Indians had been mounting against Irala for years, but by 1555 his hand was forced.[16] In that year, royal provisions came from Spain and crown officials and locals pressed him to officially assign Guaraní to encomenderos.[17] Irala's explanation for why he delayed in creating repartimientos speaks volumes about his perceptions of the land, his dashed hopes for greater conquests, and the nature of Spanish-Guaraní relations:

[Your servant] has been occupied many times in making and sustaining *armadas* to discover and conquer lands which, he was informed, contained wealth of gold, silver and great populations of people. He has dedicated himself to this effort so that God, Your Majesty, and the conquistadors, vassals of Your Majesty, could be served. He has not attempted to make a repartimiento out of this land nor an encomienda out of the natural Indians . . . because the land is miserable and contains a small and scattered population. They are a people without lord and leader to whom they should pay obeisance or with whom they should trade or provide tribute. To the Spaniards, they have only provided the service of their persons, an ancient custom of this land that has been kept and guarded. All the Indians or a great part of them are connected with the conquistadors and *pobladores* by way of kinship, having given their daughters, sisters, women, and relatives so that they serve them. For all these reasons your servant has not wanted to distribute the Indians. . . . And if by doing this a scandal or disturbance or other damage occurs, may the blame and charge be to Your Majesty's officials and to their possessions, not to your servant.[18]

Irala's reluctance to institute the encomienda in Paraguay underscores the conquistador ideal to identify and colonize sedentary peoples who could integrate with political empire through tribute payment and political obeisance. Guaraní could only offer their personal service through kinship bonds. According to Irala's logic, without powerful political figures and the ability to manipulate and access the labor resources of large Guaraní political units, the encomienda was not a viable labor structure. Instead of the encomienda, Irala held, conquistadors received Guaraní personal servants "by way of kinship."

Despite his hesitation, Irala proceeded to institute the encomienda in 1556. Little is known about the logic of the original encomienda units. Irala must have considered preexisting Spanish-Guaraní kinship ties when allocating encomienda grants. For example, it is likely that Irala first determined which Spaniards already possessed kinship alliances with specific teyÿ and then sanctioned those relationships as an encomienda, and to these additional teyÿ would have been added indiscriminately. Spaniards estimated that the best encomiendas were those that were products of cuñadasgo and the less attractive encomiendas were those in far-flung regions where little or no contact had been made.[19] But even if assigned indiscriminately, it is clear from later documentation that encomiendas were shaped around the teyÿ or individual tuvichá and that, to a degree, encomenderos continued to adhere to the norms of exchanging women in Guaraní society.

After the initial assignments, contemporaries complained that Irala had created excessive numbers of encomienda and that they were too small, insinuating that in his attempt to appease everyone he had harmed everyone. Juan Salmerón de Heredia, for example, thought it unfair that the already downtrodden and impoverished conquistadors of Paraguay only received encomiendas of ten, fifteen, or thirty Indians when the typical encomienda in Peru was around four to five thousand strong.[20] One conquistador was awarded an encomienda of sixteen Indians that was situated eighteen leagues from Asunción and concluded that his grant was good for nothing.[21] The standard for local encomenderos was close access to personal servants. Nearly all the conquistadors who condemned Irala's methods for creating repartimientos also noted that he had given encomiendas to Italians, English (*bretones*), Portuguese, and French.[22] Distributing royal grants to non-Spaniards was bad enough, but giving them out to new arrivals who did not participate in the dangerous expeditions of the last two decades went too far. Nearly all the Spaniards who decried the repartimiento were members of the Cabeza de Vaca expedition that had been on the losing side during the 1544 debacle that resulted in Cabeza de Vaca's imprisonment and ouster from Paraguay. These original conquistadors were offended that they had been passed over for recent arrivals from Peru. Juan Pavón went so far as to claim that the newly arrived Peruvian Spaniards were traitors, suggesting that they had been party to the execution of the viceroy Blaco Núñez Vela during the bloody Peruvian civil wars of the 1540s.[23] Even *conquistadoras* weighed in. The resilient Spanish woman doña Isabel de Guevara, who arrived in the region with the Mendoza expedition, addressed her grievances to the Spanish Princess, doña Juana. She explained that Irala had not given her "the service of a single Indian," an injustice that ignored her valiant career as a participant in the conquest. During the most tumultuous episodes of the conquest, especially when the expedition starved at Buenos Aires, Guevara and other women of the Mendoza expedition cared for sick men, cooked food, cleaned clothes, and even fought off enemy Indian attacks. Doña Guevara's husband, Pedro de Esquivel, a Spaniard from Seville and member of the Cabeza de Vaca expedition, was on Irala's bad side and was not awarded an encomienda, so doña Guevara asked for an "encomienda be granted to me in perpetuity" and a political office for her husband.[24]

To be sure, Irala's repartimiento was shaped by nepotism, patronage, and regional affiliation (a Viscayan, Irala was quick to award his fellow compatriots), but indigenous norms also informed the original distribution. One clue that Irala drew on indigenous social organization to allocate encomiendas is that so many encomiendas were granted: a total of 320.[25] The size of the encomiendas ranged, but generally they were small: fifty to sixty tributaries. The crown defined *tributaries* as men between the ages of eighteen and fifty. A group of nearly one hundred conquistadors received dismally small units of between fifteen to thirty Guaraní.[26] Units of this size would have been equivalent to one or two teyÿ. Considering the deep rifts among the settlers, it is reasonable to conclude that Irala's move to create so many encomiendas was an attempt to appease his enemies and award his cronies. However, it is also true that the practice of cuñadasgo was not possible with large groups of Guaraní. A single Spaniard did not have the resources to negotiate with dozens of caciques to arrange labor gangs. Had Irala disregarded kinship and Guaraní social units, then he would have made much larger encomiendas and fewer encomenderos, but this was simply not possible and so Spanish colonial institutions were poured into indigenous molds. However, this over-lay was not a perfect fit, and new encomenderos acted as if their authority over Guaraní was derived from colonial dominion.

The most disruptive repartimientos were those that abrogated long-estab-lished kinship relationships. The conquistador Diego Tellez de Escobar related that the Indians wanted to flee because they were not allowed to "serve or go to the houses of Christians they were accustomed to serving."[27] Enough Guar-aní became enraged by the new impositions that flight or armed resistance became the only viable options. In 1560, some Guaraní violently resisted Span-ish demands. The uprising was instigated by Guaraní who had recently returned from a failed expedition led by Nuflo de Chávez in 1558. Motives for the rebellion are not clear, but the timing points to Spanish mistreatment of Guaraní during the expedition, as well as onerous encomendero demands.[28] The rebellion was quelled by the new governor Francisco Ortiz de Vergara (elected 1558). Another Guaraní rebellion congealed in 1556 under the direction of an unnamed shaman who claimed to be a god or the son of god and offered his followers alternative baptisms. The cleric Martín González explained that Guaraní followed this shaman because the newly arrived bishop, Pedro Fernández de la Torre, had excommunicated a number of Guaraní, supposedly for idolatry. If we follow de la Torre, the source of Guaraní discontent was not the encomienda but religious in nature.[29]

Irala issued his ordenanzas or regulations for the encomiendas on May 14, 1556, and they reflect his unrealized ideals regarding encomienda labor. The ordenanzas attempted to control and restrain Guaraní political leaders, legally transforming them into officials whose authority was tethered to local regal authority. The principals, mayorales, or caciques, as Spaniards com-monly called indigenous leaders, were to be the intermediaries between encomenderos and tributaries. But this system required that Guaraní com-moners recognize their tuvichá's enhanced political authority within the new colonial system. In fact, many Guaraní disobeyed their caciques, for Irala explicitly demanded that Guaraní were "obliged to obey their *principales*."[30] As part of his effort to control Guaraní authority, Irala hoped to halt the tuvichá's power to direct women and relatives to other tuvichá and especially to other Spaniards. The goal was to restrict the exchange of women and reciprocal obligations to the encomienda. This was effective to a degree. Gradually, it became impossible for Spaniards to go independently into a Guaraní community, to become kin, and to receive women, a right that after 1556 was under the legal purview of the governor. While Irala was able to restrict cuñadasgo to encomenderos, he was not able to control relationships between encomenderos and tuvichá. Tuvichá continued to interact in the encomienda through the cultural ties of cuñadasgo and women exchanged in the encomienda continued to carry similar political weight.[31]

Many of the assertions made above are built on a relatively small batch of *probanzas* (proofs of merit) and relaciones. Analysis of litigation records and attempts to reform the encomienda complement and expand this appraisal of the encomienda. A criminal investigation from the eastern region of Guairá foregrounds the networks of cuñadasgo as they operated within the legal framework of encomienda. Guairá was even less developed than Asunción, with only 150 vecinos distributed in the region's two cities of Ciudad Real and Villa Rica. In the year 1557, Ruy Díaz de Melgarejo, an enemy of Irala, led a group of conquistadors and mestizo settlers who were not granted encomiendas or who were assigned dismally small encomiendas to settle the eastern territory of Guairá. Spaniards maintained very little real control over the Guaraní in the region but brought with them the frameworks of legal tribute in the form of the encomienda. Unlike Asunción, where cuñadasgo preceded the encomienda by two decades, in Guairá cuñadasgo was forged simultaneously within the legal framework of encomienda. This timing is crucial because the legality of the encomienda generated lawsuits that provide an unusually detailed portrait of early interethnic relations of cuñadasgo.

Tovajá-Tributaries

In April of 1577 in the area of Ygatú, a company of Spaniards led by Captain Ruy Díaz de Melgarejo were moving upriver on their way back to Villa Rica.

They had recently pacified a group of "rebellious" Natives and were likely exhausted from their activities and travels. As they and their native auxiliaries crawled up the river with vigorous paddle strokes, the current became increasingly difficult and the rapids treacherous. Just above the "salto grande" (perhaps the marvelous Iguazú Falls), they took lodging at a Guaraní village to rest for a few days. Spaniards had access to this village because at least one member of the company, Ortuño Arbildo, possessed an encomienda in the village and was therefore a tovajá to a prominent tuvichá in the village. It is difficult to gauge how the Guaraní villagers perceived the Spaniards' arrival, but it was probably mixed. Some may have received Arbildo, a brother-in-law, and the company of Spaniards warmly at the prospect of receiving cloth and iron tools. Others may have suspected that they might be sent with the Spaniards as criados and feared the drastic changes they would experience.

While it is unclear what Guaraní thought about the Spaniards' arrival, the documents reveal that Spaniards were filled with trepidation. They feared a powerful mburuvichá in the region named Maçaru who exercised a degree of political authority over this particular village as well as surrounding villages; according to the Spanish captain, Maçaru was the "key to the whole land."[32] Given the current atmosphere of Guaraní resistance, Captain Melgarejo feared that Maçaru could have called on his allies to attack the Spaniards if they behaved poorly. Melgarejo therefore gave strict orders to his men that they should respect the villagers. Moreover, he ordered that Maçaru's granddaughter was not to be touched. While her age was never recorded, it is clear that she was baptized, for Spaniards referred to Maçaru's granddaughter as María. It turns out that she was an important person and, when it came to marriage, was reserved for someone of higher status than a Spanish encomendero: Maçaru had arranged for María to marry another tuvichá named Alonso (also baptized) in the same village.

It appears that Arbildo was upset that one of his tributaries (María), who Spanish witnesses claimed was rather beautiful, was betrothed to a Guaraní cacique. Moreover, María and Alonso's potential union represented the loss of a woman from Arbildo's encomienda, which meant the loss of not only physical but also sexual labor, for women perpetuated the encomienda population. But the issue goes beyond access to labor. Arbildo's offense at being passed over as Maria's future husband reveals how deeply encomendero-tovajá were entrenched in Guaraní social practice. As a conquistador polygamist, Arbildo competed with other Guaraní leaders over access to women and he lost. This turn of events publicly revealed that Arbildo's position in the Guaraní politico-filial landscape was lower than other competing Guaraní men.

Taking offense at being passed over, Arbildo ignored his superior's orders and met with Maria's brother, Sebastián, to request that he give up his sister. This kind of negotiation between tovajás was typical in early colonial Paraguay. Arbildo approached Sebastián while the latter was resting in his hammock under the shade of his longhouse. After making his proposal and offering several items of clothing, Sebastián rose from his hammock in anger and cast the offering of clothes aside. Later that day, the relentless Arbildo demanded that María untie her hammock from Sebastian's longhouse and take it to his own. She refused. Intent on succeeding, Arbildo sent a friend named Juan Ruíz, a younger man of around twenty-six years old, to take María by force and bring her to a hut some distance from the village. Ruíz brought María to Arbildo and hung her hammock next to Arbildo's hammock. María resisted Arbildo and defended herself from Arbildo's sexual advances, but she was not successful. Upon hearing that Arbildo had raped María, Sebastián went directly to Captain Melgarejo to protest. Arbildo was promptly apprehended and shackled inside a longhouse in the village. Melgarejo immediately began an investigation and took several depositions in the village. Perhaps concerned that they would suffer retribution, Melgarejo ordered that the Spanish company resume its journey to Villa Rica by river, with the now humbled Arbildo chained to the ribbing of one of the canoes. Once in Villa Rica, more depositions were taken, Arbildo's goods were inventoried, and he was sent to Asunción, where the governor was to oversee the rest of his trial.

Arbildo's use of sexual violence against María is a reminder of the traumatic and painful experiences brought about by the Spanish conquest. However, if we read the criminal investigation against Arbildo only as a story of Spanish dominance then we miss an opportunity to analyze the colonial encounter as a transcultural political process. Arbildo's actions and the subsequent investigation demonstrate that at least in the early years of colonization, Spaniards did not reign over their tributary populations. Arbildo himself demonstrated the typical pattern for acquiring Native female tributaries in colonial Paraguay during the sixteenth and early seventeenth centuries when he approached María's brother and offered him clothing in exchange for wives. The seemingly utilitarian and economic motives of these exchanges possessed social and cultural meanings shared by both Guaraní and Spaniards. The translator for the Spanish company, Francisco Montañés, described Arbildo as Sebastián's "brother-in-law encomendero."[33] At least in this moment, cuñadasgo and the encomienda functioned more within Guaraní sociopolitical logic than Spanish colonial logic.

Maçaru's and Sebastián's behaviors further illustrate the relationship between political authorities in Guaraní communities. The Spanish captain fretted that Maçaru, as "the key to the whole land," could unite Guaraní for war, suggesting that Maçaru was regarded as a mburuvichá of a guará who maintained kinship networks with Sebastián's and Alonso's respective teyÿ.[34] Given Sebastián's prominent role in determining María's marriage partner, why did Maçaru also wield authority over her? Although the translator rendered María as Maçaru's "granddaughter," it was probably not that simple. In Guaraní society, children called their fathers' brothers "father" and mothers' sisters "mother"; likewise, all grandchildren called their grandfathers' brothers or cousins "grandfather."[35] Maçaru had profound power over women who called him "father" or "grandfather," just as Sebastián had power over women who called him "brother." Maçaru desired to unite his "granddaughter" with Alonso, a cacique in Arbildo's encomienda. That María's brother, Sebastián, so earnestly refused Arbildo's offer and attempted to honor Maçaru's desires suggests that he recognized Maçaru's authority— or at least the authority to arrange marriages with women in his teyÿ. Not willing to give up María, Sebastián offered Arbildo four other women. These women were probably Sebastián's cousins, sisters, or nieces. Exchanges of women often occurred between tovajás, as was the case in the negotiations between Arbildo and Sebastián.[36]

Arbildo's interest in María's hammock suggests that he symbolically hoped to communicate his possession of María as a bride. That her hammock was placed next to his perhaps indicated that a sexual relationship had ensued; by raping María, it appears that Arbildo was engaging in what he understood to be a kind of conquest of her. From a Spanish perspective, a man's rape of a woman could taint her and her family's honor and make a future marriage very difficult.[37] But this was not true among Guaraní, where monogamy was not yet an ideal. In fact, for María the rape did not serve as an impediment to her marriage, for she was promptly married to Alonso (the tuvichá Maçaru intended to unite with María) by a cleric in Villa Rica.[38]

This episode from Guairá shows that in some contexts, Spanish-Guaraní relations in the postencomienda context changed, but mainly for Spaniards. A Spaniard's access to cuñadasgo was restricted to those fortunate enough to receive an encomienda. Moreover, encomenderos were prohibited from augmenting their network of cuñadasgo outside of the community they were assigned. While the mechanics of cuñadasgo had not changed for Guaraní, the ability of tuvichá to negotiate with individual Spaniards was restricted to official encomenderos. Nonetheless, as this example from Guairá shows, tuvichá continued to arrange unions between villages. While cuñadasgo was channeled through the colonial apparatus of the encomienda, Guaraní patterns of reciprocity and meanings of relatedness grew up around it and tuvichá continued to exercise authority over the women subject to an encomendero. The relationships and networks analyzed in this episode in Guairá were specific to a period when Spaniards had little to no real authority over Guaraní groups. In the following section, we turn back to Asunción to understand how Spaniards attempted to strengthen their grip on Guaraní communities in the context of the early Guaraní reducciones.

Fixing the Guaraní

As in the case of Ortuño Arbildo, the independence of tuvichás sometimes frustrated encomenderos' efforts to extract more labor from Guaraní teyÿ. Many Guaraní leaders were not willing to submit to Spanish authority and simply relocated their villages when colonials' demands pushed them to the breaking point. In fact, when Guaraní communities removed themselves from Spanish territories, Spaniards called this "rebellion" and often attempted to bring them back.[39] In addition to fleeing, many Guaraní openly resisted Spanish authority in the region. Several sources speak of general rebellions led by loosely connected mburuvichás and shamans.[40]

Louis Necker counts eleven Guaraní resistance movements against Spanish power from the 1530s through the 1570s and concludes that these rebellions reflected a vortex of Spanish violence as a result of their waning control over Guaraní populations.[41] Necker argues that Spaniards went from kin to becoming harsh oppressors, thus leading the Guaraní to completely reject Spaniards. As we will see, this was not entirely true and Guaraní responded in a variety of ways that included flight, rebellion, and uneven acceptance of Spanish power. The challenges to colonial rule and changing priorities of Spanish governors led to renewed efforts to fix Guaraní communities and convert them to Christianity. For this they turned to priests.[42] With the assistance of Spanish militias and indigenous auxiliaries, Franciscan priests worked to create sedentary Indian pueblos or reducciones. Unlike the Jesuits who sought extreme independence from encomenderos, the Franciscans worked closely with the encomendero class. This was not necessarily by choice, for the largest conglomerations of Guaraní near Asunción were already assigned in encomienda. In fact, the role of encomenderos in the pueblos was so pronounced that Governor Ramírez de Velasco referred to the Franciscan reducciones as the "pueblos de encomenderos."[43]

The first Franciscans arrived in 1575 and were active in founding reducciones from the 1580s to around 1630, with a few reducciones founded in later years, including San Isidro de Itapé in 1682.[44] Under the leadership of their most lauded priest, fray Luís de Bolaños, they founded twenty-one reducciones.[45] Spaniards and secular clergy were also involved in founding pueblos during the same period, though many of these communities did not endure on their own and were lumped into Franciscan reducciones.

Historians have dedicated relatively little attention to Franciscan methods for evangelizing Guaraní. In the most important work on the Franciscan reducciones, Louis Necker argues that the Guaraní were converted to the missionaries rather than to Christianity.[46] Recognizing their distinct social position and spiritual power, Guaraní saw the Franciscans as similar to itinerant shaman or karaí. Europeans noticed degrees of shamanism among the Tupí-Guaraní in Paraguay and Brazil. Most villages had pajé or shamans, but karaí were more powerful and rarer. Karaí moved from village to village, might possess multiple wives and servants, were eloquent orators, possessed elaborate and powerful songs, could imbue objects with spiritual power, and prophesied.[47] Similar to karaí, Franciscans preached in Guaraní, used spiritually charged objects, and possessed gifts that initiated bonds of reciprocity. Eloquence and generosity, the characteristics essential for any karaí, were the same characteristics that made Franciscan efforts bear fruit. Franciscans usurped the power of Guaraní shamans, who were the primary instigators of rebellion, thus eliminating a key hindrance to the creation of pueblos. Necker's thesis that Franciscans essentially became shamans is groundbreaking, but his argument that Franciscans saved the Guaraní from imminent destruction at the hands of Spaniards is overblown. Following Service and Susnik, Necker contends that the encomienda nearly exterminated Guaraní culture.[48] Relying primarily on priestly accounts, Necker argues that Franciscans appeared in Paraguay at a time of general rebellion and that they forged a new path toward a peaceful colonial compact. Franciscan fray Felipe Franco in 1618 said that the Spaniards wanted to subdue the Guaraní with "iron and force of arms," but the Guaraní were saved when Franciscans swept in and converted the Guaraní and "put them in *policía*."[49] The root of *policía* is *polis*, or "city," and the term implied converting Indians to Christianity, organized in sedentary communities with orderly governance. Thus, *policía* referred to the condition of "good order" in the reducciones.[50]

While Spanish abuses certainly occurred, the narrative of a Franciscan rescue mission is unrealistic. If the Franciscans were so crucial to reviving and sustaining peace, then how can we explain such prolonged peace in some reducciones when Franciscans were rarely present? Moreover, Franciscans did not work alone but cooperated with Spaniards in founding new reducciones. Like other Spanish American regions, Paraguay did not have enough priests to go around. From their base in Asunción, Franciscans frequented the Pueblos of Los Altos, Itá, and Yaguarón, but they were rarely stationed in the pueblos. Priests paid even less attention to the northern pueblos in Itatín. To maintain obeisance in the pueblos, Franciscans followed their encomendero counterparts' lead and distributed tools and cloth to Guaraní when they came to Asunción to fulfill their tribute obligations, thus maintaining their status as generous leaders.[51] Of course, conquistadors had already established this pattern decades earlier and encomenderos continued to distribute similar objects well into the seventeenth century. In fact, Spaniards' unwritten metric for evaluating whether or not one was a "good" encomendero was determining how many goods he/she gifted to his/her encomendados. In a 1603 suit over an encomendero's poor treatment of his tributaries, the encomendero assembled witnesses who spoke to his consistent and liberal gifting of knives and hatchets to his tributaries.[52] There were similarities with priests. For the Jesuits, gifting was a primary method for founding reducciones. Once gifts like cloth, hatchets, and knives had been distributed and caciques had been baptized and christened, Jesuits believed that a permanent pact had been created between themselves and the native community.[53] Thus, trade and reciprocity were at the center of the reducción-founding process. If violence was employed to bring Guaraní to submission, reciprocity and cuñadasgo were the main methods for maintaining obeisance.

Comparing Guaraní and colonials' accounts of the genesis of individual reducciones, we find divergent perspectives. The first is that of a Guaraní cacique who in 1652 recounted to a Spanish official the origins of his *parcialidad* in Tobatí pueblo (founded in the year 1583 or 1597), when he was only a child.[54]

> I came from [the] Jejuí [region] where many Indians went into the forests. My father, being a good Christian, searched for Spanish lands and came to this pueblo [Tobatí] with some of his vassals. . . . I have always heard it said that others of my father's vassals remained in the forests and these have gathered and populated Arecayá [another reducción] and pay the mita.[55]

The second account is from a Spanish vecino who in 1611 served as a lengua and *protector de indios* (a crown-mandated legal representative of indios) alongside the Franciscan fray Luís de Bolaños and other Spaniards in establishing the pueblo of Yuty.

> [With Bolaños] we both entered the forests, each in his own office, and turned to our duties. God was served that we took from the forests a great quantity of Indians and caciques and we populated and gathered them in the pueblo of Yuty. Among these caciques the first that we took from the forests was the cacique Cururú with his vassals and he told me

he was of the encomienda of Lázaro Gribéo [an Italian conquistador who came with the Mendoza expedition] and was counted as a subject when he was just a young lad.[56]

The first passage by the Guaraní cacique requires careful interpretation because it was produced by a cacique raised in a pueblo, perhaps under the close tutelage of a priest. His claim that his father was a "good Christian" and chose to seek out Spanish lands and join a reducción reflects a desire to demonstrate a loyal Christian identity. Even so, as the next chapter will demonstrate, it was not unusual for Guaraní to seek out reducciones. The reasons caciques abandoned their villages to live in a reducción were many: tools, food, protection from Spaniards or Guaicurú, spiritual power they found in priests, and reconnecting with kin who had already congregated in a reducción. But as the cacique cited above suggested, the choice to join a reducción could be divisive.

Whereas the cacique suggests that his people sought out a reducción, Captain Vallejo's account indicates that he and Bolaños "took" (*traer* and *sacar*) Guaraní out of the forests and settled them in pueblos. But the language of force is deceptive: "to take" Guaraní out of the forests implied a range of activities, including gifting, preaching, and forging kinship. A second point of interest in Vallejo's account is that Yuty was founded as a joint Franciscan-Spanish venture. Franciscans promoted the idea that they alone went into the forests with the word of God and brought Guaraní into the light of Christian civilization.[57] And while there were some reducciones settled with minimal settler involvement, Spaniards often accompanied Franciscans. Spaniards were involved in settling Yuty likely because they were seeking out Guaraní who they knew had once been encomendados. Vallejo noted that among the Indians they "took" from the forest, one cacique who had previously been granted in encomienda to a first-generation Italian conquistador. So when Vallejo said that the Guaraní he sought were "in rebellion," this meant that they had fled encomienda demands. Thus, the creation or regeneration of reducciones and encomiendas were interrelated processes.

The reducciones had a profound impact on Guaraní. Just a few years after a reducción was founded by Bolaños in 1615, another priest named fray Felipe Franco gave his estimation of how the reducciones had changed the Guaraní:

"Today they live in great order (*policía*) and doctrine. Their houses are protected by tile roofs and supplied with provisions."[58] In the priest's mind, sedentariness was related to production and surplus. Moreover, it was in the reducciones that polygyny and cannibalism were gradually eradicated. Social organization was transformed as shamans were replaced by priests and the inheritance of political power was ordered according to lineage and primogeniture. Encomenderos benefited from these transformations and were therefore supporters of the reducción project. With stable sedentary populations, encomenderos could draw more heavily on Guaraní labor from the pueblos on a rotational basis. But, as the next section argues, the inchoate reducciones did not immediately transform Guaraní into pliant tributaries, for cuñadasgo was still the dominant paradigm.

Suits and Suitors: Policing Kinship

A systematic review of court records from the Asunción National Archive reveals a litigious spike between the 1570s and the 1640s. During this period, encomenderos frequently sued each other over the possession of an individual, usually female, tributary. That Spaniards were embroiled in expensive and lengthy legal lawsuits often over a single female tributary underscores the importance of Guaraní women in the encomienda-cuñadasgo system, the persistence of Guaraní sociocultural norms, and Spaniards' reliance on these norms to create and maintain viable labor forces. The reason for the increased litigation is related to the formalization of the encomienda and the creation of the reducciones. The institutionalization of cuñadasgo under the encomienda shifted the regulation of those relationships to the purview of civil authorities. In the pueblos, gubernatorial and priestly oversight provided the bureaucratic weight necessary to maintain such a system. But the system still relied on modified forms of kinship and the power of Guaraní tuvichás to mobilize community members.

The spike in litigation is related to the fluidity of kinship networks running up against the fixity of encomienda units. Typical Guaraní unions, especially between powerful tuvichá, were exogamous unions between distinct teyÿ. But because many encomiendas overlapped with teyÿ, when an interteyÿ union took place, an encomendero lost a tributary. Some of these

TABLE 1.   Distribution of 24 Disputes over Tributaries, 1570–1640

DISPUTES OVER A FEMALE TRIBUTARY	DISPUTES OVER A MALE TRIBUTARY	DISPUTES OVER A FAMILY OF TRIBUTARIES	DISPUTES INITIATED BY INDIOS
15	4	5	4

Sources: 1590, vol. 1987, no. 2, CJ, ANA; 1592, vol. 1810, no. 4, CJ, ANA; 1593, vol. 1966, no. 4, CJ, ANA; 1596, vol. 2117, no. 6, CJ, ANA; 1598, vol. 1941, no. 3, CJ, ANA; 1600, vol. 1810, no. 10, CJ, ANA; 1605, vol. 1811, no. 6, CJ, ANA; 1605, vol. 2185, no. 1, CJ, ANA; 1610, vol. 2010, no. 3, CJ, ANA; 1615, vol. 1685, no. 3, f. 1–36, CJ, ANA; 1617, vol. 1362, no. 2, CJ, ANA; 1707, vol. 71, NE, ANA; 1552, vol. 5, f. 19–69, SC, ANA; 1594, vol. 12, f. 75, SC, ANA; 1594, vol. 12, f. 103, SC, ANA; 1595, vol. 12, f. 177–251, SC, ANA; 1595, vol. 12, f. 109–10, SC, ANA; 1595, vol. 12, f. 130, SC, ANA; 1596, vol. 13, f. 26–56, SC, ANA; 1598, vol. 13, f. 73–170, SC, ANA; and 1602, vol. 14, f. 72–190, SC, ANA.

unions were arranged by other encomenderos in order to augment their tributary populations; in other cases, tuvichá had arranged for the exchange of women. Governor Irala attempted to address these issues when he required that "no [cacique] allow Indians from foreign *repartimientos* to move into their own *repartimiento*," but Guaraní social customs were not consistent with this regulation.[59] The congregation of Guaraní in reducciones contributed to interencomienda unions because higher numbers of teyÿ lived in closer proximity to each other. A description of the following lawsuit illustrates how Guaraní social patterns played out within the encomienda.

On August 14, 1595, Pedro Sánchez Valderrama sued Antonio Denis for taking a Guaraní woman named Francisca out of his encomienda population.[60] The suit dragged on for sixteen months, generated dozens of claims, counterclaims, and multiple rounds of depositions. It began after Denis removed Francisca from a pueblo, placing her in his home in Asunción. Valderrama claimed that Francisca was not Denis's tributary and he persuaded a local magistrate to place her in protective custody until an official sentence could be issued. Valderrama's claim on Francisca hinged on proving that her mother, Mariana, was part of the original encomienda that Valderrama had inherited. This was a common tactic in these kinds of disputes. Francisca was from a pueblo known as Juan Farel. (The pueblo was named after a conquistador who gave his name to the chieftain of said pueblo and it was located in the Itatín region).[61] This pueblo had a historical relationship with encomenderos and at the time of the suit it was likely in the process of being connected to a reducción. On Valderrama's insistence, a notary was sent to the pueblo to take depositions. The witness examinations were designed to establish that Mariana descended from an encomienda that Valderrama had inherited, and indeed witnesses affirmed as much, further revealing that Mariana was the daughter of a powerful cacique named Mocarapé. However, witnesses for the defendant (Denis) testified that although Mariana had once belonged to Valderrama's encomienda, she had since joined Denis's encomienda through marriage to her second husband, also a cacique. Witnesses' explanations of their kinship with Francisca and Mariana reveal that Guaraní kinship terms like *sister/brother* and *mother/father* did not easily map onto Spanish notions of kinship. One witness named Elvira said that she and Mariana were "sisters." The interpreter explained that "they are sisters . . . according to their customs" and then clarified that this implied cousins in the European context.[62] Remember that children of two sisters referred to each other as siblings, not cousins. Aunts, by European terms, were often referred to as "little mothers" by their nieces and nephews.[63]

Ultimately, the magistrate sided with Denis, providing him access to Francisca's labor and the labor of her children. The magistrate explained that Denis convincingly showed that Francisca's mother, Mariana, had effectively been "annexed" (*aneja*) to Denis's encomienda through marriage, despite the fact that she had originally pertained to the encomienda that Valderrama had inherited.[64] The litigants employed two conflicting legal logics: one demonstrated the tributary's descent from her grandfather, while the other demonstrated descent through the mother's line, identifying her mother's most recent marriage. In the suits over individual female tributaries, this latter logic won out. Thus, rather than following Spanish preference for paternal descent, officials in Paraguay molded legal decisions around the indigenous social reality, which was marked by fluidity and movement of women between teyÿ. In another suit, from 1596, the Spanish defendant won a dispute over a female tributary named Malgarida because he demonstrated that even though she was connected to the plaintiff's encomienda through her grandfather, that patriarchal connection was superseded by the grandmother's marriage to a cacique in the defendant's encomienda.[65] The rulings on these cases underscore the right of a woman to marry and maintain *vida maridable* or married life with her spouse, even if that meant relocating outside an encomienda.

These suits reveal that Spanish encomenderos engaged in widespread manipulation in order to bolster their units. In the 1595 lawsuit involving the encomendero Denis, one of the witnesses, a Spanish vecino named Juan Jiménez, explained that Francisca was cohabiting with a cacique named Francisco in his encomienda, with whom she had produced at least one child. Seeing an opportunity to augment his encomienda population, Jiménez asked Francisco to marry Francisca under the auspices of the Church, a legal act that would officially annex Francisca to Jiménez's encomienda. But Francisco refused, perhaps because he understood the legal weight of a Spanish marriage, which would ostensibly limit him to Francisca. Many encomenderos employed this tactic of arranging a marriage to augment their repartimiento populations.[66]

As in Jiménez's case, the common pattern was for encomenderos to arrange marriages between their male tributaries and foreign females because if litigation ensued, a magistrate would uphold a couple's right to live together, as long as the woman lived with her husband's encomienda population. Local legislation addressing the issue of cross-encomienda unions followed this pattern. In November 1593, Lieutenant Governor Bartolomé Sandoval Ocampo ordered that male Indians from the pueblos could not marry a yanacona in Asunción and take her back to the pueblos because it was draining Asunción of its labor force. Ocampo ordered, therefore, that any male Indian marrying a female yanacona was required to remain in his encomendero's house in Asunción as a yanacona, taking his wife to live with him. The legislation had unintended consequences and three months later, on February 5, 1594, Ocampo rescinded the decree. He explained that "some . . . maliciously persuaded and incited their Indians (yndios) to marry foreign Indians (*yndias*) so that they could bring these [foreign *yndias*] to their houses and use them as servants."[67]

Historians who have noticed these tactics and the litigation that ensued have concluded that they reflect Spanish dominance over the Guaraní.[68] But the cases reviewed here suggest a degree of Guaraní agency, autonomy, and social reproduction. Caciques like Francisco did not allow Spaniards to treat them as pawns to be married to whomever could augment their encomendero's tributary population. Moreover, Guaraní caciques exercised authority over women in their teyÿ and Spaniards relied on caciques' powers to acquire personal servants. In a suit from 1596, two encomenderos, Pedro de Lugo and Miguel López, each claimed labor rights to an indigenous woman. This dispute arose when López went to a pueblo named Palmares (later called Ypané) to acquire a female Native for service in his home. He explained that "while I was in my encomienda pueblo, I needed an *yndia* for my house. A cacique from Pedro de Lugo's encomienda said that I should not take [the Indian I had chosen], but Malgarida instead."[69] López conceded and took Malgarida back to his chacra in Asunción. This cacique ultimately determined which females could be taken from his pueblo and where they were channeled.

On the surface, these suits appear to be about Spanish dominance over Guaraní populations, but in fact they open a revealing window onto the transcultural networks of relatedness and tribute forged between encomendero and Guaraní communities. Moreover, the suits underscore the importance of female service in the encomienda and caciques as purveyors of personal service.

During the period when these suits over individual tributaries proliferated (1580s to early 1640s), colonial officials attempted to reform the encomienda. The legal wrangling over tributaries helped persuade Spanish governors that the encomienda required reforms. Moreover, officials were concerned that disease was weakening Guaraní populations, further spurring protections for indios. Colonial officials believed that the ongoing Franciscan and Jesuit efforts to organize Guaraní in reducciones would help consolidate Guaraní populations, but ironically these efforts contributed to the spread of disease.[70] To address the problem of migration within and between encomienda units and the obvious contradictions of colonialism that cuñadasgo produced, several governors and visiting officials attempted to reform the encomienda. The reform efforts of Juan Ramírez de Velasco (1597), Hernando Arias de Saavedra (1603), and the general inspection by Charcas audiencia judge don Francisco de Alfaro (1611–1618) reveal much about the tangled system of Guaraní kinship and colonial exploitation.

To limit Guaraní movement in and out of their assigned encomienda units, Governor Saavedra prohibited encomenderos from forcing Indians to marry, set down guidelines for residence, and requested that patrilocal residence be the norm. When a couple married, the children of that union were to remain in their father's encomendero's house, even if the mother left the encomienda. The explicit purpose of this regulation, Saavedra noted, was to "avoid lawsuits between vecinos."[71]

Governor Velasco hoped to change the language encomenderos used to describe their tributaries. He demanded that encomenderos stop using the phrase "my Indians," reminding them that, in fact, Indians were vassals of the crown.[72] For officials, this language of possession was symptomatic of encomenderos' improper assumption of power over their tributaries and their close social contact with them. Thus, while the ordenanzas aimed to eliminate any semblance of Indian slavery in Paraguay, they also tried to eradicate the indigenous patterns of alliance and kinship that defined the encomienda. It was presumably for this reason, rather than simple intransigence, that most of the provisions Velasco and Saavedra issued were ignored. This is evidenced by the fact that the same issues were discussed in another reform effort, this time in the form of a royal inspection.

Between 1610 and 1618, don Francisco de Alfaro, a judge of the Audiencia of Charcas, attempted to remodel the encomienda in the Río de la Plata along Peruvian lines and eradicate personal service. He hoped to replace personal service with a wage and a more formalized mita system. Historians of colonial Paraguay suggest that Alfaro's reforms were for Paraguay what Viceroy Francisco de Toledo's reforms of 1570s were for Peru, insofar as they successfully channeled more tribute to the Spanish crown and profoundly restructured Native cultural lifeways through increased demands and formalized reducciones. This claim is overstated, for while Alfaro's reforms provided important legal boundaries regarding limits on periods of labor, the key regulations—namely, the wage and the abolition of personal service—were all but ignored.[73] In short, Alfaro's reforms largely failed because cuñadasgo, not wages or legalistic mechanisms, framed relations within the encomienda.

Friendship and Kinship

Alfaro's reforms addressed Spanish misconduct, personal service, and the yanacona system.[74] When Alfaro came to Paraguay, he observed Guaraní families living with Spaniards on their estates. Surprised by the high rate of racial mixing, Alfaro warned that this social arrangement would result in the disintegration of the "republic of the Indians." His remedy was to create a pueblo close to Asunción in which all yanacona would settle permanently and abolish tribute payment in personal service.[75]

Alfaro built on the reforms of Governors Velasco and Saavedra, who restricted the amount of time mitayos served their encomenderos, with two months of service being the norm. Moreover, both governors took a stricter stance regarding the number of mitayos that could serve from a pueblo: Velasco said only a quarter of an encomienda's male tributaries could serve on the mita at one time, while Saavedra put the number at one-third.[76] Alfaro went a step further and replaced personal service with a head tax on male tributaries (ages eighteen to fifty) that could be paid directly to the encomendero in cloth and/or other agricultural goods (la moneda de la tierra). If a tributary still wanted to pay an encomendero in personal service, then the encomendero would be required to effectively rent a tributary's labor based on a fixed day wage. Alfaro fixed mita service to sixty days and restricted the kinds of work Guaraní mitayos could perform. In performing agricultural work, for example, tributaries were to go on the mita only once per year for sixty days during the harvest period, eliminating year-round personal service. Alfaro also prohibited Spanish contact with Native villages and emphasized the need to settle Natives in urban villages where they could be instructed in the Catholic faith.[77]

As a royal visitador, Alfaro's reforms represented a major increase in royal attention to Paraguay; even so, local encomenderos, priests, and Guaraní resisted and ultimately rejected most of these reforms. The encomendero class suggested that they could rely solely on personal service as tribute because it was built into the indigenous social milieu. Representing the priests of the Mercedarian monastery in March 1612, Father Jerónimo Luján de Medina argued that Alfaro's new regulations would tear apart the bonds that created Paraguay's encomienda community. Father Luján de Medina's strongest piece of evidence came from the Guaraní themselves. Alfaro noted that "the majority of the Indians, especially those in Asunción, say that they do not want to pay the tax. Most say this because they do not know what the tax is. Others say they oppose it because they can serve their encomenderos when and how they want and in return the Spaniards give them some kind of recompense not by way of the tax nor service, *but as kin*."[78] Alfaro concluded that "[Guaraní] would rather serve their encomenderos as they always have."[79] Father Luján de Medina emphasized the idea that encomenderos' estates had become yanaconas' natural homes. He explained that Indians had not been denaturalized from their original communities and that "the majority of [the yanacona] were born in the same houses, plantations, and farms as their encomenderos, growing up in the company of the Spaniards' sons from infancy. An almost natural love (*amor casi natural*) between the one and the other, has been conserved to this day."[80] In fact, Luján de Medina suggested, encomenderos and their Guaraní tributaries were almost family: "they live with their Indians with such love as if they were from the same place to such a degree that the Indians call the Spanish their kin."[81]

Luján de Medina's use of the term *natural* to describe encomendero-Guaraní relations points to the fraught boundaries between socially and biologically derived kinship. Luján de Medina articulated a local Spanish-Guaraní framework that, using Janet Carsten's term, we can call "relatedness." For example, an encomendero might sire a mestiza/o child with one of his yanaconas and that child may be groomed as a Spaniard or may be allowed to remain with her/his mother and inherit her tributary status. The biological "truth" about the mestiza/o is expressed differently depending on whether or not the father decides to socially constitute his relationship with the child.[82] In the networks of cuñadasgo, many encomenderos felt obliged to treat tributary relatives with a degree of respect and reciprocated with the giving cacique. All of this suggests that relatedness in Paraguay required work on the part of the encomendero and Guaraní.

While there was the potential for kindness in these relationships, "kinship and friendship" were firmly rooted in material benefits and reciprocity. Personal service was not free. During the battle over Alfaro's reforms in 1612, Pedro del Toro emphasized that encomenderos reciprocated with tangible goods, not just their "civilizing effect." Encomenderos provided material goods to their encomendados, including mules, tools, cloth, seed, and whatever else was necessary for their fields and crops. Father Luján de Medina noted that on their deathbeds most encomenderos provided material goods for their yanaconas and paid for masses on their behalf.[83]

A review of fifty testaments from the early 1540s to the end of the seven-teenth century suggests that many encomenderos did in fact bequeath resources to their criados/as.[84] Many encomenderos paid a few pesos for masses, prayers, and candle vigils on behalf of their deceased "indios de servicio." While it appears to have been far less frequent, some encomende-ros bequeathed material goods to their yanaconas. In 1593, for example, Damián Muñoz requested that each of the Indians in his service receive a two-piece set of clothes.[85] These bequests were small, to be sure, but the fact of a donation is reflective of the many social nuances found in cuñadasgo, similar to the complicated meanings associated with deathbed manumis-sions.[86] It is difficult to interpret bequests of these kinds, but whatever feel-ings encomenderos had for their tributaries, many regarded them in their wills as servants or domestics who had become part of an extended family unit.

Spanish apologists argued that if they had heeded Alfaro's reforms and installed a head tax Spaniards "would have no obligation to give the Indians" material goods and Christian examples of righteous living.[87] These argu-ments resonate with similar arguments in response to the crown-issued New Laws of 1542. In that era, Spaniards argued that they had a civilizing effect on Indians, treated Indians like their own children, and could not survive with-out Indian tribute.[88] The appeals from Asunción encomenderos were distinct insofar as they highlighted kinship and emphasized the "ancient customs" that had sustained encomienda relations since the conquistadors arrived. Above all, they claimed that personal service was the only option to maintain a viable encomienda system in Paraguay. Encomenderos' claims that cuña-dasgo was preferable to a head tax can be easily brushed aside as simple avarice but must be seen in the light of Guaraní responses to the reforms.

Guaraní rejection of Alfaro's reforms is difficult to interpret. With such a strong encomendero reaction, we might suspect (and some officials did) a display of Spanish ventriloquism.[89] Yet when we consider that Alfaro himself noted indigenous opposition to the reforms, we can move forward with the evidence that follows with less skepticism. As local officials attempted to con-firm and initiate Alfaro's reforms, Guaraní expressed their opposition. Lieu-tenant Governor Francisco González de Santa Cruz was charged with announcing Alfaro's reforms and receiving indigenous leaders' official consent in several reducciones near Asunción and among the yanacona population in Asunción. He held his first meeting on August 12, 1613, in the parish church of San Blas (the Indian and black parish) with the yanacona population. It did not go as planned. Santa Cruz explained to the tributaries that by Alfaro's decree they were to resettle in a designated pueblo just outside the city, where they could learn trades and work for a wage. Several *ladino* indios among them immediately rejected the reforms, explaining that "[they] wanted to serve their encomenderos as they always have done."[90] A little over a week later, on August 22, the protector de indios, Juan Escalante, met with the yanaconas in San Blas and again requested that they accept the reforms. The yanaconas repeated their prior answer and claimed that "their encomenderos love them and treat them like their own children."

Over the course of the next year, the same process was repeated in the Pueblos of Itá, Altos, Yaguarón, and Tobatí, all pueblos within a one- or two-day journey from Asunción. In every pueblo, the logic employed to reject Alfaro's reforms was the same: a head tax would undermine the pattern of service through kinship and friendship. In each pueblo, a *cabildo abierto* was called and all the indigenous leaders of the pueblo were asked to confirm Alfaro's ordenanzas. In the pueblo of Itá, Native officials (alcaldes and regidores) presented a statement that emphasized their concern about instituting a system like the one in Peru. Their disapproval of the Peruvian system was related to the social impact of the head tax and day wage: "we have seen in these parts that *naturales* who contract themselves out and provide service for pay do not endure the difficult work and servitude they find themselves in."[91] They added that one of the cabildo members had been to Peru, observed the labor system firsthand, and was discouraged by it.[92] Itá's cabildo officials concluded that tribute demands should remain connected to an encomendero. Similar responses were recorded in the remaining pueblos' cabildos. The Guaraní's preferred obeisance to Spanish labor demands was embedded within concepts of friendship and kinship. Members of the Altos's cabildo stated, for example, that they preferred to serve their encomenderos as their fathers had done "anciently" and because of the "love and kinship [encomenderos and their tributaries] share."[93]

Several years after Alfaro's departure from Paraguay, Governor Saavedra noted that Alfaro's reforms had been neglected.[94] The central goal of the reforms to eliminate personal service had failed and personal service continued throughout the colonial period. During the proclamation of the reforms in the pueblos, the lieutenant governor conceded to the Guaraní's wishes that customary labor relations remain, officially confirming that those elements of the reforms would not be adopted.

Evidence from another visita conducted nearly forty years after Alfaro's reforms, from 1651 to 1653, by the audiencia judge don Andrés Garabito de León, demonstrate that the central characteristics of cuñadasgo survived Alfaro's reforms. Guaraní described their relationship with the encomendero using the language of love and family, as they had in 1612. Moreover, several Guaraní indicated that their encomenderos treated them well and gave them little work and that they felt obliged to serve them because of their old age and good treatment. These statements certainly do not mean that all tributary-encomendero relations were harmonious. Even so, Guaraní criticism of encomenderos came from an expectation that as "relatives" they deserved better. Garabito de León's visita is an important source because he made great efforts to provide Guaraní the opportunity to speak freely about their encomenderos, resulting in an array of sincere observations about encomienda relations.[95] Interviews with tributaries were conducted in private, and the *oidor* (judge of the audiencia) frequently encouraged tributaries that they should not withhold information and even asked if their encomendero had asked them to lie.

Many yanaconas freely expressed familial obligation toward their encomenderos, as was the case for three blacksmith yanaconas in Asunción (Spaniards often employed indio tributaries and African slaves to run businesses).[96] Yanaconas Pedro, Juan, and Mateo explained that they gave some of their earnings to their encomendera, doña Francisca, but added that she "does not ask them for anything." The yanaconas felt obliged to care for their encomendera even when she did not demand it. In fact, the yanaconas had two of their children, Pedro and Isabel, serve doña Francisca in her house. As prescribed by Alfaro's reforms, doña Francisca gave cloth to her tributaries, but Pedro, Juan, and Mateo explained that because of her need and poverty they did not want to accept the cloth. They asserted that they served their encomendera "with good will."[97]

Other Guaraní similarly indicated that they would not accept their encomendero's payments because of the good treatment they received. Several tributaries belonging to encomendero Francisco Rolón noted that at the end of every year their encomendero had offered them payment in cloth, but they had not wanted to accepted it because they felt grateful for the "love" he had for them in curing their illnesses. They added that they were able to sustain themselves with their own *chacras* or garden plots.[98] A handful of Guaraní claimed they served their encomenderos out of sincere concern. The thirty-year-old widower Miguel explained that he served his sixty-year-old widow encomendera because he had pity for her.[99] A young woman of fourteen named Magdalena left her reducción of her own accord to serve her enco-mendero's wife, doña Marcella, because of the "love she has for [her]" and because "she treats her well and teaches her the Christian doctrine and *buena policía*." For these reasons, the young Magdalena explained, "she did not want to return to the reducción."[100]

The language Guaraní and encomenderos used to describe their tributary relationship transcends the categories of labor or servitude to include a diverse array of relationships created within cuñadasgo. Both Guaraní and encomen-deros used the term *love* to describe their respect for each other. When the encomendero Simon Albertos said that he loved an adult indio of his enco-mienda because the former "raised [the indio] as a son," the encomendero connected the natural love of family with tribute.[101] What did it mean for enco-menderos and tributaries to share love in a colonial context? When the young Guaraní Magdalena said that she served her encomendero because of her love for her, the meaning of that word is not straightforward. We can assume that the Spanish interpreter translated "love" from *mborayhu*, which was the same word Jesuit Antonio Ruíz de Montoya used to describe the Christian concept of God's love.[102] But *mborayhu* is a complicated term. Ethnographers have found that among some modern Guaraní groups, *mborayhu* is related to com-munity and reciprocity. Pierre Clastres argues that the word means "tribal solidarity," while Hélène Clastres translates it as "reciprocity."[103] Assuming Guaraní used *mborayhu* when they said they "loved their encomendero," it seems that the term had specific meanings as it related to reciprocity, commu-nity, and even kinship. Carlos Fausto argues that as love was incorporated in Guaraní-Christian communities, the concept replaced vengeance, predation, and the practice of anthropophagy: "in order to found a new ethic of love (*mborayhu*)—which was probably built on Native concepts of generosity and reciprocity and nurtured by the 'love thy neighbor' ethic of the Christian message—the Guarani concealed the footprints of the jaguar."[104] The predatory consumption paradigm used to transform objects or humans was replaced in the reducciones with the imperative of love. As a social mechanism in the encomienda community, *love* was a highly productive term that evoked relationships of kinship, friendship, dependence, and reciprocity. Defined in this way, *mborayhu* speaks to the ambiguities of relationships built on kinship and coercion, reciprocity and force.

Encomenderos similarly fell back on relatedness as a paradigm for explaining their relationships with encomendados. When Garabito de León asked the encomendero Captain Pedro Rodríguez why he did not keep an account book of his yanacona's labors and his yearly payments, he retorted that he had had no need to keep one, nor would his encomendados have wanted him to because they were like family. Some of the older yanaconas in Rodríguez's unit practically "raised" him. Rodríguez believed that his "love" and "good conduct" toward his encomendados precluded a contractual relationship and that the feeling was mutual.[105] Other Guaraní made similar statements reflecting a paradigm of relatedness. Úrsula and María, two yanaconas working for the encomendero Francisco de Espínola de Santa Cruz explained that their encomendero and his wife treated them "like daughters."[106] The yanacona Ana said that her encomendero had raised her from a young age "like his own daughters." Cuñadasgo's effect on the encomienda is reflected in this rhetoric of kinship, friendship, and love. The existence of this language does not require that encomienda relations be romanticized or artificially constructed as more harmonious, as in Gilberto Freyre's description of slave-master relationships in Brazil.[107] Indeed, subsequent chapters will detail the serious abuses, sexual or otherwise, encomenderos inflicted on the indios who served them. What this language does tell us, however, is the profound impact of cuñadasgo and the existence of an institution that drew on both Guaraní and Spanish cultural imperatives.

Conclusion

In 1688, crown officials attempted yet again to resettle Paraguay's Guaraní yanacona population in pueblos outside the city, just as Alfaro had attempted to do in 1613. The encomenderos, represented by Asunción's *procurador*, Juan Ortiz de Zárate, recited the formula for decentralized authority that allowed local officials to contest crown mandates: "we obey but do not execute."[108] Ortiz de Zárate backed up his position by rehearsing the same arguments used decades before. That personal service remained so dominant in Paraguay throughout the colonial period is not simply a reflection of Spanish aptness in avoiding royal mandates, but the effects of the early patterns of cuñadasgo on the encomienda. Examining the encomienda from its inception into the mid-seventeenth century allows us to perceive the changes and continuities in Guaraní-Spanish relations.

By the late sixteenth and early seventeenth centuries, direct kinship linkages between tovajá-encomenderos and the tovajá-Guaraní faded away. This was a result of the radical changes to Guaraní social norms (like the eradication of polygyny) within the new reducción communities and the formalization of yanacona populations as encomiendas. The best evidence for this trend is the absence of suits over individual female Guaraní after the second decade of the seventeenth century. The language and values of kinship and reciprocity, however, never entirely disappeared. In the 1694 census of the Asunción yanaconas, the governor found an adult tributary named Juan Pasqual among encomendero Juan de Encinas's yanaconas. After examining the physical aspects of Juan Pasqual, the governor determined that he was mestizo.[109] Juan Pasqual, however, desired to remain an "indio" and tributary. The notary recorded that "for the love that he has for his encomendero, Juan de Encinas, and the good treatment and pay he receives [Pasqual] never abandoned the encomienda."[110] We can only speculate about Pasqual's reasons for remaining as an encomendado when he had the opportunity to be free of tribute, but certainly the patronage, housing, agricultural plot, and other resources his encomendero offered the yanacona of this encomienda made striking out on his own unattractive. Pasqual's case is rare, but the language used to describe his connection to an encomendero is rooted in cuñadasgo and underscores some of the elements that bound the encomienda together.

During the conquest period, it was kinship that created servants, the Guaraní criadas who appear in the conquistadors' earliest testaments. And even as real kinship ties between conquistadors/encomenderos and tuvichá became less common, the social context of live-in service on Spanish estates allowed kinship to remain. Spaniards' "gente de servicio," especially the yanacona population, were family, receiving spiritual blessings in Spanish testaments and modest material protections. Many Guaraní explained their relationships with encomendero/as using the word *mborayhu*, which implied reciprocal benefits and a sense of community. If we interpret these networks through Spanish-European lenses, then we could conclude that they are simply networks of patronage or vassalage. But this was not a European institution. Cuñadasgo was rooted in Guaraní notions of reciprocity, community, and kinship that underwent significant changes but were never entirely subsumed under exploitative imperatives.

CHAPTER 3

Embodied Borders

Conflict and Convergence in Guairá, 1570s–1630s

CHAPTERS 1 AND 2 demonstrate that Spaniards and Guaraní in the Asunción region forged relationships of cuñadasgo that were eventually institutionalized as the encomienda. Guaraní political power was reconfigured in reducciones cocreated by Spaniards, Franciscan priests, and Guaraní chieftains from the 1580s to the 1640s. Similar patterns for interethnic relations and colonial institution-building occurred in Guairá, colonial Paraguay's easternmost territory (see Map 2). But the patterns of colonial experience in Guairá diverged from Asunción in two important ways. First, Franciscans maintained a small and peripatetic presence in Guairá, and by 1609 the fiercely independent Jesuits replaced them as the primary evangelical force. Second, the political landscape of Guairá was complicated by the proximity of Guairá to the Portuguese settlement of São Paulo and the presence of other indigenous polities. Portuguese slavers from São Paulo and their indigenous allies invaded Guairá targeting reducciones supervised by encomenderos and Jesuits, thereby setting off a massive exodus from the region in 1628. Thousands of Guaraní fled Guairá with Jesuit priests to establish a new homeland in the southern Paraná River and Uruguay River territories, a region that would become the heartland of the Guaraní-Jesuit mission zone.

Important scholarship on sixteenth- and seventeenth-century Guairá examines the genesis of the Jesuit reducción project, the transcultural dynamics of evangelization among Guaraní, the social character of slavers, the plight of deracinated Natives, and the effects of interimperial politics and Atlantic markets on colonial actions. These histories often treat Jesuits, Spaniards, and Portuguese distinctly without much consideration for the tensions between diverse colonial institutions and distinct indigenous

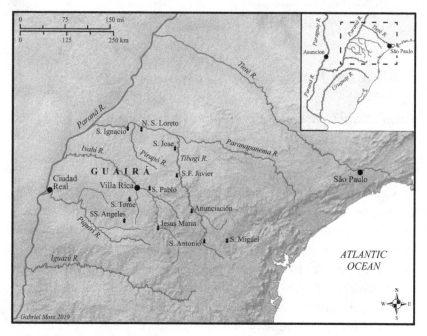

MAP 2. Guairá, ca. 1628

leaders. Other accounts focus on Natives, but they often do so from the van-
tage point of Spaniards, Portuguese, or Jesuits.[1] This chapter elucidates the
differences and similarities between colonial institutions and actors. Moreover, a frontier and borderlands paradigm reveals the political impact of
diverse indigenous groups on colonials' decisions and strategies. Jeremy
Adelman and Stephen Aron's frontier/borderland framework allows for multiple and conflicting sources of power and colonial relations. These authors
define *frontier* as a "meeting place of peoples in which geographic and cultural borders were not clearly defined." Intercultural mixing and accommodation marked interethnic relations, not outright conquest. A borderland
constitutes the "contested boundaries between colonial domains."[2] According to this definition, Guairá was simultaneously a frontier and a borderland.
From 1570 to the 1630s, Spanish Guairá was a space of intense intercultural
exchange, evidenced by the emergence of a variety of transcultural institutions, practices, and actors. While the two small Spanish cities of the region,

Villa Rica (one hundred vecinos) and Ciudad Real (fifty vecinos), wielded significant power over several Guaraní communities, the majority of the region's Natives were claimed as colonial subjects on paper only. Spaniards survived in Guairá because they adopted Guaraní patterns of interethnic alliance or cuñadasgo. If the lack of clear Spanish domination over Natives marks the region as a frontier, then the intense exchange and conflict between Spaniards and Portuguese mark it as a borderland. Spanish Guairá was roughly delineated by the Piquiri, Paraná, Paranapanema, and Tibagi Rivers. The rivers of Guairá—flowing from east to west and into the Río de la Plata basin—served as highways of commerce and mobility and facilitated the economic and social exchanges between Spanish, Portuguese, and indigenous domains. What further contributed to interimperial exchange was the union of the Portuguese and Castilian crowns from 1580 to 1640. The official boundary between the two imperial realms, the Tordesillas demarcation line of 1494, was all but ignored.

As with most borderlands, political identities on the Spanish-Portuguese borderland were unfixed, and individuals demonstrated distinct priorities that may or may not have aligned with their king's priorities.[3] Even though the Jesuit mission enterprise in Guairá partially aligned with Spanish imperial goals, its particular evangelical mission and corporate aspirations often placed it at odds with *Guaireño* (Spanish settlers of Guairá) interests.[4] A focus of this chapter is, therefore, on the oftentimes divergent priorities of colonial actors (simplified as Jesuits, Spanish Guaireños, and Portuguese Paulistas) in the context of an indigenous frontier. Tamar Herzog argues that local interests and actors, not crown officials and royal armies, defined Spanish-Portuguese borderlands throughout the Atlantic world. Indeed, in Guairá, the borderland "agents"—Natives, encomenderos, slavers, and priests—contributed to the process of enacting territories.[5] Natives in Guairá sought autonomy, protection, and community integrity even as colonials sought to claim authority over their communities. The principal objects of colonial ambitions were indigenous bodies and souls, not demarcated geographic territories. The claims colonials made in Guairá correspond to recent scholarship on sovereignty in the early modern world. Lauren Benton argues that colonial "agents" generated sovereignty through geographic corridors such as rivers. In Guairá, Paulistas, Jesuits, and Guaireños generated sovereignty not only by traveling through geographic features but by claiming indigenous bodies.[6] Unlike the contestants for colonial domains in eighteenth- and early nineteenth-century British, French, and Spanish North America, colonials in Guairá did not define political boundaries as spatial territories. Instead, mobile Native communities and the juridico-spiritual assertions that colonials made on them marked boundaries for colonials, a logic of embodied borders. Paulistas, Guaireños, and Jesuits each made specific claims on which bodies they had the right to enslave, demand labor from, or claim as spiritual subjects. Guaraní and other groups often confounded these claims when they moved their communities in and out of colonial jurisdictions. Like unmoored but autonomous buoys in open water, Native communities were perceived by colonials as moving borders whose alliances were in a state of flux due to colonial pressures and interethnic rivalries. For their part, many Native communities actively exploited the competition among colonials by taking sides with the groups that could offer them the most beneficial arrangement. At times this meant allying with the Jesuits, sometimes the Guaireños, and even Paulistas.

The Paulista slave operations reviewed here were among the most destructive to occur on South American soil.[7] Between 1628 and 1640 in Guairá and the neighboring Tapé regions, slavers from São Paulo and thousands of Native auxiliaries captured tens of thousands of Guaraní from villages and reducciones. Paulista slavers who led expeditions to the *sertão*, or Brazilian frontier, came to be known in the twentieth century as bandeirantes (bearers of the flag) and their expeditions as *bandeiras*. The bandeiras to Guairá resulted in the enslavement of approximately thirty-three thousand Guaraní from 1628 to 1632 alone.[8] Working from a Portuguese or Atlantic perspective, several excellent monographs examine the socioeconomic factors and ideological justifications behind Indian slavery. Most notably, John Monteiro's classic *Negros da terra* employs civil documentation from São Paulo to elucidate the social practice of enslavement and slavery in the São Paulo plateau.[9] Following the work on Paulista slavers, scholars have flattened colonial agents in the borderlands, suggesting that Spaniards and Portuguese alike enslaved Indians. This idea lends itself to a narrative of Jesuit heroism: trapped between Spaniards and Portuguese, Guaraní fled to the open arms of the Jesuits in their reducciones.[10] Historians writing from nationalist

(Brazilian or Paraguayan) positions absolve frontiersmen from any wrong-doing or credit them with performing the morally ambiguous work of "clearing the path" for civilization.[11] Recent ethnohistorical research elucidates Guaraní attitudes toward the Jesuits, but it does not take into account the complexities of borderland politics. The nascent reducciones directly challenged the embodied borders logic under which Guaireños and Paulistas operated, thus leading to accelerated slaving activities that culminated in the devastating 1628–1632 slave operations. Ironically, at the same time as Paulistas launched increasingly damaging raids, Guaraní and other Natives took advantage of the competing colonial practices in Guairá to pursue their own agendas.

The story of Guairá is one of intense human suffering and dislocation but also indigenous assertion and colonial pliability. Guairá was a place of contradictions, where Spaniards and Jesuits often played by Guaraní rules while simultaneously subjecting Guaraní to incredible heartache and loss through forcible relocations and harsh labor demands. These contradictions existed among the Paulista slavers as well, who might acquire Guaraní through gifting on some occasions but on others used brute force. A colonial frontier and borderlands par excellence, Guairá challenges straightforward narratives of colonial dominance and indigenous decline. This chapter charts the emergence of Spanish and Portuguese colonial settlements in Guairá in the 1550s to the period of Jesuit reducción formation between 1609 and 1628. It concludes with a brief account of the devastation of the region at the hands of slavers from São Paulo between 1619 and 1632.

Genesis of a Colonial Borderlands

Guairá was home to a large concentration of around 160,000 to 200,000 Tupí-Guaraní peoples, as well as an unknown number of other non-Tupí-speaking groups.[12] Eastern Guairá was a site of encounter between two distinct language-groups: Tupí-Guaraní and Gê. The Tupí-Guaraní included Guaraní, Tupí, Tememinó, Carijós, Camperos, Guañanos, and Caayguas, among others.[13] The Gê-speaking groups included Guayaná, Carajá, Ibira-baquiyara, and Maromomi. These names are "imposed identities" or colonial ethnonyms and do not reflect Natives' own notions of themselves in relation to others.[14] Ethnic names corresponded with colonials' needs to distinguish between groups.[15] Iberian colonial powers were aware of Guairá's dense Native populations in the sixteenth century and established settlements in or near the region in order to exploit and evangelize them. The origins of Guairá as a colonial frontier and borderland must take into account three colonial powers: Spanish Guairá, Portuguese São Paulo, and the evangelical reducción enterprise.

The story of Spanish Guairá begins after the controversial 1556 Asunción repartimiento, or distribution of encomiendas. Those conquistadors not on good terms with Governor Irala were either passed over for encomiendas or were given very small units. Many disgruntled conquistadors left Asunción. More precisely, Irala strongly encouraged these conquistadors to settle Paraguay's eastern territories—a kind of soft purge.[16] This was a typical pattern in conquest-era Spanish America that has been dubbed the "relay" pattern of conquest.[17] Like Cortés's expedition to Mexico or Pizarro's initial foray into Peru, the expedition to Guairá was directed by the ambitious but politically disadvantaged conquistadors moving out from one center in the hope of creating a new one.

The first city of Guairá was called Villa de Ontiveros (1554), situated on the eastern side of the Paraná River, near the salto grande (present day Iguazú Falls). Members of the early colonizing expeditions to Guairá included Spanish, French, English, Italian, and Portuguese settlers, as well as Spanish mestizos, all perceived by Irala to be untrustworthy. The settlers lived up to Irala's expectations. Led by an Englishman named Nicolás Colman, a group of settlers took issue with local leadership and caused serious divisions in the city. Internal feuds were compounded by attacks from Natives and the city fell apart. Most of the settlers from Ontiveros moved north in 1557 to accompany Ruy Díaz Melgarejo, who had been sent by Irala to found another city three leagues north of Ontiveros named Ciudad Real, situated near the confluence of the Paraná and the Piquirí Rivers. Shortly thereafter, Melgarejo founded Villa Rica del Espíritu Santo, thirty leagues to the east of Ciudad Real on the Ivaí River and the mouth of the Corumbataí River. These two cities, Ciudad Real and Villa Rica, were the two main poles of Spanish power in Guairá. Santiago de Jérez was founded far to the north, but it was even more isolated and sparsely populated than the former two.

Following established practices in Asunción, colonials who settled in Guairá sought to acquire Indian servants and corvée laborers under the encomienda system. As chapter 2 argued, Spanish officials molded the legal framework of encomienda around Spanish-Guaraní relations, which were rooted in Guaraní kinship. Through the political and affinal networks of cuñadasgo, Spaniards acquired personal servants who lived in their homes and granted them access to corvée laborers living in pueblos. A similar process occurred in Guairá, but instead of the encomienda following cuñadasgo, as was the case in Asunción, the encomienda and cuñadasgo were created simultaneously.

Little is known about these encomiendas and their encomenderos' social positions and their economic activities. Reflecting Guairá's position as a borderland with São Paulo, a few encomenderos were Portuguese.[18] The evidence is so sparse that reliable estimates of how many Guaraní were subject to the encomienda in Guairá are unavailable.[19] A few of the earliest encomienda units (1590s) were rather large in size, ranging from 200 to 650 indios.[20] For example, the encomienda granted to García López contained fourteen *principales* with a total of 560 souls.[21] Typical of other encomiendas, López's encomienda was not a unified village but instead a collection of villages from various locales. One of García López's assigned caciques, Miguel Pindo Bitin, governed eight fuegos, or a unit of thirty-two individuals. Most Guaraní assigned to encomenderos remained in autonomous villages but were sometimes subject to an encomendero's labor demands via cuñadasgo. A relatively small population of Guaraní were congregated into a few pueblos managed by Guaireños and a handful of Franciscan or secular priests. There is little information about how these early pueblos operated and so it is not clear how priests, encomenderos, and caciques shared power. Smaller encomienda units were made up of handfuls of what Spaniards called yanaconas, or indios removed from their communities. These were granted to widows.

Similar to Guaraní in the Asunción region, their counterparts in Guairá enthusiastically sought out metal tools from colonials. This demand for metal tools, especially axes, was partially driven by conflict between indigenous groups, not to mention the threat of slavers. Axes helped to speed up the construction of defensive palisades around villages. One Spaniard in the 1580s delivered axes to a group of Guaraní for the specific purpose of building a defensive wall against Tupian attacks.[22] Just like in early Asunción, metal tools became so central to the political economy that officials in Ciudad Real and Villa Rica made them the official currency, setting specific values for each iron object.

But how did Guaireños acquire these important trade items when they were at such a great distance from Asunción? The answer is that they made their own. Conquistadors traveled to Guairá in the 1540s and 1550s, long before they established permanent settlements there. In those earliest expeditions, they discovered raw ore in Guairá, but they lacked the technical knowledge to begin mining operations.[23] In subsequent expeditions, however, settlers with technical knowledge of mining and metallurgy migrated to the region. Mining operations were located at a site Guaireños called the Campos de Coraçy Berá, forty leagues north of Ciudad Real.[24] With indigenous laborers and probably African slaves, Guaireños produced cuñas and other tools for gifting. Unfortunately, no other extant documentation exists to shed light on the operation of the mines.

The Guaraní name for the mining region, Coraçy Berá, is not easy to interpret. It is possible that the name is not related to the mines since the placename "Campos de Coracivera" appears in other documents without reference to the mines.[25] Nonetheless, given the importance of the mines, the appearance of a placename incorporating Guaraní words deserves speculative attention. *Berá* often means "resplendence," "brightness," or "shine," but when attached to certain words *berá* can also mean "agitated."[26] Translating *coraçy* is more problematic. Ruíz de Montoya renders the word *quaraçî* as "sun" and *quaraçî berá* as *resplandor* (resplendence).[27] When broken down, *quaraçî* forms a syntagma and can be associated with "hole" (*qûa*), "pain," "adversity," or "difficulty" (*açî*). If brightness is the key concept in Coraçy Berá, then perhaps the name evokes the incandescent ore as it was formed into axes, knives, and other tools. Resplendence was also associated with prophetic or spiritual power, an otherworldliness. The word *hole* might be related to the extraction of ore in tunnels or open pits. If certain parts of the words were dropped as in *co(g)(r)asay*, then it may have referred to a "chacra" or place of cultivation that was associated with pain and suffering. These philological possibilities suggest that the Campos de Coraçy Berá was a place of contradictions: hard toil but also bright possibilities.[28] Guaraní leaders who maintained ties to encomenderos did so for a variety of reasons that included coercion and the threat of violence, but cuñadasgo and iron tools were also factors. One cacique explained that he left with his people to live under Spanish dominion because of the constant warfare that existed among neighboring groups. He also cited the "gifts and tools" that the encomenderos gave them as a primary reason for remaining subject to Spaniards.[29]

Despite the exchange of iron tools for kinship, Guaireño demands on Guaraní communities pushed many to the breaking point. In the earliest years, Spaniards recognized several important regional Guaraní caciques (Tayaoba, Araberá, Yaguaracuré, and Maçaru) who possessed neighboring villages and had the power to raise war parties against Guaireños.[30] As the episode involving María, Maçaru, and encomendero Ortuño Arbildo described in chapter 2 demonstrates, Spaniards were wary of the potential for violence and recognized that a broad Guaraní coalition could have wiped them out. When faced with violence or flight, Guaireños were quick to respond with a show of force. They frequently organized military campaigns to subdue rebellious or migrating communities, and these expeditions were always bolstered by Guaraní allies.[31] In the aftermath of skirmishes, Spaniards often took women and children as captives and used them as personal servants, legitimating their practices under the laws of "just war." Guaraní also did not hesitate to flee from Spaniards. An anonymous Jesuit priest in 1620 succinctly described how relationships of kinship could descend into violence: "after the Indians saw that the Spanish did not treat them like brothers-in-law and kin but like servants, they began to withdraw, not wanting to serve the Spaniards."[32]

Kinship, gifting of iron tools, and violence animated the region, setting already semimobile peoples on the move, either pulling them closer to Spanish centers or repelling them. Thus, there was no authoritative Spanish conquest of Guairá but a complex and prolonged negotiation. In 1630, an encomendero named Francisco de Vallejos provided his opinion that the Spanish presence was indeed fragile: "these Indians . . . were not reduced, or baptized, or conquered, nor did they pay the labor draft of right and obligation; rather, it was service of their own free will in exchange for payment [axes]."[33] The migrations in and out of colonial jurisdictions and the heavy reliance on gifting and kinship placed Guaireños in a position of weakness. There was very little immigration to Guairá and perhaps more attrition. By the 1620s, when the first reliable population estimates appear in the sources, there were around fifty Spanish vecinos in Ciudad Real and one hundred in Villa Rica.[34]

By the seventeenth century, most of the settlers of Guairá were creoles or mestizos. In describing his firsthand account of Guairá to the crown, one governor remarked, "These, your subjects, have lived as barbarians these last ninety years. Their houses are like those of gypsies."[35] Jesuit reports from Guairá similarly commented on the population's humility and provincialism. Regarding Guaireños choice of foods, the Italian Jesuit provincial Nicolás Durán condescendingly noted that Guaireños "eat nothing but cassava cakes; they have no cattle or sheep; the meat that they rarely eat is from chickens or pigs or sometimes from tapir when they catch them in the mountains or rivers . . . content with sustaining themselves day to day on vegetables and fish from the river."[36] For early modern Europeans, you were what you ate. Humoral medicine dictated that if one ate Native foods then one could become a Native.[37] Durán seemed to hint that Guaireños were transforming into Indians, or at least that they had lost the virtues of their Spanishness. But if acquiring Guaraní cultural practices and knowledge looked like degeneration to outsiders, to insiders it was a boon. The story of a single español named Hernando Díaz, a second-generation conquistador-encomendero, and his local relationships and conflicts helps to elucidate the kinds of political, social, and cultural possibilities at play in Paraguay's eastern frontier.

Hernando Díaz appears in the documentary record because he attempted to create a rebellion against a local Spanish leader. Díaz accompanied the first entrada to Guairá and was awarded an encomienda, which was eventually distributed to a nonheir in 1597 sometime after his death. Contemporaries noted that Díaz was a troublemaker and a "malevolent young lad."[38] Apparently upset with Domingo Martínez de Irala for unstated reasons, Díaz aided a group of Guaraní (it may have been Tupí) in raiding a Spanish company while they were traveling downriver. The governor apprehended Díaz, but he escaped and attempted to make his way to Brazil. Along the way, he ran into a Spanish captain who exiled Díaz to a river island used as a makeshift prison. The island-prison did not hold him for long and Díaz made his way to Ciudad Real, where he remained and established a life for himself.

Surrounded by others who likely shared his disdain for Irala, Díaz enjoyed full citizen rights as a vecino and even came to possess an encomienda. From a man on the run to a vecino and encomendero, Díaz's career in Paraguay was tumultuous but not unusual for new colonial territories in Paraguay or throughout Spanish America where competition for encomiendas was fierce.

In the year 1582, Díaz, now in his fifties, got entangled once again with Spanish authorities and was accused of fomenting a Guaraní rebellion against the Spaniards.[39] Employing Tupí-Guaraní symbols of power and warfare, he attempted to provoke a powerful Guaraní chieftain named Gaspar Tayaoba to rebel against the Spaniards and specifically to attack Lieutenant Governor Ruy Díaz Melgarejo.[40] Gaspar Tayaoba maintained political connections with several Guaraní villages in the Ubay River valley, where many of Guairá's encomenderos possessed cuñadasgo networks. According to several witnesses, Melgarejo was Tayaoba's brother-in-law. In other words, Díaz urged Tayaoba to terminate his politico-filial bonds of cuñadasgo with Melgarejo. Díaz gained access to the powerful Tayaoba and other regional chieftains because they too regarded him as a nephew.[41] In Guaraní social terms, the nephew-uncle relationship implied a political bond of unequal power with the nephew subservient to the uncle.

Díaz gave Tayaoba *maracás*, or calabash rattles adorned with feathers ("calabaças de plumería"). Tupí-Guaraní maracás were objects that could possess powerful spirits associated with warfare. Hans Staden, a German captive among the Tupinambá near São Vicente (Brazil) in 1549, noted that all the males possessed a maracá but only the shaman could imbue it with its power and ability to speak. Once prepared, the shaman declared that the maracás needed war captives to feed on.[42] Tupí-Guaraní cared for maracás as if they were individuals. Small houses were built for them and they were offered food. The maracá was less an instrument for producing music than a magical tool associated with prophecy and warfare.[43] For the contemporary Araweté, the rattle or *aray* can carry souls who speak to the shaman and contain lightning bolts to ignite the earth.[44]

Several witnesses noted that Díaz sent only feathers to Tayaoba, and one witness suggested that the feathers were intended to adorn the chieftain's arrows. Díaz's gifting of these objects during a time of potential violence recalls an episode from the 1540s when the adelantado Álvar Núñez Cabeza

de Vaca received gifts from his Carío-Guaraní allies. Just before a battle with
the nonsedentary Guaicurú, Cabeza de Vaca's indigenous allies, the Carío-
Guaraní, gave him bows and arrows richly adorned with ochre-colored paint
and embellished with feathers.[45] The association between feathers and
arrows may have been similar to that between feathers and maracás. Among
the Tupiniquim in coastal Brazil, shaman invited men to attach feathers to
their maracás to activate the spirits within them, giving them power.[46] The
richly colored parrot feathers attached to arrows received by Cabeza de Vaca
had spiritual power that would help the adelantado take many captives.

Díaz's gifts to Tayaoba can be interpreted with these ethnographic possibilities in mind. If Díaz saw Tayaoba simply as a leader-warrior, then the
feathers would have assisted the latter in rejuvenating his prowess and his
tools of war. One Guaraní witness suggested that Díaz was providing Tayaoba with new, resplendent feathers to adorn and spiritually animate his
weapons of war.[47] It is striking that the españoles who investigated Díaz paid
such careful attention to the gifts he gave Tayaoba. Local officials understood
these objects as spiritually and politically charged. Hernando Díaz's experience may appear unusual because of his extreme politics, but as a cultural
product of his time and place, he was typical. His ability to speak Guaraní
and engage deeply in the politics of cuñadasgo were not abnormal in Guairá.

Portuguese São Paulo, Spanish Guairá, and the Economy

Similar to Spanish Guairá, outsiders described Portuguese São Paulo as a
colonial backwater. Few Portuguese ventured to the São Paulo *planalto* in the
decades following Pedro Álvares Cabral's first contact with Brazil in 1500.
The expansive São Paulo tableland was separated by the Serra do Mar Mountains, making access to the region difficult. Efforts to colonize the region
began only after the 1532 arrival of the first Portuguese governor-general,
Afonso de Sousa. In 1553, the Vila de Santo André da Borda do Campo was
established, followed shortly by the founding of the Jesuit college in 1554. In
the 1550s, Jesuits and settlers clashed over rights to settle Indians, leading the
governor-general Mem de Sá to initiate in 1560 *aldeias d'el rei*, or Indian villages of the king. Jesuits administered the aldeias but Paulistas used them for
their labor needs. Throughout the sixteenth century, Paulista settlers took on

Indian concubines and referred to their Indian allies as kin and friends. Paulistas of mixed Native and Portuguese parentage were abundant, often referred to by Portuguese and Spaniards as mamelucos.

For much of the sixteenth and seventeenth centuries, São Paulo remained a poor colonial backwater dependent almost entirely on Native labor. Priests and settlers alike gifted copious amounts of iron tools to establish relations with Natives. Paulistas exploited conflicts between indigenous groups and enslaved captives taken in war. Tupí-Guaraní groups dominated the region, but there were also Gê speakers in the vicinity.[48] Paulistas applied a variety of ethnonyms to identify the Natives they encountered, but they came to call Indians with whom they fostered reciprocity "Tupí." Over the years, real kinship linkages faded and were replaced with forced enslavement. Portuguese did, however, maintain a fiction of kinship by calling their Indian slaves "relatives" and sometimes adopting them as godchildren.[49] As the population of São Paulo grew in the late sixteenth and early seventeenth centuries, the internal market economy expanded, which in turn prompted Paulistas to venture into Spanish Guairá to acquire more labor hands for their farms and ranches.[50]

In 1614, the Jesuit provincial of Paraguay, Fray Diego de Torres, wrote that Guairá was the "last corner of the earth, the most distant place from human commerce."[51] Despite Guairá's seeming isolation, transatlantic commerce had a strong pull on the territory, motivating Paulistas to enslave thousands of Natives. Luiz Felipe de Alencastro's analysis of African and Indian slave labor in colonial Brazil demonstrates just how deeply the Paulista bandeiras were embedded in Atlantic dynamics. When the Dutch invaded and occupied Portugal's colonial holdings in the 1620s and 1630s, the Portuguese African slave trade fell sharply: 150,000 Africans from 1600 to 1625 dropped to 50,000 Africans from 1625 to 1650. The decline in African slave imports in the Brazilian northeast had a direct impact on the demand for Indian slaves throughout the colony.[52] In the 1620s, Indian enslavement increased dramatically, and as a result from 1625 to 1650 the trade in Indian slaves surpassed the trade in Africans. But many of these slaves were not destined for the sugar plantations of the northeast. John Monteiro demonstrates that most Indians who were ripped from their homelands were put to work in the wheat fields, plantations, and trade networks around São Paulo.[53] Alencastro confirms Monteiro's argument but adds that there was a causal relationship between the Atlantic African trade and the bandeiras to Guairá-Tapé.[54] During the Dutch-Portuguese wars, the price of African slaves in Brazil doubled, driving up the cost of basic provisions. Paulistas saw a market opportunity and transformed the São Paulo plateau into the breadbasket for the northeast. São Paulo also supplied Río de Janeiro and Bahía with goods for the militias and Portuguese naval fleet, who were constantly on the move against the Dutch. Paulista hacienda owners exported all kinds of goods, from tallow to cotton to corn, nearly all of which was produced by the sweat and toil of enslaved Natives.[55] This context indicates that the extensive slaving activity in Guairá was intimately linked with volatile but powerful transatlantic commerce and imperial politics.

Comparing Spanish and Portuguese patterns of colonization on the planalto and the Río de la Plata basin, two main differences stand out. With a larger colonial population than Guairá, São Paulo put greater pressure on indigenous communities. Combined with their population disparities, the two colonies' different patterns of colonization—encomienda and cuñadasgo versus slavery—led the Paulistas to take a more expansive and aggressive attitude toward their neighbors, while Guaireños maintained a rather precarious position.

From their inception, these two poles of Ibero-American colonialism began forging social networks and developed a moderate exchange. By the early seventeenth century, officials in Asunción hoped that Guairá would forge commercial networks with São Paulo and vice versa. In 1604, lieutenant governor Antonio de Añasco, the highest local officer in Guairá, ordered that locals open a road to São Paulo. Paulista officials authorized the same action.[56] Local officials estimated that the distance from Villa Rica to São Paulo was 120 leagues (one league is equivalent to around three miles) by river and another 20 on foot. One year later, a vecino of Villa Rica named Francisco Benítez loaded up with trade items and made his way to São Paulo, where he married the daughter of a Paulista vecino, Joseph Camargo.[57] These kinds of social networks further fueled economic linkages. From 1580 to 1640 the Spanish and Portuguese crowns were united, complicating all of these local dynamics. Following the death of the last heir of the Portuguese Aviz dynasty in 1578, a war of succession determined that Philip II would become the ruler of the two kingdoms. Although Philip II prohibited free interimperial trade and communication, there was little stopping the networks that already existed, and locals during this period used the farce of political unification to move people and goods freely between the two kingdoms.[58] Paulista traders brought to Guairá goods of all kinds from Brazil, including African slaves from Guinea.[59] This trade was illegal, so it is difficult to measure its impact on the local economy.[60] While Paulistas developed an agricultural complex to supply the northeast, Guaireños directed a portion of their encomienda laborers toward yerba maté production. An indigenous tea, yerba maté became a regional commodity in the late sixteenth century and gained in importance from around 1600 to 1630. By at least 1616, the tea was being shipped from Paraguay across the Andes to Chile and Peru. By the 1620s and 1630s, yerba maté had a strong consumer base in cities such as Lima, Cusco, and Potosí. Guairá was strategically located near the wild yerba maté groves of Mbaracayú, located to the west of Guairá and the Paraná River.

The rising importance of yerba maté caught the eyes of crown officials. A newly appointed governor, don Luis Céspedes Jeria, arrived in Guairá in September of 1628. After surveying the economic landscape, one of his primary goals was to systematize and regulate the yerba maté trade.[61] Céspedes Jeria referred to the wild yerba maté groves as "mines," thus allowing him to claim the groves of wild trees as subterranean and therefore subject them to the royal *quinto*. Defining trees as mines in order to tax and regulate them was also part of the crown's strategy to block the Portuguese from accessing them and the silver wealth of the Andes. In the decades following these reforms, church and crown officials referred to the wild yerba maté groves of Paraguay as "the gold and silver of this region."[62] Individuals who hoped to "mine" the yerba maté were required to obtain a lease from the crown through the governor.[63] On the question of labor, Governor Céspedes Jeria sided with encomenderos against the Jesuits, who argued for exempting all neophytes from the encomienda and therefore labor in the yerba maté groves.

The center of the yerba maté trade was the remote city of Mbaracayú to the west of Guairá. Members of the Mbaracayú cabildo referred to their city as "purgatory."[64] Mbaracayú was no more than a work zone with very little by way of a local market, churches, and housing. Before the 1630s, a significant portion of the workers sent to harvest and process yerba maté in

Mbaracayú were encomienda indios from Guairá, presumably because Mbaracayú was easier to reach from Guairá. Even so, the biggest financial beneficiaries of the yerba maté economy were the traders from Asunción, Santa Fe, and Corrientes. The producers who remained in Mbaracayú and Guairá remained poor and were forced to sell cheap.

The trade in yerba maté drew to the region a number of Paulistas who managed work gangs and supplied the region with black slaves and other miscellaneous materials or foodstuffs. In 1629, there were twenty-two Paulistas in Mbaracayú out of a total of around 100 to 150 vecinos.[65] In Villa Rica there was a similar ratio, with seventeen Paulistas out of a total of 100 vecinos.[66] This Paulista minority had important social ties in the region. Of the twenty-two Paulistas in Mbaracayú, three were married and two were betrothed to women in Asunción. One declared that his wife was Portuguese but lived in Asunción; two had wives in Mbaracayú; three in Villa Rica; five were bachelors; and four claimed their wives were in São Paulo.[67] These marriages suggest the outlines of a socioeconomic strategy: yerba maté producers in Mbaracayú forged kinship ties to families in Asunción or São Paulo who were involved in the shipment and sale of yerba maté in regional markets.

Since he was the first governor of Paraguay to visit Guairá, Céspedes Jeria's visit signaled that Paraguay finally had a viable export product in yerba maté. Céspedes Jeria was also the first governor to come to Paraguay through São Paulo, and he used his trip to Brazil to enhance his social networks. As a freshly minted governor, Céspedes Jeria employed his new social prestige to contract an illustrious marriage to doña Victoria de Sá, niece of the infamous governor Martim de Sá and cousin to Salvador de Sá, governor of Río de Janeiro. He also bought several plantations in the São Paulo plateau, which were worked by Guaraní slaves.[68] Céspedes Jeria's interest in Guairá represented the growing economic opportunities of the Guairá borderlands, as well as the need for mediation between encomenderos and the increasingly powerful Jesuits.

Catholic Evangelization and the Native Political Context

The first priests to arrive in Guairá were Franciscans, and eighteenth-century sources indicate that they established two reducciones in 1580 called Pacuyu

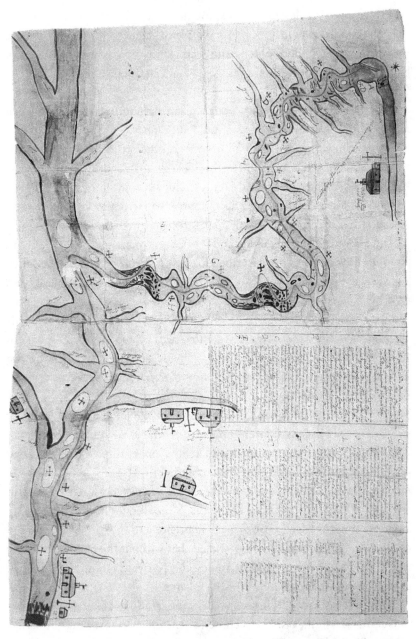

FIGURE 1. Map drawn up under the direction of Governor Céspedes Jeria detailing his voyage from São Paulo, Brazil, to the cities of Ciudad Real and Villa Rica in Guairá. Source: AGI, Seville, MP, Buenos Aires, 17.

and Curumiai. While Franciscans initiated evangelization in the Guairá, they maintained a peripatetic presence. Overwhelmed with their work with the nearly twenty reducciones in the Asunción region, Franciscans did not have the number of priests nor resources to make Guairá an evangelical priority.[69]

Christian evangelization in Guairá began a second phase in 1609 when Jesuits threw themselves into founding reducciones in Guairá.[70] Jesuits had been preparing to enter Guairá for several years before 1609. In 1595, officials from Asunción in cooperation with officials in Ciudad Real granted the Black Robes lands in Guairá and a few yanacona servants for their headquarters in Villa Rica.[71] In their own accounts of their activities in Guairá, Jesuit priests often trumped up their own accomplishments, or rather God's accomplishments through them, and the dangers of missionizing. The Jesuit Antonio Ruíz de Montoya described his entrance into a territory he called Tayaoba, a region controlled by a powerful but resistant cacique, like a lamb entering a den of wolves—the lone priest armed only with faith and a cross against hordes of uncivilized gentiles. Reading between the lines of his account, it is clear that Ruíz de Montoya was accompanied by scores of Indian neophytes, some of whom were armed. Moreover, Ruíz de Montoya and the other Jesuits took copious amounts of iron tools as gifts. By the 1620s, the Jesuits could offer Natives not only axes but also firearms and protection in fortified villages with larger numbers of allied Natives. In short, Jesuit strategies for evangelizing were informed by the local political context of interethnic warfare and resistant leadership. Some groups fiercely resisted Jesuit invitations to build reducciones and convert, while others quickly accepted the offered gifts and used these as leverage against more powerful enemies or at least competitive neighbors. Moreover, Jesuits did not operate alone. At times they relied on armed Guaireños and the threat of Guaireño retaliation. Jesuit Nicolás Durán related that without the Spaniards, there would be no fear of retribution among the Natives.[72] Jesuit and Spanish power were competing but imbricated spheres.

Between 1609 and 1628, Jesuits oversaw the creation of fifteen reducciones in Guairá. The Jesuit order was chosen as the order to carry out the settlement of Guairá because of their strong presence in Peru and their local connections in Paraguay. Governor Hernando Arias de Saavedra became a champion of the Jesuits and he petitioned the crown to allow the order to begin establishing reducciones in the region.[73] Trusting in the reducción project already underway in the Asunción region under the Franciscans, Saavedra hoped that the Jesuits would help to *reducir* Guairá. Saavedra's ultimate aim was to create a commercial bridge between Guairá and São Paulo but also to maintain a buffer against Paulista settlers. Saavedra suggested that eastern Guairá would be settled with reducciones, not encomienda pueblos, believing that Jesuit-managed reducciones would be more economically productive than encomiendas and provide stronger trade networks with Atlantic Brazil. Through his lieutenant governor in Guairá, Saavedra ordered that Guaireños were not to enter the territories in which the Jesuits operated.[74] The broader political context was that the Jesuits entered Guairá during a moment of intense debate about the legality of the encomienda in Paraguay. As described in chapter 2, in 1611 the audiencia judge don Francisco de Alfaro arrived in Asunción and, over the next several years, issued a series of reforms that sought to severely restrict encomenderos' claims on tributaries. A friend of the Jesuits and father to a Jesuit priest who would work in Paraguay, Alfaro exempted from encomienda service all Jesuit reducciones that formed independently of encomendero pueblos. This context was not lost on Guaraní and may have informed their decisions to join reducciones.

Magnus Mörner suggests that it was the Jesuits' offer of tribute exemptions that lured Guaraní to join the reducciones.[75] This became a dominant explanation in the literature on the Guaraní reducciones, but it is not entirely accurate. While many Guaraní did flee encomienda pueblos, other Guaraní remained. Recent scholarship has shown that Natives joined reducciones in Guairá for a variety of reasons, including chieftains' and shamans' desires to protect their communities and the perceived spiritual-material power of the priests.[76] Placing these attitudes in the context of a frontier and borderland further deepens our understanding of why Guaraní joined or rejected reducciones.

When dealing with territories of Guaraní-speaking peoples, the Jesuits rarely invented ethnonyms but spoke instead of the "lands" or "province" of a particular leader. Differences in naming territories and peoples emerged where imperial politics impinged on claims of sovereignty. For example, both

Jesuits and Guaireños referred to the generic "Tupí," as opposed to the name of their chieftain, because they did not typically claim Tupí as subjects. Other groups who were perceived to be culturally different were given ethnonyms. For example, the Jesuits contacted a people they called "Camperos Cavelludos" (a rough translation might be "shaggy field-dwellers") because they lived in open fields (not in the river valleys or in the forests like Guaraní) and because they wore their hair to their shoulders, trimming their bangs to the level of their ears. The Camperos spoke a distinct language from Guaraní, probably a Gê language.[77] In this way, the colonial practice of naming Natives was informed not by some timeless colonial mentality but by a borderland context of contested sovereignty claims.

Despite the region's linguistic diversity, Jesuits focused on Guaraní-speaking groups. Understanding the early reducciones in Guairá requires an understanding of Guaraní supravillage institutions for interaction. Branislava Susnik argues that at the moment of contact, Guaraní between the Paraguay and Paraná Rivers were organized in fourteen supravillage units or guarás. Ruíz de Montoya translated *guará* as "country," "region," or "nation" and defined it as a conglomeration of teko'a. Organized around a single mburuvichá (leader of a guará) who extended his network of subordination over "subject" villages through polygynous marriages to other tuvichá, the guará was a loose political unit. The guará possessed real social meaning when the unit gathered to wage war on neighboring groups or for communal ceremonies, including festivals and anthropophagous feasts.[78] María Cristina Santos convincingly argues that Susnik's model for guarás relies too heavily on ethnographic observations rather than historical evidence.[79] Even so, scattered evidence indicates that supravillage affiliations did in fact exist.

Chapter 2 details the experience of a Guaireño encomendero named Ortuño Arbildo who was tried in 1577 for raping María, granddaughter to Maçaru, who exercised a degree of political authority over villages in which he did not reside. The major issue for Arbildo was that he forcefully took a girl who Maçaru had betrothed to another tuvichá, suggesting that he had arranged a marriage to enhance his kinship bonds with subject villages. The Spaniards recognized Maçaru as the "key to the whole land" and feared his ability to organize large war parties that could wipe the Spaniards off the face of Guairá. All of these clues point toward Maçaru's real powers as a mburu-vichá (supravillage leader). Supravillage gatherings also appear in the historical record. In 1612, local officials investigated a Guaraní "rebellion" in the region of Villa Rica. In that year, officials sent messengers among Guaraní villages to announce Alfaro's new reforms, but instead of receiving them, the Guaraní warriors captured, killed, and consumed the messengers. Native witness testimony described a gathering of several villages that involved copious drinking, dancing, and consumption of their human captives, including the visitador's messenger. A Guaraní witness named Mborocatira emphasized how the communal activity cancelled out any potential animosity between participants.[80] Another witness, a cacique named Pedro Tabaca, noted that during these events, "old grudges" were forgotten.[81] These documents from Guairá suggest that supralocal affiliations existed, especially when it came to the management of politically important marriages, warfare, and festivals. But as Guillermo Wilde notes, these regional units "would have been highly unstable and inclined to fracture, in favor of [smaller] groupings with higher degrees of autonomy."[82] Wilde's emphasis on the fragility of supravillage alliances is justified, considering the frequency of violence among Guaraní peoples.

Guaraní Uses of *Reducciones* and Jesuit Responses

When Jesuits began working with communities in the earliest phases, they described a "bellicose" or "warlike" quality among some groups. These generalizations work to discursively construct Natives as barbaric and obfuscate the cultural meanings of violence.[83] Tupí-Guaraní violence should not be understood as purely political or simply motivated by self-preservation. These are modern Western understandings of violence, which tend to see violence as socially destructive. But as Neil Whitehead explains:

> The violence of capture, killing, and consumption of enemies is itself a ritual form understood by both perpetrator and victim, and for this reason can be seen as expressing agreement or accord over the wider issues of sociocultural reproduction, since both killers and victims participate in the same cultural quest for cosmological status. Accordingly, violence

and warfare may actually represent interaction, familiarity, and exchange.
... Violence sometimes appears both appropriate and valuable and is not
necessarily understood as dysfunctional and pathological.[84]

Ruíz de Montoya translates war as *guarîni*, the same word used to describe
an entire ethnic group. It is unclear if *guarîni* was regularly used to describe
violent acts by Guaraní in the sixteenth and early seventeenth centuries, but
by the time a "reducción Guaraní" language had formalized in the reducciones in the eighteenth century, the word was regularly used in writing.[85]
Among the modern Tupian Parakanã, anthropologist Carlos Fausto notes
that their cognate of *guaranïnï* is *warinio* and is rarely used; instead, combat
is explained through the use of various verbs describing violent acts. What
unites these acts is not some notion of warfare where distinct political groups
engage in violence for a state-sanctioned purpose. Instead, killing is at the
heart of violence. Fausto explains:

> Our [Western] typologies are founded on an opposition between war
> and private revenge. Yet the latter only becomes private where juridical
> regulation of interindividual and interfamilial conflicts exist; in other
> words, when there is a state apparatus determining when a type of armed
> conflict belongs to the kinship domain rather than the public sphere. In-
> digenous societies, however, in practicing warfare according to a criteria
> of scale, may conceive of war as an interminable series of acts of revenge,
> which are not private but necessarily public and socialized.[86]

The social and cultural meaning of violence among Amazonia peoples transcends Western concepts of state-sponsored warfare. An anthropological
understanding of violence among Tupí-Guaraní peoples helps explain the
reports of "bellicose" Indians in Guairá. Moreover, given the importance of
violence among Guaraní, it stands that Jesuits leveraged violence to keep or
gain the loyalties of Natives.

The Jesuit Claudio Ruyer observed warfare in the new reducción of Santa
María del Iguazú, in the southwest reaches of Guairá. "At this time," he
explained, "the Indians had a little war (*guerrilla*) with those they called
Caayguas, which means Indians who live in the forests without shelter or

houses. These are great scoundrels and traitors, who have committed great offenses in the past years, killing a great many [Guaraní associated with the reducción]. . . . They have a foreign language that is very difficult, similar to the Guaicurú language, of which one cannot understand a word."[87] Ruyer's characterization of Caayguas as murderous barbarians and culturally puzzling had a purpose: to frame them as other in relation to the Guaraní in the process of conversion and justify Guaraní killing. The connection Ruyer drew between the Caayguas and Guaicurú further served to construct the former as eternal enemies. Guaraní from Santa María del Iguazú reducción attacked the Caaygua, killing many and capturing ten men and three women. Ruyer was disturbed to learn that Guaraní from the reducción took these captives to a camp some distance from the reducción, where they killed and cannibalized them. Absolving himself of collusion with the Guaraní killers, Ruyer noted that he gave three strong sermons against cannibalism. The unsettling reality was that the reducción enhanced Guaraní abilities to wage war against their enemies. The reducción provided enhanced numbers, strengthened defenses, and potentially lethal weapons in firearms and metal tools.

The divisive nature of supravillage associations, the social necessity of violence, and the menace of slavers made reducciones an alluring possibility to many Guaraní. A group called Camperos, who joined the Jesuit Nuestra Señora de la Encarnación reducción in eastern Guairá, approached the Jesuits precisely to gain a competitive edge over their enemies. When the Jesuits entered their territory, called Campos de Coracivera (perhaps the iron mining region), Tupí were at war with Camperos. Tupí had apparently sold several hundred Campero captives to Paulistas.[88] With their community under threat of destruction, the Camperos requested the Fathers' protection. The Jesuits interpreted all such overtures as a contract to reducir.[89] Responding quickly and decisively, before Tupís could do any more damage, the Jesuits convinced a group of Guaraní warriors associated with a nearby reducción, led by a cacique named Pindoviiu, to attack the Tupí village and free the captured Camperos. Of the freed Camperos, nearly 160 relocated to the reducción of Encarnación, while an uncertain number returned to their original settlements.[90] From the Jesuit perspective, this specific conflict between Camperos, Tupís, and Jesuit-allied Guaraní revolved around

captivity and redemption. Jesuits apparently justified directing Guaraní violence as an active temporal redemption that would lead to a spiritual redemption for the Camperos in the reducción. The Guaraní warriors, however, may
have seen these activities as an opportunity to acquire more allies for their
defensive or offensive campaigns against Tupí and Paulista slavers.

One of the most difficult territories for the Jesuits in Guairá was Tayaoba,
where a chieftain of the same name loomed as a menacing force. Tayaoba was
in frequent conflict with his neighbors, especially over the control of wild
yerba maté groves. The Jesuits had to make three attempts to establish themselves in Tayaoba. When they first arrived, they were expelled by Pindoviiu
(the same mburuvichá from the campaign to protect the Camperos, but
before his alliance with the Jesuits). Before contacting the Jesuits, Pindoviiu
and several other caciques, including one named Zuruba, led their people to
gather yerba maté in a region under the control of Tayaoba. Tayaoba attacked
them and Zuruba was killed. Ruíz de Montoya relates that Pindoviiu escaped
thanks to the Paulista armor and weaponry he had acquired in an encounter
with bandeirantes. Recognizing his precarious position in relation to the
great chieftain Tayaoba, the Jesuits, the Paulistas, and the Guaireños, Pindoviiu requested that the Jesuits establish a reducción in his community. This
action would have provided Pindoviiu with more Native allies, protection in
numbers, stronger fortifications, and powerful weapons and tools in the
form of firearms and axes, as well as the spiritual power he may have perceived in the Jesuits.[91] The formation of alliances between Native groups and
Jesuits, sometimes formalized through participation in reducciones, provided Guaraní with greater political and material security in the context of
local violence and increasing threats from outsiders.[92]

Jesuits' frustrations with the inconstancy and the resistance of Natives
could reach such a height that they turned to violence to bring Natives into
reducciones. Jesuit Claudio Ruyer flirted with raising a war party from his own
reducción to attack a Guaraní village that had stubbornly resisted his overtures
to join the reducción. It is not clear if he followed through with his plans.[93] In
practice, violence became part of the evangelical reality. When Ruíz de Montoya entered Tayaoba around 1624, he did so with fifty indios, and some of
these may have been armed with rifles the Jesuit provincial had acquired in
Buenos Aires in 1618.[94] Ruíz de Montoya made two attempts at entering

Tayaoba, but he and his company were repelled. On his third attempt, Ruíz de Montoya joined a group of seventy Spaniards with five hundred Native allies. Ruíz de Montoya claimed that he had opposed the Spanish entering the region, but he accompanied them nonetheless to "defend" Guaraní from the rapacious Spaniards.[95] Even with the armed Spanish-indio company, the expedition failed: nearly seventy Spaniards, five hundred Indian allies, and an untold number of the Jesuits' allies were broken up and surrounded by an overwhelming force organized by Tayaoba. Eventually, Ruíz de Montoya was successful in establishing a reducción in Tayaoba, but only after repeated attempts and considerable effort.

Throughout his account of the beginnings of the Guaraní-Jesuit reducciones, entitled *The Spiritual Conquest* (*La conquista espiritual hecha por los religiosos de la compañía de Iesus, en las Provincias del Paraguay, Parana, Uruguay, y Tape*, published in Madrid in 1639), Ruíz de Montoya uses the españoles and the notion that they only relied on violence to acquire Indian laborers as a foil for Jesuit preaching, suggesting that a true conquest, a "spiritual conquest," of Guaraní could only be accomplished with the spiritual tools of miracles and the word of God. He constructed the province of Tayaoba in metaphorical terms as a "citadel," protected by the devil's dark forces and swarming with "sorcerers" that could only be defeated with spiritual powers. In this rhetorical framing, Ruíz de Montoya downplayed Jesuits' reliance on violence and the complicated political dynamics of the borderland. Several Guaraní caciques who organized militias to assist the Spanish in their campaigns in Tayaoba testified that their military actions were necessary and that the Jesuits required them. The cacique principal, San Miguel Rivera, who participated in the campaign to found the Jesuit reducción of Los Ángeles, declared that the Indians there were so "obstinate" that the use of force was necessary.[96] In sum, Jesuits resisted violent actions against potential neophytes, but when they felt it was necessary they organized or fomented violence.

Spanish and Jesuit approaches to Guaraní differed in many ways but were identical when it came to reciprocity: both gifted copious amounts of iron tools.[97] One Jesuit remarked that "with one ax you could win an entire lineage of Indians."[98] This Jesuit noted that the ax was so important because it was the Natives' preferred tool for "making the garden," suggesting that the ax was put to use clearing ground for planting. Ruíz de Montoya explained that when he went to Tayaoba he "succeeded in attracting some [Guaraní] to visit me" by offering gifts.[99] In many cases, iron tools brought Jesuits and Guaraní together. It appears that Jesuits brought iron with them into Guairá, but once they were established they began exploiting local sources of iron at Campo de Coraçy Berá, just as their encomendero counterparts did.[100] If the Jesuits accessed local iron deposits in Guairá, they were not dependent on them. With their resources and interprovincial connections, they could bring iron from maritime ports.[101]

Natives in Guairá saw the Jesuits as suppliers of firearms and other tools useful in a context of sustained violence. Jesuits initiated a discussion of arming reducción indios after 1611, the year of the first major bandeirante raid in Guairá. Jesuits not only decided to deliver arms to reducción Indians but to organize them as militias and encourage them to confront the bandeirantes in open battle. In 1618, the Jesuits purchased one hundred firearms in Buenos Aires and shipped them to the reducciones in Guairá. After catching wind of the transaction, the Asunción cabildo complained to the governor that these same firearms had been destined to the Spanish militias in Asunción, who were in much greater need than the reducciones. The cabildo's missive initiated a decades-long dispute over the Jesuits' right to arm and train Guaraní, a fight Jesuits ultimately won.[102] Guaireños were alarmed by these actions, contending that Guairá was the only province in all of the Spanish empire where Indians were given firearms. This was not true; nonetheless, arming Indians was rare in Spanish America.[103] Guaireños and Asunceños were especially disturbed by Jesuits issuing firearms to indios because firearms and swords served as symbols of socioracial status.[104]

Once the weapons arrived in Guairá, the Jesuits set to work at training reducción militias. Applying their own military training, they instructed Native militias to engage the enemy "en campo abierto" or "on the open field." The idea was to combine the strength in numbers with the power of firearms to break up large slaving expeditions. Jesuit officials instructed the Fathers that they were not to bear arms themselves nor were they to lead the militias as captains; therefore, Jesuits trained caciques to lead reducción militias.[105] From the Jesuits' perspectives, these efforts bore fruit, but not in the ways we might anticipate.

The firearms and training, before they were directed toward Paulista slavers, were used against Guaraní's enemies. Writing about the easterly reducciones of Javier and Encarnación, Ruíz de Montoya reported in 1628 that "[the Guaraní militias] have made a good catch of the Tupís, capturing them and taking the captives they carried as well as their loot, including many axes, machetes, bucklers, and other arms. . . . We sent the captives to [Villa Rica] to help Father Pablo, but the [Spanish] lieutenant . . . has taken some of these away to his *chacaras*."[106] Ruíz de Montoya provides no explanation as to why the reducción Guaraní attacked the Tupí, but the actions were presumably justifiable because the Tupí were allied with Paulistas.

After the Jesuits had established reducción communities in the east, some Guaraní in western Guairá who were dissatisfied with their situations saw these new communities as a boon and relocated. These migrations occurred for a variety of reasons, including internal divisions, the attraction of gifts in the reducciones, and conflict.[107] The divisions and exodus from the Guaraní pueblo of Santa Ana provide a useful case study. Santa Ana was an important encomienda pueblo for Guaireños. Located at the nexus of the Paraná and Ivaí Rivers, Santa Ana was in close proximity to Ciudad Real and Villa Rica. The documents do not reveal when the pueblo was created, but it was not the pueblo of the same name founded by the Jesuits in 1633.[108] Santa Ana pueblo had a church with a Guaraní-led (but Spanish imposed) administrative structure, including an unknown number of caciques, a cacique principal, alcaldes, other minor officials, and a mayordomo who oversaw the church and its financial assets. Sometime between 1625 and 1628, there was a division in the pueblo and a cacique and mayordomo named Bartolomé Pana abandoned Santa Ana with all his "subjects" and several other caciques with their kin. Their destination was the recently created Jesuit reducción of Los Ángeles.[109] The documents do not reveal why Pana left Santa Ana. Perhaps Pana had kin on the Jesuit reducción of Los Ángeles and received word that the situation was better there.

Whatever their reasons, Pana and the other Guaraní's departure caused shockwaves in Santa Ana. To add insult to injury, Pana took the swine that belonged to the church. The cacique principal, San Miguel Rivera, expressed his dismay at the exodus and did everything he could to retrieve his absconded community. Acting decisively and without prior approval from

Spanish authorities, he sent an emissary, an indio named Pablo, to Los Ánge-
les with the order to convince Bartolomé Pana and his followers to return.
Pablo accepted the assignment, but when he caught up with Pana in Los
Ángeles and attempted to persuade him to return, his words went unheeded
and Pana even threatened to tie him up and strip him of his clothes. Pablo
likely left Los Ángeles in a hurry for fear of losing his life and returned to
Santa Ana with the bad news. With no other recourse, the cacique principal
Rivera reported these happenings to Guaireño officials. Santa Ana was one
of several other communities that experienced divisions and flight to Jesuit
reducciones.[110] We can guess why Guaraní would leave these communities,
but the documents also shed light on why many Guaraní chose to stay.

Cacique Rivera from Santa Ana and the other caciques who persisted in
alliance with Guaireños remained because they saw their Guaireño encomenderos as kin. A cacique named Pedro Jupiay noted that the Indians in
Guairá were like "brothers" to the Spaniards.[111] These caciques also recognized that their relationships with Spaniards yielded peace and security,
similar benefits proffered by the reducciones. But these caciques represent
the power-holders in their communities, and their political position
depended on keeping the community united. To be a cacique within the
networks of cuñadasgo meant inhabiting a modified form of tuvichá social
power, one that was connected not only to the Guaraní values of eloquence
and generosity but also to a degree of loyalty to Spanish power. As the case
of Bartolomé Pana in Santa Ana demonstrates, not everyone shared this sentiment and saw the Jesuit reducciones as a way out of the onerous demands
of cuñadasgo.

Pajé as Priest and Other Challenges to the Reducciones

Adding to the political and physical forces working on Guaraní allegiances
in Guairá were shamans or pajé. Because their activities involved the meta-
physical world, pajé pitted themselves against colonial competitors who
claimed to have possessed prophetic and spiritual power. The contests
between pajé and Jesuits over Guaraní adherents involved the fluid meanings
of physical objects.

Jesuits often approached Guaraní villages with scores of Guaraní assistants and porters, bearing artwork displaying powerful saints and angels. When he went to the province of Tayaoba, Ruíz de Montoya was accompanied by thirty Guaraní and he carried an image of the seven arch-angels.[112] Once Jesuits established a reducción and began offering the sacra-ments to catechumens, even more objects entered the spiritual field of power. Pajé paid special attention to the holy liturgical objects associated with bap-tism and communion. Guaraní frequently observed priests using their vest-ments, the chalice with its wine, the paten with the host, and the monstrance in association with powerful blessings and words. To counter the priests, pajé responded by co-opting and deploying Jesuit rituals and objects. For exam-ple, the formidable Miguel Artiguaye, a baptized cacique who turned against the priests, led his community in a kind of countercommunion. In "pretend-ing to be a priest," Ruíz de Montoya reported, Artiguaye donned his own version of the liturgical vestments: a robed mozzetta of brilliant bird feathers. In his sacramental garb, he performed a mass for his flock using manioc cakes and maize wine.[113] In another example, a pajé named Nezú killed three priests before donning their vestments and performing a counterbaptism. The counterritual involved scraping young neophytes' tongues of the purify-ing salt applied before baptism and washing away the oil that had been placed on the neophytes' bodies. These debaptisms were important to many pajé because, in their minds, the priests' baptism inflicted death; precisely during the Jesuits' most active periods in Guairá there was a serious plague that swept through the region.[114] Even so, these debaptisms seem to differ from other kinds of Guaraní "healing" activities, for healings often involved suck-ing infected portions of the body to remove the evil or foreign substance.[115] Thus, debaptisms may have been more an attempt to usurp the priests' pow-ers, symbolically removing his spiritual actions and replacing them with the pajé's. In other words, these actions were not an attempt to destroy every-thing that was Catholic, but instead to co-opt and redeploy; the pajé fought fire with fire. Elevated by the hands of a pajé, the eucharistic honey beer and cassava cakes morphed into something other than the blood and body of Jesus.[116]

Guaraní pajés were not the only challenge Jesuits faced in the early reduc-ciones. Onerous Jesuit demands related to labor and daily schedules, the change of heart of a Guaraní leader, or the introduction of a better option introduced by encomenderos or Paulistas all worked against Jesuit efforts to build lasting reducciones. Moreover, reducciones struggled when Jesuits pressed Guaraní on eliminating socially disruptive practices, especially polygyny. Jesuits recognized how disruptive monogamy was to Guaraní social organization and so delayed teaching monogamy for two years after first contact.[117] But once instruction on the sixth commandment (the Augustinian division) began, many tuvichá and pajé resisted and convinced others that such a policy was part of a Jesuit attempt to eradicate Guaraní communities and political power. Other impositions included Jesuit requests to relocate a village and tasks oriented toward maintaining surpluses of food.[118] Most Jesuits explained away Guaraní reluctance as the work of the devil or as a reflection of Indians' natural inclinations. Claudio Ruyer observed that Guaraní were naturally disinclined toward obedience because they lacked a formalized political organization.[119] Jesuits' accusations of "fickleness" are borne out of their ethnocentrism. Indeed, Guaraní were prone to division long before Christianity arrived. Hélène Clastres has demonstrated that tuvichá and pajé were sometimes requested to verify their legitimacy as leaders through battles or prophecy.[120] If Jesuits were put to the test and failed to demonstrate their authority—perhaps by not yielding a good prophecy, by not catching a jaguar, by being associated with social disruption (as in the prohibition of polygyny)—a tuvichá may have chosen to break the alliance and relocate. Ruíz de Montoya related the experience of a cacique who had resided in a reducción but became dissatisfied with "the life of the Christians" and when another tuvichá from the area approached him about combining their lineages to form a new village, he joined him and abandoned the reducción.[121]

Jaguar Killers

If pajé co-opted the power of priests, priests adopted some of the social and cosmological roles of the pajé. In the context of a politically unstable and ethnically mixed frontier, Jesuits were forced to creatively appeal to their indigenous audiences. The following narrative, constructed from Jesuit Claudio Ruyer's letters, provides an example of Jesuit attempts to minister to the needs of their Guaraní neophytes in ways that resonated across Catholic and Guaraní cultural fields.

During the dark of night, a large jaguar snarled before ending the life of a young girl. The child had been sleeping in a hammock next to her mother when the *yaguareté*, as they were called in the Guaraní language, stealthily approached her and pulled her from her hammock into the nearby forest. The young girl's mother witnessed the horrifying scene and called out for help. Men in the village rushed into the forest and tried to catch the feline. Armed with a bow and arrows, the girl's grandfather demonstrated incredible bravery when he located the creature and scared it away from the girl's lifeless and mangled body; the jaguar had already consumed a good portion of her. The Guaraní hamlet where these events occurred was only a short distance from a new reducción, Santa María del Iguazú, situated near the confluence of the Paraná and Iguazú Rivers and not far from the awe-inspiring Iguazú Falls. When the jaguar attacked, the reducción had only been around for a year, having been founded in 1627. Many Guaraní in the hamlet, including the young girl, had been baptized and interacted regularly with the Jesuits in the reducción, but they did not reside within the mission town's emerging urban complex. What happened next suggests that Guaraní saw in the Jesuits powerful shamanic and leadership abilities and that the Jesuits actively promoted themselves within Guaraní paradigms of spiritual power while simultaneously pronouncing themselves as apocalyptic emissaries of a new religion.

Several of the men from the village ran to Santa María del Iguazú to inform the two Jesuit priests about the yaguareté attack and solicit their help.[122] When a powerful being like a jaguar attacked a villager, it required the intervention of shamanic power to locate and capture it. These Guaraní perceived that the Jesuits possessed these powers. At the Guaraní's urging, the following day Jesuit Claudio Ruyer and his companion led a group to the site where the Jaguar had killed the girl. They resolved that they would catch the predator and, with the help of their Guaraní neophytes, built a trap. It is what the Jesuits did next that likely drew the attention of Guaraní onlookers. Ruyer and his companion blessed the site by performing a mass and petitioning Saint Charles—a favorite of seventeenth-century Jesuits— to intercede on their behalf and capture the jaguar. With their spiritual labor concluded, the Jesuits and their Guaraní retinue returned to Santa María del Iguazú.

Early the next morning, Guaraní from the hamlet joyfully entered the reducción compound to announce that the yaguareté had been captured and killed. With the entire community present, the priests celebrated their victory over the jaguar and mourned the loss of the young girl. They held a mass for the dead child and buried her. Having dealt with the corpse of the girl, now it was the Guaraní's turn to deal with the corpse of the jaguar. Several Guaraní brought the "fierce massive beast" before the entrance of the church and skinned it, then fed its corpse to the dogs.

What did these events mean for Guaraní and Jesuit participants? Claudio Ruyer provides some clues when he noted that after these dramatic events, Guaraní from surrounding areas recognized the Jesuits as "jaguar killers" and enthusiastically joined the reducción.[123] To be a "killer" of enemies in Tupí-Guaraní societies was positive. Young men longed for an opportunity to kill, as it marked their passage from boy to man and provided them with a new name. The benefits of killing were not limited to warriors but were dispersed throughout the community. Ruíz de Montoya wrote that when an enemy was killed in an anthropophagic ritual, members of the village participated in the violence and thereby received new names.[124] But killing a jaguar was not the same as killing a human enemy. "A jaguar, as a symbol of cannibalism, was treated as if he were a human: his head was smashed. An enemy, on the other hand, was treated as if his captors were jaguars: he was eaten." While jaguars ate uncooked meat, humans possessed fire and ate cooked meat. Similar ideas may have been at play among the Guaraní at Santa María del Iguazú where, instead of consuming the jaguar, the Guaraní quartered it and fed it to the dogs, allowing other animals to consume its uncooked flesh.[125]

Ruyer reported another episode involving jaguar predation and Jesuit intervention. In the vicinity of the Santa María de Iguazú reducción there were four caciques who resisted Jesuit overtures to join the reducción. To punish their obstinacy, Ruyer's God sent a jaguar among them, killing several people. Guaraní leaders from these villages requested the Jesuits' help, so a priest went to help lay the trap and bless it. When the jaguar was captured, these Guaraní villages were more receptive to the priests' overtures.[126] A dramatic example of transculturation, jaguar trapping became an important evangelical method for Ruyer and his companions. Ruyer noted that because of their fame throughout the land as jaguar killers, many Guaraní came from the surrounding region and joined the reducción.

In their own writings about their evangelical actions, Jesuits used the metaphor of prey and predator, lamb and lion, when referring to themselves as against enemies of the faith, especially Guaraní shamans. The humble and meek priests were not afraid of predation but expected it. The "sorcerers" or Guaraní pajé were like predatory jaguars, who lurked in the forest ready to pounce on priestly prey. Pajé even growled at priests.[127] But in ways that perhaps the Jesuits did not fully recognize, they willfully became predators themselves. Dressed in black robes, carrying crosses, perhaps images of saints, and with liturgical accoutrements, the priests used their distinctive image and special powers to perform rituals and prayers at the site of the jaguar traps. Guaraní onlookers would have remembered the priests' actions as directly impacting the capture of the yaguareté. Jesuit incarnational spirituality is at work in Ruyer's account, but reading ethnographically it is clear that Jesuit behaviors and tactics were being "guaranized" at the same time as the Guaraní were experiencing what Fausto calls a "dejaguarization," when the Catholic ideas about love replaced predation.[128]

There are many other examples of priests doing shaman-like things, but tales of jaguars will suffice. For now, it is important to recognize that the same frontier dynamics that informed Hernando Díaz's decision to give a tovajá feathered maracás led Jesuits to trap jaguars. The transcultural behaviors of colonials in Guairá are part of a broader narrative of shifting alliances and political subjectivities. The Jesuits' presence in Guairá had profound repercussions to the east and the west. Whereas the Franciscans had worked closely with encomenderos to establish pueblos in the Asunción region, Jesuits in Guairá sought greater autonomy and resisted the encomienda. Franciscans in Guairá had worked with Guaraní communities in close proximity to Villa Rica and Ciudad Real but did not expand their influence beyond the reach of the encomenderos. The Jesuits, by contrast, pushed east into territories where encomenderos had fewer or no kinship networks. Moreover, as Jesuits moved east, they encountered Natives that Paulistas claimed. To add to the tension, some Natives who joined reducciones were at odds with Tupian groups allied with Paulistas. This increased threat of losing Indian slaves to the Jesuit reducciones as well as Atlantic market forces led the Paulistas to intensify their recruiting and slaving activities in Guairá.

Borderland Flux

Excellent historical scholarship on the Jesuit reducciones in the Portuguese-Spanish borderlands of Tapé in the late seventeenth and eighteenth centuries describes the many treatises, geopolitical factors, and local actors that made that space a dynamic Spanish-Portuguese borderland.[129] The borderland conflicts in seventeenth-century Guairá did not share all the same dynamics, especially when it came to imperial interests in defining borders. While the 1494 Treaty of Tordesillas provided a vague demarcation of imperial territories, local officials on either side largely ignored it. For Paulistas, territorial boundaries meant little; the primary goal was to find slaves. The small population of Guaireños also sought labor, but they pursued it through cuñadasgo, not enslavement en masse. The Jesuits, for their part, sought to create fixed communities free of the encomienda and safeguarded from Paulista enslavement. Natives navigated these three nodes of colonial power carefully, becoming adept at pitting groups against each other in order to acquire allies, kin, and metal tools.

Guaireños claimed Indians through their status as encomenderos. Encomenderos in Asunción relied heavily on the registers of their encomienda Indians in the padrón or census to legitimate their claims over Natives when such claims were contested by their colonial peers. In Guairá, colonial officials conducted very few inspections (visitas) of Indian pueblos, leaving encomenderos with irregular legal records that could validate their claims on Indians. Furthermore, the registers that were produced were made rather arbitrarily and did not reflect real colonial control. An español captain named Francisco Vallejos commented on the slipshod censuses that served as a legal foundation for Spanish rule over indios in Guairá. After explaining that Spaniards essentially bought Indian personal servants with axes, he noted that local officials decided to "distribute in encomienda the Indian villages, gathering information through their caciques about their location in relation to rivers and how many fires each village possessed, without ever having seen them. And with this confused knowledge they counted, distributed, and gave out the encomiendas."[130] This Guaireño admitted that the encomienda was not a system of colonial subjugation but rather a system of reciprocity. When Jesuit reducciones began attracting encomienda Indians to their communities, encomenderos responded by demanding the return of their Indians to their original villages. But with few padrones, encomenderos had very little legal recourse and therefore relied on force or persuasion to bring Guaraní back to encomienda pueblos.

For their part, Jesuits made jurisdictional claims on indigenous bodies based on the status of their souls. While Jesuits accepted Natives from all corners, they made legal claims on Natives by arguing that they were first baptized in the reducciones, not among Guaireños or Paulistas. Castilian law charged encomenderos with evangelizing encomienda indios so, according to Jesuit logic, if Indians had not been baptized, they were not encomendados. These contrasting methods for colonial sovereignty can be seen in the following episode.

In November of 1628, the encomendero-friendly Governor Céspedes Jeria sent Captain Francisco Romero to all the Jesuit reducciones to conduct an inspection and verify the status of the Indians the Jesuits claimed. In short, Romero was sent to reclaim encomienda Indians Guaireños had claimed were unlawfully taken by the Jesuits. The governor also ordered Romero to identify any "Tupís" or "Mbiobes" in the reducciones and return them to São Paulo via Villa Rica. This last order underscores the notion of embodied borders in Guairá.

Romero began the census in San Francisco Javier, one of the newest reducciones. Romero claimed that many of the indios there had relocated from encomienda pueblos. As a delay tactic, the Jesuit father asked the indios to declare to Romero whether they preferred to submit themselves to royal authority as opposed to encomenderos. The Jesuit apparently hoped to provide a legal record that the indios in his reducción were blank political slates, coming under imperial subjectivity for the first time, and therefore nullifying any encomendero or Paulista claims. Romero retorted that indios could not be presented as crown subjects anew and demanded that the priest stop this "ruse." Romero believed that he had sufficient evidence to accuse the Jesuits of harboring encomendados. Father Ortega responded that "you cannot *encomendar* unbaptized Indians, and if they were found in this state, their status as encomendados would be null and void."[131] For the Jesuits, defending their claim on Indians was a matter of determining if they were baptized in the reducciones.

Paulistas' approaches to Indians evolved over time, but they are marked by a tendency to construct Indians as heathens who could be subject to "just war" and enslavement. John Monteiro shows that bandeiras were not colonizing activities along the lines of territorial expansion; rather, they were "depopulating" activities, and "virtually every aspect of the formation of São Paulo during its first two centuries was tied in some fundamental way to the expropriation, exploitation, and destruction of indigenous populations."[132] Paulistas, unlike Guaireños, fully embraced Indian slavery, and the language they employed to describe Indians reflects this. "Expressions such as *'peças do gentio de terra'* [native heathen pieces]or *'negros da terra'* [native blacks] paralleled the terms *'peças do gentio da Guiné'* [Guinea pieces] or *'negros da Guiné'* [Guinean blacks], which designated African slaves."[133] But Paulistas were never given a green light to enslave Indians. They constantly negotiated the ambiguous legal position of Indian slavery in Portuguese law and contended with the Jesuit order who pressured them to liberate Indians and deposit them in villages or aldeias. Over the course of the seventeenth century, however, local Paulistas were victorious in defining Indians as slaves.[134]

Guaireños, Jesuits, and Paulistas each had their own methods for claiming Natives, reflecting the local construction of border and authority. But despite these differences, a consensus emerged among Guaireños and Paulistas that specific ethnic groups belonged to each realm.

Testing and Transgressing Embodied Borders

Historical work on the bandeiras has emphasized their no-holds-barred colonialism. There is no disputing the destructive nature of the bandeiras; however, the historical record indicates that for a time they operated under the embodied borders logic. It is precisely because Paulistas perceived that the Jesuits had breached the embodied borders pattern for claiming Indians that they ramped up slaving expeditions in the reducciones. By looking carefully at the borderlands, we see that bandeiras responded not only to Atlantic market forces but also to the contested claims on the borderlands itself.

Paulistas' methods for enslaving Natives developed gradually over the course of the late sixteenth and early seventeenth centuries, evolving from kinship and political networks to small-scale "trade and raid" campaigns to huge mobilizations. Columns of bandeiras were often led by culturally ambiguous mamelucos (mestizos) whose kinship connections with groups in and around São Paulo provided them with allies.[135] Eventually, the kinship relationships between Paulistas and the groups they targeted for slavery faded. Individuals and groups mounted expeditions not regulated by the Portuguese crown.[136] As market forces allowed, and as borderland politics dictated, these slaving activities evolved into massive expeditions, culminating in the largest bandeiras of 1628–1632 and 1635–1637.

The bandeiras were composed of a core group of mamelucos, but much of the hard labor was performed by indigenous allies and slaves who served as warriors, porters, and servants. Neil Whitehead and Brian Ferguson describe indigenous participation, either through coercion or enticement, in colonial- or state-led violence as "ethnic soldiering."[137] Spaniards described all Paulista Native allies as Tupí; in reality, Paulista allies were ethnically diverse. Some of these Natives went willingly as hired agents motivated by interethnic rivalries, while others were conscripted to fight, having just recently been made slaves.[138] Soldiering on Spanish Portuguese borderlands was part of many Natives' new enslaved experiences.

Paulistas first targeted Carijó, or Guaraní who inhabited a region Paulistas called the Sertão dos Patos and the Sertão dos Carijós. This latter region included Spanish Guairá. Because Guairá was a relatively short distance of a forty- to sixty-day march from São Paulo, it soon became the principal destination for Paulista slavers. The expeditions to the sertão became so frequent that bandeirantes began planting crops along the routes to the slaving territories.[139] To the east and north of Spanish Guairá, in the Paranapanema Valley, Paulistas encountered Tememinó (sometimes called Tupí) and Tupinaé.

But even as they launched their first bandeira in 1611 to the Guairá borderlands, they were forced to operate according to embodied borders logic. The bandeira was composed of thirty Paulistas and an unknown number of Tupí. They attacked Guaraní associated with reducciones, but a militia of similar size from Ciudad Real cut them off. The bandeira and the Ciudad Real militia confronted each other, though diplomacy won out. The Paulista captain carried a commission he claimed was from the Portuguese governor granting permission to enslave Indians. The Guaireño captain rejected the commission and demanded the Guaraní be returned. He prevailed in taking back five hundred Guaraní from the slavers and sent the Guaraní back to the reducciones.[140]

Traditional portraits of the bandeiras highlight their European origins, but Paulistas relied on indigenous knowledge and leadership to acquire captives through culturally informed coercion and persuasion, not simply brute force. A bandeira that was in Guairá between 1626 and 1627 was led by a pajé who used methods of preaching drawn from indigenous and Catholic traditions. The pajé used a cross, three triumphal arches, and lit candles to "predict success and help the group capture many Indians."[141] The presence of triumphal arches in the bandeira evokes a reducción's reception of an important ecclesiastical or royal official, except that when accompanying a bandeira the arches portend the triumphant arrival of slavers. Triumphal arches were an important part of reducción life and Guaraní were accustomed to dressing these arches up with all kinds of objects and flora.[142] The image of a bandeira composed of mameluco Paulistas and Tupí warriors being led by a pajé bearing a cross and other Catholic liturgical objects recalls the methods of the Jesuits, who arrived in Native territories accompanied by scores of Indian auxiliaries, bearing crosses and paintings of archangels. It appears that the pajé with the bandeira hoped to communicate that the bandeira arrived as an alternative to a reducción. Apparently, bandeira leaders frequently employed pajé. These transcultural methods for slaving speak to the effect of Tupí-Guaraní knowledge and religion on colonial activities in Guairá—activities that have consistently been depicted as "Atlantic" or "Portuguese." Thus, the pajé's presence reveals the ontological slippage implicit in slaving activities. Similar to the ways that some scholars have called the conquest activities in Mesoamerica less a "Spanish conquest of Mesoamerica" and more a "Mesoamerican conquest of Mesoamerica," so too we can discern in Guairá the "guaranization" of the bandeiras.[143]

Besides shamanic prophets, Paulistas also used the practice of gifting iron tools to persuade Natives to settle in São Paulo. In 1612, a rather large group of Guaraní abandoned pueblos on the Piquirí River subject to encomenderos in Ciudad Real. The departing group was led by thirteen tuvichá and consisted of nine hundred souls. As these Guaraní relocated, they convinced other Guaraní members of nearby Jesuit reducciones and other independent villages to join them in their migration. While in transit, Paulistas caught up with them and convinced them to relocate to São Paulo. But the consensus among the migrants was weak, for as the group moved eastward, divisions and violence derailed the group. Several people were killed. A few witnesses stated that cannibalism occurred during the migration, a claim that would have given Guaireños license to halt the migration and forcefully relocate people to encomienda pueblos. Officials from Ciudad Real sent a militia to stop the migration. It was successful in bringing three hundred back to the Ciudad Real area. The rest of the group broke up, following diverse paths: two hundred fled into the forests under the leadership of a great pajé, while five caciques with an untold number of followers were led by the Paulista Sebastián Preto, who "took them with pure gifting [iron tools]."[144]

Slavers made claims on Indians not only through ethnic designations but also through their religious status. Ruíz de Montoya recounts that a group of Paulistas came into Guairá and took an untold number of Guaraní, some of whom were from villages connected to the reducciones. Unsure if their captives were members of the reducciones, the Paulistas submitted the captives to a "doctrinal examination," which typically was a request to recite the Paternoster. Finding many of these to be catechized, they set them free, but not before providing them with the enticements of axes and hooks. The Guaraní that could not "pass the test" were labeled gentiles and taken as slaves to São Paulo.[145] That the Paulistas took such a cautious approach reveals the importance of the local context. With Jesuits arming and training Guaraní in the reducciones and the threat of large mobilization, the Paulistas calculated that caution was the better option.

After the initial bandeira expeditions in 1611 and 1612, the looming threat of future expeditions prodded Guaireños to more carefully consider which Natives pertained to encomenderos, Jesuits, or Paulistas. Guaireños and Paulistas seemed to agree that Tupí and Mbiobe Indians belonged to São Paulo. As we saw earlier, when Governor Céspedes Jeria arrived, he ordered any Jesuit or encomendero who found Tupí or Mbiobe in their communities to return them to São Paulo via Ciudad Real.[146] But as the Jesuits pushed eastward and created reducciones closer to São Paulo, the ethnic groups designated for each colonial group were mixed together, setting the stage for jurisdictional confusion and increased Paulista aggression.

As the Jesuit reducciones became more renowned, indio slaves from São Paulo fled to the reducciones, drawing the ire of Paulistas. Responding to these trends, Manoel Preto (brother to Sebastián, mentioned above) traveled from São Paulo to the cabildo of Ciudad Real in 1619 with twenty soldiers. He came representing the vecinos of São Paulo and submitted an official petition to the Ciudad Real cabildo to reclaim Indians who had fled to Guairá from haciendas in São Paulo. In his petition, Preto lashed out at the Jesuits in the reducciones of Pirapó and Nuestra Señora de Loreto for taking in Indians who were not theirs and breaking canon law by keeping Indians who were married in the Paulista-controlled aldeias of Pirapó from returning to their spouses.[147] Operating under the embodied borders logic, the Ciudad Real cabildo gave Preto permission to go to the reducciones and take the Indians belonging to the Paulistas, specifying "Tupí and Tememino" ethnic groups.

Preto arrived at Ciudad Real in late 1619. By mid-January 1620, Preto was in the reducciones of San Loreto de Pirapó and Ypaunbuçu with cabildo permission in hand to request that Tupí and Tememino Indians be turned over to him. The Jesuits refused. Preto was incensed and threatened to destroy their reducciones. The Jesuits responded by asking the caciques to confirm Preto's claims that they were married in São Paulo. The caciques responded that they had been married by the Jesuits in the reducciones, lending weight to the Jesuits' position. In a scene that could have come from the pages of a wild west novel, Preto and his soldiers fired their weapons into the air as they withdrew from the reducciones and threatened to return with more soldiers and destroy the reducciones. Preto left for São Paulo nearly empty-handed, but his words would prove prophetic: Preto commanded one of the largest columns during the devastating 1628 bandeira.

After 1619, the frequency and size of the bandeiras increased.[148] In the years after the 1623 bandeira, six new Jesuit reducciones were established, suggesting that many Guaraní joined Jesuits to build reducciones for the protection they offered.[149] By September 1628, when Governor Céspedes Jeria arrived, the situation for Guaireños was dire. Natives throughout the region were abandoning encomienda pueblos to seek out new opportunities in the reducciones or were escaping the threat of Paulistas.

Céspedes Jeria attempted to use his clout as governor and his supplies of gifts to try to regain Natives' allegiance and bring about calm amid the mercurial political landscape he found in Guairá. He called a meeting with two powerful chieftains, Tayaoba and Maendí, who had relocated their communities to a Jesuit reducción. The two caciques initially ignored the governor's invitation but eventually agreed to see him in Villa Rica. As Tayaoba and Maendí traveled to meet the Spanish governor, their Jesuit priest accompanied them, but he did not command or lead them. The governor received the caciques with as much pomp and circumstance as he could muster, including a gun salute, banquet, and many gifts (presumably axes and cloth). Céspedes Jeria's deferential approach suggests just how fractured the political landscape had become and the desperate position encomenderos found themselves in by the late 1620s. Guaireños were optimistic that Tayaoba and Maendí would return to pay tribute under the encomienda, but it seems plausible that Tayaoba and Maendí were playing Jesuits and Guaireños off each other to acquire more gifts or beneficial arrangements for their communities.[150]

Before he came to Guairá in 1628, Céspedes Jeria had learned of an impending bandeira; in fact, he had observed its organization in São Paulo and had traveled with one of the columns up to a certain point.[151] Céspedes Jeria made no moves to stop it because, according to the embodied borders logic, Paulistas were free to claim certain categories of Indians. Céspedes Jeria instructed the Guaireños that if the Paulistas came into the reducciones to take Indians rightly *reducido* under Jesuit or encomendero auspices, they were to arm themselves, assemble friendly Indian warriors, and "die fighting."[152] He also ordered that if the bandeirantes attacked the reducciones, the lieutenant governor was to bring all indios to Villa Rica so as to better protect them. He added, however, that if the Paulistas came to take *indios infieles* (unbaptized gentiles), Tupí, or Tememino, the Spanish-Guaraní militias were to leave them alone.

Columns of the bandeira finally arrived in Guairá in late 1628. When the attacks on the reducciones began, the lieutenant governor moved to congregate all Indians to Villa Rica. Ruíz de Montoya suspected that Guaireños were trying to enslave the Indians, and so he forced his way through Villa

Rica and led the exodus of thousands of Indians south to the Paraná region. Scholars working from the Paulista perspective suggest that Guaireños and Céspedes Jeria were in cahoots with Paulista slavers, presumably to make profits off the sale of slaves.[153] No doubt some Guaireños conspired to sell indio slaves, but given Céspedes Jeria's orders and the fact that Guaireños engaged in combat with bandeiras, it seems unlikely that there was a general agreement between Spanish Guairá and São Paulo over Indian enslavement.[154] Nonetheless, thanks to Jesuit litigation initiated at the audiencia in Charcas, Céspedes Jeria was charged with colluding with the slavers and ultimately lost his governorship over the matter.[155]

The bandeira that began in 1628 destroyed thirteen reducciones and enslaved thousands of Natives. The bandeira was massive: over 2,200 Tupís and 900 Paulistas. According to Jesuit sources, they committed terrible atrocities, slaughtering elderly and children who held up travel as they advanced eastward.[156] Two Jesuit reducciones survived but migrated to the southern Paraná region. In 1641, at the battle of Mbororé, an armed Guaraní-Jesuit army routed a bandeira, dealing a devastating blow to Paulista confidence. Thereafter, Paulistas mounted much smaller and more nimble expeditions to the reducciones in the Paraná and Tapé regions. With the indigenous population decimated, Ciudad Real and Santiago de Xérez were abandoned and Villa Rica relocated to the west of the Paraná River. Several other bandeiras attacked Paraguay, including a devastating raid in 1676, which forced the migration of thousands of Indians south from Itatín (north of Asunción to the east of the Paraguay River), an episode examined in chapter 5. Spanish officials did not attempt to reclaim Guairá until the eighteenth century when they sent colonists to established the fort of Curuguaty just to the west of the Paraná in order to stop the advance of Portuguese settlement.[157] Unlike the borderlands activities of the early seventeenth century focused on indigenous bodies and souls, the eighteenth-century imperial borderlands reflected state goals related to the demarcation and defense of imperial territories.

Conclusion

Two Jesuits who operated in Guairá, Justo Mancilla and Simón Manceta, accompanied their enslaved flock as they were forcibly marched to São Paulo.

Their goals were to observe, recount, and then seek redress from the Brazilian governor in Bahía. Observing the brutalities committed against captives during the journey and the horror they felt at losing their inchoate godly communities, these Jesuits contemplated the reasons for the destructions that beset them.

> We have been the cause of [the Guaraní's] captivity, and their selling off like animals. Having been gathered together under our promise that with us, in our villages as Christians and children of God they would be safe from the Portuguese and from captivity. With these promises they gathered and if we had not promised them so much security they never would have gathered so swiftly and therefore many of them would probably be free.[158]

These Jesuits' recognition that the reducciones played a role in the widespread enslavement of thousands of Guaraní points to the complex dynamics in Guairá.[159] Centuries detached from these harrowing events, historians should resist framing the narrative through a guilty-innocent paradigm.[160] Guairá was a space of political flux that saw competing yet partially overlapping colonial goals and actors and it was these dynamics, coupled with the Atlantic market incentives, that explain the region's descent into chaos. In the absence of strong regal motives and imperial identities among Guaireños and Paulistas, colonial boundaries were literally mobile Native communities. Indigenous bodies constituted jurisdictional borders, and since those borders were mobile, they were impossible to fix. Paulistas used this borderland logic to legitimate their enslavement of the entire region's inhabitants.

Guairá was largely abandoned by Spaniards and Jesuits alike following the 1628 bandeira, but the movement of people affected by these slaving campaigns continued to inform lives throughout the province and reflect the distinctions between Guaraní life under the Portuguese in São Paulo and life under Spaniards in Paraguay. Take Luís, a second-generation slave born to Guaraní parents who had belonged to a Jesuit reducción in the vicinity of Villa Rica when the Paulistas came in 1628. His parents were forcefully removed to São Paulo and made slaves. Luís's mother gave birth to him after her enslavement in São Paulo. Later, as a young man, he and his uncle were conscripted into a bandeira that went to Paraguay. It must have been terrifying for Luís to be forced to engage in a form of violence that had previously destroyed his parents' world. Unhappy with his situation, Luís and his uncle escaped from the bandeira and fled to Villa Rica, then Mbaracayú, before landing in the Asunción region. Once in Asunción, Luís was assigned by a city official to an encomendero. Having moved from one form of subjugation to another, he decided to relocate to Caazapá, a Franciscan pueblo subject to encomenderos. Luís's experiences reflect the borderland dynamics of eastern Paraguay and provide a social portrait of a small number of Indians who survived the bandeira ordeal and forged new lives for themselves in Spanish Paraguay. Their movements highlight Natives' use of porous borderlands to seek better lives but encountering a stark reality where "Indian" status required inhabiting a place on a continuum of subjugation.[161]

As the birthplace of the Jesuit enterprise among Guaraní in Paraguay, Guairá deserves close scrutiny. Jesuit reducciones emerged out of a relationship of tension and mixed cooperation between Spaniards, friars, Paulistas, and Guaraní actors. By emphasizing indigenous agency and internal conflict, the reducciones appear more prominently as strategic communities that Guaraní used to navigate the political and social transformation brought about by the various goals of colonials and Natives. Employing a frontier/borderlands framework highlights the many factors influencing Guaraní communities' actions and adds nuance to a narrative of conquest and conversion that has traditionally favored conquistadors, pathfinders, and priests.

Part 2.

Challenges

CHAPTER 4

Resplendent Prophets and Vengeful Warriors

Guaraní Rejection of Colonial Rule

THIS BOOK HAS demonstrated that Guaraní came into the orbit of colonial power for a variety of reasons including kinship, material benefits, protection, and spiritual power, as well as the coercion and force of colonials. Whatever their pathway into relationships of subjugation under Spanish colonialism, after a period of time within the encomienda and/or reducciones many Guaraní discovered that their social structures and traditions were at risk. Some chose to resist onerous demands and social strictures through "everyday forms of resistance."[1] Others, however, chose outright rejection of Spanish colonial rule. This chapter analyzes two episodes of Guaraní rebellion. The first occurred in 1625 and was directed by a pajé named Juan Cuaraçí who promoted himself as a kind of "antipriest" trying to build an "antireducción." He used his prophetic gifts and a network of shaman-disciples to convince other Guaraní to abandon what he believed were the socially destructive demands of the priests and draw Guaraní away to live in a renewed society where its members could practice polygyny. The second resistance movement occurred in 1660 in the relatively young pueblo of Arecayá, which sat on the Jejuy River in the northern region of Itatín. Unlike Cuaraçí, who often hid from colonial authorities and tried to draw Guaraní away from reducciones, the Arecayá pueblo tried to decapitate Spanish power in the region. Starting with the governor himself, the ringleaders of the rebellion sought to completely eradicate Spaniards in Paraguay and then take their women as slaves. Their anger stemmed from abusive Spanish officials who had killed a prominent cacique in the community a decade before.

While only Arecayá became radically anti-imperial and violent, both rebellions included pajé. Occurring nearly a century after contact, these rebellions (especially Cuaraçí's) provide unique perspectives on Guaraní religious expression during a period of time when the reducciones were solidifying. In other words, these rebellions give us a portrait of Guaraní religion that had "cannibalized" Catholicism.[2] Similar to the way Guaraní warriors believed that by consuming an enemy they could receive his strength, Guaraní pajé engaged in semiophagous displays to counter the priests and enhance their own power.[3] The analogy of eating here is meant to imply that the symbols of power were transformed through their consumption.[4] Unlike other indigenous rebellions, like that of New Mexico, where many things perceived as foreign were destroyed, Guaraní were highly receptive to external elements and consumed foreign ideas and objects as a way of expanding their selfhood.[5]

Conditioned to find religion in institutions and art, Ruíz de Montoya and other Jesuits believed that Guaraní were not prone to religion or that they were even "atheists."[6] Of course, this was not true, for Guaraní had an array of deity, spirits, and spiritual objects.[7] What confused and confounded the priests even more was how Tupí-Guaraní could one day enthusiastically adopt Christianity and the next day disregard it. A renowned Portuguese Jesuit, Antonio Vieira, who missionized among Tupian and other Natives of Brazil, wrote a famous sermon in 1657 that likened the Indians of Brazil to statues of myrtle. Unlike statues of marble (i.e., former gentiles of the Old World), which are carved with great difficulty but forever keep their shape, myrtle is easy to shape but constantly changes. If the gardener removes his hand for a moment, the myrtle statue quickly acquires a new shape: "in four days a branch sticks out that runs through the statue's eyes, another one jumbles its ears, two more turn its five fingers into seven, and that which shortly before was a man is now a green confusion of myrtle."[8] Jesuits connected the perceived problem of Indian inconstancy to their lack of strong political authorities like kings. Viveiros de Castro argues that what priests called fickleness was in fact a reflection of Tupí-Guaraní "ontological incompleteness" or a tendency to desire to be something Other.[9] This perspective is useful to understanding pajé actions and attitudes and when coupled with a robust historical contextualization, some of the utility of these actions comes into focus. When it came to pajé who resisted the reducciones, they absorbed Christianity to use it as a weapon. As one scholars puts it, pajé "'guaranized' elements of the Christian message in order to counteract the power of the Christians."[10] Not only did shamans use Christian objects like chalices, vestments, or even the host, they also readily inserted concepts like resurrection or images of saints and devils into their cosmologies. But beyond Catholic symbols of power, Guaraní also adopted methods and tactics of rebellion in a frontier context where encomenderos, Catholic priests, independent Guaraní, reducción Guaraní, and Chaco Indians all engaged each other in an intense cultural exchange. This chapter analyzes the "unnatural" and "monstrous" forms in Vieira's metaphorical garden of myrtle statues, which took shape on Paraguay's porous political and ideological frontiers.

Most of the research on Guaraní resistance movements has been informed by priestly narratives. By contrast, this chapter creates a narrative of Guaraní resistance by triangulating a criminal suit, official documentation, and traditional priestly sources. The results demonstrate that Guaraní were more mobile than previously imagined. Both Juan Cuaraçí and the Arecayá communities forged interethnic relationships with independent Native groups as well as with Guaraní in reducciones and Spanish cities to enhance their power. Moreover, there was a great deal of mobility between and communication across pueblos and Spanish towns or cities. Examining these two resistance movements together elucidates the diverse and creative strategies a minority of Guaraní employed to assert greater autonomy and reclaim waning social practices.

The *Pajé*'s Words

As the rope of the garrote tightened around his neck, he gasped, drawing his last breath, but despite his efforts he could not speak. The eloquent concepts that he had so loved to vocalize, his "word" or "ñe'ẽ ayvu," were gone. A Guaraní pajé's words were a source of power. Eloquently expressed or sung, words could draw people together around concepts that united the past and the present, the living world and the world of spirits.[11] Through the 1620s and perhaps earlier, Juan Cuaraçí had relied on his prophetic words to convince many Natives to believe in his antipriestly agenda with his warnings that the priests sought to destroy everything that was good about Guaraní existence.

But now on an unspecified date in 1625, the colonial administrators who oversaw the execution could breathe again. They were relieved to hear Cuaraçí's voice fall silent, for he had sowed chaos in the province: seven young Guaraní reducciones were on the verge of collapse because of his actions. For several years, Cuaraçí had openly challenged priests' authority in both Franciscan and Jesuit reducciones, threatening decades of work and encomenderos' tributary base. To be sure, there were Guaraní onlookers there that day, but we can only guess what Cuaraçí's death meant to them. Cuaraçí had several wives, and one of them resided in Asunción. Had she witnessed the scene, she would have been horrified by the gruesome death of her politically and spiritually influential partner and father to her children.

Cuaraçí's prophetic career was not exceptional. Between 1537 and 1735 there were fifty documented shamanic movements in Paraguay. Scholars have interpreted these movements and their implications for colonialism and Guaraní religion in a variety of ways.[12] Generally, the scholarship shows that shamanic messianism was marked by its opposition to priests' usurpation of their authority and the transformation of Guaraní social structure, especially the eradication of polygyny. These movements were conducted by one or more pajé who often claimed divine status. The pajé's theosis was often combined with a redeployment of Christian concepts or objects. While Cuaraçí was typical of other pajé in his spiritual practice, he was exceptionally threatening to provincial secular and ecclesiastical authorities, underscored by the fact that he was tried by secular officials in Asunción. By contrast, most other pajé were contested directly by priests and their indigenous allies in what Ruíz de Montoya termed a "spiritual conquest." Because Cuaraçí's activities attracted the attention of secular officials in Asunción, his activities and life have been recorded in greater detail.[13]

Mobile Prophet

Cuaraçí was from a village in the region of Guairá he called "Pueblo de Roque" in the Ivaí River valley.[14] The Ivaí River was an important corridor for Spaniards since the city of Villa Rica was situated near the headwaters of the river. At the time of his trial in 1625, the magistrate estimated Cuaraçí was forty years old, which means he was born around 1585. Given the timing and his village's proximity to Villa Rica, Spaniards had been familiar to Cuaraçí from birth. At best, Spaniards were powerful and useful allies who provided revolutionary technologies and were affinal kin; at worst, they were tyrannical taskmasters and political usurpers. Cuaraçí likely saw both ends of this spectrum and everything in between. The documents reveal little else about Cuaraçí's early life in Guairá, but Cuaraçí did testify that he was baptized by a priest named Velasco and that his encomendero was named Joseph de Sayas.[15]

This information suggests that Cuaraçí was not part of a Jesuit reducción but was part of a village or pueblo with close ties to encomenderos. In his early adult years, Cuaraçí likely paid tribute to his encomendero, Sayas, and he would have done so through personal service or performing any number of tasks for his encomendero, including agricultural work, hunting, fishing, building construction, or harvesting yerba maté. At some point, Cuaraçí began working under a different Spaniard named Juan Jiménez, a vecino of Ciudad Real.[16] Jiménez could have been Cuaraçí's new encomendero or another Spaniard who paid him (or his encomendero) for work. It appears that Cuaraçí was sent to work in the yerba maté groves at Mbaracayú. We can surmise that if he labored in the "mines of Paraguay" he came away from the experience with less regard for Spaniards. In Mbaracayú, colonial officials first noticed that Cuaraçí was a pajé and they apprehended him for sorcery (*hechicerías*). Cuaraçí explained that he had learned these *hechicerías* from "Indians that were in the forest" around Mbaracayú.[17] Cuaraçí's admission that he was educated in spiritual knowledge by *monteses*, as Spaniards called unconquered Indians who resided in the forests, underscores the porous boundaries between Spanish-Christian and autonomous Indian spaces.

What did it mean for a Guaraní in colonial Paraguay to become a pajé? As stated in chapter 2, early European observers of Tupí-Guaraní throughout Brazil and Paraguay distinguished between pajé who were member-residents of a village and other renowned pajé called karaí who traveled from village to village. Lesser pajé were men and women who could transcend the realms of the spirits and humans. A pajé gained spiritual knowledge and power that could be used to cure illness or inflict disease, bring abundance or scarcity, discover the names of newborns, and portend good or evil events; thus, pajé could be agents of positive or negative spiritual power. But only those pajé

who were sufficiently powerful were regarded as karaí. The power of the shaman was reflected in the size of his following, the effect of his prophecies, the
number of concubines he possessed, and the beauty of his words. Karaí often
led multivillage ceremonies but lived apart from the village.[18] Given his
mobility, number of adherents, peripatetic existence, and religious and political actions, Cuaraçí was one of these greater pajé. (To avoid confusion and
following the sources, which generally do not use "karaí," I refer to Cuaraçí
as "pajé.") But a pajé was not a static category and Cuaraçí lived at a time
when pajé were at once accepted and rejected by Guaraní. Guillermo Wilde
shows convincingly that in the reducciones the role of the pajé was elimi-
nated while the tuvichá or chieftain was transmuted into an "acceptable"
position within the mission governing structure as caciques, corregidores
(indio governor), and other kinds of leaders.[19] So while the social need for
pajé was being squeezed out of the reducciones, on Paraguay's frontiers, like
Mbaracayú and Guairá, Guaraní remained in contact with pajé. It was the
porousness of the frontier that allowed Cuaraçí to acquire spiritual knowledge from monteses.

The documents do not reveal how long Cuaraçí was in the Mbaracayú jail,
but eventually he either escaped or was set free.[20] Cuaraçí probably used
Mbaracayú as a home base from which to travel to the reducciones of Itatín
to the northwest to spread his message. Eventually Cuaraçí went south to
Asunción. The reason for his travel to Asunción was apparently personal, as
he had a wife (one of several) there with whom he had children he "loved very
much."[21] His partner may have been from Guairá and was brought to Asunción by an encomendero. That Cuaraçí risked appearing in Paraguay's provincial capital to see his wife and his children reveals a personal and intimate
side to this Guaraní prophet. In Asunción, encomenderos were very vigilant
when it came to their tributary populations and most encomenderos would
have noticed an unknown male Indian visiting their female tributary. Thus,
it was most likely under the cover of darkness that Cuaraçí entered and
departed the provincial capital.

The highest official present in Asunción, the lieutenant governor general
Pedro Hurtado, received a letter from the official in Mbaracayú informing
him of Cuaraçí's presence in Asunción. But before they could capture him,
Cuaraçí had fled Asunción to the distant city of Santa Fe, where he lived

among a Native group Spaniards called the Charrúa, a nonsedentary group that resisted Spanish power. Cuaraçí never explained why he traveled 560 miles to the Santa Fe region to join a non-Guaraní-speaking group, however he did indicate that there was a great shaman among them with whom he performed spiritual rites. While Santa Fe was distant from Asunción, there were strong social networks between the two cities thanks to the growing yerba maté trade. Cuaraçí may have joined the Charrúa because they had been at war with the Spaniards in Santa Fe and he hoped to find like-minded indios. Regardless of his reasons, it is impressive that Guaraní and Charrúa cooperated.

Unfortunately for Cuaraçí, Spanish troops on an expedition against the Charrúa captured him. With a knack for avoiding confinement, Cuaraçí escaped and with several of his followers returned to Paraguay. He began preaching in the secular-sponsored reducción of Yaguarón, situated south of Asunción. He was able to stay under the radar of the priest at Yaguarón, Father Juan de Gamarra, by residing in the vicinity of the reducción. His connections inside the reducción were apparently strong because several caciques created kinship bonds with him and offered their daughters. One witness indicated that three wives accompanied Cuaraçí and we can assume these were the caciques' daughters. As a pajé operating in between reducciones, Cuaraçí received Guaraní from the reducciones, preached to them, administered rites, and imparted spiritual knowledge. Cuaraçí had competition in Yaguarón, for there was another pajé (described as an "hechicero"), an unnamed old man who was accompanied by his wife, but they were eventually caught by Father Gamarra and punished. After establishing himself in the Yaguarón region, Cuaraçí traveled to other reducciones in the Paraná region, including Caazapá (Franciscan), Yuty (Franciscan), and San Ignacio (Jesuit).[22] As he taught, he acquired more followers and built up a small community. Cuaraçí's settlement was probably very small and mainly served as a base of operations for his preaching missions and perhaps as a place of gathering for his adherents. All of these activities speak to the fluid boundary between the reducción and groups living outside or, as in the case of Cuaraçí, in between colonial institutions. But the fluidity was physical *and* ontological. That Guaraní caciques inside a reducción would offer their daughters to a shaman speaks to an ambiguous Christian identity in the reducciones.

Cuaraçí covered impressively expansive distances in his travels as a prophet. It appears that he understood how to exploit the frontiers and cracks within colonial society in order to identify and find those who would listen to him and share in his visions for the future.

Cuaraçí and the Antireducción

Cuaraçí never provided a comprehensive vision of what he desired, but his actions demonstrate that he hoped to invert the reducción and make himself the pajé-priest. By taking what he perceived to be useful or powerful from the reducción, he hoped to create a kind of "antireducción." Through his spiritual power, Cuaraçí worked to purge his community of the sicknesses he believed the priests had inflicted on Guaraní and to return to practices that he understood to be socially regenerative, especially polygyny. Cuaraçí claimed that otherworldly powers called him to be a "true priest." This prophetic call came in the form of a vision he had experienced during a yerba-maté-induced trance.

The vision came to Cuaraçí during a trance he experienced with his Charrúan counterpart. In the midst of a fast, the two consumed large quantities of yerba maté, to the point that they vomited. They picked up the yerba maté–bile mixture from the ground and threw it into the air. While tossing this substance they exclaimed "colomi yubete" or "yerba be calm."[23] The vomiting of this substance is consistent with modern Tupian groups where beverages used in ceremonial or shamanic practices are considered trance-inducing substances.[24] The words "yerba be calm" are puzzling, but the simple fact that the pajé addressed the yerba maté reflects the spiritual qualities of the substance. After repeating the process of vomiting, throwing the yerba maté, and speaking the words "colomi yubete," Cuaraçí and the other shaman had a vision of demons ("diablos") whose bodies took the form of indios and Spaniards. A few indio-demons were nude while others wore shirts. Demons in the shape of Spaniards appeared with beards and dressed in more elaborate garb. One demon appeared under the brilliance of the noonday sun. He was running with a trumpet made of iron, and exclaimed "I am *tacua vera*" (I am brilliant bamboo).[25] Other demons appeared, some sumptuously arrayed in feathers while others were chimerical: one had the feet of a mule and the body of a man. This parade of demons had an important message for the pajé: call to all the indios and tell them to leave the Spaniards.[26]

The figure holding the iron trumpet reminds us of an angel-turned-devil inspired by catechismal materials from the reducciones and the iron tools used to initiate and maintain diplomatic relations with Natives.[27] Priests commonly used paintings and sculpture to instruct Guaraní in Christian doctrines and to inspire a fear of hell and God. Images of chimerical demons being trampled by Saint Michael, for example, may have inspired Cuaraçí's human-mule figure. The words of the trumpeting demon, "I am brilliant bamboo," correspond with other anti-Spanish shamanic activities. For example, in 1579 a pajé led an uprising against Asunceños and his name was Oberá, which means "brilliant" or "resplendent." Brightness was an important concept in Guaraní culture, signifying power and spiritual strength. Bamboo also held sacred significance for the Guaraní. Among some modern Guaraní groups, bamboo is used to make the drumming instruments women use to keep rhythm while men dance.[28] This impressive vision reflects the syncretism at work in Cuaraçí's cosmology. Filled with a rich material culture, the vision seems to turn Christian visions of holiness on their heads. The figures calling the prophet are not angels but demons. What was once evil in the reducciones becomes holy in Cuaraçí's spiritual world. More correctly, the vision reflects the breakdown of a stark division between good and evil.

One of Cuaraçí's most important activities as pajé was to teach his followers how to make their agricultural fields abundant: Guaraní witnesses called him "god of the chacaras (agricultural plots)." He instructed his listeners to say the following incantation after they planted: "ybatinbire yapaiquie cheiañandua" (the fruit of the plant withers, this is what I feel). The meaning of the incantation may be impossible to decipher because the transliteration is likely faulty.[29] What matters is that Cuaraçí was acting as a spiritual midwife to agricultural abundance, an important characteristic of pajé. In another ritual that might have been related to cultivation, Cuaraçí scratched the sign of the cross into the dirt, as if he were planting seeds, and poured yerba maté into the marks.

Like other shamans of his time, Cuaraçí affirmed his apotheosis, proclaiming himself to be "the god of the earth" and "the sun."[30] His godly nature was also reflected in his name: *Cuaraçí* is Guaraní for sun.[31]

Resplendence was a familiar theme among Guaraní, but Cuaraçí innovated by adding Christological overtones.[32] He claimed that he had died at the hands of a priest and had become a resurrected being so that he could seek his revenge.[33] Vengeance was an important cultural concept among the Tupí-Guaraní.[34] When a member of a community died at the hands of enemies, a shaman might inspire the group to go to war, take a captive, and then perform ritual anthropophagy. The desire for revenge was an important explanatory principle in these practices, though there are many others. Did Cuaraçí intend to kill priests and cannibalize them? This is unlikely, since, as Fausto notes, Jesuit priests were often avoided as objects of consumption. Instead, their bodies were dismembered and burned, suggesting a desire "to reduce them to nothingness in order to avoid shamanic vengeance and deny them the posthumous immortality they had proclaimed in life"—a true Guaraní murder.[35] The idea that Cuaraçí wanted to kill the priests came from a priest; Guaraní witnesses only mentioned his goals of creating an antireducción. If Cuaraçí believed himself to be a resurrected being, he sought to lead his followers to a better existence outside the reducciones rather than leading them to war.

Despite his resurrected state, Cuaraçí understood that he could be killed anew and that by his own power he could again raise himself from the dead. Ruíz de Montoya relates the story of a Guaraní neophyte who was cannibalized by a gentile village. When threatened with death, he exclaimed: "kill me, for you will only kill my body and not my soul because it's immortal. When I die I hope that I will go to heaven to partake of God's eternal joy."[36] The young Guaraní-Christian was expressing a dualistic theology of body-soul where the soul is purer and glorified in God's presence, leaving behind the body to return to dust. The problem is that these were not the Indian's words, they were Ruíz de Montoya's. It is entirely possible that he had other conceptions of the body-soul, as did Cuaraçí, who articulated a more fluid body-soul relationship. Guaraní believed that the remains of an individual (especially a pajé) contained power and remained as sociospiritual actors.[37] Cuaraçí's reimagined doctrine of resurrection likely resonated with other Guaraní-Christians whose priests had instructed them about a man who had been killed by a powerful empire but raised himself from the dead and promised to return to the earth in terrifying glory. Despite his messianism,

Cuaraçí's goals were rather practical. He did not prescribe an interminable migration to a "land without evil" or a negation of the social, as Clastres argues, but rather a reconstitution of social integrity through an eradication of practices he perceived were destroying Guaraní.[38]

Cuaraçí argued that the priests' sacraments were the kiss of death. In 1606 and 1607 a disastrous epidemic swept through Paraguay and we can safely assume that Cuaraçí was witness to terrible biological carnage.[39] Like other pajé of his time, he explicitly warned against taking salt from a priest at baptisms. (As part of the Catholic ritual of baptism, the priest put salt on the neophyte's tongue.) A contemporary of Cuaraçí performed a kind of "debaptism" when he symbolically scraped the baptismal salt off of infants' tongues, smudged the oil used for anointing, and washed the person from foot to head.[40] Cuaraçí performed similar rites: marking infants' chests with the sign of the cross in charcoal and giving them new names. When an individual took ill and there was concern that they might die, the priests gave the last sacrament or extreme unction and it was this rite, Cuaraçí believed, that would produce maggots ("criar piojos") in the Indians.[41] This reference to putrefaction is culturally significant. When objects or bodies putrefied, Tupí-Guaraní saw it as a sign of dishonor or thought that it portended evil. Tupinambá would halt a war party if their food spoiled during the journey; the spoiled food was a sign that their enemies would capture them, kill them, then let their bodies rot. The ultimate honor for a warrior was not to be killed in battle but to be consumed by the enemy.[42] Cuaraçí's claim that the priests produced putrefaction in Guaraní went to the heart of Guaraní ontology: with rancid bodies, the Guaraní became ineligible for warfare, consumption, and, therefore, cosmic realization.

Like other pajés, Cuaraçí decried the priests' prohibition of polygyny.[43] He associated polygyny with the dramatic population loss from epidemics (generated through priestly sacraments) to argue the priests had created a program of population eradication.[44] This call for the return of polygyny is understandable, since polygyny provided a socioeconomic base for chieftains and shamans alike. Moreover, polygyny and the ability to create kinship ties was an important aspect of intervillage politics. That caciques within a reducción created kinship relationships with Cuaraçí by giving him their daughters reveals that the practice had remained attractive and that monogamy had not been universally embraced. But if polygyny was limited to Guaraní leaders, then how did women and nonleaders perceive it? Aware of polygyny's potentially limited appeal, Cuaraçí encouraged all males to practice polygyny: one witness remembered hearing Cuaraçí say that seven or eight was acceptable.[45] By universalizing polygyny, Cuaraçí broadened his message outside of the leadership class. It would appear that Cuaraçí's message was directed to men, assuming that polygyny was unappealing to women. But such an assumption would impose Western notions and values on a people who only recently had been introduced to monogamy. Perhaps women found prestige in being associated with powerful polygynous men or they believed in the social benefits of polygyny for their society writ large. Until more evidence surfaces that can tell us about women's responses to neopolygyny, it will be difficult to comprehend how it was perceived and understood.

Both priests and Guaraní residents in the reducciones noticed that Cuaraçí's teachings had shaken things up in the reducciones. Gaspar of the Jesuit reducción of San Ignacio noted that the Indians of the Paraná were all in "revolt and that the reducciones were on the verge of ruin." One of the reasons for Cuaraçí's success was his innovative use of disciple-shamans. Instead of preaching solo, he relied on disciples to spread his message. Fernando of the Yuty reducción (Franciscan) indicated that all the pueblos from the province were "scandalized and in revolt" as a result of the "speech that [Cuaraçí] sent through other Indians he dispatched."[46] With his disciple-shamans, he was able to "send his speech throughout the entire province."[47] Cuaraçí's use of messengers is an unexplored aspect of Tupí-Guaraní shamanism in the colonial period. We have already seen that Cuaraçí was in dialogue with monteses shamans in Mbaracayú, as well as Charrúan shamans in the Santa Fe region. Like ad hoc apprenticeships, these interactions were apparently an important way of acquiring shamanic power and learning spiritual rites. Exchanging or combining spiritual knowledge is one thing but relying on messengers to disseminate the message is another. The literature emphasizes the concentration of the shaman's power in his "ñe'ẽ ayvu" ("word"), something supposedly intrinsic to the pajé. Instead, Cuaraçí dispersed his *ñe'ẽ ayvu* through messengers. One possible explanation for Cuaraçí's use of messengers is that he borrowed the practice from Jesuits. Jesuits regularly used neophyte Guaraní to soften the ground, so to speak, before they arrived in a new gentile territory. The neophytes would enter a territory with gifts and speak to chieftains about the priests' messages. If the chieftain was receptive, the neophytes would return and report to the Jesuits, who would then initiate more aggressive evangelization.[48]

Cuaraçí may have borrowed priestly methods, but he also redeployed symbols of political power within the reducciones. When priests organized a reducción, they endowed Guaraní chieftains with staffs of justice (*varas de justicia*) as a symbol of their political power. By controlling who received the symbols of political authority, priests and officials hoped to monopolize and manipulate the political system of the reducciones. But as with most objects in the Guaraní-Christian world, the *varas* quickly took on their own meaning. In the mature reducciones, the alguacil mayor (constable) received a staff; the Guaraní name for this position was *ibiraruzu* ("the first of those who carry the staff in their hand").[49] These staffs had a lasting effect on Guaraní groups, for among the modern Guaraní-Kaiowá, assistants to shamans charged with protecting "insignia rods" (*ywyra'i*) are called "rod owners" (*ywyra'ija*).[50] Cuaraçí made use of these staffs and distributed them to his disciples so that those who listened to their speeches would "obey," "respect," and come to listen to his speech.[51] Cuaraçí forged a social position that melded the roles of pajé and mburuvichá, combining the animated rattles with the staff of justice.

Turning the Jesuit paradigm for missionizing on its head, which required leaving the civilized space of the reducción to seek out the barbarous gentiles in the shadows of the forest, Cuaraçí deployed shaman-disciples to go "out" into the reducciones and call Guaraní back to the safety of the forests—what had been outside became inside. The European symbols of indio authority in the reducciones, Cuaraçí assumed, would communicate to neophytes that he too was a purveyor of authority and a direct challenge to the priests. To be a pajé did not mean the same thing it did before the European conquests; being a pajé was to be a "true priest," which involved adopting many of the priests' methods.[52] Cuaraçí's words and actions reveal just how intimately he understood the effects the reducción program was having on Guaraní society. His disturbing prophecies of putrefaction struck a chord with many Guaraní who recognized the effects of the social and demographic changes they were

experiencing. While Cuaraçí acted like other pajé who readily adopted Spanish-Catholic objects and concepts, the record documenting his activities
allows us to see a more holistic picture of his rebellious program. From the
visions of demon-like figures, to his apotheosis as the son/sun of God, to his
use of disciple-pajés and staffs of justice, Cuaraçí drank deeply from the
spiritual and practical power of Spanish-Catholic objects and concepts.

Justice

Having caught wind from his followers that he was being pursued by author-
ities, Cuaraçí fled to a location on the western bank of the Paraná in the
southeast, where he lived with an older pajé who also called himself "the
Sun."[53] Shortly thereafter, Cuaraçí was captured by indio soldiers from Yuty
and Caazapá (both Franciscan reducciones) who had received a tip from the
Jesuit father Roque González. Cuaraçí's Guaraní captors transported him to
Asunción, where he was held in the Jesuit college under the surveillance of
Father Juan Pastor.[54]

   Cuaraçí's trial was swift, lasting only eleven days from start to finish. The
trial reflected officials' real concerns about the potential for a growing rebellion. Because Cuaraçí's actions were both heretical and anticolonial, his case
combined ecclesiastical and criminal justice. While a city magistrate oversaw the case, Cuaraçí was imprisoned in the Jesuit college, not the city jail,
and the provisor and vicar-general (an ecclesiastic official authorized to act
in the name of the bishop) was asked to provide his opinion. Following patterns of ecclesiastical justice for prosecuting Indian sorcery, Cuaraçí was not
allowed to call any witnesses for his defense.[55] While the court gave Cuaraçí
free legal representation—under Spanish American law all Indians were
granted this right—his defender was no lawyer, only an Asunceño vecino
and captain in the city's militia. The suit was unusual in that it drew on three
separate institutions: the Jesuit order, the bishopric, and municipal government. Cuaraçí's prosecution was brought under the purview of the civil government for two principle reasons. First, he was captured in the territory of
a Franciscan reducción managed by religious and secular authorities. Second, he had committed the serious offense of usurping Spanish symbols of
authority (i.e., the staffs of justice) and distributed them among his disciples.

The existence of the civil-religious prosecution of Cuaraçí is evidence of its gravity. Father Juan Pastor, rector of the Jesuit college in Asunción, made a statement of concern and urged officials to proceed swiftly with the trial for he was concerned that Cuaraçí was not secure in the Jesuit college and believed that Indians in Asunción sympathetic to him would help him escape.[56] Jesuit narratives, like those of del Techo and Montoya, written years after the events they described, emphasized the gravity of crises in the missions brought about by the emergence of a powerful pajé, but in their narratives the tension is quickly resolved with God's intervention and the downfall of the shaman. Ruíz de Montoya claimed that the reducción Concepción de Nuestra Señora "as well as all the rest" of the pueblos were "seminaries of sorcerers." But before describing the details of the crisis, Ruíz de Montoya reassures his readers that they were "defeated by divine preaching."[57] This narrative strategy of highlighting crisis and danger then quickly resolving it serves to reinforce the central message that God is in control. But this move is so repetitive that it causes the modern reader to be skeptical of the Jesuits' claims that Guaraní shamanic movements posed real threats. By contrast, the criminal suit against Cuaraçí was recorded at a closer proximity to the events and therefore reflected a deep sense of alarm. Indeed, this episode demonstrates the tenuous and fragile nature of the early reducciones.[58]

Cuaraçí's movement caused chaos in the surrounding reducciones as more and more Guaraní believed that he could produce results. In the colonial Guaraní experience, we find a pattern where Guaraní moved back and forth between shaman and priest with relative ease. Guaraní only supported priests and pajé who made promises and produced results. Priests, the reducciones, and the power they possessed were not closed off to other forms of power. As Carlos Fausto explains, "the main problem for the Guaraní was . . . how to appropriate the powers that the Europeans, especially the priests, seemed to possess."[59] Cuaraçí adeptly claimed the reducción's powers, especially in its organizational and political methods. By reimagining a Guaraní society that incorporated objects and concepts across ontological divides, he provided his adherents with an alternative social space that harmonized with their experiences in the reducciones. In his antireducción, Guaraní could return to the practices necessary for social reproduction, while also charting a path of change through their plasticity and "exteriority."[60] Cuaraçí's program is not an example of a "new Christianity" but elements of Christian signs inserted into a Guaraní spiritual universe.[61] By crossing multiple ethnic and jurisdictional boundaries, Cuaraçí challenged the categories colonials hoped they could implant in their subjects. Moving between reducciones, encomenderos, colonial cities, and spiritual universes, Cuaraçí was the epitome of indigenous mobility in colonial Paraguay.

Arecayá: A Troubled *Reducción*

In 1660, thirty-five years after Cuaraçí was executed, an armed uprising occurred in the pueblo of Arecayá, situated in the northern region of Itatín. This rebellion possessed similarities with Cuaraçí's movement insofar as there was at least one pajé involved, but Arecayá was different in that it evolved into an extensive armed uprising resulting in the death of several Spaniards. It was perhaps the most radical armed rebellion of colonial Paraguayan history. Scholars have traditionally viewed the Arecayá rebellion as a Guaraní reaction to the oppressive nature of the encomienda system and general anticolonial sentiment.[62] These interpretations are useful but lack the ethnohistorical context of the movement.[63] Arecayense's willingness to take up arms and propose a radical political configuration must be explained in the context of indigenous interethnic exchanges and Guaraní modes of warfare, spiritual power, and vengeance.

The 1660 Arecayá rebellion reflects the slow crawl of the conquest and the varied historical trajectories of reducciones in Paraguay. Nuestra Señora de la Concepción de Arecayá was founded circa 1632 on the Jejuy River, between Mbaracayú and the Paraguay River along the yerba maté transport route. At the time of the rebellion, Arecayá was a small pueblo consisting of around 160 families, equaling nearly 640 individuals.[64] It was organized under the aegis of encomenderos and Franciscans, but it quickly became a secular reducción.[65] Almost nothing is known about the nature of its founding, but it appears to have been created with a great deal of coercion and a minimal amount of the reciprocal benefits of cuñadasgo. Encomenderos from both Asunción and Villa Rica possessed encomiendas in Arecayá, and tributaries were directed to work in the yerba maté harvests as well as in the transport industry. Others still served their encomenderos in Asunción as yanacona.

A slipshod census conducted in the year 1651 reveals that the pueblo was divided up into ten encomiendas. A large portion of the population was not in the pueblo: 104 men, women, and children. Of these, nearly 75 percent were in the household of an encomendero in Asunción or Villa Rica serving as yanaconas. Twenty-seven were considered absentees in the charge of an unassigned encomendero, suggesting that many Arecayense fled their encomendero to work for another. All of this suggests a very heavy-handed Spanish treatment, one that reflects Spaniards' frustrations with a pueblo that did not want to stay put and was reluctant to pay the mita.[66] Indeed, in the years before the 1660 rebellion, encomenderos reported that many Arecayense refused to appear for their mita service. Labor demands on the pueblo were weighty, but this does not go far enough to explain why the pueblo revolted.

Arecayá was situated on a frontier where monteses or independent Guaraní groups and Guaicurú circulated frequently. The presence of these groups had a profound effect on the pueblo. Groups that were reducido on paper actually circulated in and out of the reducción with ease. This had the effect of weakening the community's allegiance to priests and encomenderos. One official explained that on two occasions over Arecayá's existence the community had abandoned the pueblo for the forest, "returning to their faithlessness and barbarism." This official added that the Arecayense had taken turns rotating in and out of the pueblo to keep up the appearance that the community permanently resided there—a Guaraní version of a Potemkin village.[67]

Contributing to Arecayá's high degree of freedom was the absence of a full-time priest. To check in on the community and see to their spiritual needs, a secular from the nearby parish of Villa Rica regularly visited, but these priests had bad reputations. One priest, named Francisco Chaparro, illegally sent tributaries from Arecayá to Asunción to work in the home of a Spanish client.[68] When the priests were not sending away tributaries, they were critiquing the pueblo's lack of Christian zeal. Arecayense cared little for their community's church, allowing the building to decay until alarmed officials admonished them to repair it.[69] From the perspective of Spanish officials and priests, Arecayá lacked "policía cristiana."

With no permanent priest, a church in shambles, and a Guaraní community slacking in its mita duties, the pueblo's loyalties to encomenderos and

Spanish officials were weak. Allegiance to Spaniards was further dampened by a highly independent and untethered leadership. A prelude to the 1660 rebellion came in 1650 when the pueblo "rebelled." In reality, the "rebellion" was more of a walkout, for the documentation does not mention any armed insurrection. Leading the group in 1650 was the community's Spanish-appointed corregidor, Rodrigo Yaguariguay, who was later accused of being a "sorcerer." Not willing to let the community abandon the pueblo, Spanish officials organized a militia and rounded up the community in the same year, a process that took around four months. Yaguariguay was apprehended and sentenced to be executed, although he was freed for reasons that go unexplained in the documentation.[70] While Yaguariguay was let off the hook, another cacique, named Pedro Tiesu, was executed—this decision would come back to haunt Spaniards ten years later. The 1650 "rebellion" was a turning point for the community that steeled their determination to end their subjugation to Spaniards once and for all.

Arecayá carried on after these punishments, but it was not subdued or pliant. It was during the intervening years that pueblo leaders began organizing a broader rebellion. The goal was to draw Guaraní from the surrounding area into the conflict, then march on Villa Rica and Asunción and eliminate the Spanish men. The rebels also intended to take the Spaniards' women and keep them as slaves. Above all, the motivation was fueled by the desire to "avenge their fathers" for the abuses they experienced in 1650.[71] In the months before the rebellion broke out, Arecayense raided and plundered Spaniards traveling on the rivers. To avoid retribution, they disguised themselves as Payaguá Indians, a nonsedentary group that plied the region's rivers. These raids were likely an attempt to supplement the pueblo's supplies or perhaps an attempt to gain access to Spanish firearms. Arecayá's leaders also worked to gather allies to their cause. Ironically, a government *mandamiento*, or public works project, in 1659 provided Arecayense leaders with an opportunity to network with Guaraní from other reducciones. The project was to build a new fort along the Paraguay River, called San Ildefonso de Tapua (see Figure 2).[72] Besides providing an opportunity to communicate with indios from other reducciones, the labors associated with construction surely contributed to an anti-Spanish sentiment. At San Ildefonso and in other clandestine meetings, Arecayá leaders secured the support of Guaraní from other reducciones, including fighters from Yaguarón, Terecañy, Tobatí, and Atyrá. Months after construction began, Arecayá launched their armed rebellion.

The Violence of 1660

The leaders of the rebellion did not begin with an all-out assault on Asunción but instead waited for the governor to come to them on his regular visita. Governor Figueroa left Asunción for his round of visitas in late September 1660, accompanied by thirty Spaniards, including royal officials, notaries, encomenderos, and fifty Guaraní auxiliaries. He arrived at Arecayá around October 12. As the formalities and procedures of the visita played out, several Spaniards observed that the Arecayense were "anxious." Shortly after their arrival, Figueroa learned that the pueblo's corregidor, Rodrigo Yaguariguay, was also a "sorcerer." Yaguariguay claimed that he was God the Father, his wife was Saint Mary, and his daughter was Saint Mary the Younger ("Santa María la chica"). He instructed his flock to wash in a special ointment made with boiled bark from a local tree, perhaps another form of debaptism.[73] Like Cuaraçí, Yaguariguay imbibed the "yerba mala" in order to receive prophecies and spiritual knowledge. The governor decided to replace Yaguariguay as corregidor with another cacique, Mateo Ñambayú, but in an effort to save Yaguariguay from embarrassment and avoid further agitation in the pueblo, the governor had told him that he had been removed because of his old age.[74] The governor's cautious approach to these matters reveals the lack of firm control that Spaniards exercised over Arecayá. At the same time, the governor did not want to appear weak, so when several Guaraní did not show up to be counted, the governor publicly hit the new corregidor, Ñambayú, with his cane. Incensed by the governor's mistreatment of their leaders, thirty Arecayense withdrew from the pueblo and, in the darkly poetic language of one Spaniard, "tuned their bows."[75] Perhaps sensing that the pueblo was on the brink of rebellion, the governor abstained from punishing the entire pueblo for its neglect of the mita and offered a general pardon.

The visita now concluded, Governor Figueroa left Arecayá for Atyrá, Ypané, and Guarambaré, reducciones to the north of Arecayá. While he was away, Arecayense warriors prepared for their assault, knowing that the governor would return to their pueblo because Spaniards used it as a way station between the reducciones to the north and Villa Rica to the east. The governor returned to Arecayá on October 28. In the interim, ten Spaniards arrived at Arecayá to escort the governor to Villa Rica. Having arrived before the governor, these Spaniards caught wind that Arecayense had been preparing for an assault. The rebellion began the very night of the governor's arrival. At dusk, as the surrounding forest cast long shadows over the clearing of the pueblo, the governor and his entourage heard the ominous orchestra of war cries from the darkness: muffled shouts, the fluttering sounds of wooden or bone flutes, the rhythmic beat of calabash rattles, and the human mimicry of birds and jaguars. Figueroa, now sincerely alarmed, summoned the newly appointed corregidor, don Mateo Ñambayú, and demanded an explanation. The corregidor claimed that his sentinels suspected the Payaguá were approaching and began the war cries to prepare to defend the pueblo. Despite his suspicions, the governor allowed the Guaraní leader to return to his lodging but also ordered his men to be ready to fight at a moment's notice.

Just before dawn, the attack began. Around 350 warriors descended on the Spanish in their lodge with cudgels and bows and arrows.[76] Arecayá warriors did not act alone. They were joined by Guaraní from Yaguarón, Terecañy, Tobatí, and Atyrá. A few of these participants in the rebellion were taken from their pueblos during the previous visitas and were traveling with the governor in order to pay their mita in Asunción.[77] Several Guaraní from foreign reducciones wore disguises like false hair to hide their identities from encomenderos or other Indians who might have recognize them.[78] Besides mitayo defectors, there were also a few indio pages, most of whom were yanaconas from Asunción. Among the defectors was a Portuguese mulatto from São Paulo, a servant ("criado") of Governor Figueroa. According to Spanish testimony, the governor's criado was the most violent of the defectors, stealing one of the governor's firearms and munitions to use against the Spaniards. As the rebels pressed their offensive, they burned the lodge where the governor and his entourage had been sleeping. In a mad scramble, forty Spaniards escaped to take shelter in the sturdiest area of the church. As they retreated, the governor snatched up a barrel of gunpowder that his soldiers had left behind. The gunpowder proved to be the Spaniards' saving grace in the four-day siege that ensued. The governor ordered that the straw on the roof of the church be removed to fireproof the building and that embrasures be bored in the walls of the church, allowing his soldiers to fire their muskets at their enemies.

Violence during the siege became brutal, reflecting the Arecayense's former grudges. During one dramatic moment, a warrior decapitated a Spaniard named Pedro Chaparro and paraded his detached head around the pueblo like a trophy (ironically, *chaparro* means "squat" or "short"). Present at the rebellion was Bartolomé Tiesu, son of Pedro Tiesu who was executed during the 1650 episode. Glaring at the Spaniards cowering in the church, Bartolomé Tiesu angrily proclaimed that he was meting out vengeance upon the Spaniards for having executed his father. In an expression of retributive justice, Tiesu specified that he would hang the official who had executed his father—the same method used on his father.

The threatening and displays of violence at Arecayá point to the role of Guaraní vengeance as a primary factor in the uprising. The earliest settlers in South America noticed that violence and vengeance were inseparable for Tupí-Guaraní. Cabeza de Vaca's experience with Guaraní warriors led him to declare that the people were "very vindictive."[79] In chapter 1 we saw that the words for vengeance, trade, and kinship were connected to reciprocal relationships and ontologies. The Arecayá uprising presents an example of Guaraní insisting on reciprocating with Spaniards in violent exchanges: Bartolomé Tiesu demanded the hanging of the official who had killed his father. As discussed previously, vengeance among Tupí-Guaraní at contact was wound up with warfare and anthropophagy.[80] When a member of the community was killed in warfare, usually a relative of the deceased was urged to seek vengeance by taking an enemy warrior captive. The captive was then submitted to a number of practices that reflected his "pet-like" or adoptive status in the community. But inevitably the captive was destined to be killed and the warrior who dispatched him and others who inflicted violence on him received new names. All of this suggests that anthropophagy propelled social reproduction. In the reducciones, Guaraní cannibalism was forbidden and, despite a few deviations (as described in chapter 3), the practice was swiftly eradicated. So what did vengeance mean for a group like the Arecayense who had ostensibly been removed from cannibalism and vengeance warfare? Carlos Fausto suggests that among Guaraní in the reducciones, a process of "dejaguarization" occurred whereby cannibalism's association with shamanism and social reproduction were replaced by love.[81] Perhaps Arecayense displayed a partial dejaguarization, for there is no indication that the Arecayense planned on consuming the governor and the other Spaniards, but their war cries—which likely included the sounds of jaguars—and exclamations of vengeance suggest that the theme of predation was still a strong cultural concept several decades after incorporation into a reducción.

Fate of the Pueblo

Despite their ambitious planning and strong early offensive, the warriors at Arecayá failed to capture the Spaniards in the church. Warriors attempted to dig under the walls of the church, but all their efforts failed. Fending off the attacks and suffering through hunger and thirst, most of the forty Spaniards survived. Several Spaniards attributed their survival to heavenly intercession, claiming that at a point of severe desperation when their water and food supplies had run out, God had sent rain that puddled inside the church and mana from heaven in the form of a pig that wallowed conveniently near the church door. Several encomenderos explained that Figueroa was their anchor, giving them heart when they were ready to despair: "My brothers and friends, for God and for King life is nothing." As the church became the Spaniards' sanctuary and fortress, defending its sacred objects took center stage in a few Spaniards' accounts. But the Spanish heroism and heavenly intercession would have been insufficient were it not for the arrival of three hundred Guaraní soldiers from Atyrá, Ypané, Guarambaré, and Caaguazú (the only Jesuit reducción of the four). After the attack had begun, the governor's Guaraní attendants escaped and called for aid. As Guaraní soldiers arrived, Arecayense fled to the forests, but most were captured, including many of the warriors and ringleaders of the uprising. All told, four Spaniards were killed and twenty-two wounded.

Officials meted out a swift and harsh justice on Arecayá. While still in the reducción, the governor determined that the entire Arecayá community be subjected to perpetual servitude and become yanaconas in Asunción, citing a 1618 precedence for such actions against Guaicurú and Payaguá. The prosecutor reasoned that "[Arecayá] should not be permitted to remain as one body but should be divided. In this way they will easily enter into the Faith and Christian law." When the Arecayá community was taken to Asunción, nearly 160 families were distributed to local encomenderos.[82] En route to Asunción, Governor Figueroa decided to execute the ringleaders, reasoning that the opportunity for their escape was too high. Thirteen individuals were garroted, including the governor's page, the "mulato mameluco" named Domingo.[83] Other alleged conspirators were executed after the group arrived in Asunción. Figueroa ordered that the bodies of the executed be displayed and the head of their leader, Rodrigo Yaguariguay, be placed atop a pike in plain view. As for Guaraní participants from other pueblos, apparently none were officially prosecuted.

Paraguay's bishop, Andrés Cornejo, frowned on the governor's severe treatment of Arecayá and its leaders and accused the governor of excessive cruelty. The subsequent investigation revealed that some indios had not been present in Arecayá during the rebellion but had been submitted to perpetual servitude nonetheless. Pressure from Bishop Cornejo, the crown, and other parties mounted against the governor and the cabildo, and they eventually moved to reconstitute Arecayá as a pueblo. As officials debated the particulars of Arecayá's reconstitution, they decided that the community be kept closer to Asunción. They reasoned that because of increased Payaguá raids, the community was not safe on its own, so in 1669 Arecayá was joined with Los Altos, one of the pueblos in closest proximity to Asunción.[84] In reality, officials meant to control the Arecayense and keep them connected to an allegiant reducción and reducción leadership. In 1669, the governor of Paraguay, Juan Díaz de Andino, collected donations from Asunceño vecinos for the transmigrated pueblo of Arecayá. Spaniards volunteered horses, mules, beans, corn, and metal tools as a kind of start-up kit for the reconstituted pueblo.[85]

In 1673, the governor conducted a visita of the Arecayá/Altos pueblos, providing a social snapshot of the reconstituted community. The Arecayá population contained 120 tributaries divided into 12 encomiendas, averaging 10 tributaries each. Interestingly, some Arecayense had not given up on their former lives and social networks in Itatín. Fourteen tributaries (including a handful with their entire families) had abandoned the new Arecayá pueblo to take up residence in a reducción to the north named Atyrá, not far from the original site of Arecayá. Ten more tributaries had made their way in the yerba maté transport industry and were in Corrientes.[86]

Historians cite the Arecayá rebellion as evidence of the repressive nature of Spanish colonialism in Paraguay, and they are correct to do so. From the rapid and legally dubious executions of the rebel leadership, to the forced removal of the entire community to Asunción where they were subjected to a severe form of servitude, these actions were profoundly disruptive. But this kind of intense violence was more rare than common. Figueroa's treatment of Arecayá before the rebellion was more typical and mirrors what occurred in Guairá. When confronted with a disruptive pajé, officials removed him or priests shamed him. When tributaries slacked in their payments of the mita, the reprisals targeted only the top leadership. We should not be surprised that a pueblo like Arecayá—a pueblo that hosted a shaman instead of a Catholic priest, maintained its cultural integrity through interaction with unsettled Guaraní, and was a partial mita payer—existed for so long. Despite its final and adamant objection to colonialism, Arecayá was typical of a relatively new reducción on the frontier.

Conclusion

The prophetic career of Juan Cuaraçí and the violent rebellion of Arecayá represent two overlapping but divergent patterns of Guaraní resistance to colonial rule. In the case of Cuaraçí, the movement hovered around the words of a pajé and his prognosis for a healthy society. Epidemics and social change spurred Cuaraçí. He preached that with one hand the priests were trying to eliminate Guaraní through rot-inducing rituals like baptisms and with the other hand they restricted social regeneration and reproduction through the eradication of polygyny. Having been born into a world where Spaniards were familiar, Cuaraçí saw no contradictions in borrowing from the powerful objects and methods used by colonials. To attract Guaraní to leave the reducciones, Cuaraçí proclaimed himself a true priest of an antireducción. The Arecayá rebellion also possessed shamanic elements, but it was rooted in the desire for vengeance. After witnessing the execution of one of their leaders in 1650, Arecayense warriors hoped to unite other Guaraní and eradicate Spanish power.

These two movements drew strength from their ability to exploit Paraguay's frontiers and the porousness of the region's communities. Cuaraçí acquired pajé knowledge from monteses in Mbaracayú and from Charrúa in the Santa Fe region. Similarly, Arecayense were frequently in contact with monteses who contributed to the vitality of pajé knowledge and autonomy. This does not mean they rejected everything Christian but instead rejected those things that seemed most onerous, especially labor demands and infringements on their movement. Arecayá was a part-time home for groups of Natives who found it temporarily useful. Cuaraçí moved in and out of places like Asunción, Yaguarón, and San Ignacio with relative ease, fostering interethnic social networks spanning great distances. Similarly, Arecayense rallied indios from Asunción and other reducciones to their cause. This mobility and the creation of social networks followed colonial trade and tributary routes. Cuaraçí made his way to Mbaracayú likely through his service in the yerbales and no doubt got to Santa Fe on routes familiar to all colonials who traveled throughout the region.

Both Cuaraçí and the Arecayá community created and drew on syncretic religious images and expressions. The pajé of Arecayá, Yaguariguay, and Cuaraçí each claimed divinity that was an amalgam of things old and new. Anthropologist Carlos Fausto finds that this Tupí-Guaraní "use and abuse" of Catholic imagery "indicates that from the native point of view, what was at stake was not a conflict between two 'religions' in the sense of two mutually exclusive orthodoxies. . . . The reduction system did not consist of two watertight worlds divided by an impermeable frontier; it formed a social network involving not only the circulation of goods but also a constant flow of reinterpreted signs. The missionaries had no control over the meanings produced in their interactions with natives: once placed in circulation, their ideas acquired autonomy."[87] Fausto's comment about a "constant flow of reinterpreted signs" evokes the image of microcurrents in a vast river. Almost imperceptibly, the water moves as a whole in a certain direction, but when focusing on small patches in the river, one sees a swirl of currents, eddies, and waves moving in different directions. So too with the changes in the emerging colonial Guaraní culture. The diversity of cultural currents and influences is impressive. A specific example of a reinterpreted sign in the Arecayá rebellion has to do with slavery. Several witnesses, including indio and español, indicated that Arecayense warriors hoped to kill Spanish men and take their wives as slaves. What did it mean for Arecayense to desire to take Spanish women as slaves? What did slavery mean for a people who had resided in a reducción for nearly thirty years? Arecayá may have drawn on concepts of captivity important to Payaguá and Guaicurú, who consistently raided pueblos and Spanish towns in Paraguay, taking humans as captives. Was the goal to take Spanish women a kind of retributive justice in response to cuñadasgo and the loss of women? Or did Arecayense have in mind the socially and morally degrading elements of Africans slavery? All of this is to say that the Guaraní rebellions of the seventeenth century were a product of and response to porous ideological and physical boundaries in a context of colonial oppression.

The Arecayá and Cuaraçí movements ultimately failed. The reasons for this are varied, but there is one common denominator: Guaraní who opposed them. Cuaraçí was captured by indios from a nearby reducción and the warriors of Arecayá were cut short of their massacre of Spanish officials by the timely arrival of a Guaraní militia. The failure of these two episodes then can be directly attributed to different positions of Guaraní on a spectrum of loyalty to Spanish authorities and the mobilization of Guaraní militias. The next chapter addresses the threat that Guaicurú Indians posed to Spaniards and Guaraní alike and argues that they served as a catalyst for a sustained Spanish-Guaraní alliance.

CHAPTER 5

Indios Fronterizos and
the Spanish-Guaraní Militias

AFTER HIS LIFELESS body was removed from the pole on which he was garroted, the executioner fulfilled the governor's orders to divide the sorcerer Juan Cuaraçí's body into four parts. Each dismembered portion was to be placed on the caminos reales, the official roads that connected Asunción to its hinterlands, making the gore visible to indios traveling in and out of the city. The head was ordered hung on the pillory in the pueblo of Yuty in the Paraná district, where Cuaraçí had caused considerable disruption. Finally, the governor ordered that one of the limbs be taken to the other side of the Paraguay River where it was displayed on a road Guaicurú frequented.

This order is curious since Cuaraçí had no connections to Guaicurú west of Asunción and suggests that for colonial officials there was a symbolic connection between Guaraní resistance and the nonsedentary Chaco groups who consistently raided colonial Paraguayan cities and villages and who represented the opposite of reducción civility. Even though there was no evidence of it, the very possibility of a Guaraní-Guaicurú alliance disconcerted Spanish officials. Taking Cuaraçí's sentence alongside the dubious accusations of an Arecayá-Payaguá alliance, we can clearly discern a deep-seated Spanish anxiety about the rise of a Guaicurú-Guaraní confederacy. Spaniards were indeed insecure on the Chaco frontier. This chapter addresses these fears with a focus on the impact of threats on Guaraní and Spanish communities and demonstrates that violence and reactions to violence helped shape a colonial community and Guaraní-Spanish interdependence.

Historical accounts of the genesis and expansion of Spanish authority in the Americas often begin with the infamous conquests, often conceived of as a finite period of time when Spaniards asserted their control over Natives and began to construct a colonial state. According to this framework, whenever and wherever widespread violence ends, governance begins. In other words, a state becomes a state when it effectively monopolizes violence or at least promotes the idea of its control over violence. But as Sean McEnroe argues for New Spain's northeastern frontier, warfare was not simply "a function of the state or a force that dissolves the state. . . . Social organizations occasioned by war can also construct the state."[1] Similarly, communities and identities are forged through acts of warfare and the identification of a shared enemy. In eastern Paraguay and in the Banda Oriental on the borderlands between the Spanish and Portuguese realms, the Guaraní-Jesuit reducciones developed in a context of violence and continual attacks by bandeiras. In fact, the Guaraní-Jesuit alliance was further strengthened by the creation of institutions capable of violence.

In response to the bandeiras, Jesuits organized militias in many reducciones. By 1680, there were approximately three thousand Guaraní soldiers spread throughout the Jesuit reducciones.[2] These militias were highly organized with a variety of officials and equipped with horses, swords, lances, uniforms, and even cannons and rifles. Indeed, the Guaraní-Jesuit militias were the most sophisticated fighting force in the Río de la Plata until the expulsion of the Jesuits.[3] Historians demonstrate that Guaraní's defensive responses to bandeiras played an important role in the long process of ethnogenesis or tribalization that contributed to a unified mission complex and communal identity.[4] Historians assume that the process that occurred in the Guaraní-Jesuit reducciones was unique in the Río de la Plata, but they largely ignore the similar processes that occurred among Guaraní in the Asunción region.[5] This chapter describes the nature of indigenous military service in Paraguay, focusing on Guaraní soldiers from secular- or Franciscan-sponsored reducciones and argues that Paraguay's violent frontier dynamics were bound up with cuñadasgo and contributed to the creation and evolution of Paraguay's colonial community.

Histories of colonial Paraguay are replete with intrepid español conquistadors, suggesting that colonizing activities were the domain of Europeans. In these histories, Guaraní appear only as subjected groups or as oppositional forces to colonialism. The reality was that Guaraní were the backbone of the colonial state, not only in terms of labor but also in terms of its military strength. These findings dovetail with developments in the new conquest histories, a historiography that shifts its focus from conquistadors and priests to indigenous actors who participated in the conquests by way of indigenous sources.[6] When indigenous sources are unavailable, scholars read Spanish sources with an eye toward contradictions and gaps in Spaniards' knowledge, opening up opportunities to see Native agency without eliminating or domesticating indigenous ways of knowing.[7] Mesoamericanists have gleaned from indigenous accounts of conquest activities a new narrative of the conquest that amplifies the diverse actors and motives. For some Natives, the conquest may have been almost a nonevent, while for many others it was an utterly destructive moment. Other indigenous people sensed an opportunity and so joined or co-opted conquest expeditions. Natives who participated in conquest activities later learned to leverage their services and enhance their political positions within the new colonial system. Beginning with the assertion that the Spanish conquest of Mesoamerica would have been impossible without Native allies, these scholars suggest that we understand the conquest as a Mesoamerican conquest of Mesoamerica.[8]

Participation in the conquest provided crucial leverage for Natives and Spaniards alike in the new colonial order, but Spaniards rarely extended the privilege of holding official positions in militias to Natives after the sixteenth century. An exception to this was the community of Ciudad Vieja in Guatemala, founded by Nahua, Zapotec, and Mixtec who fought in the conquest of that region. Mexicanos, as the residents of this town came to be known, maintained their status as a conquistador community through active participation in annual pageants and by sustaining a militia that assisted the community's local officials in keeping the peace.[9] The Mexicanos of Ciudad Vieja are exceptional, and colonial officials rarely organized militias made up of Natives (or blacks) in the immediate aftermath of the conquest. The reason for this delay was that Spaniards associated the military with the chivalrous traits of the nobility and military service as a pathway for social mobility. What eventually prompted Spanish officials to diversify the ranks of the militias with blacks and indios was a sense of emergency on the frontiers and an increased trust in Indian and black loyalties. Over the course of the seventeenth century, but especially during the military reforms of the late eighteenth century, the Spanish crown organized Indian and black militias throughout the realm.[10]

In contrast to most other regions, Guaraní militias were a direct extension of the earliest joint expeditions against common enemies. The Guaraní-Jesuit militias emerged in the 1610s to the 1640s on Paraguay's eastern frontier with Brazil in the context of the bandeirante raids. A Spanish-Guaraní alliance emerged as early as the first expeditions to the Gran Chaco in the 1540s and 1550s, followed by a lull after the creation of the encomienda in 1556. In the early seventeenth century, Spanish officials organized Guaraní militias in the reducciones to counter the rise of powerful and damaging Guaicurú confederacies that had formed up in the intervening years.

The Gran Chaco and Guaicurú Dominance

As a geographical and ecological space, the Gran Chaco is a large alluvial plain sloping toward the Paraguay/Paraná River systems and covers parts of Argentina, Bolivia, Brazil, and Paraguay. From the south along the Salado and Dulce Rivers, the Chaco extends north to the Mato Grosso plateau. From west to east, the Chaco is bounded by the foothills of the Andes Mountains and the Paraná-Paraguay River systems. Scholars further subdivide the Chaco into three regions by the three rivers that run across it. The southern Chaco extends from the Salado River to the Bermejo River and is marked by semiarid steppe vegetation. The vegetation in the central Chaco, between the Bermejo and Pilcomayo Rivers, is denser and spotted with large patches of forest. Finally, the Northern Chaco—where Asunceños and Guaraní militias most frequently engaged Chaco groups—extended from the Pilcomayo River north to the Apa River. The Northern Chaco was perhaps the most difficult territory for Spanish-Guaraní militias to navigate. It contained impenetrable palm forests and experienced seasonal floods that made parts of the region nearly impassable for a good portion of the year. Despite the difficulty of the terrain for Spaniards, various Native groups thrived in the Northern Chaco by remaining mobile and following seasonal crops and game.[11]

At contact, there were a variety of semi- and nonsedentary groups who inhabited the Gran Chaco. During the conquistadors' expeditions to the Andes, they encountered several semisedentary agriculturalist groups, including the Guaná (or Chané) and Maskoy. The Guaná were the only Arawak-speaking groups in the Chaco, and their culture reflected a strong

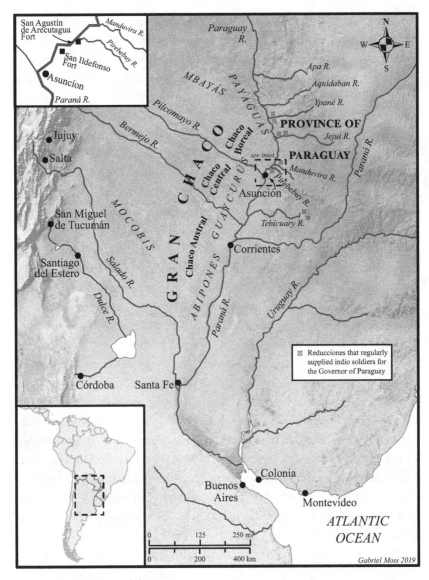

MAP 3. Gran Chaco and the Paraguayan Frontier

Andean influence. The most dominant groups of the Northern Chaco were nonsedentary Guaicuruan-speaking peoples, among which Spaniards discerned different groupings, including the Mbayá and Payaguá. Just as with terms like *Guaraní* and *Tupí*, these ethnonyms do not describe the political and ethnic reality, but they do show the outlines of political and cultural divisions. Spaniards had a whole host of other names for Chaco groups they deemed their enemies, including "indios enemigos" (enemy Indians), "indios fronterizos" (frontier Indians), "infieles fronterizos" (frontier infidels), or a combination of these terms and other ethnonyms. (When no other ethnonym is given, I use the term *Guaicurú*.) At contact, Guaicurú aggressively asserted themselves over other groups in the Chaco, including the sedentary Chané of the Northern Chaco.[12] Guaicurú had frequent contact with Asunción and its subject populations, especially those in the Itatín region, north of the Jejuy River. Asunción was situated on the edge of the frontier with the Gran Chaco, and the waterways pulsing past Asunción and into the reducción territories served as highways for Chaco peoples to penetrate Spanish-controlled territory and regularly trade with or raid local populations.

Guaicurú dominance on the frontier began in the late sixteenth century and grew over the course of the seventeenth century, reaching its apogee by the first decades of the eighteenth century. Chaco groups crossed the Paraguay and Paraná Rivers to attack not only Spanish communities but also Guaraní pueblos. Thanks to Guaicurú attacks in the 1670s, as well as a massive bandeirante invasion in 1676, colonial Paraguay retracted considerably. By the last quarter of the seventeenth century, several reducciones had been abandoned or relocated closer to Asunción. From the Spanish point of view, Guaicurú inflicted the most damage on western Paraguay. In 1675, on the heels of several devastating Guaicurú attacks, the members of the Asunción cabildo concluded that "[the Chaco Indians] have had us on our knees from the first conquests."[13] Indeed, the late sixteenth and seventeenth centuries were periods of Guaicurú ascendance and dominance on Paraguay's frontiers. Guaicurú behaviors suggest that they saw Spanish and Guaraní communities in the province of Paraguay as tributary communities who provided them with valuable opportunities for captives, livestock, and other goods. Eighteenth- and nineteenth-century sources suggest that Guaicurú defined all non-Guaicurú neighbors as their potential slaves or tribute providers, using the word *nibotagipi* (pl.) to describe captives, slaves, servants, subjects, or vassals.[14]

A few scholars paint Chaco peoples with a broad brush, calling them "bellicose" or defined by a strong "warrior ethos," but ethnohistorical perspectives reveal the historicity of Guaicurú raiding activities.[15] The introduction of European livestock, especially the horse, contributed to significant changes among Chaco groups. Mbayá, who inhabited the northern reaches of the Northern Chaco, became able equestrians. The Jesuit Martin Dobrizhoffer commented on the horse's utility as a transport vehicle among the Abipón (a Guaicuruan group of the southern Chaco) when he described an Abipón woman atop her horse laden with any number of saddlebags, vessels, bundles, and skids draped along the flank of her animal. In these pouches, noted Dobrizhoffer, women even carried their children and puppies.[16] This same observer also noted that above the ax, knife, scimitar, or any other instrument of war, Abipón viewed the horse as their principal weapon.[17] Payaguá did not adopt the horse, preferring their canoes as vehicles to hunt, fish, raid, and migrate.[18] Similar to Guaraní, Guaicurú people's adoption of iron tools profoundly affected their way of life, especially their prowess in warfare, their ability to hunt, and their potential for trade. Moreover, Guaicurú responded creatively to the introduction of European livestock, which occurred apace after around 1569. Initially, they were avid hunters of slow-moving grazing animals, but as the years progressed they adopted pastoralist strategies and raised their own herds of cattle and sheep. When Guaicurú entered Jesuit missions in the eighteenth century, they brought into the reducciones large herds of livestock.[19]

Guaicurú's increased mobility, facility in hunting, and access to iron tools and livestock translated into the ability to acquire surpluses and increased exchange of goods. These factors drew Guaicurú into frequent contact with Spanish-Guaraní society and with other Chaco groups to create expansive trading networks. The riverine Payaguá were pulled into these changes through their alliances with Guaicuruan groups. The specifics of this trade are murky for the Northern Chaco, but the basic outline that emerges suggests that Spaniards gave iron tools, livestock (especially horses), and yerba maté to Guaicurú in exchange for hides (from guanaco or cattle), honey and wax, and other miscellaneous items. It is likely that the trade items that moved in and out of the Chaco passed through multiple hands. Scholarship on eighteenth-century Chaco groups of the central and southern Chaco demonstrates that some groups served as middlemen in this exchange, passing goods acquired from Santa Fe to groups to the west.[20] The Chaco was thus a landscape of intense movement and exchange. Via trading and raiding, Chaco groups acquired goods from the Spanish frontier (Asunción, Corrientes, Santa Fe, Córdoba, Santiago del Estero, Tuchman, Salta, and Jujuy) of the oval-shaped Chaco region and then circulated these goods within the Chaco, creating networks based on kinship and trade.

Historians know little of the nature of political networks in the Gran Chaco before the sixteenth century.[21] When Spaniards arrived in Paraguay, the Carío-Guaraní were not on friendly terms with Chaco groups. In the earliest expeditions to the Chaco, Carío allies took advantage of the opportunity to kill and capture Guaicurú enemies. But during the 1545–1546 Guaraní insurrection against the Spanish, the Carío created an alliance with the Agaces or Payaguás. Apparently the alliance was hampered by mistrust and the Payaguá never fought alongside the Carío. In response to the Carío insurrection, Spaniards turned to Chaco peoples, the Guatatas and Yaperús, and decimated the Carío resistance. Spanish chroniclers recounted that the Yaperús took advantage of the military victory to enact a harsh revenge on the Carío, massacring and enslaving hundreds of their enemies. But Guaicurú's alliance with the Spanish was short-lived because they never agreed to submit to Spanish political authority, nor did they sustain bonds of kinship to Spaniards like the Guaraní. And with no unifying political structure among Guaicurú in the vast Chaco territory, individual bands chose how to react to Spaniards. During Irala's disastrous expedition between 1547 and 1549, Payaguá attacked the Spanish-Guaraní company, killing eighty Spaniards. This attack was likely retribution for Irala's 1539 expedition in which Carío slaughtered and enslaved hundreds of Payaguá. In sum, it may have been Spaniards' increasing connection to Guaicurú's long-standing Guaraní enemies that hindered a lasting Spanish-Guaicurú alliance, not some vague bellicose instinct.[22]

After the last entradas to the Gran Chaco in the 1550s, Spanish-Guaicurú diplomatic encounters were less frequent or at least less effective. From the 1550s to 1600, Chaco-Paraguay interactions transitioned to an uneasy relationship of trading, raiding, and reprisals. By the 1590s, Spanish officials were reporting raids by "indios enemigos" as well as increased trading between Spaniards and Guaicurú on farmsteads throughout the region.[23] The intensity of this raiding and trading only increased after the 1590s. The most common trade items included honey, wax, animal skins, and salt, which Guaicurú exchanged for iron, horses, and mules. (As will be explained below, Guaicurú also traded with human captives.) Spaniards were sufficiently desirous of Guaicurú trade objects that they continued to allow trading even when they knew Guaicurú were engaged in raids. In an attempt to regulate Guaicurú's activities and limit Guaicurú movement in the city, the Asunción cabildo designated a port in Asunción on the banks of the Paraguay River as the official trading zone for Guaicurú. This policy was also intended to forestall trading between Guaicurú and Spaniards on individual chacras, where negotiations could turn violent. Moreover, it was feared that after such trades, Guaicurú would sneak into the city to lay in wait for an ambush or pass into the interior of the province to attack Guaraní pueblos.[24] Governors frequently requested that vecinos or mitayos cut down the trees and brush thickets that occupied swaths of the cityscape because these served as hiding places for Guaicurú warriors.[25]

Spaniards' ambivalent position on Guaicurú trading when they knew that trading and raiding went hand in hand is puzzling. One explanation is that Guaicurú responded to Spanish demands for scarce commodities like hides, wax, and salt. Trade may also have been a part of Spanish officials' strategy to pacify Guaicurú.[26] These explanations for Spanish-Guaicurú trading seem possible but ignore the obvious: Spaniards traded with Guaicurú because the latter compelled them to do it. When Guaicurú showed up on the eastern banks of the Paraguay River, Spaniards could either wave them off and expect a reprisal or try to control trading activities in the hopes of staving off potential violence and raiding. Guaicurú trading parties could be rather large and their arrival put locals on edge. In December of 1668, the cabildo noted that "enemigos fronterizos" had arrived in peace to trade. They consisted of six parcialidades, led by several caciques. We might translate *parcialidad* in this context as "bands" of extended families whose sizes may have ranged from 10 to 100. If these six parcialidades were each composed of 20 individuals, then the group would have totaled 120. Because of the large size of this trading party, the cabildo feared that the Guaicurú were staging an attack and cautioned that they were not to pass beyond the trading site into the city and beyond into Asunción's chacras. Almost like hostages, the cabildo urged the governor to use the "gentlest means" to desist the Guaicurú from moving past the coastal trading site into the city.[27]

Guaicurú actions suggest they saw themselves as the dominant actors in many of their trading encounters with Spaniards and that the latter were tribute-paying slaves. In 1613, the cabildo wrote:

> [The Guaicurú] enter [Spanish] homes and chacras under the pretense that they are there to trade and sell their things, but they leave the people scandalized and fearful. From some [Spanish homes] the Guaicurú take whatever they can. To others the Guaicurú issue threats that if [Spaniards] do not let them take what they want, [the Guaicurú] will kill them. The Guaicurú have acquired so much freedom that they mock Spaniards to scorn in their fields, even tugging on their beards in contempt.[28]

This last comment about Guaicurú tugging on Spaniards' beards communicates a high degree of Spanish shame; to pull on a Spaniard's beard was an act of incredible effrontery.[29] For the beardless Guaicurú, Spaniards' beards may have marked them as distinct and inferior. Entering homes, taking possessions at will, issuing death threats, and mocking Spaniards' appearances, Guaicurú perceived Spaniards as subordinates.

Besides the material goods and livestock, Guaicurú promoted an exchange of human captives. Guaicurú practiced an expansive form of slavery, with slaves serving both men and women. Guaicurú preferred children or adolescents as captives because they could be raised in Guaicurú culture, and they sought out female captives so they could be used as "servicio" or domestic servants in their households.[30] When whole communities were defeated, Guaicurú treated them as subordinates and required tribute payments and military assistance during major mobilizations.[31] If Guaicurú slavery and captive-taking was a strong practice before the arrival of Europeans, it expanded during the colonial period, fueled by demand on either side of the frontier.[32] The Franciscan father Luís de Bolaños in 1614 reported that supposedly friendly Guaicurú hid in the city with the intention of setting it ablaze and taking all of the city's women as servants.[33] Ironically, Spanish demand for captives likely promoted Guaicurú raiding of Guaraní and Guaicurú communities.[34] Spanish motivations for purchasing captives transcended labor needs to include religious motivations, for they believed that purchasing captives was a form of "redemption."[35] The redemptive meaning of these purchases depended on the slave: if she were Christian she would be restored to her community and kin, but if she were Guaicurú she would be "redeemed" through Christianization and incorporation into the yanacona population or indio pueblo. Individuals like Marcela, a Guaicurú woman whom a Spaniard acquired through barter, were destined for personal service among Spaniards. But when captives were taken in military expeditions, some were turned over to neighboring reducciones. This was the case for several Guaicurú women taken after an expedition in 1672 who were placed in the care of a Jesuit reducción in Itatín.[36]

Guaicurú learned that Spaniards had a soft spot for captives, especially Christian captives, and exploited these attitudes to engage in trade. On September 15, 1675, the cabildo reported that the "Guaicurú and Mbayá" appeared in Asunción to trade Christian captives (most likely Guaraní) as well as sacred liturgical objects like chalices, platters, and monstrances.[37] The Guaicurú had taken these "sacred ornaments" and captives from the Guaraní reducción of Atyrá, which they had razed in 1672 after killing nearly one hundred Guaraní and the chaplain. Burning with righteous indignation, the cabildo vowed that they would do everything in their power to "rescatar" or redeem the liturgical objects and Christian souls from the "power of the enemy."[38] That Spaniards were compelled to purchase these items underscores the power of Guaicurú in the region.

The robust exchange between Spanish-Guaraní society and Guaicurú was a love-hate relationship. Just as soon as Guaicurú concluded bartering, Spaniards worried they would attack outlying farms, pueblos, or even Asunción. For example, after Guaicurú had appeared in Asunción to trade in 1613, and receiving reports of stolen canoes and horses, the cabildo suspected they were planning to raid Asunción on Holy Thursday. Later that year, the cabildo noted that Guaicurú had begun trading only for horses or mules, which further stoked fears of an imminent Guaicurú attack. At night, one could hear droves of canoes and paddles sloshing down the river and sounds of ominous war cries from the opposite shore of the river.[39] The arrival of so many people in canoes from the north led the cabildo to suspect a joint Guaicurú-Payaguá raid of nearly two thousand warriors. With such a sizable force, Asunceños feared the city could be wiped out. Fortunately, an attack of such a size never materialized.

Raids were often seasonal, occurring during the summer months, between November and March, and this timing may have been related to the availability of game and edible fruits and vegetables. Not all Guaicurú raids were for economic gain; some were punitive. Sometime between 1615 and 1620, governor Hernando Arias de Saavedra conducted a "war of fire and blood" against Guaicurú in the Chaco, massacring eighty individuals. In retribution, the Guaicurú attacked chacras in Asunción and captured Saavedra's sister and niece.[40] It is not clear if the Guaicurú had targeted the governor's family, but given the Guaicurú's access to Asunción as regular traders, it seems likely the abduction of a high-status woman and relatives of the region's top official was premeditated.

Guaicurú raids took a heavy economic toll. In 1674, vecinos abandoned a number of important wheat farms in the Valley of Tapeca after a devastating Guaicurú raid. The crops from these wheat farms were so important to Asunción's survival that the cabildo ordered a group of fifty Guaraní from a nearby pueblo to harvest the wheat, with the protection of a Spanish contingent of soldiers.[41] Guaicurú also targeted Asunción's herds of horses and cattle, which were easy and plentiful targets. Near Asunción at a site called the Valle de Tacumbú, the cabildo owned pasturelands and corrals, which housed essential mules and war horses for the city's militia. This livestock was under constant threat from indios fronterizos. In one entry, the cabildo also mentioned that the herds were frequently attacked by "tigers" and "lions," references to the region's healthy population of jaguars. Mentioning the Guaicurú and ferocious tigers in the same breath was a literary technique in the conquistador accounts and the early histories of the region. For example, Cabeza de Vaca recounts that in the 1540s, as he was leading a group of Carío-Guaraní against an encampment of enemy Guaicurú, the Guaraní spotted a "tigre" or jaguar, which caused them to withdraw in fear. To the Guaraní, the jaguar was a powerful being whose appearance portended destruction or danger.[42] The connection between Guaicurú and feral predators in this rather ordinary cabildo entry might be nothing more than a faithful recounting of the damages to the herds, but it nonetheless recalls a deep-seated Spanish fear of Guaicurú.

A large portion of the booty Guaicurú acquired came from Guaraní-Christian pueblos. Attacks on Guaraní pueblos and reducciones became so severe in the northern Itatín region from the 1660s to the 1670s that the region was largely abandoned in the late 1670s. The Atyrá pueblo was a Franciscan-sponsored reducción founded in the late sixteenth century near the Jejuy River and was a favorite target of Chaco groups. It sustained continuous attacks from the early seventeenth century to its demise and relocation in 1672. In 1614, a cacique from Atyrá explained to a Spanish official that he had no more Guaraní "vassals" because they had all been killed or carried away captive by Guaicurú.[43] Because the reducciones were fortified with a palisades, Guaicurú often targeted Guaraní residents during the harvest season while they worked in the chacras and estancias outside the reducción walls.[44] An attack in the year 1661 on the Itatín pueblos of Ypané, Guarambaré, Caaguazú, and Guaranambí resulted in the deaths of six hundred Guaraní.[45] A large Guaicurú raid in 1674 devastated the Atyrá pueblo and an estimated 120 individuals were either taken captive or killed, including the secular priest who resided there. All of the pueblo's sacred objects, as well as its livestock, were also taken.[46] Several Jesuit reducciones were targeted during these years, and one Jesuit estimated that seven hundred Guaraní had been taken captive. This devastation was followed by a massive bandeira attack in 1676 that dealt the final blow to Itatín. Most communities along the rivers north of the Jejuy in Itatín evacuated and resettled closer to Asunción or to the Paraná region.[47]

The size of Guaicurú raiding parties ranged from around two hundred to five hundred warriors.[48] That Guaicurú assembled such large groups of warriors is impressive; colonial officials could rarely muster a militia of Spanish vecinos larger than four hundred. Guaicurú never lived in groups as large as their raiding parties; instead, they coordinated with their Chaco neighbors. As early as 1613, Spaniards observed that Guaicurú and Payaguás created *confederaciones* for the purpose of making war. Guaicurú-Payaguá raiding parties were increasingly common in the last half of the seventeenth century.[49] Historians of Guaicurú have emphasized that these moments of political unification were fleeting and quickly dissolved into competition after the raids concluded.[50] Nonetheless, Chaco groups' willingness to coordinate on such a grand scale is an underappreciated innovation in response to Spanish-Guaraní society in the Northern Chaco.

Colonials generally denounced Guaicurú as enemies, and attempts to reducir bands of Guaicurú in the seventeenth century were short-lived, further reinforcing colonials' antipathy toward the Chaco and its peoples. The short experiment with reducciones in the Chaco occurred between 1609 and 1626 under the direction of the Jesuits. The Jesuits offered material goods and a band of Mbayás called the Codalodis agreed to inhabit a reducción, but the process was largely determined by Codalodis leadership. Chief Guayicota and his people welcomed Jesuits Vicente Grifi and Roque González de Santa Cruz to Guazutinguá, situated to the west of Asunción.[51] Other Mbayá bands saw the material benefits of the reducciones and joined the experiment. But by the late 1620s these reducciones had failed. Diseases and the severe contradictions Guaicurú found in sedentary life caused the experiment to crumble, leading them to resume their nomadic existence. Guaicurú would not attempt to inhabit reducciones again until the 1730s when ecological changes made them more vulnerable and open to negotiation with Spanish officials and Jesuits.[52]

In 1614, the Franciscan fray Luís de Bolaños was asked to provide his opinions about the Indian frontier. He lamented that Guaicurú and Payaguá "have never been punished, reducido, or conquered" and concluded that they were "enemies" to the colonial state and to the reducciones.[53] Bolaños's comments, made in the midst of the Jesuit experiment with Mbayá reducciones, underscore the fact that colonials experienced a variety of Guaicurú attitudes simultaneously. At the same time as the Jesuits were beginning to see the fruits of their investments among Mbayá peoples, Asunción contended with Guaicurú attacks in Itatín, the Paraná, and Asunción. The Asunción cabildo recorded their frustration with indios fronterizos, explaining why they believed they were completely incompatible with colonial society:

> The frontier enemies, the Guaicurú and Mbayá, and other infidel enemies of Christianity have never desired to embrace the Catholic faith nor desist from persecuting the faithful. They are without profession, life,

or habit. They sustain their art of war without a town, labor, nor other assistance. Instead, they wander naked as vagabonds with their portable shacks, without any impediment other than the management of their arms, which they use on foot or on horse. In their agility on land and water they are insurmountable. They suffer through thirst, hunger, or any inclemency. When they retreat they swim across many mighty rivers and when they attack they appear from different parts of our lands without being detected. Because the bank of this river is forty open leagues, it is impossible to defend it, not even with the twelve forts we already have along her banks. . . . [The Guaicurú's] lands are cunning, full of marshes and floods. During the dry season there is no water, and during the rainy season it floods. This makes it impossible for them to have villages nor labor and impossible for us to locate them.[54]

Guaicurú peoples' abilities to navigate terrains and waterways, impassible to Spanish military forces, confounded Spaniards. Even the Guaicurú's lands possessed "cunning" and deceptive traits, almost as if the people and their homeland were spiritual kin locked in alliance against the Spanish. Spanish officials believed Guaicurú were incompatible with colonial civility. This ethnocentrism and ardent opposition underscores the fact that Guaicurú possessed their own kind of dominance on the frontier.

Defending the Province

As local government developed in Paraguay, a formalized militia structure was created to organize defenses and provide social capital to its Spanish participants. Militias were military units of varying organizational sophistication composed of local citizens that formed up and disbanded as needed. The governor was by default the captain general of the militias. There were a whole host of other minor militia officers, including dozens of captains. By the year 1614, Paraguay had three companies of soldiers. Companies of infantry and cavalry varied from fifty to one hundred soldiers.[55] In 1676, during the largest expedition of the seventeenth century, seven infantry companies and one cavalry company were mobilized, with several officials assigned to each company. Militia service was fairly unprofessional and provided soldiers with little formal training or weapons. When governors mustered the militia, soldiers were required to bring their own weapons and vecinos of the city were asked to cough up donations in cattle, horses, iron, steel, and rope. For example, in the 1676 expedition, there were around 400 Spanish soldiers with 250 firearms. The crown and city governments provided only 22 percent of the firearms.[56] During periods of intense raiding, citizen-soldiers were prepared to assemble at a moment's notice. One Spanish official noted that Asunceño vecinos were constantly preoccupied with defense, sleeping "with their weapons under the pillows."[57] Besides the punitive expeditions, the Spanish militia was charged with occupying forts. In the 1660s and 1670s, there was a flurry of fort building and by 1706 eleven forts dotted the Chaco frontier—nine on the Paraguay River and two at the pueblos Itá and Tobatí. While Spaniards of the lowest rank were ordered to occupy the forts, indios were called on to build and repair them. The Castillo of San Ildefonso (built in 1660) was continuously occupied by twenty-five soldiers who held their post for one week at a time before being relieved.[58]

Forts, or "castillos," came to embody the Spanish defensive apparatus in the province, as evidenced in two visual representations. In Figure 2, an anonymous artist depicts the Castillo of San Ildefonso, situated on the banks of the Paraguay River just to the north of Asunción. The drawing is divided in half by the Paraguay River, presenting the viewer with a discernible borderland. On the upper half, the artist depicts the "land of enemy Indians." From the shore, Guaicurú led by a cacique fire arrows at the fort. Some of them have painted skins and colorful plumes adoring their heads. Two of these figures are playing long flute-like instruments. Spaniards knew firsthand that before a raid or battle Guaicurú would play music on flutes and shout war cries in an ominous cacophony that signaled their intent to attack. On the river, canoes carrying two to three Natives advance on the fort. These figures may have represented the "river pirates" or Payaguá.[59] The bottom half of the drawing shows an imposing castle standing in defiance of the oncoming Guaicurú horde. The straight lines and foreboding stone walls communicate steadfastness while soldiers fire their muskets from ramparts at each of the four corners of the fort. Figure 3 is a drawing of the fort San Augustín de Arecutagua, constructed in the early eighteenth century, situated just north of the San Ildefonso fort, where the Piribebuy River joins the

Paraguay River. This drawing similarly communicates Spanish strength, grandeur, and permanence. Both of these drawings attempt to display Spanish imperial power and authority. In the drawing of San Ildefonso, the discursive undercurrent is that even though Chaco groups were not settled in reducciones, they were at least kept out of Spanish territory and held at bay on "la otra banda" or the "opposite shore of the river."

Indios Amigos

The message of Spanish strength implicit in these images does not reflect the reality. In the first place, these forts were made of wood and mud and were constantly being repaired by Guaraní tributaries from nearby reducciones.[60] Moreover, the most important defensive weapons were not forts or Spanish soldiers but Guaraní militias. In all the punitive expeditions against Guaicurú or bandeirante incursions, Guaraní soldiers were the majority. Spanish officials who documented expeditions rarely mentioned indio soldiers in any detail, leaving the historian with very little information about the leadership structure of Indian militias, the nature of their service, and the arms they bore. Guaraní were so ubiquitous in any military venture that they often go unmentioned or are mentioned in passing as "indios amigos."

Velázquez estimates that there were thirty-five military expeditions under the aegis of Asunción officials during the seventeenth century.[61] The actual number of expeditions was likely much higher considering uneven record-keeping associated with expeditions and lost documentation. Table 2 lists expeditions led by the provincial government of Paraguay in the seventeenth century for which data on the number of indio soldier participants is available. This tabulation represents Guaraní soldiers originating from Franciscan-, secular-, and Jesuit-sponsored pueblos. While many reports did not register indios, by reading between the lines, it is clear that indio soldiers, porters, and guides were involved in each of the thirty-five expeditions for which there is data. The numbers of indio participants in these expeditions is significant and adds a new dimension to our understandings of the demands on Guaraní in colonial society, as well as a truer understanding of who defended the province of Paraguay.

Paraguayan governors requested soldiers from nearly all the pueblos

FIGURE 2. Drawing of Fort San Ildefonso, February 20, 1660. Source: "Plano del castillo de San Ildefonso, a orillas del río Paraguay," AGI, Seville, MP, Buenos Aires, 225.

FIGURE 3. Drawing of Fort San Augustín de Arecutagua, July 24, 1719. Source: "Representación del castillo de San Agustín de Arecutagua, situado en la confluencia de los ríos Paraguay y Piribebui," AGI, Seville, MP, Buenos Aires, 15.

TABLE 2. Military Expeditions with Documented *Indio* Soldier Participation

YEAR	NUMBER OF INDIO SOLDIERS	NUMBER OF ESPAÑOL SOLDIERS	DESCRIPTION
1604	400	5	Expedition of exploration to the Gran Chaco. Anticipated military action
1623	50	24	Punitive expedition against Payaguás
1662	100	—	Punitive expedition against Guaicurú
1662	600	120	Punitive expedition against Guaicurú
1664	500	70	Punitive expedition against Guaicurú, Mbayá, and Payaguá
1672	100	50	Villa Rica militias aid Atyrá Pueblo
1674	200	—	Punitive expedition against "*indios fronterizos*"
1676	700	322	Punitive expedition against Guaicurú
1676	650	400	Expedition against Paulistas in Itatín
1677	200	—	Punitive expedition against "*enemigo fronterizo*"
1688	300	200	Punitive expedition against Guaicurú

Sources: 1604, 27, R8, N22, Charcas, AGI; 1623, vol. 15, SC, ANA; 1662, vol. 2, no. 27, 28, SH, ANA; 1662, vol. 2, SH, ANA; 1664, vol. 324, f. 137, NE, ANA; 1672, vol. 2, SH, ANA; March 1681, Sección Jesuitica, IX 6–9-4, doc. 45, AGN; [1674], vol. 11, f. 447, AC, ANA; 1676, vol. 17, f. 109–10, SC, ANA; 1676, 33, Charcas, AGI; 1677, vol. 11, f. 686, AC, ANA; and 1688, vol. 37, no. 3, SH, ANA.

Note: A few of these numbers are requests for soldiers, not real numbers of soldiers who participated. The requests should not be discounted, however, because real and requested numbers often come close to matching, as in the case of the 1676 expedition.

and reducciones subject to the encomienda, including select Jesuit-sponsored reducciones. The militias of Guaraní-Jesuit reducciones and non-Jesuit reducciones differed significantly. The Jesuits actively promoted and built militias in their reducciones and used them as leverage to receive royal exemptions from the encomienda. The exceptions were officially granted in 1647 but practiced from the inception of the reducciones.[62] In officials' eyes, Guaraní-Jesuit reducciones were the primary line of defense on the eastern borderlands against bandeirantes, while Asunceños held the western frontier against Chaco Indians. The Guaraní serving in militias from non-Jesuit pueblos went largely unrecognized by royal officials even though they received small tribute exemptions or direct payments in local currencies. Given the Jesuits' extensive resources and impressive organizational structure, the Guaraní-Jesuit militias were much better equipped and trained than the other Guaraní pueblos.

Paraguayan officials regularly solicited soldiers from the Jesuit reducciones of San Ignacio de Caaguazú and Nuestra Señora de Fe. Of all the military expeditions that the Jesuit-sponsored Guaraní militias participated in, 43 percent were to the Gran Chaco. Of these, the government of Paraguay (not Buenos Aires) was the largest recipient of Guaraní help.[63] The requests for auxiliaries from reducciones were determined by their proximity to the area under attack and the availability of tributaries. If indios from reducciones were harvesting yerba maté or engaged in other productive tasks, they normally were not called on. In February 1662, Guaicurú attacked various pueblos in the Tebicuary region, including the Jesuit missions of Nuestra Señora de Fe and San Ignacio de Caaguazú, and the governor requested one hundred indio soldiers from the nearby Caazapá and Yuty pueblos (both Franciscan sponsored), as well as troops from the Jesuit reducciones that were attacked.[64]

For expeditions to the northern regions, officials frequently called on select pueblos in the Asunción area. For example, in a 1688 punitive expedition, the governor requested soldiers from the following pueblos: Itá, Altos, Ypané, Guarambaré, and Atyrá. Of these, only Itá was under Franciscan jurisdiction. It is difficult to determine why officials selected these specific pueblos, but it was not for their demographic strength, for all but one of these pueblos had 120 tributaries or less in 1674.[65] Other factors that officials considered when selecting pueblos for militia service may have included the pueblos' familiarity with expedition activities and the degree of cooperation they could expect from caciques and corregidores. Besides Indians from the pueblos, encomenderos sometimes took yanacona on expeditions as squires (*escuderos*).[66] Household servants/fiefs accompanied their Spaniards into battle as servants and protectors, while the men of subject villages were called to muster under Spanish leadership.

It is unclear if Guaraní-Jesuit militias were subsumed under the same structure or led separately by their own officers. When Guaraní soldiers assembled for an expedition, they were led by their respective pueblo corregidor and caciques. This seems to have been the extent of the official militia leadership structure for the non-Jesuit Guaraní militias. Again, we can surmise that the absence of official status bestowed on secular- and Franciscan-sponsored reducciones had to do with Spaniards' goals to monopolize these positions. The result was a partially desegregated militia, wherein Guaraní and Spanish citizen-soldiers served side by side. By contrast, the militias of the Jesuit reducciones boasted the formalization of official militia units, with infantry and cavalry companies and a variety of official posts, including captains, field masters, lieutenants, sergeants, standard-bearers, and buglers.[67]

While a minority of soldiers in militias from the Jesuit reducciones likely bore firearms, other indios amigos probably wielded only bows and arrows, lances, knives, and swords. Evidence suggests that the bow and arrow was the weapon of choice (or the only option) for colonial Guaraní. As they traveled to and from their pueblos and Asunción on the mita, it was common for Guaraní men to take weapons as protection from bandits, Guaicurú raids, and jaguars.[68] While specific details about indio participation in expeditions are thin, a few accounts provide insight into the physically and psychologically rigorous nature of these activities, as well as the kinds of tactics employed by combatants. Immediately following a Guaicurú attack in the Itatín region in October or November of 1688, the governor sent a vanguard company to force a retreat. The plan backfired. Guaicurú vastly outnumbered the Spanish-Guaraní force and overwhelmed them, killing twenty-three Spanish soldiers and one "indio amigo." After hearing of this devastating blow, the governor called a war council and requested a militia of 250 Spaniards and 400 Guaraní auxiliaries. The expedition's commander,

Maestro de Campo Juan de Vargas Machua, relied on a tracker called Juan Payaguá. The army was divided into several companies, each led by a Spanish captain. On June 27, 1689, with the militias finally assembled, the expedition marched out of the Valley of Pirayú, a settlement just north of Yaguarón, with 2,450 head of cattle, 600 horses, and 20 mules. On August 27, the militia arrived at the Jesuit Caaguazú reducción, where they remained until mid-October, thoroughly frustrating the Jesuit priests there who were surely burdened by the extra hordes of people, animals, and, surely, demands on their food and yerba maté stores.[69]

On October 14, the expedition finally located a large Payaguá settlement and a melee ensued. Spanish soldiers fired their muskets, killing four Payaguá, including the principal Payaguá cacique's son.[70] A few more skirmishes occurred as the Payaguá retreated to the western shore of the Paraguay River. From November 1 to 4, the Spanish-Guaraní troops repelled Payaguá attacks from canoes and finally crossed the river in pursuit. On November 5, they located the Guaicurú's trail, thanks to an individual named Ignacio Mosquera who had special knowledge of Guaicurú settlements. Mosquera had been a captive of the Guaicurú but had been "redeemed" by Spaniards in a prior expedition. As the troops continued their march through the difficult Chaco terrain, Mosquera identified signs of Guaicurú civilization, including small huts and seasonal horse pastures Guaicurú used to feed their horses.

The march continued for seven days without further sign of the enemy. Then suddenly, on November 14 at noon, a large number of Guaicurú warriors attacked from all sides. A sergeant major took thirty men to defend the horses while the remaining four companies attacked and forced the Guaicurú warriors to retreat. If the Spanish-Guaraní militia had been pleased with their successes thus far, their joy quickly turned sour. Seeing the militia's foray into the Chaco as an opportunity to raid, Guaicurú returned that same night, encircled the encampment, and attacked, targeting the expeditions' horses and cattle. After two hours, Spanish-Guaraní forces were able to force the Guaicurú into the surrounding forests, but from their hideouts in the trees Guaicurú shot arrows at their enemy throughout the night, wounding cattle, horses, and a few soldiers.

The next day, the militia followed the Guaicurú's trail through deep swamps, which nearly swallowed the soldiers, the water rising up to their chests. The commander noted with disgust that Guaicurú favored this kind of terrain, for this was the "land in which they were born and raised, as wild beasts in the thickets and brambles."[71] These notes of utter frustration with the land, weather, and enemy belie the commander's loss of morale and sense of defeat. Shortly thereafter, Vargas Machuca assembled his captains and they unanimously decided to retreat and return to their stronghold on the eastern shores of the river. During their retreat, Guaicurú warriors mounted another damaging attack, resulting in the loss of more livestock. Humbled by the experience, the general explained that repeated invasions of the Guaicurú's lands would change nothing. There was no hope in mounting more attacks since the "land was not capable of supporting a Spanish army, not even a small one."[72] Nearly all expeditions to the Chaco ended in similar defeat.

Spaniards and Guaraní paid a high price on the Chaco frontier. In the year 1680, a devastating Guaicurú attack resulted in the depopulation of a place named Valle de las Salinas, just to the east of Asunción. Many Spaniards died in the attack. At the behest of the cabildo, the governor ordered that the Valle be resettled and called for two hundred vecino volunteers to relocate and establish a villa, or village fortified by a defensive wall. Incentivizing the colonization scheme with paid houses and land (presumably to be built with indigenous labor), the governor attracted 229 vecino volunteers. Along with Spanish vecinos, the governor ordered the relocation of the Guaraní pueblo of Atyrá to Salinas. The Atyrá pueblo had just a few years earlier been transplanted from Itatín to a reducción called San Benito, just east of Asunción. The governor reasoned that the two communities together would "give each other a hand" and that "uniting their forces they could achieve . . . the conservation of this province . . . and the security of this city [Asunción]."[73] This statement summarizes seventeenth-century local Spanish policy on frontier defense: both Spanish-Guaraní settlements and fighting forces were the bulwark against invasion.

The Guaraní-Jesuit reducciones and militias of eastern Tapé were a strategic string of defensive communities, forestalling Portuguese incursion in Spanish territory. Similarly, Guaraní pueblos on Paraguay's western frontier functioned as a loose system of defense against Guaicurú. One reducción that dealt frequently with Guaicurú and Payaguá attacks was Tobatí, which was situated on the Manduvirá River before it was relocated to the Piribebuy River, closer to Asunción.[74] By at least the 1620s, Payaguá targeted the pueblo seasonally. Tobatí residents noted that the attacks usually came during the harvest season, when large numbers of Guaraní were outside working the fields, suggesting that Payaguá targeted human captives. During one particularly frightful attack sometime before 1652, Payaguá nearly burned the pueblo to the ground.[75] Because of Tobatí's strategic location on the yerba maté route, the pueblo was designated as a fort. The governor even stored powder and shot in the pueblo and provided supplies to strengthen its walled fortifications.[76]

Guaraní Soldiers and Internal Conflicts

Besides expeditions to the Chaco, indio militias were also involved in internal civic disputes and threats from other European powers. To cite just two examples among many, Guaraní-Jesuit militias from Tapé were deployed to Buenos Aires for fear of a French invasion in 1657 and to Colonia do Sacramento (now in Uruguay) in 1680 against a Portuguese army. All of these actions were directed by the governor of Buenos Aires.[77] The non-Jesuit reducciones in the Asunción orbit were never asked to travel so far afield, but they were pulled into local political conflagrations. Specifically, Guaraní soldiers were asked to fight in the two small civil wars commonly referred to as the Comunero Revolts of 1649 and the 1720s–1730s. Underlying both episodes were the eternal struggles between Asunceño encomenderos and the Jesuit order. In both conflicts, the Jesuit faction won out after Guaraní-Jesuit militias defeated the opposing forces and occupied Asunción.[78] Of these two conflicts, the civil strife that erupted in 1649 has received the least historical attention and merits consideration here. It is one of the few instances where Guaraní from Jesuit reducciones and Guaraní from non-Jesuit reducciones faced each other in open battle.

The cause of the conflict can be traced to the year 1638, when a creole Franciscan friar named Bernardino de Cárdenas was appointed the bishop of Paraguay. After waiting three years for the papal bulls legitimating his spiritual office, Cárdenas grew impatient and pushed his ordination through in 1641 without official Roman sanction. Once in Asunción, Cárdenas and the governor, don Gregorio de Hinestrosa, became embroiled in rivalries typical of governors and bishops. Cárdenas became increasingly bitter about the Jesuits' wealth and power in the region. After a series of heated exchanges with the new bishop, Governor Hinestrosa feared that Cárdenas might sequester Jesuit properties, so he ordered that guards protect the Jesuit college from the Cárdenas faction, consisting of Asunceño encomenderos. The Jesuits threw their support behind Governor Hinestrosa and ordered Guaraní-Jesuit militias to occupy Asunción and protect the college for a short time. The move worked and Hinestrosa forced Cárdenas to flee to Corrientes. In the aftermath of this prelude to a larger confrontation, Cárdenas ignored the Audiencia of Charcas's orders that he present himself in Charcas to answer to the claims Hinestrosa and the Jesuits made against him. In 1647, a new governor of Paraguay was appointed in don Diego de Escobar Osorio, who took a more neutral position in the conflict. This gave Cárdenas the window he was looking for, and he returned to Asunción. When Osorio suddenly died on February 22, 1649, the Asunción cabildo elected Cárdenas as the interim governor, further provoking Cárdenas's enemies and setting the stage for a larger conflict.[79]

On March 6, 1649, Cárdenas ordered the expulsion of the Jesuits from the capital. According to Jesuit sources, a mob broke down the doors of the Jesuit college and violently removed the fathers and looted the college.[80] The Jesuits used their connections in Peru to get a judge from the Audiencia of Charcas to come to Asunción, restore the Jesuit college, and put down the Cárdenas faction. Audiencia judge don Sebastián de León y Zarate accepted the assignment, but when he attempted to enter Asunción he was blocked by Cárdenas's partisans. In response, Oidor León y Zarate asked his Jesuit allies to assemble a Guaraní-Jesuit militia force of three thousand soldiers with one thousand of these wielding firearms. These were joined by two dozen Asunceño exiles, enemies of Cárdenas.[81]

The uncompromising Cárdenas assembled his own military force to meet the Guaraní-Jesuit militia consisting of a militia of Asunceño vecinos and four hundred "indios amigos" or Guaraní from the non-Jesuit reducciones.[82] These two opposing forces met on an open field three leagues from Asunción and a bloody battle ensued.[83] On Cárdenas's side, there were twenty Spanish and six Indian deaths. A memorial that is biased toward Cárdenas's position claims that 385 Guaraní-Jesuit soldiers were killed, but this must have been an exaggeration.[84] Descriptions of the battle scene from this same source emphasize the Jesuit mission Indians' cowardice: "if the Indians had not been so interested in stripping dead Spaniards they would have killed all of [the Spanish]. But scarcely had a Spaniard died when over twenty Indians began arguing over which would take the dead man's clothing and supplies."[85] The battle at San Lorenzo ultimately determined Cárdenas's fate. A few days after the battle, Cárdenas fled and the Guaraní-Jesuit militias occupied Asunción.

Imagining both factions battling, each with indigenous partisans, complicates how we understand colonial politics in Paraguay. Until now, scholars have imagined the Jesuit missions as the main sites of Guaraní indigenous power and resources, but this episode demonstrates that Asunción was also a site of Guaraní military power. With no indigenous comments on this episode, an understanding of why Guaraní participated in these actions will always be out of reach. Mercedes Avellaneda argues that Guaraní from the Jesuit *reducciones* saw the conflict as an extension of their flight from Guairá, which was to escape the tyranny of the encomienda, and to depose Cárdenas, who they perceived would limit their autonomy. She also adds that militia service was a way of reinforcing power structures among the Guaraní ruling classes.[86] Both of these arguments are reasonable, but the participation of Guaraní on Cárdenas's side provides a different perspective on Guaraní militia service. Of course, the indio militias from Paraguay may have been coerced into fighting, but given the lack of evidence of coercion in every other mobilization to the Chaco, this seems unlikely. For example, there are no extant accounts of indio desertions during expeditions. By all accounts, Guaraní served, if not willingly, then faithfully in military expeditions.

For the King and the Public Good?

Understanding why Guaraní performed military service is not easy to discern from the available records and requires a degree of speculation. While officials reported that "indios amigos" served out of a desire for a public good and to serve their king, the sources point to other possibilities. The first joint Spanish-Guaraní military activities in the 1530s and 1540s emerged out of a sense of shared alliance but with extremely divergent motivations: Guaraní fought to enact vengeance on their traditional enemies and claim captives while Spaniards hoped to find sedentary populations and a route to the Andes. As Guaraní society and culture changed in the reducciones, military activities became associated with community protection and self-preservation. In the case of the Guaraní-Jesuit communities of Guairá, military activities emerged out of regional conflict between contending Native communities and the Paulista-led raids. In both cases self-preservation was a major factor.

The long historical experience with violence against bandeirantes, especially, allowed Guaraní in the eastern reducciones to inscribe the concept of vengeance into a shared identity and purpose. The cultural meaning and practice of vengeance were transformed in the reducciones, but it never entirely disappeared. The contentious politics of the 1750s allows us to glimpse expressions of vengeance alive and well among Guaraní communities. In 1750, the Spanish and Portuguese crowns signed the Treaty of Madrid, which moved the demarcation line separating the two realms' territories in the Banda Oriental. With the stroke of a pen, seven Guaraní-Jesuit reducciones were designated as belonging to the Portuguese crown. The Spanish crown demanded that these seven reducciones relocate west of the new boundary line and abandon their homes, fields, and churches. Indigenous leaders mobilized pen and then sword to resist the order. Guaraní leaders articulated their opposition to the treaty and subsequent relocation order through an acute anger with the Portuguese. In a letter written in the Guaraní language, the corregidor from San Juan Bautista, Miguel Guaiho, reminded the Spanish official that Guaraní had fought ferociously against the Portuguese at Colônia do Sacramento in 1735. In a striking passage, Guaiho rhetorically shifted his gaze from the Spanish official to his Portuguese enemies to revel in the potential past vengeance Guaraní troops had inflicted on them: "remember, remember well Portuguese, we made ashes out of your fathers at Colônia, only a few [got away]."[87] This and other letters articulated a collective memory of the Paulista bandeirantes as savage brutes and the object of the militias' vengeance. Vengeance played an important part in Guaraní memory and political posturing that was likely reinforced by religious art. In the reducciones, a favorite theme that Guaraní artisans

FIGURE 4. Michael and the demon, San Cosme y Damián Reducción, 18th c. Source: colonialarchitectureproject.org. Photo courtesy of Gauvin Bailey.

FIGURE 5. Michael and the demon, Yaguarón Reducción, 18th c. Source: Photo courtesy of David Peery.

depicted for their churches was that of Saint Michael defeating a demon, and in some of these sculptures the demon bears resemblances to a human being, perhaps a Paulista.

These sources suggest that vengeance was an important aspect of militia activities in the Jesuit-sponsored reducciones, but what motivated Guaraní in non-Jesuit reducciones in the Asunción region? Spanish official commentary on why Guaraní served emphasized "public good" and "service to the crown."[88] But Spanish officials knew that Indian militias were not free. The costs of military service on Guaraní communities were mainly associated with labor, not material resources. Guaraní who served on expeditions could be absent from their communities for nearly six months, which would have been taxing on their pueblos. While the tax in time and labor on Guaraní reducciones was significant, the material costs associated with defense fell

FIGURE 6. Yaguarón retablo, 18th c. Source: colonialarchitectureproject.org. Photo courtesy of Gauvin Bailey.

FIGURE 7. Drawing of Guarani-Jesuit Reducción San Juan Bautista with Indian Militias Processing, ca. 1750. Source:

most heavily on the Spanish vecino population. While forts were built by mostly Guaraní hands, expeditions were funded almost entirely by vecino donations in livestock, iron, yerba maté, and tobacco.[89] This pattern contrasts with eighteenth-century New Mexico, where Pueblo communities provided the majority of Indian soldiers, with these soldiers often being better equipped than their vecino counterparts, at least during the first half of the eighteenth century. Moreover, a large portion of the burden to provision military expeditions in New Mexico fell on the shoulders of Pueblo communities.[90] The burden of military service certainly seemed higher for Pueblos when compared with Guaraní.

Not only did Spanish vecinos provide most of the victuals for expeditions in the form of yerba maté, cattle, and tobacco, they also outfitted Guaraní with the necessary tools and weapons. In the 1689 expedition reviewed above, the Spanish official called on the vecinos to donate four hundred axheads (*cuñas*) and one thousand lengths of rope.[91] The axes were for the indigenous soldiers who used them as weapons and for clearing paths in the forest. Provisions of these kinds should not be underestimated: four hundred axes carried a hefty value in Paraguay. Axes used on expeditions were improved for battle by covering parts of the head with steel, which served to strengthen and sharpen the axe.[92] Payments to Guaraní for participation in expeditions were not always quid pro quo but were meant to bolster the defensive capabilities of a frontier pueblo. As discussed above, Tobatí reducción was a vital community in the defensive network of forts and reducciones near Asunción. After suffering several devastating Guaicurú attacks in the 1660s, which forced the community to relocate, the governor sought to "redeem" the pueblo from Guaicurú invasions with donations from the vecinos of Asunción. These included 120 head of cattle and thirty arrobas of yerba maté, as well as iron and steel for their tools.[93] The governor recognized that the Tobatí reducción was too important as a defensive asset and subsidized its recovery.

Besides material goods, Spanish officials provided Guaraní communities exemptions from encomienda labor, mandamientos (state public works projects), and the beneficio de yerba, or yerba maté harvest. The few Jesuit reducciones subject to the encomienda were particularly effective in receiving these exemptions. For example, in 1668 after the Jesuit reducción of San

Ignacio assisted the governor on a campaign to defend Villa Rica, he granted them a year exemption from tribute.[94] In 1677, a year after a major bandeira invasion and a series of devastating Guaicurú raids, the governor restricted the use of tributaries for the yerba maté beneficio for three pueblos: only twenty-five from San Blas de Itá, fifteen from San Pedro de Ypané, and twenty from Todos Santos de Guarambaré were allowed to pay tribute.[95] The restriction of tribute requirements was common and had two goals: reward Guaraní for militia service and keep Guaraní soldiers near their pueblos where they could quickly assemble for campaigns.

While there are no extant records of Guaraní leaders requesting payment or tribute exemptions for military service rendered, there are several examples of Guaraní requesting payment for construction work related to defense. In 1671, three Guaraní representatives from Ypané appeared before a magistrate in Villa Rica (they made their petition in Villa Rica because the rains had made river travel to Asunción impossible) and explained that they had not yet been compensated for constructing ten war canoes for the governor. The Spanish official denied their request, noting that other pueblos had previously constructed war materials and had not been compensated. The official invoked the idea that Indians served simply out of a sentiment of "public good," but this record indicates that Guaraní expected payment for their labor.[96]

Guaraní did not provide their martial labor for free. Officials gave tribute exemptions and materials in order to maintain a relationship of reciprocity. These remunerations were significant but a small price to pay for the continued existence of the colony in Paraguay.

Conclusion

The seventeenth century was a period of retraction for the Spanish colony of Paraguay under the jurisdiction of Asunción. With the bandeiras on the eastern frontier and Guaicurú on the western frontier, Paraguay was hemmed in by enemies. Reducciones and towns retreated from the peripheries to occupy places closer to the administrative center of Asunción and the major Guaraní reducciones of the region. The rapid ascension of Guaicurú power, which ran almost parallel with the rise of the Guaraní reducciones in the

Asunción region, speaks to the importance of interindigenous relations and diverse indigenous responses to the colonial presence. From before contact, Guaicurú and Guaraní had been enemies, and this mutual hostility continued and expanded in the colonial period. While the expeditions of the 1530s and 1540s would suggest a Guaraní ascendance, Guaicurú responded by the 1590s with increased raiding, aided by their adoption of horses. Guaicurú behaviors suggest that they saw Paraguayan populations as slaves and tributaries. Using the frontier as a seasonal warehouse, they took captives and livestock, which they in turn circulated back into the societies who made the Chaco their home.

To stop the bleeding and keep the province from being wiped off the map, officials turned to Guaraní communities and local Spanish militias. The backbone of the province's defenses were Guaraní from both Jesuit and non-Jesuit reducciones. Paraguay contributes to a growing body of scholarship that demonstrates that Natives were the most important factor in explaining the conquest and continued existence of Spanish colonial society in the Americas. Guaraní participated in militia service for a variety of reasons that included self-defense, community autonomy, remuneration in the form of tribute exemptions, coercive encomenderos and officials, and an evolving concept of vengeance. With such dire threats, Paraguay was a frontier society, frequently on alert. These circumstances affected interethnic social and political relations. Fighting and dying together, Spaniards and Guaraní forged bonds of community through their shared experience of militia service. Of course, Guaraní and Spaniards were not considered social equals, but by engaging a common enemy they were drawn into an interdependence. The following chapter turns from Guaraní martial labor to labor more broadly and the role of reducciones in the regional economy.

Part 3.

Communities

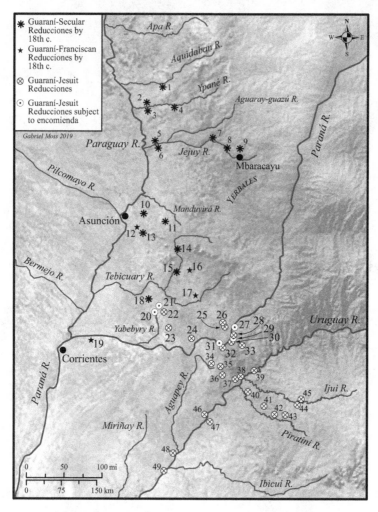

MAP 4. Select *reducciones* of Paraguay

1. Perico Guazú	14. Itapé	27. Corpus Christi	40. S. Nicolás
2. Ypané	15. Ntra. Sra. del Pilar	28. S. Ignacio Mini	41. S. Luis
3. Guarambaré	16. Caazapá	29. Loreto	42. S. Lorenzo
4. Tacuatí	17. Yuty	30. Sta. Ana	43. S. Miguel
5. Atyrá	18. Yaguaracamigtá	31. Itapua	44. S. Juan
6. Jejuy	19. Itatí	32. Candelaria	45. S. Angel
7. Terecañy	20. S. Ignacio Guazú	33. Stos. Martires	46. Sto. Tomé
8. Ybyrapariyara	21. Sta. Maria de Fe	34. S. Carlos	47. Sao Borja
9. Candelaria	22. Sta. Rosa.	35. S. José	48. Cruz
10. Altos	23. Santiago	36. Stos. Apostoles	49. Yapeyu
11. Tobatí	24. S. Cosme	37. Concepción	
12. Itá	25. Sma. Trinidad	38. Sta. Maria Mayor	
13. Yaguarón	26. Jesús	39. S. Javier	

CHAPTER 6

Beyond the Missions

Guaraní Reducciones *in Asunción's Orbit*

THIS BOOK HAS examined the themes of kinship, borderlands and frontiers, shamanic resistance, and militias but has not yet focused on economic, political, and social life in the reducciones. The vast majority of studies of Guaraní treat the Jesuit reducciones, but this chapter shifts focus to reducciones subject to Asunceño encomenderos, which included Franciscan, secular, and a handful of Jesuit reducciones. Analyzing missions across jurisdictional boundaries runs the risk of flattening Guaraní experiences, but this is not the intention. Institutional affiliations profoundly affected a community's religious, economic, and social life. However, there is strong evidence that cuñadasgo as it existed within the encomienda was an enduring aspect of colonial life, and therefore all reducciones that were touched by it merit consideration together. So, while institutional boundaries (e.g., Franciscan, Jesuit, and secular) are a fruitful way of analyzing reducciones, this chapter examines the impact of the economy and encomienda on a variety of Guaraní communities in Asunción's political orbit.[1]

This chapter is by no means a comprehensive treatment of reducciones within the regional economy; instead, it focuses on fluidity and political and social divergence within the reducciones. Specifically, it addresses the themes of shifting jurisdictional status of the reducciones, the fraught position of indigenous leaders, absenteeism, and mestizaje. Historical work on the non-Jesuit reducciones has tended to describe the integration of the reducciones into the regional economy as the primary factor explaining their disintegration, leaving little room for an understanding of how Guaraní contended with each other and with society outside the reducciones to shape their communities.[2] All of this change was compounded over time by the fluidity of the reducciones. Unlike their Jesuit counterparts, the reducciones that paid tribute in personal service to encomenderos were demographically dynamic spaces. So, while the reducciones remained spaces of indigenous community, they were not fortresses against outside society. In fact, the pueblos were more like magnets that could at once repel and attract. Indios came and went from the reducciones for a variety of reasons. The travel in and out of the reducciones was not limited to indios, for españoles and blacks were also frequent visitors in the pueblos. The effect of this movement of people, goods, and capital on the reducción as an institution is the subject of this chapter.

Surveying the Colonial Economy

As the yerba maté market picked up steam in the early seventeenth century and producers and traders demanded more laborers, Spanish vecinos in Asunción sought to gain greater access to Guaraní in the reducciones.[3] As the provincial capital in closest proximity to Mbaracayú, Asunción was poised to become a regional powerhouse. But Asunceños' access to labor in the reducciones suffered serious restrictions in the first quarter of the seventeenth century. First, don Alfaro's visita beginning in 1611 initiated a string of legislation that restricted encomenderos' use of mita laborers. Second, in 1617 the crown divided the Province of Gran Paraguay to create the Province of Buenos Aires, which included Corrientes and Santa Fe as its most important cities. The governorship of Paraguay was reduced to Asunción, Villa Rica, and Ciudad Real. These jurisdictional shifts paralleled the shift in economic power from Asunción to other key cities in the region. Santa Fe, Buenos Aires, and Tucumán became the main hubs for intra- and interregional trade, while Paraguay remained a supplier of raw materials. In the sixteenth century, cattle hides, sugar, tobacco, honey, wax, wine, and crude cloth were some of the major exports destined for regional markets. With their profits, Paraguayan vecinos and reducciones purchased iron, tools, slaves, fine cloth, clothing, and wheat.[4]

By the seventeenth century, yerba maté had caught on in the Río de la Plata and Peru, despite priestly warnings against its perceived addictive and degenerative effects on Christians.[5] The tea became a staple throughout Paraguay and a desired import in places like Potosí, Cusco, Santiago de Chile, and even Mexico City. By the 1630s, yerba maté overtook sugar and wine as

Paraguay's biggest export.[6] The colonial governorship of Paraguay competed with the Jesuit reducciones for dominance in this market, but the Jesuits overcame Asunción in the eighteenth century. Nonetheless, yerba maté remained the strongest product in the Paraguayan economy. In fact, yerba maté served as the primary coinage for the royal treasury in Asunción and in Paraguay generally. Slaves, cattle, and labor were all sold and bought in quantities of arrobas of yerba (one arroba equaled around twenty-five pounds of tea).[7]

As with other export economies in colonial Spanish America, the groups that stood to gain the most from a primary export were the intermediaries, not those exploiting the resources. While the vecinos from Asunción, black slaves, and Guaraní mitayos from the reducciones were the ones who organized yerba maté expeditions, collected the leaves, toasted them, bagged them, and transported them on barges or mules, they received only the smallest compensation. As the tea moved out of Asunción, the gains on the tea grew. The yerba maté trade initiated in Asunción then moved south, either on the Paraguay and Paraná Rivers or overland on mule carts, to Corrientes and then Santa Fe. From Santa Fe, the tea was sent south to Buenos Aires or northwest to Tucumán, then to Chile or Peru and beyond. Along this route, the tea was sold to local populations. The traders or *mercaderes* who moved the yerba maté along this route for various lengths of its journey were primarily from Buenos Aires, Tucumán, Santa Fe, and Corrientes. Most Asunceño vecinos lacked the capital and the social connections to break into the trade beyond Asunción.[8] Traders involved in the production and transportation of yerba maté at its earliest stages maintained connections with the Paraguayan governor and local officials. Many spent a considerable amount of time in Asunción, where they owned houses and ranches. While most of these were *residentes*, not vecinos, thereby limiting their access to local political office, they nonetheless wielded important economic and political power in the city. Through their patronage networks with city officials and the Paraguayan governor—who frequently resided in Corrientes, Santa Fe, or Buenos Aires—these traders gained access to the yerba maté groves.

Governor Céspedes Jeria (r. 1634–1636) is often attributed with the regulation of the yerba maté trade, but yerba maté groves were defined as crown possessions decades earlier.[9] As early as 1603, officials were renting out yerbales (groves of yerba maté trees) to traders who could assemble teams of laborers and transporters. In that year, royal officials in Asunción "rented" and "auctioned" the "coca or yerba de Mbaracayú" to a high-status encomendero named Lucas de Balbuena for a period of forty days at a cost of 510 pesos.[10] The existence of this auction record at such an early date, before Alfaro's reforms, is surprising considering that the governor of Paraguay issued a prohibition against the consumption of yerba maté that very same year.[11] Local crown officials recognized very early the economic importance of yerba maté and found it to be a suitable commodity for taxation. This document also highlights the relationship between coca and yerba maté. Coca was an important stimulant for Andean mitayos working the mines. That yerba maté was referred to as "coca" suggests that yerba maté was intended as a supplement to coca and therefore connected to Potosí and the mining economy.

As the yerba maté trade surpassed other commodities, royal officials began characterizing the tea as a subterranean resource, thereby creating a framework of legality for collecting the royal quinto.[12] In the decades following these reforms, church and crown officials referred to the wild yerba maté groves of Paraguay as "the gold and silver of this region."[13] The governor granted access to the green mines of yerba maté and indigenous tributaries by auctioning leases, called *beneficios*, to the highest bidding trader. The beneficios included access to the yerba maté groves for a specific period, as well as an allotment of Guaraní mitayos. The so-called beneficio general occurred regularly, at least once per year. For example, in the 1697 beneficio general, the governor issued a called for "agents" to bid on the beneficio, and the successful agents essentially leased the rights to harvest the crown's yerba maté "mines" as well as a *tropa* of mitayos from the nearby reducciones. Following Alfaro's regulations, these tropas were limited to no more than two months but they usually lasted as long as six months to a year.[14] Each agent received around ten to twenty mitayos. While certain governors restricted the mitayos' labor to only harvesting and preparing the yerba maté, most tropas were also employed in transporting the tea in barges or overland in oxen-pulled carts. In the year 1697, a total of 296 Indians were allotted out to agents. Yerba maté tropas were composed of not only Guaraní but also black slaves, who often served as mayordomos or simple laborers. Upon their return to Asunción, the agents paid a certain percentage of yerba maté to the governor for the royal treasury at the *estanco* or state monopoly.[15] Many of the agents who bid on the leases were often from Corrientes and Santa Fe, though between 35 and 50 percent were encomenderos from Asunción or Villa Rica.[16] To summarize, an agent typically went through the following process: acquire a lease from the governor, take or send a tropa of laborers to Mbaracayú, prepare the tea, then transport the product downriver where they often changed hands with other traders. Besides the beneficio general, there were other licit and illicit means for harvesting yerba maté. The governor issued so-called *beneficios simples*, which could happen at any time and were often based on specific needs.[17] For example, beneficios simples were used to pay off debts incurred on military expeditions to the Chaco or for other expenditures related to public works or festivals.[18] Agents also organized illicit yerba maté expeditions, which were frequently condemned but rarely caught and prosecuted.[19]

The bulk of the labor associated with the yerba maté economy—harvesting and preparing the tea, building transport vehicles like carts and barges, and transporting it at any point along the trade routes—was performed by Guaraní from the reducciones subject to the encomienda. Before the devastating 1676 bandeira and string of Guaicurú raids, the reducciones closest to Mbaracayú performed most of the beneficio labor. These included Jesuit, Franciscan, and secular pueblos near Villa Rica. After the 1676 attacks and subsequent abandonment of Itatín, the burden shifted to reducciones farther south, which included the reducciones in the vicinity of Asunción as well as the Alto Paraná and Tebicuary: the Franciscan reducciones of Caazapá and Yuty and the Jesuit reducciones of San Ignacio, Santiago, and Nuestra Señora de Fe.[20]

While yerba maté was the most important export, producers also exported a variety of other goods, including hides, tallow, cotton, cloth, crude sugar, honey, and wax. Guaraní laborers were involved at every level of production and distribution. Thanks to their obligation to pay tribute directly to the provincial governor and to their encomenderos, mitayos were rapidly drawn into the yerba maté trade and regional economy. The signs of this integration are identifiable in two developments: first, the transfer of many reducciones from Franciscan to secular sponsorship and, second, the attitudes and behaviors of reducción indigenous leaders and priests. Each will be addressed in turn.

From Regular to Secular

The development of the regional economy and the rise of the yerba maté trade paralleled the increasing influence of encomenderos over reducciones in Paraguay. Table 3 shows the institutional affiliation of the principal reducciones subject to encomienda service. Out of a total of fourteen reducciones founded under Franciscan supervision, only four remained Franciscan by the end of the seventeenth century. This secularization was the effect of the lack of Franciscan priests and pressure from the encomendero class to move pueblos under secular administration. Guaraní leaders became embroiled in the disputes over the secularization of their reducciones and lobbied to pursue their chosen priests.[21]

A rare record of a conflict over the status of Yaguarón in 1622 illustrates how actors on different sides pursued their interests. Yaguarón was founded by the Franciscan fathers Luís de Bolaños and Alonso de Buenaventura in 1586. The pueblo remained under Franciscan leadership until Bolaños asked a trusted secular priest, Hernando de la Cueva, to serve in Yaguarón for a time, presumably before 1600. When de la Cueva died in 1622, Franciscan leaders sought to get one of their own appointed to Yaguarón. The bishop appointed a Dominican as interim priest, but the Franciscans had arranged for one of their own to reside in the reducción. Spanish vecinos claimed that the Franciscans had "violently and forcibly" taken control of Yaguarón and evicted the bishop-appointed interim cleric. The vecinos obviously had ties to the bishop-appointed priest while the Franciscans wanted to hold onto the reducción. But what did the indigenous leadership think of the matter? A rare report from the pueblo's indigenous cabildo tells us that the indigenous leaders supported Franciscan sponsorship of their community. When de la Cueva died, the Guaraní cabildo of Yaguarón sent messengers directly to Caazapá to petition the Franciscan visitador and request a Franciscan priest.[22] In their written petition, the members of the cabildo argued that because Franciscans had helped found the reducción, a Franciscan should remain its priest:

> The Franciscans, who discovered and settled these provinces by order and command of His Majesty, were the first to preach the Holy Gospel

TABLE 3. Institutional Status of Principal *Reducciones*

PUEBLO/REDUCCIÓN	FOUNDED BY	CHANGED TO
Ypané (or Pitum)	Franciscan (ca. 1579)	Secular (ca. 1600)
Altos	Franciscan (ca. 1580)	Secular (ca. 1600)
Itá	Franciscan (1585)	—
Yaguarón	Franciscan (1587)	Secular (ca. 1600)
Guarambaré	Franciscan (ca. 1598)	Secular (ca. 1600)
Atyrá	Franciscan (ca. 1580–1600)	Secular (ca. 1600)
Candelaria	Franciscan (ca. 1580–1600)	Secular (ca. 1600)
Mbaracayú	Franciscan (ca. 1580–1600)	Secular (ca. 1600)
Perico Guazú	Franciscan (ca. 1580–1600)	Secular (ca. 1600)
Terecañy	Franciscan (ca. 1580–1600)	Secular (ca. 1600)
Ybyrapariyara	Franciscan (ca. 1580–1600)	Secular (ca. 1600)
Caazapá	Franciscan (1606)	—
San Ignacio Guazú	Jesuit (1610)	—
Yuty	Franciscan (1611)	—
Tobatí	Franciscan	Secular
Arecayá	Secular (ca. 1632)	—
San Benito de los Yois	Secular (ca. 1632)	—
Itapé	Franciscan (ca.1673)	—
Caaguazú	Jesuit	—

Note: Yaguarón came under the supervision of a secular priest sometime before 1600. In 1622, the secular priest Hernando de la Cueba died and the Franciscans moved in to assert supervision. Asunción vecinos disputed the action. See 12 December 1622, CACh, vol. 755, ABNB. The Yaguarón cabildo also submitted its own position in favor of the Franciscans. 4 November 1622, CS, ANA. See also 159, SH, ANA. For Altos, see Necker, *Indios Guaraníes y chamanes franciscanos*, 66; and Durán Estragó, *Presencia franciscana en el araguay*, 1538–1824, 134. For Ypané, see Durán Estragó, 107. For Guarambaré, see Durán Estragó. Guarambaré relocated closer to Asunción in 1682. Ybyrapariyara was destroyed by Paulistas in 1672 and the remnants of the pueblo relocated to San Benito de los Yois. Terecañy was destroyed by bandeirantes in 1672. Durán Estragó, 111. Mbaracayú and Candelaria were destroyed by bandeirantes in 1672. According to Azara, Itá was founded by Ayolas in 1536 and then reinforced by Franciscans in 1585. San Ignacio Guazú may have been founded by Bolaños, but it immediately transferred to Jesuit supervision. Durán Estragó, 157. On Yuty, see Durán Estragó, 159. San Benito de los Yois was founded after the 1628–1632 bandeirante from Guaraní associated with Santiago de Jerez, which also was destroyed. Garavaglia, "La demografía paraguaya," 25. Arecayá was likely founded with assistance from Franciscans but largely under secular supervision.

to us and our ancestors. They took us out of the forests and the idolatries in which we resided and they settled us in pueblos where they instructed us in the things pertaining to our Holy Catholic Faith, teaching us Christian policía and obedience to our natural Savior and King. . . . And we have always desired that the Fathers continue assisting our pueblo for our teaching and that of our children and for the good and gain of our Republic.[23]

This statement was signed by the Yaguarón cabildo, as well as a number of caciques. Interpreting this kind of source is difficult considering the many unknowns surrounding its creation. It was recorded in Spanish, but it may have been translated from Guaraní. The language of the petition—with its references to evangelization, policía, and the relationship between forest and idolatry—takes on a tone very similar to priestly narratives. This suggests that some Guaraní leaders had absorbed concepts of reducción and therefore were supportive of priests who could sustain such a program or that a priest composed the letter on the cabildo's behalf. Given other evidence of a small minority of educated Guaraní leaders, it is safe to assume that Guaraní leaders composed the letter.

The Guaraní leaders of Yaguarón may have preferred Franciscans over seculars for the additional reason that clerics were deeply connected to the encomendero class and economic interests. Seculars often sent mitayos on the beneficio de yerba or assigned them to vecinos in private short-term labor contracts, despite prohibitions against these contracts.[24] Just as in other regions of Ibero-America, we see in Paraguay the classic family strategy for elites to place one son in the government and one in the clergy. For example, the priest at Tobatí in the mid-seventeenth century, Diego Núñez de Añasco, was the son of a prominent Asunceño encomendero. Thanks to his connections, the former received a beneficio de yerba in 1652. These networks firmly bound the encomienda class and strengthened their grip on Indian labor.[25]

Even so, the secular-regular divide was not always so clear-cut. The fact that Bolaños appointed a secular priest to Yaguarón indicates that patronage could trump institutional affiliation—apparently Bolaños raised de la Cueva like a son. The Yaguarón cabildo's petition suggests that Guaraní leadership only accepted the secular de la Cueva because he was trusted by Father

Bolaños. If this was true, then Bolaños—a master of the Guaraní language—likely raised a priest who was a highly skilled Guaraní speaker and therefore more attractive to Guaraní leadership. Bolaños's appointment of a non-Franciscan also underscores the fact that the Franciscans were understaffed. So, while Franciscans fought the good fight in trying to hold back the secularization of the reducciones, they did not have the personnel to manage the reducciones on their own. Franciscan loss of authority over the reducciones occurred rather quickly, with the majority of reducciones turning over to the curate by 1600. By 1655, the Franciscans only controlled Caazapá and Yuty in the Tebicuary region and Itá along the Paraguay River.[26]

The Contested Authority of Guaraní Leaders

Given the withdrawal of Franciscans from many reducciones and the peripatetic presence of secular priests, much of the administration of the Indian towns was left to indigenous leaders. Managing social relations, tributary duties, economic activities, and continual religious observances in mission towns averaging around one thousand souls required a strong leadership structure. Indigenous leadership in Guaraní reducciones was similar across secular, Franciscan, and Jesuit reducciones, although future studies will surely describe the finer points of variation. When a reducción was founded, the friars identified the most prominent political leader or leaders and attempted to overlay the new authority of the reducción onto the traditional authority of the tuvichá. As the community developed, priests dispersed power to a variety of other indigenous officials. Initially, these leaders negotiated the new relationship between the community and the priests, and if priests could convince a core group of leaders to support the reducción, their work would advance rapidly. Writing about the founding of the San Ignacio Guazú, the Jesuit Father Lorenzana explained that "nine caciques . . . have offered to come with their people and some of them have begun cultivating their garden plots, which is the best signal we could have."[27]

As the reducción matured, priests created new institutions for governance. Each reducción had a cabildo with a core set of officials. The corregidor was the top indigenous official and was the head of the cabildo. Other officers of the cabildo included four regidores (councilmen), one or two alcaldes mayores (municipal magistrate), alférez real (royal ensign), alguacil mayor (constable), procurador (steward), and sometimes an *alcalde de la santa hermandad* (lower-ranking justice of rural territories).[28] The social and political meanings of these positions were captured in their Guaraní translations. *Corregidor* was *poroquaitara* ("he who commands what should be done"); *regidor* was *cabildoiguara* ("he who pertains to the cabildo or council"); and *alguacil mayor* was *ĭbĭraiyâ ruçú* ("the first of those who carry the staff in hand"). This last term referred to the staff of justice the alguacil carried, an object that, as we have already seen, took root quickly in Guaraní culture.[29] These cabildo positions rotated annually or biannually, while the corregidor held longer terms. The governor, with priestly advice, confirmed new officials during visitas and appointed corregidores as needed. Guaraní leaders whose political authority was at stake frequently petitioned authorities.[30]

In the Jesuit reducciones with formal militias, we can add to the list of official positions the sundry military officials (see chapter 5).[31] Priests or administrators also appointed cooks, barbers, blacksmiths, carpenters, and other skilled artisans.[32] All the reducciones had formal offices associated with religious life. *Cantores*, *fiscales*, and sacristans respectively sang or assisted with sacred music, administered church resources and moral justice, and aided in performing holy rites. The office of fiscal, or church assistant, was an important one. The 1603 synod for the Río de la Plata indicated that the fiscal should be the eyes and ears of the priest: he was to be among the community and keep his eyes open for sin, especially concubinage. He also was tasked with ensuring that youth and children were instructed in Christian doctrine and that the church remained clean.[33]

Cabildo officers also played an important role in internal government, especially when it came to crime and justice. For example, in 1693 a woman was taken into custody for having murdered the six-year-old child of a cacique with whom she quarreled. The alcaldes responded decisively to the reported crime, detained the accused, identified the body of the victim, and took depositions, all before notifying Spanish officials in Asunción. They even conducted a coerced interrogation (they whipped her) until they extracted a confession. Shortly thereafter, Spanish officers appeared at the pueblo and took over the proceedings.[34] Few records have survived, but Indian cabildos held elections and created inventories of their goods.[35] These mechanisms of indigenous administration were crucial because most non-Jesuit reducciones functioned without a resident priest.[36] The few surviving sources speak to a high degree of autonomy.

One of the most important institutions in the reducciones was the parcialidad or *cacicazgo*, headed by a cacique, which was based loosely on the Guaraní teyÿ or extended kinship unit. In the reducciones, the teyÿ-cacicazgo underwent profound transformation due to the loss of key Guaraní social practices, especially polygyny. Guaraní leadership at the level of the teyÿ could be inherited but was also subject to other characteristics, including generosity, warrior prowess, and eloquence. Unsettled by the lack of continuity in the Guaraní leadership structure, colonials propagated a system of primogeniture, whereby a leader passed his authority on to his kin. In the reducciones subject to encomienda service, the caciques were endowed with the status of Native nobility and exempted from tribute service, thereby incentivizing the position.[37] Guillermo Wilde demonstrates that while the Jesuits successfully instituted a system of political inheritance for indigenous leaders based on the management of the symbols of authority and filial inheritance, the reality of indigenous leadership was more complex. Wilde calls the "true caciques" those leaders that wielded real authority and "caciques on paper" those who possessed authority from the priests. Jesuit internal documents demonstrate that Guaraní brought into the reducciones a framework for political power that was inherently contingent: leaders' eloquence, generosity, warrior prowess, and charisma, not primogeniture, gave form to their real authority. This authority continued unofficially within the reducciones.[38] Julia Sarreal shows that when caciques lacked leaderships qualities, they served as "placeholders" or figureheads of the cacicazgos.[39]

Evidence from the non-Jesuit context confirms these findings. Even when Spanish officials and priests recorded inheritance of a cacicazgo through lineage, more complex realities of authority emerge, as the following example from a 1652 visita conducted in Tobatí illustrates. After examining a parcialidad headed by the cacique Agustín Yarabay, the encomendero, don Fernando Zorilla del Valle, claimed there was a pretender cacique named Hernando Candiyú who was absent from the pueblo. The visitador investigated and discovered that when Agustín's father, Miguel Yarabay, headed the parcialidad it was rather large and so he took it upon himself to divide the parcialidad.

Miguel Yarabay identified a capable Guaraní named Martín Candiyú, father
of the perceived pretender, to head the new division. Yarabay's decision to
divide up his parcialidad seems nonsensical, since a larger unit had the potential to increase the power of its leader. It may have been the case that a priest
or encomendero intervened, but perhaps there were other logics at work.
Miguel Yarabay may have divided his parcialidad with Martín Candiyú
because the former sought to reciprocate with the latter. As we have seen
previously, a primary privilege of a Guaraní tuvichá was to distribute family
members to men within and without the village. In other words, this document may be attesting to the continuation of Guaraní patriarchal privileges
within the reducciones. Martín Candiyú received his status as cacique from
an interindigenous transaction, whereas his son, Hernando Candiyú, received
his privileges through the colonial system of primogeniture.[40]

Indigenous intermediaries inhabited fraught political positions. Go-
betweens like Malintzín (La Malinche)—Cortes's translator, emissary, and
concubine—have been portrayed as either pawns or victims of their own
betrayal.[41] Writing from a materialist perspective, some scholars argue that
colonial economies shifted indigenous leaders' priorities from the needs of
their communities to the avaricious and exploitative demands of the market.
Once fully "converted" to colonial hierarchies and economic forces, indigenous leaders turned against their communities and adopted symbols of social
distinction (e.g., Spanish clothing) and fully cooperated with the colonial
state, in what Steven Stern terms the "tragedy of success."[42] More recently,
scholars have delved into the nuances of indigenous leadership, paying attention to how the tactics of mediation were informed by cross-cultural knowledge and local political contexts.[43] Yanna Yannakakis notes that indigenous
power brokers in the Villa Alta district of colonial Oaxaca walked a fine line
as they attempted to appease colonial authorities and the Native communities
to which they belonged, especially when their authority became intrusive.
Yannakakis argues that because indigenous go-betweens' authority was legitimated by two opposing spheres, they operated within two systems: an official
state system and a "shadow system" that consisted of invisible human networks that transcended indigenous communities. When colonial officials
detected a shadow system was at work, the indigenous broker's authority was
suspect and he could be reprimanded or deposed.

This framework for understanding indigenous go-betweens does not apply well to Paraguay, where the go-betweens were rarely indios and more often españoles. While the corregidores (indigenous governors) and caciques were responsible for ensuring the consistent payment of tribute, this burden also fell on the shoulders of encomenderos and their agents. Guaraní leaders who found themselves at odds with Guaraní residents were despised not because they were too closely aligned with colonial representatives but because they were exploitative or were strict adherents to reducción rules. In other words, a "shadow system," framed by the binary systems of colonial and indigenous power, was not necessary in Paraguay because many españoles and Guaraní coalesced around a shared Guaraní language and a cultural framework for service or cuñadasgo.

The corregidor possessed the greatest authority in the reducciones and was the crucial link between the community, priests, and the regional economy. Early colonial officials recognized the importance of Indian corregidores for maintaining *policía cristiana*, ensuring the regular payment of personal service, and mustering indio soldiers. Given the importance of this office, colonial officials selected the most ostensibly loyal Guaraní. In many cases, these were Guaraní of "noble" families who received special schooling from the priests in the reducción. This training resulted in a figure who was often bilingual and literate. The broad authority of the corregidores inevitably led to conflicts. A 1654 dispute between the corregidor of Altos and a Guaraní family provides an example of the way corregidores could abuse their positions. A thirty-year-old Guaraní named Pedro Quattí, his eighteen-year-old son Domingo Quattí, and Domingo's wife Ana appeared before a magistrate in Asunción to request that officials stop their pueblo's corregidor, Juan Pasqual, from pressuring them to return to the pueblo. In essence, this family wanted the magistrate to legitimate their flight from the reducción to the home of their encomendera. This family's plight began with a plague that killed many of the members of Pedro Quattí's family, as well as the cacique of their parcialidad. Aside from ravaging the reducción population, disease also took Quattí's encomendero, leaving them with no indigenous or Spanish lord. Domingo Quattí related that the corregidor Juan Pasqual took advantage of their "vacant" status and claimed them as members of his cacicazgo. Juan Pasqual was no benevolent cacique.

In the first place, Pasqual took Ana, Domingo's wife, as his own—Pedro Quattí suggests there was sexual abuse. Moreover, Juan Pasqual ordered the family to perform all kinds of tasks for the pueblo, as well as for private individuals, including renting them out to Asunceños and yerba maté agents running beneficios in Mbaracayú. Tiring of Juan Pasqual's onerous labor requirements, Domingo Quattí complained. In his defense, Juan Pasqual reportedly justified his requests as necessary work for the pueblo, invoking a sense of community moralism, but the Quattí family did not buy it. Pedro Quattí summarized their situation when he explained that Juan Pasqual acted as if he "were the absolute Lord of the family."[44] Fed up with the corregidor's abuses, the family left Altos and took up residence with an encomendera named doña Mariana Resquín near Tobatí Pueblo. Juan Pasqual could have been a bad encomendero's indio doppelgänger: he rented Indians out to private individuals, made claims on vacant Indians, demanded excessive labor, and took other men's wives.

Similar abuses occurred in the same reducción under the leadership of don Juan Tucuray just a few years before Juan Pasqual's term as corregidor. Several indios complained that Tucuray had illegally created work contracts for Guaraní residents and had retained Spaniards' payments for himself. After Tucuray asked a man in the pueblo to go on a beneficio with a Spaniard named Melchior de los Reyes, this indio had suspected the contract was not official and determined to inquire with officials in Asunción. His suspicions were confirmed, and he returned to Altos with written proof that the contract was bogus. The corregidor became incensed with the man and punished him severely. Stripped of his clothes and locked in the stocks (which were normally situated at a central location in every reducción), Tucuray whipped him.

Obliged to give his side of the story, Tucuray submitted in his own hand a defense that brushed aside the denunciations:

> I say that for justice [these accusations] should not be heeded because it is ordinary [for the inhabitants of the reducción] to cast the corregidor and caciques as the enemy . . . for reprimanding them in things touching the care that they should have . . . for their policía, good doctrine, and instruction.[45]

Tucuray seemed to say that "the indios don't know what's good for them." By linking policía and good doctrine, this corregidor articulated a classic description of the goals of the reducción.

Literate and austere, these corregidores saw no problem drawing distinctions between themselves and the rest of the reducción population. In the year 1602, Alonso, the cacique principal and corregidor of Tobatí, petitioned the governor to intervene on his behalf. This rare petition was composed in Spanish by Alonso, who cast himself as different from the rest of his community by virtue of his political office and responsibilities: "the indios resent me because I make them keep the doctrines and good customs. I do not want to please them by drinking wine with them, according to their ancient customs."[46] That Alonso refused to imbibe wine with the community is significant. Communal drinking of honey wine was a practice that preceded contact and continued in the reducciones well into the seventeenth century despite frequent prohibitions. Drinking festivals were organized whenever a significant social event occurred, including harvest, hunts, or when captives were consumed. The association between drinking and cannibalism is pronounced in priestly sources and therefore helps explains colonials' and Guaraní-Christians' strong negative reactions to them.[47] Even so, the opportunity for social encounters and public ritual did not seamlessly transform into the ideal practice of the Christian festival. Communal events involving drinking attracted nonindios from Asunción, some of whom provided the wine.[48] Alonso's rejection of these social gatherings seems to have turned the community against him and caused him to lose effective authority in the pueblo.

Alonso explained that the Indians of his pueblo regularly disobeyed his orders to cultivate garden plots for the pueblo, which he believed would bring misery on their own heads: "it is my charge to command them to cultivate their fields so they can feed themselves and their children . . . but they do not want to do it."[49] Alonso also voiced his concern that many Guaraní did not return to Tobatí after their mita period ended. On one occasion, he sent messengers to demand that they return to the pueblo, further inciting anger against him. Alonso believed that the Tobatí residents' "bad behaviors" were exacerbated by Spanish encomenderos who strove to turn loyalties from the pueblo to the encomendero. Specifically, an encomendera named doña María Pineda incited other indios to refuse Alonso's authority and encouraged them to remain on her farmstead.[50] Alonso claimed that doña María further weakened his authority by spreading false rumors about him in Tobatí and by convincing a Spanish official to conduct an inquiry into his alleged abuses of office. The governor who reviewed Alonso's petition was supportive and ordered that he maintain his post as corregidor and that outsiders stop meddling. Alonso's case suggests that indigenous leaders in the Asunción orbit were enmeshed in social networks that transcended the pueblo. In this case, what pushed indios away from the pueblo was their corregidor's burdensome demands and the prospect of a less stringent lifestyle with an encomendera.

While Guaraní had strong leaders before the reducciones, colonialism strengthened a hierarchical organization in Guaraní communities and multiplied the opportunities for stratification. The most contentious issue pitting commoner Guaraní against corregidores was labor. In 1608 in the Itá Pueblo, the corregidor hit a Guaraní woman named Ana with his staff of justice because she was not completing a previously assigned task for the pueblo. The symbolic potency of this violent act surely was not lost on the Itá community; it certainly was not lost on Ana's husband, who responded by attacking the corregidor.[51] The demands on Guaraní mitayos were already onerous, and if a corregidor pushed his community too hard, they resisted.

Analyzing social distinctions and tension in the reducciones demonstrates that ethnogenesis was not monolithic. Officials like Pasqual and Alonso represented a new Guaraní ruling class in the reducciones who learned to use their positions and distinct educations to enhance their own situations as they related to the regional economy. Corregidores and other Native leaders fully adopted the ideology of reducción, which often placed them at odds with Guaraní who bristled at the toilsome demands of reducción life and labor. Many Guaraní chose to flee the pueblos to reside on encomenderos' farmsteads. Thus, Guaraní leaders were not always positioned as intermediaries between their communities and the avaricious demands of encomenderos. Instead, they often applied pressure on their communities to maintain the pueblo, thereby prompting many Guaraní to relocate. The cross-ethnic networks proved an important safety valve on the reducciones, allowing the political pressure indigenous leaders produced through the effective operation of the reducción's moral and economic mechanisms to dissipate outside of the pueblo.

Tribute and Labor

The reducciones were important sites of economic activity. At any given time, Guaraní were involved in mita, community, or contract labor, which included cultivation of community fields, yerba maté beneficios in Mbaracayú, barge transports, building construction in Asunción, care for livestock, cloth production, etc. Guaraní categories of labor and tribute service can be summarized in the following way: mita labor; mandamientos, or public works projects requested by the governor or cabildo; the yerba maté beneficio; wage labor or *conchabo*; and pueblo or community tasks. This last category was referred to in the reducciones as *tupambaé* (God's possessions), which implied productive tasks directed toward the community, while *abambaé* (man's possession) was labor to support one's own family.[52] Historians of the Guaraní-Jesuit reducciones use the categories of tupambaé/abambaé as a framework for understanding daily life in the reducciones and note that the Jesuits' ideals were different from the reality. In the Jesuits' writings, Guaraní were busy every waking hour either in religious activities or labor, but internal sources document resistance to rigid schedules and heavy workloads through flight and aversion. In the Guaraní-Jesuit reducciones, caciques or heads of individual families were given access to gardens to cultivate their own goods. These goods were stored in warehouses and distributed to families or cacicazgos at regular intervals. Tupambaé labor was theoretically limited to two days per week, while abambaé labor took place during the remaining four days of the workweek. This schedule may not have been tenable in the encomienda reducciones, who frequently left the community for tribute or contract labor.[53]

Discerning "daily life" and internal economic activities in the non-Jesuit reducciones is difficult, but civil documentation sheds light on the variety of Guaraní labor tasks. For Guaraní in the vicinity of Asunción and the Alto Paraná, cattle ranching was an important source of food and income. Many reducciones had their own grazing territories with small huts for the "cowboys," or vaqueros, and their families. The size of these herds of cattle varied. For the most prosperous reducciones, they could be rather large: in 1673, Yaguarón had two thousand head of cattle among other livestock.[54] By 1790, Yaguarón possessed ten thousand head of cattle in estancia Pirayuby.[55] The

work indios performed in the reducciones often spilled over to private vecinos and traders. For example, español cattle ranchers relied on indigenous
hands from reducciones to move their herds. In July of 1659, a vecino from
Corrientes signed a contract in Asunción with the vicar of Altos and several
members of the Altos cabildo to take sixteen indios to the Alto Paraná district and drive eight hundred head of cattle up to Asunción. The contract was
for five months, and each indio earned a quantity of cloth for his labor. It is
not clear if these proceeds were destined for the community warehouse or
for the individual, but given the priests' involvement, it is likely that a portion
of the earnings went back to the community or priest.[56] After private ranchers, the city government called on indios to deal in livestock. Spanish governors and the Asunción cabildo relied on mandamiento labor to acquire
cattle to fund the city's needs. For example, in 1675, the cabildo organized a
state-sponsored beneficio to pay down debts associated with militia activities. To provision the beneficio, the city ordered twelve indios from various
reducciones to accompany a Spanish captain to go on an *arreo*, or roundup
of cattle owned by the cabildo.[57] Some of the city's herds were in Guaicurú
territory, making arreos dangerous affairs. In one year, several vaqueros were
killed by Guaicurú during a roundup.[58]

Arreo and other labor contracts moved Guaraní not only between Spanish cities of the upper Río de la Plata and Guaraní pueblos but also between
reducciones of diverse jurisdictions. Around the year 1698, the Franciscan
pueblos of Itapé and Caazapá made a sizeable purchase of four thousand
head of cattle from the Guaraní-Jesuit reducción of Itapúa for the price of
two thousand arrobas of yerba maté. Spanish royal authorities got wind of
the transaction and intervened before the two Franciscan pueblos could
make the payment. The governor explained that contracts of this kind—
those involving yerba maté—had to be cleared with the governor. The governor requested that the corregidores and members of the cabildos from Itapé
and Caazapá travel to Asunción to hear his admonishment. He ultimately
approved the transaction but requested that the yerba maté be taken from
yerbales on their own lands and not from those controlled by Villa Rica. The
governor's orders reveal that at least some non-Jesuit reducciones had their
own yerbales, even when all wild yerbales were ostensibly owned by the
crown. That these pueblos bought cattle with yerba maté indicates their

access to a significant source of wealth, providing them with alternative ways of provisioning themselves.[59]

While male Guaraní tributaries are the focus in official records, women also performed a tremendous amount of labor. At contact, most agricultural work was performed by women, but the gendered division of labor gradually changed as men were incorporated as servants on the conquistadors' and later encomenderos' farmsteads. Spanish law stipulated that all nonnoble male indios between the ages of eighteen and fifty pay tribute. Female indias were ostensibly exempt from tribute in the form of personal service because it provided too many opportunities for interracial sexual relationships.[60] The legal definition of tributaries as male was largely ignored and many women followed their husbands on the mita and served alongside them in agricultural, spinning, and other domestic tasks. Female Guaraní also acquired labor tasks that, according to Spanish officials, were appropriate to their sex, especially cloth production. Spinning cotton and weaving became important tasks for women across all the Guaraní reducciones during the colonial period. Officials and overseers called indias engaged in spinning tasks *hilanderas*. Karen Graubart analyzes the gendered reorganization of labor in the colonial Andes and demonstrates that in pre-Columbian society weaving was performed by both men and women, but under the new colonial order weaving came to be gendered as a female activity.[61] In contrast to Andean societies, weaving was not a high priority for the Tupí-Guaraní at the time of contact and, while they produced cloth, it is unclear if it was strictly gendered as female work.[62] But for Spanish governors who recognized the absolute necessity of female labor within the legal framework of the encomienda, which defined tributaries as male only, spinning was an ideal form of female indigenous labor because women would not be required to travel to perform their labor. So Spanish officials and encomenderos put women in the reducciones to work spinning cotton. To governors' chagrin, encomenderos' wives often oversaw the work of the hilanderas and managed the manufacturing of cloth in the reducciones closest to Asunción. Governor Velasco explained that the "encomenderos' women go to their encomienda pueblo, causing great damage to the *naturales* and especially to the Indian women, making them spin cotton every day. And when they return to their homes they attempt to take Native girls (*chinas*) with them as servants."[63] That encomenderos' wives provided oversight for this work, not a hired mayor-domo, reflects encomenderos' lack of resources to hire mayordomos, as well as being a testament to their linguistic abilities. In later periods, spinning also occurred among the yanacona in Asunción, only on a much smaller scale than in the reducciones.[64] There were no large textile *obrajes*, or work-shops, in Asunción. This decentralized hilandera system is a result of the small size of the encomiendas and the lack of financial capital in Asunción.[65]

All of these economic activities inevitably led to abuses and, when given the chance, male and female Guaraní tributaries sought redress. The most common complaints regarding labor included unlawful periods of mita ser-vice, failure to pay mitayos the required amount of cloth each year, not pro-viding mitayos with sufficient days off to cultivate their own fields, and physical abuse. In 1618, Oidor Alfaro established regulations for mita service when he stipulated that no more than one-quarter of the male tributary population of each pueblo was allowed to serve on the mita at the same time and that the period of service was limited to sixty days. This was the ideal, but the reality was that encomenderos often stretched or divided up this time to serve their own particular needs. In Yaguarón, the encomendera doña Beatriz de León y Peralta had four mitayos who served on her farmstead for thirty days before returning to their pueblo for two months, at which point they returned again to their encomendera. If this occurred yearly, then doña León y Peralta's mitayos would have been on her estate for a total of four months out of the year.[66] Some encomenderos with small cacicazgos required that their mitayos serve one at a time for two months' time, at which point another single tributary replaced the former. In this way, the encomendero always had at least one tributary on his or her estate.[67] These customized mita service periods were common and reflected encomenderos' specific needs. Poorer encomenderos with small encomienda units preferred to keep at least one personal servant on their estates, while encomenderos with larger ranches or farms required larger groups of laborers to perform agricultural or ranching activities for shorter periods of time.

Many Guaraní suffered severe abuse during mita service. Working in close proximity to their encomendero family and their neighbors, Guaraní experienced whippings, beatings, and other physical abuses. One Guaraní from Itatín told a royal inspector in 1653 that his encomendero kept the mita group for months over the limit and that his encomendero had tied him up so that he would not leave—the encomendero was fined and lost his encomienda.[68] Other Guaraní complained that their encomendero did not provide for their physical needs. One encomendera had no garden plot for her mitayos and forced them to sleep in a hut that did not provide adequate shelter. In Tobatí, several Guaraní complained that Captain Juan del Valle, the alguacil mayor, physically abused them. One said that after mistakenly pulling up immature mandioca (cassava) roots his encomendero tied him up and beat him with a stick. Another mitayo said that after he returned with firewood del Valle beat him because the load was too small. Other Guaraní from the pueblo claimed that del Valle forcefully kept two mitayos permanently on his farmstead.[69]

Guaraní tributaries were frequently away from their communities performing contract labor, cattle roundups, mita service, yerba maté beneficios, and transport activities. Of all these activities, the yerba maté transport industry was one of the most disruptive to Guaraní communities. The route could take indios from their home pueblos to Asunción, where transport gangs assembled. From Asunción, they might travel to Mbaracayú and back again. Other gangs would take the second leg of the journey and travel from Asunción south to Santa Fe, Corrientes, or Buenos Aires. This labor often took Guaraní away from their pueblos for a minimum of six months. After their labor was done, some chose not to return home.[70] The labor demands on Guaraní contributed to a high degree of flight. But violence and exploitation do not go far enough in explaining why Guaraní moved from reducción to Asunción or beyond, for there were many push-and-pull factors and these could be entangled with cuñadasgo.

Fixed and Unfixed Populations

A primary purpose of the reducciones was to fix indigenous communities in one place where they could realize a Spanish-Catholic form of civilization. It is ironic, then, that the reducción-encomienda system in Paraguay returned Guaraní to a kind of colonial semisedentary existence. Many Guaraní lived for around ten months of the year in their pueblos, while another two months were spent in Asunción with their encomenderos, thus creating two locales

at which they realized their lives. The reducción required Guaraní sedentariness, but colonial demands asserted a new kind of semisedentariness. Until
recently, historians have viewed migration as a last-ditch effort of subjugated
peoples to escape from colonial pressures. But as Karen Vieira Powers asserts
for Andean peoples in the Quito region, flight or migration were acts of
assertion in the face of colonial governments that strove to situate indigenous
peoples in one locale.[71] In the case of the non-Jesuit reducciones in the seventeenth century, cuñadasgo informed individuals' decisions to leave their
pueblos. But before analyzing individual accounts of migration, a numerical
portrait of absenteeism is necessary.

Given the lack of systematic absentee categories in the censuses, it is difficult to tabulate absentee destinations. Even so, the data allows for some
generalizations. Guaraní tended to leave their pueblos to seek a new life in
the following three destinations: Asunción and its surrounding farmsteads;
Santa Fe, Corrientes, or other cities río abajo; and other reducciones. A big
picture of absenteeism in the reducciones and pueblos can be partially distilled from a 1674 report drawn up by the notary and secretary Alonso
Fernández Ruano, who tallied basic demographic figures from seventeen
Guaraní reducciones, including the Jesuit reducción of San Ignacio Guazú.
The total tributary count was 2,780, and out of these 187, or 7 percent, were
absentees. But this figure is not altogether accurate as it does not include
Guaraní away from the pueblo serving on the mita.[72] Examining the reducción of Yuty, a Franciscan pueblo on the Tebicuary River in the Paraná district, the Ruano report indicates there were 32 absentees, or 6.4 percent of the
total tributary population. But when compared with an individual census, it
appears that Ruano either underreported or did not have access to more
realistic absentee figures. Just three years before the Ruano report, in 1671,
the governor recorded extremely high absentee figures in Yuty. Out of 581
tributaries, 58 (10 percent) were absent on the mita and 174 (30 percent) were
absent in Paraguay or río abajo. This latter group included individuals who
should have been in the pueblo but were not.[73] Combining these two figures,
39.9 percent of all male tributaries were absent from the pueblo at the time of
the census.[74] A more universal portrait of absenteeism culled from individual censuses demonstrates that, on average, most reducciones were missing
19.1 percent of their tributary population (see Table 4).

TABLE 4. Absentees in Select *Reducciones*, Various Years

YEAR	*REDUCCIÓN*	MALE TRIBUTARIES	ABSENTEES	PERCENTAGE OF TRIBUTARIES ABSENTEE	TOTAL POPULATION
1614	Atyra	280	16	5.4	839
1657	San Ignacio	267	1	0.3	1,344
1669	Arecayá	125	7	5.3	482
1671	Yuty	349	232	39.9	1,649
1672	Atira	121	9	6.9	584
1673	Arecayá	120	25	17.2	445
1673	Caasapá	486	42	7.9	1,820
1673	Ita	434	55	11.2	1,999
1673	Yaguaron	262	37	12.3	1,309
1673	Ypane	356	12	3.2	1,292
1687	Caasapá	376	116	23.5	1,419
1688	Altos	212	59	21.7	932
1694	Altos	244	71	22.5	1,111
1694	San Blas	67	27	28.7	293s
1694	Yaguaron	250	111	30.7	1,254
1694	Ypane	110	33	23	431
1699	Yuty	284	57	16.7	1,252
1714	Guarambaré	58	23	28.3	234
1714	Yaguaron	225	69	23.4	1,127
1714	Yuty	239	247	50.8	1,560
1724	Altos	134	37	21.6	583

Sources: Visita, Atyra, 1614, vol. 160, NE, ANA; Visita, San Ignacio, 1657, IX, 18-7-7, AGN; Visita, Arecaya, 1669, vol. 160, NE, ANA; Visita, Yuty, 1671, vol. 160, NE, ANA; Visita, Atira, 1672, vol. 212, no. 7, NE, ANA; Visita, Yaguarón, 1673, vol. 28, no. 5, NE, ANA; Visita, Ita, 1673, vol. 185, NE, ANA; Visita, Ypane, 1673, vol. 212, no. 8, NE, ANA; Visita, Caasapá, 1673, vol. 354, NE, ANA; Visita, Altos, 1688, vol. 185, NE, ANA; Visita, Caasapa, 1687, vol. 354, NE, ANA; Visita, San Blas, 1694, vol. 39, no. 1, NE, ANA; Visita, Yaguarón, 1694, vol. 212, no. 1, NE, ANA; Visita, Ypane, 1694, vol. 212, no. 2, NE, ANA; Visita, Arecayá and Altos, 1673, vol. 177, NE, ANA; Visita, Yuty, 1699, vol. 209, no. 1, NE, ANA; Visita, Yaguarón, 1714, vol. 350, no. 1, NE, ANA; Visita, Guarambaré, 1714, vol. 350, no. 2, NE, ANA; Visita, Yuty, 1714, vol. 350, no. 3, NE, ANA; and Visita, Altos, 1724, vol. 28, no. 4, NE, ANA.

Note: When available, I combined *ausente en mita* with *huido* or the more general *ausente* categories.

The high degree of absenteeism challenges the notion of a reducción as a fixed community. Moreover, the fact that so many indios fled reducciones to locations a great distance from Asunción throws doubt on the idea that proximity to Asunción and españoles caused greater community disintegration.[75] The numbers from Yuty—the Franciscan pueblo farthest from Asunción—contradict this paradigm. What explains a pueblo's absenteeism is the degree of social connections through cuñadasgo and the integration of the community in the regional economy. Yuty had one of the highest numbers of tributaries of all the reducciones and was therefore enmeshed in a variety of economic activities. Officials in Asunción correctly viewed high rates of absenteeism as a severe threat to the colonial system, and some officials took action to remedy the situation. On February 23, 1697, the alcalde de la hermandad (justice over rural areas around Asunción) observed that there were many young "Indians" living in Spaniards' homes when they should have been living in their pueblo, Itá. He recorded the names of over two dozen young male and female absentee Guaraní who resided in Spanish homes and noted that all of these Natives were eventually returned to their pueblos.[76] Evidence for these kinds of door-to-door relocations are rare and, given the effort and resources required to conduct them, it seems unlikely that they were a regular occurrence.

Guaraní men migrated more frequently than women, and this slowly drained the reducciones of men. In 1694, two Franciscans lamented the state of the reducciones, noting that a population tally from seven reducciones showed that there were nearly 2,000 women and only 196 men. They explained that 800 men had been called to work on a mandamiento and another 1,000 had fled to other provinces.[77] The gender imbalance in the encomienda reducciones surely contributed to lower birth rates when compared to the robust rates in the nonencomienda Jesuit missions.[78] Juan Carlos Garavaglia refers to the flow of mitayos to Asunción and the draining of the pueblos of its populations as the "yanaconization of the mitayo" or the transformation of reducción indios into indios residing permanently on Spanish estates. In 1652, out of a total of 14,360 tributaries, 3,381 (24 percent) were yanaconas. While the total number of tributaries had declined to 11,254 by 1682, the percentage of yanaconas remained nearly the same.[79] Garavaglia characterizes the yanaconization of the mitayo as generally coercive and driven by the colonial economy.[80] This conclusion is not completely off the mark, but it lacks an examination of the social networks that facilitated migration. As noted above, Guaraní corregidores joined encomenderos in exploiting Guaraní labor, which inspired some Guaraní to abandon their reducción for permanent residence with their encomenderos. A prime example is the 1654 case (reviewed above) of three Guaraní from Altos who disputed their corregidor's claim on them and opted to live with their encomendera, doña Mariana Resquín. The indio Domingo explained to a Spanish official that his encomendera treated him and his family "like kings" and that his situation with her was much better than it had been in the pueblo. Domingo also noted that he chose "for his *pueblo* the chacra of doña María, his encomendera." Echoing his kin, Pedro Quattí requested that the magistrate accept doña María's chacra "as his *pueblo and reducción*."[81] Domingo understood that his fate rested on articulating why it was better for him to remain with doña María than return to his reducción. He made his argument by drawing a connection between his encomendero's farmstead and a reducción. The colonial logic of indio conversion required a town, a place of belonging, where one could be part of Christian society, and Domingo suggested that his encomendera's estate was just such a place. In other words, the encomienda was the reducción. In the following chapter, I will elaborate on the many ways that relatedness informed the movement of individuals back and forth between reducciones and Spanish households, but as Domingo's statements suggest, cuñadasgo was one of many factors informing decisions to relocate.

Reducción populations were in motion not only in terms of out-migration but also in terms of immigration. Monteses frequently joined reducciones and a few pueblo populations were the recipients of refugees fleeing Guaicurú or bandeirante attacks, while others fled encomenderos. After the 1628–1632 slave raids in Guairá, refugees sought to build new lives in the easternmost reducciones. Caazapá, for example, had a whole group of individuals who did not pertain to an encomendero and were therefore classified as *forasteros*, or groups who could not claim a natal pueblo or encomendero. This group mainly consisted of Guaraní who inhabited pueblos subject to Villa Rica encomenderos but who were forced to flee their original pueblos.[82] Several Guaraní witnesses explained that after the attacks they had fled to Paraguay, where they were claimed by or assigned to vecinos as yanaconas. But some disliked their situation in Asunción and migrated to various pueblos before landing in Caazapá. A Guaraní named Juan provided a brief narrative of his experience of migration during a visita. Juan's parents were from a pueblo named Nautinguy, which had been abandoned before the bandeirante raids. His parents went to a Jesuit reducción but were then forced back to Villa Rica because of the raids. From Villa Rica, Juan and his parents fled to Mbara-cayú, then Tobatí. In Tobatí, Juan said his parents had heard good things about Altos and so they relocated, remaining in Altos for five years. Juan said he and his parents had been treated well in Altos and had never been assigned to an encomendero. At some point, Juan made his way to Caazapá, where he was finally assigned an encomendero.[83] Juan's mediated narrative is sparse and leaves much untold about what made one pueblo better than another. We can assume that the indigenous reducción leadership and the prospects of serving an encomendero were major factors. The picture that emerges is one in which Guaraní frequently picked up and relocated, blending into the general context of mobility, until they found a suitable location with fewer restrictions on their freedoms and demands on their labor.

Besides refugees and intrapueblo migrants, the reducciones were also sites of immigration for unassociated groups, or monteses. In 1688, Guaraní from Yaguarón who were on the yerba maté beneficio in Mbaracayú told a Spanish official that they had encountered monteses while hunting in the forest. The Guaraní came upon a small band of twenty-one Natives who spoke Guaraní and explained that they wanted to become Christians and join Christian society. The group was mostly composed of widows, small children, and several older couples. A few in this group had Christian names, suggesting that they had at one point been baptized.[84] The governor decided to assign the group to Caazapá, supposedly because it was the closest to yerbales, ostensibly their original homeland. This kind of encounter was not uncommon. For example, the Jesuit reducciones of Corpus and Jesus accepted Guayaná Indians, a Gê-speaking group.[85] This in-migration of both Guaraní-speaking and non-Guaraní-speaking peoples had important cultural implications. The presence of "gentile" groups in the reducciones makes us consider the influence they had on community culture. At the same time, we can also assume that the minority groups would have adopted some of the habits and practices of the reducción population. The ethnogenic process of becoming "Guaraní" involved a variety of ethnic groups with distinct timelines and relationships to the colonial reducción.[86]

The encomienda reducción populations were subject to a variety of variables that moved people between and out of reducciones: market forces, coerced labor, raids, and abusive administrators, priests, or encomenderos all contributed to patterns of forced, free, and coerced migration. The reducciones and encomenderos' farmsteads provided choices for Guaraní residence. These forces were specific to the reducciones in the orbit of Asunción even if they did share a number of factors with Jesuit missions of the Tapé, including incorporation of unconverted groups. But one of the most important distinctions between encomienda reducciones and nonencomienda reducciones was the presence of españoles in social life.

Españoles in the Pueblos

Españoles were familiar with Indian towns, especially the non-Jesuit reducciones. (The Jesuits maintained much stronger restrictions on Spanish access to the reducciones, even those who paid tribute to encomenderos.)[87] Reducciones saw españoles come and go: from encomenderos' wives checking in on cotton production, to encomenderos accompanying the governor during his visitas, to officials like the protector de indios who frequented the pueblos to conduct business and carry out their duties. But Spanish dealings with the reducciones were not all business. Some Spaniards visited indio communities because they had lovers or friends there. This level of engagement in the reducciones challenges our definition of *reducción* as a space closed off from Spanish social and biological influence. While the reducciones subject to the encomienda in Paraguay were ostensibly protected from Spanish influence, the ties of cuñadasgo, the cultural trajectory of Spaniards and Guaraní, and the impact of the regional economy made them much more interconnected.[88]

Spaniards were permanent fixtures in the reducciones. Nearly every non-Jesuit reducción had a *poblero*, or español who lived permanently in or near the reducción and was charged with protecting encomenderos' interests.[89] Juan Carlos Garavaglia notes that pobleros were the "eyes and ears of the encomendero."[90] It is not clear when pobleros became regulars in the reducciones or exactly what roles they performed. It is likely that the social position of pobleros grew out of the role played by lenguas during the first generation after contact. These were often mestizos and castaways with deep indigenous cultural experience. In the period between 1556 and the 1580s, Spaniards began acquiring the Guaraní language and the role of the lengua was dispersed broadly in society. The emergence of the term *poblero* in place of *lengua* signaled a shift from the context of conquest where a social figure who derived his authority through his cultural capital in the indigenous sphere to a more official representative. If, as Dorothy Tuer argues, the lenguas inhabited an ambivalent political position between the Spanish and Carío worlds, the poblero was more firmly a representative of colonial, especially encomendero, interests.[91]

Royal officials and priests were concerned that pobleros would have a negative impact on Guaraní communities. Governor Ramírez de Velasco, in his 1597 ordenanzas, is one of the first officials to mention the pobleros, and his rules regulating them speak to a perception of them as delinquent and sexually mischievous. Reasoning that the quickest fix to this problem was related to sexual life, Velasco ordered that henceforth all pobleros be married and that their families live with them near the pueblos. Pobleros were also accused of physically abusing Guaraní, extracting personal servants for encomendero patrons and maintaining illicit relationships with Guaraní women.[92] Despite officials' harsh opinions of pobleros, they were never removed from the reducciones, and it appears that at least one poblero (along with his family) was present in most non-Jesuit reducciones. From officials' perspectives, they were a necessary evil who played an important role in surveilling the reducciones. In 1603, Governor Saavedra charged pobleros to monitor Guaraní behavior in the reducciones, specifically asking them to prohibit *borracheras*, or communal drinking.[93] In a 1608 litigation proceeding for which the poblero served as interpreter, his wife and daughter testified about a crime they witnessed at Yaguarón.[94] This family lived on a ranch within the pueblo territory and freely moved in and out of the village complex.[95] While the poblero was a controversial figure in the early years of the reducciones, his infamy waned as reducción communities and nonindio settlements became more familiar to each other.

Officials' concerns that pobleros' proximity to Indian communities would foster interracial unions also extended to the broader male español population.

In March 1608, a Spanish encomendero named Bartolomé de Miño (age twenty-five) and his companion, a cobbler named Pedro Tamayo (age twenty-eight), were imprisoned for having arranged a sexual liaison with two married Guaraní women in Yaguarón.[96] The accusations that landed the two in jail were made by the governor himself, who further accused the pair of desertion during a military expedition in Santa Fe, where Spanish troops had congregated to launch an attack on indios enemigos in the Chaco. For his part, Miño explained that the expedition had already dispersed when he arrived in Santa Fe. On his return to Asunción, Miño met up with Tamayo in Yaguarón, where they arranged a rendezvous with two Guaraní women, Elvira and Estefanía, who were respectively in their late teens and early twenties. There is nothing in Elvira's and Estafanía's statements that would indicate that Miño and Tamayo abused them. In fact, Estefanía explained that she had wanted to accompany Miño back to Asunción, but he had encouraged her to remain in Yaguarón. Because Elvira and Estefanía required translators and Miño and Tamayo did not, we can assume that the latter were bilingual. When the magistrate asked Miño why he had been in Yaguarón, he responded that he was looking for one of his yanacona and a yanacona belonging to another encomendero, by the name of Alonso Pérez. This speaks to the intimate knowledge that Spanish encomenderos possessed of their encomienda units through networks of cuñadasgo and regular visits to the pueblos.

The case of Miño and Tamayo shows that españoles' social networks of friendships, lovers, and enemies went far outside of Spanish centers to include Indian communities. Besides entering reducciones to secure or return tributaries, the Indian community was part of a broader network of relationships. Ultimately, the governor punished Miño for abandoning the military expedition in Santa Fe and sentenced him to six months of military service in one of the region's frontier forts. Tamayo was sentenced to two months of military service, two pesos, and all the court costs, and the magistrate ordered them both to never again enter an indigenous pueblo.

Conclusion

In his study of the Yucatec Maya, William Hanks provides a key to analyzing Natives in missions through his etymological reading of *reducción* (noun) and *reducir* (verb). Drawing on Covarrubias's 1611 dictionary, the words did not mean "to reduce" but "to convince, persuade, or to order." Hanks identifies three colonial goals associated with reducciones and the goal to "reducir" indios: congregate Indians in settled communities, change dispositions and conduct, and make the indigenous language intelligible and translatable for evangelical purposes.[97] This process was deemed necessary to "convert" Indians, but "conversion" in the communal sense of the term, not the individualistic or personalistic aspects of religiosity that interest observers of the modern age. "We tend to think of conversion," Hanks explains, "in terms of a charismatic change in an individual's religious beliefs. In the colonial context, however, the concept is primarily collective, not individual; we are talking about the social and cultural conversion of entire ethnic groups as part of colonial domination."[98] In secular, Franciscan, or Jesuit reducciones, Guaraní experienced this program of colonial domination. From the loss of polygyny and anthropophagy to the accrual of modified cosmologies and languages, Guaraní were transformed in the reducciones. Reducción served as a metonymy for a civilized existence under colonial rule. But for some Guaraní, daily life in their physical reducciones was unbearable, and so they chose for their reducción households of españoles.

Indigenous leaders were crucial contributors to the reducción project, actively encouraging and coercing Guaraní to adhere to religious and labor demands. As "children" of the priests, raised with special educations and possessing rare bilingualism among indios, corregidores inhabited an awkward position in their communities. Their unusual cultural upbringing, strong adherence to the goals of reducción, or perhaps their avarice, earned them enemies within their own communities. Corregidores' special status and role points to the multiple layers of conversion and transformation among the Guaraní, one that was an aberration from the rest of the community.

The reducciones have commonly been described as sanctuaries from the coercive and abusive behaviors of españoles, but little attention has been given to the push factors, especially abusive corregidores. The notion that proximity to Asunción determined the degree of disintegration a reducción experienced does not hold up in light of the data on absentees. The missions could be fluid demographic spaces for a variety of reasons, including proximity to other pueblos, human networks connecting communities in Asunción and pueblos, and abusive encomenderos, as well as the allure of a better life as a small farmer or wage laborer. Social networks were important factors in shaping out-migration. Mitayos spent a considerable amount of time on their encomenderos' farmsteads where they rubbed shoulders with yanacona Guaraní. These associations inevitably led to attachments, and many couples chose to remain in Asunción. One of the surprising aspects of absenteeism in the reducciones is that some Guaraní left to live with encomenderos not because the encomendero coerced them but because they felt they could have a better life with their encomendero. The next chapter elaborates on the interethnic networks in Asunción that made these kinds of attitudes possible.

CHAPTER 7

The Other *Reducción*

Asunción's Indios

THE GRANDEUR OR humility of Spanish colonial cities reflected their status in the imperial system, economic importance, and social structure. The grand cathedrals, monasteries, convents, government buildings, plazas, and homes of cities like Lima, Cuzco, and Mexico City communicated political and economic power.[1] But what did the peripheral and humble cities of Spanish realm communicate besides their marginality? When the wealth and power of a city's citizens and institutions were insufficient to raise lofty bell towers or replace dusty roads with cobblestone, can peripheral cities tell us more than their inability to tame their surroundings with markers of policía? Recently, ethnohistorians have shined a light on cities as indigenous spaces, revealing Natives' impacts on urban layout, social structure, and architecture. This chapter examines Asunción as a physical and social space continually shaped by Guaraní, other Natives, and paradigms applied to indios.[2] In a 1668 dispute (reviewed in the previous chapter), a Guaraní man described his encomendera's farmstead as his chosen reducción. The dispute involved a family of Guaraní who had fled an abusive corregidor to reside permanently as originarios with their encomendera. The Guaraní father and son each explained separately to the Spanish official that they wished to remain on the chacra of their encomendera, adding that they claimed their encomendera's farmstead as their "reducción, pueblo, and origin."[3] These three categories communicated fixity, stability, and socioreligious space where Christian policía could be realized. By defining their encomendera's farmstead as their reducción, these Guaraní displayed legal and political savviness. They were aware of how much stock colonial officials put in the reducciones as civilizing and evangelizing institutions, and by associating the reducción with their encomendera's home, they legitimated their illegal relocation outside of their assigned pueblo. More-over, crown law provided indios with the right to claim as their reducción a locale outside their original reducción.[4] Seen in this way, Asunción and the many farmsteads under its jurisdiction were different kinds of reducción in the region—a community that hosted significant indio populations and pretended to reform them according to colonial ideals.

Many indios claimed Asunción as a home. In 1609, Asunción was report-edly home to two hundred vecinos and six thousand "indios de paz."[5] In 1652, the number of yanaconas was 3,381, or 23 percent of the total encomen-dado population in Paraguay.[6] Analyzing Asunción as a site of Indian com-munity and identity provides a new vista onto Guaraní and indigenous experiences in Paraguay. This framing contrasts with many histories of Guaraní in Paraguay, which have tended to see Asunción solely as a site of Guaraní cultural loss, accommodation, and hispanization.[7] These changes have often been indexed through the evidence of mestizaje or biological mixing, with the assumption that mestizaje always resulted in hispaniza-tion. As a static cultural model, this framing does not recognize that what it meant to be Spanish or Guaraní was in constant flux. What did it mean, for example, for an individual to be hispanized when what was español was being guaranized? Biological mixing did not determine culture. Dana Velasco Murillo elaborates on the theme of mestizaje in her study of urban Indians in the mining town of Zacatecas:

> Indigeneity, or the construction and definition of indigenous identi-ties, involves myriad factors, of which biology constitutes one among other important cultural attributes. . . . Because of their small numbers and close ties to other ethnic communities, mestizos did not develop a complex common cultural identity. . . . Rather, their evolution as an identifiable colonial group was born of colonial legalese or scripted racial categories, often reflecting an administrative system that needed to clas-sify individuals in order to determine their privileges. . . . But in practice, mestizos developed a cultural identity in relation to other cohesive eth-nic groups, such as Indians, Spaniards, or African and Afro-descended peoples.[8]

Asunción, as a space of intense mixture, is the perfect place to analyze what mestizaje meant as it related to indigenous and Spanish culture. Paradoxically, what tended to define an indio in Asunción was an individual's dependence on and fealty to a Spanish encomendero, while someone defined as mestizo-español was perceived as distant from an encomendero or tribute. These categories came into use in specific legal contexts and do not represent ethnic identification. As Joanne Rappaport frames the issue, "the central question . . . is not 'Who is a mestizo?' or 'What is a mestizo?' but '*When* and how is someone a mestizo?'"[9] The city context provides an opportunity to observe scribal moments when an individual's legal status was suspect or in dispute, somewhere between español, negro, and indio. This categorical fluidity was brought about because of physical mobility, as indios entered or exited the city and moved in between jurisdictions like encomiendas and convents. Some scholars explain indigenous migration to cities as an attempt to shed indio identity and therefore the onerous demands of tribute and racial prejudice. Donning Spanish clothing, acquiring the Spanish language, and participating in noncommunal wage labor in the Spanish free market was a kind of "tragedy of success."[10] Asunción provides a counterpoint to this paradigm. One of the reasons that Guaraní found Asunción and the encomiendas viable communities was because Spanish society was undergoing a process of guaranization at the same time that Guaraní were experiencing guaranization. The sociocultural changes were different for Spaniards than they were for Natives, but the spaces where they overlapped created room for mutual understanding or the creation of community. By bringing guaranization to Asunción, Guaraní made the urban space of Asunción a sociocultural home.

Rural-Urban and City-Pueblo Connections

Like many other peripheral cities on frontiers, Asunción was deeply connected to its rural hinterland. Farmsteads considered part of the city radiated out from the heart of the city at the cabildo and governor's mansion. The earliest reliable pictorial representation of Asunción was made in 1786 by the Spanish bureaucrat and naturalist Félix de Azara.[11] The map (see Figure 8) shows Asunción cut through by deep ravines or rivulets that could only be crossed on bridges. Contemporaneous written records confirm Azara's general layout and reveal a topographical texture. One eighteenth-century traveler to Asunción noted that buildings and complexes of houses were separated by ravines; some of these required that a person ascend a ladder or steep bridge to reach them, while others were accessed by descending a ramp.[12] Late sixteenth- and seventeenth-century records confirm that erosion isolated some of the city's main blocks from one another and required bridges and ladders to allow communication within the city. A late seventeenth-century document reveals that the Jesuit college and monastery inhabited a plot of land that seemed to have been cut off from the rest of the city except for two bridges, one that led to the Dominican monastery facing the river and another on the opposite side of the complex.[13] Azara's *plano* further shows that like many other Spanish American cities Asunción was not established along a grid with a central plaza exhibiting the city's most prominent institutions and social actors.[14] Garavaglia likened Asunción to a large hacienda peppered with houses.[15] The city lacked contiguous urban structures connected by streets and thoroughfares. Besides the canals and rivulets, the buildings and dirt streets of the city were separated by masses of vegetation—trees, bushes, and grasses—which officials struggled to keep trimmed.[16]

An interesting aspect of Asunción's rural urbanism is that the city did not possess a central market where people gathered to buy and sell goods. It was only in 1779, with the establishment of the royal tobacco monopoly and the introduction of silver coinage, that a central marketplace of any significance emerged in the city.[17] Most vecinos of the city were relatively poor and sustained themselves through their own agricultural production or through barter with neighbors.[18] Locals who engaged in commerce traded directly with each other, and if items were of significant value they called upon a notary. Many vecinos who produced commodities for consumption outside of Asunción deposited them in a publicly owned warehouse where an agent exchanged them for other goods with traders from Corrientes, Santa Fe, and beyond.[19] It is unclear if this was a true estanco system or if it was privately operated, but it makes sense in a place where traders arrived via the river at unexpected intervals. The city combined urban and rural lifestyles into one. Azara's plano, shows a patchwork of chacras and farmsteads broken up by a smattering of institutional buildings, including churches and monasteries.

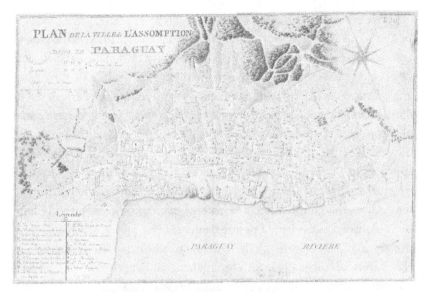

FIGURE 8. French copy of Félix de Azara's map of Asunción, ca. 1786. "Plan de la ville de l'Assomption dans le Paraguay," anonymous, ca. 1800. Source: Bibliothèque nationale de France, GED-3735.

Litigation records rarely refer to streets but rather to individuals' chacras or the camino real, the main road leading out of the city. The officials did not speak of Asunción and its "seven leagues" like Quito; however, the city did have its hinterlands. Places like Valle de Pirayú, Valle de Tapúa, and Valle del Salado hosted clumps of farms or ranches outside the main cluster of households of Asunción. These *valles* were policed by a sheriff charged with patrolling rural territories called an alcalde de la hermandad.[20] Asunción challenges definitions of urbanism. According to Jay Kinsbruner, cities possess the following characteristics: people in residence all or most of the year, few residents produce all or even most of their own food, and differentiated labor patterns and social classes.[21] Cities also have a range of crafts, specialized economies, schools, religious institutions, professionals of various types, and bureaucrats.[22] Asunción possessed nearly all of these characteristics. It falters insofar as Asunceños produced most of their own food on their chacras. In this way, Asunción can be considered a rural-urban space.

Before examining the indios of Asunción it is first necessary to understand the Spaniards who claimed them as encomendados. Spanish encomenderos in Asunción combined urban living with rurality by remaining as close as they could to the city center while maintaining a hacienda-style household, with pastures, farms, indigenous tributaries, and sometimes African slaves. Those encomenderos who were permanent residents of Asunción were generally poor. By 1622, there were around four hundred vecinos in Asunción and at least half of these were encomenderos.[23] In 1674, there were nearly 190 encomenderos in the Asunción area, and more than half of these possessed an encomienda that had been granted for two lives (i.e., heritable for two generations). Given their limited access to material markers of status such as sumptuous clothing, encomienda personal servants and black slaves served as primary signifiers of status.[24] There were, nonetheless, a few encomenderos who possessed unusually large encomiendas and engaged in the regional trade (and later in the yerba maté trade). These encomenderos were able to acquire enough wealth to mark themselves as elite. For much of the year, however, these encomenderos lived in Santa Fe or Buenos Aires; therefore, their social presence in Asunción was less pronounced.[25] Table 5 provides a snapshot from 1674 of the distribution of encomiendas based on size. The majority of encomenderos in Paraguay possessed fewer than ten tributaries. By comparison, the average encomienda in the Yucatán in the first half of the eighteenth century was 364 tributaries and the average encomienda in mid-seventeenth century Venezuela was 21 tributaries.[26] Encomenderos' poverty could reach such heights that they were forced to refuse labor from mitayos. During a visita at Tobatí pueblo in 1652, the indios of Captain Martín Suares's encomienda explained that their encomendero had to return their single tributary to the pueblo because there was not enough food in his chacra to feed an extra mouth.[27] The relative poverty of the region worked to reduce social distinctions between poor mestizos, indios, and elite españoles.[28] Guaraní and most of their encomenderos shared many experiences, among them wearing cloth made by the same hilanderas, eating the same cassava, speaking to each other in Guaraní, and sleeping in hammocks. Vecinos' last wills and testaments reveal that most possessed small wardrobes and modest estates. To declare only a few arrobas of yerba maté, a piece of land, a few weapons, one or two sets of clothing, and perhaps a slave was the norm.

TABLE 5. Number of Tributaries per Encomienda, 1674

NUMBER OF TRIBUTARIES	NUMBER OF ENCOMIENDAS
1–10	147
11–20	49
21–30	30
31–40	11
41–50	6
51–60	4
61–70	4
71–80	1
81–90	1
91–100	2
>100	1

Source: Mora Mérida, *Historia social de Paraguay,* 197.

The physical layout of Asunción was a result of ecology, economy, and cuñadasgo. Heavy rains and a lack of resources combined to create an urban space that was constantly eroding. Instead of building new canals and ravines, officials simply built bridges and ladders. These factors created an urban layout that was atomized, with institutions and farms being separated by ravines and gullies. But these ecological factors do not explain why so many españoles of status (encomenderos) lived on farmhouses and not two-story residences next to the Jesuit college, alongside the governor's mansion, or across the way from the cathedral. Because Guaraní provided only their personal service, most Spanish family units developed as relatively poor farmsteads. Individual units with plots of land proliferated, thereby moving citizens outside the main city center and into the sprawling rural-urban hinterland where yanaconas worked chacras for their encomenderos and their families. Since the vast majority of encomiendas were kept at less than ten, few encomenderos could accumulate enough wealth to build a second home in the center of the city. Thus, cuñadasgo played a major role in the rural-urban layout of Asunción. With the physical geography of Asunción in mind, it is now possible to imagine the social networks between the indigenous populations.

Some of the most important social networks in Asunción were those between residents of the city and the reducciones.[29] Asunción saw a continuous flow of migrants in and out of the city and its surrounding farmsteads. As chapter 6 demonstrates, a major portion of migration occurred from reducción to city. For example, in 1651, 12 percent of all yanaconas were born in a reducción. Many of these had been serving on the mita when their encomenderos forced them to remain in Asunción indefinitely or they chose to remain because of a marriage or other social ties.[30] The frequency of movement between reducciones and Asunción was a result of strong social networks. In an early example from 1545, a Guaraní villager who resided not far from Asunción came to the city to collect his sister, who had been serving a conquistador, and return with her to their village so she could participate in community mourning for a dead relative.[31] These kinship connections continued after the reducciones were created. A 1608 criminal investigation revealed that a yanacona from Asunción named Alonso frequented his natal pueblo of Yaguarón, where his family and close social network resided. During one of these visits, Alonso shared some drinks with a cacique and other community members. An altercation broke out between the inebriated Alonso and another cacique, named Diego, and the former stabbed the latter, killing him. Alonso and Diego had been close associates (if not friends), for they had served together as rowers on a transport barge that went as far as Buenos Aires. Alonso's social networks were typical of other yanacona who had friends and relatives that spanned Asunción and select reducciones. That Alonso, a yanacona, left his encomendero's estate to attend a social event in Yaguarón speaks to the strength of his connections to his natal pueblo and his freedom of movement.[32]

Communication between pueblo and city was often a result of tribute payment, as mitayos traveled from their reducciones to their encomenderos' farmsteads or other work sites in and around the city. But while most Guaraní carried hoes, shovels, and axes on their journey to Asunción, a minority carried violins, trumpets, and their singing voices. Guaraní musicians, especially from the neighboring Yaguarón pueblo, were frequent visitors to Asunción because of the lack of resident musicians.[33] That Corpus Christi, lent, and other religious celebrations in Asunción were enlivened by the voices and sounds of musicians from neighboring reducciones colors our vision of Asunción life and society. Guaraní men were joined by Guaraní women in sustaining expansive social networks. In 1665, officials investigated the alleged poisoning and potential hexing of a Spanish sacristan (priest's assistant) who claimed that he expelled worms from his body after an india named María served him a soup.[34] María had had frequent contact with the sacristan because of her friendship with his daughter, also named María. Investigators discovered that india María was married to an indio in Los Altos even while she maintained sexual relationships with several españoles. (The fact that María's sexual life came up in relation to accusations of witchcraft is no coincidence, for under the gaze of early modern officials a woman's sexuality was inseparable from her social standing.)[35] María's social networks were diverse and speak to her ability to move in a variety of social circles, including those located in the city and in a nearby reducción.

From Guaraní musicians traveling to the Asunción cathedral, to mitayos serving out a two-month-long tribute service on their encomendero's chacra, to yanaconas visiting family in a nearby reducción, Guaraní were frequently on the move between city and pueblos. This movement of peoples helped to promote Guaraní culture in the city, for it kept alive yanaconas' appreciation for things like communal ceremonies and kinship networks. But Guaraní were not the only Natives in Asunción, for other Native groups speaking distinct languages contributed to the uneven cultural landscape of the city.

A City of *Indios* but Many Nations

Hiding in plain sight, mixed in among Guaraní yanacona populations, were indigenous people who originated from non-Guaraní communities, especially Guaicurú.[36] Unlike some of their Guaraní counterparts, who came to Asunción by way of cuñadasgo and who maintained connections to their natal pueblos, most of these Natives were brought to Asunción through the severest forms of violence and never had the chance to reconnect with their kin.

The conquistadors' expeditions to the Chaco during the first half of the sixteenth centuries resulted in the forced relocation of many indigenous women and children. As the conflicts with Guaicurú groups reemerged in the late sixteenth and early seventeenth centuries, the population of Guaicurú captives in Asunción increased significantly. But the influx of Guaicurú captives was not always a result of Spanish expeditions, for Spaniards often purchased captives from Guaicurú to "redeem" them from what they considered a barbarous servitude. Guaicurú exchanges in slaves with Spaniards ranged from a single slave to several dozen. During perhaps the most intense period of Guaicurú hostility in colonial history, Guaicurú sold fifty-one captives to Spaniards in exchange for material goods.[37] When Guaicurú captives disembarked from canoes on Asunción's shores to be sold, they moved from one institution of servitude to another. In the Guaicurú system of slavery, captives were subordinated but they simultaneously experienced a process of familiarization and were made to become Guaicurú. This process of subordination-familiarization was visibly enacted on the bodies of captives as their Guaicurú captors painted or tattooed their slaves' faces and bodies with elaborate designs that differed from their masters' designs. This body art simultaneously marked them as slave and transitioning Guaicurú.[38] So when captives were purchased by Spaniards they may have borne these body markings, and if they had been tattooed they served as a constant reminder of their former slave status among the "indios fronterizos."

The details and voices of these captives in Asunción were largely suppressed in the documentation; however, a few fragments survived. In 1663, a Guaicurú woman named Marcela appeared before a Spanish magistrate to sue for her freedom and the freedom of her mestizo child. Spaniards had "redeemed [her] from the Guaicurú" as a young child and given her away as a servant to a Spanish couple. After her first Spanish masters died, Marcela joined or was assigned to the households of at least three different españoles for varying periods of time. Over the course of her service to these families, she had at least two sexual partners—one indio and one español—and, from her union with this last partner, Marcela gave birth to a mestizo son. Marcela's situation of being assigned to several different encomenderos seems typical of other yanaconas, but the fact that the category of Guaicurú was applied to her legal identity suggests that she either sought to retain a distinct ethnic identity or that her social peers and/or colonial officials applied it to her.[39]

Records of individual Guaicurú like Marcela are rare, but a more global portrait of the non-Guaraní Indian presence in Asunción is possible thanks to the survival of a padrón of captives made in 1688. The year 1688 was the last of nearly two decades of intense military activity on Paraguay's frontiers, and so the padrón was an attempt to record the unusually large number of captives that were brought into the city, as well as to record those who had been acquired in previous years. These mostly consisted of Guaicurú but also included Tupí and other unnamed groups.[40] Of the Guaicurú, officials counted 173 individuals: 69 adult women, 21 adult men, 41 boys averaging 10 years of age, and 42 girls whose ages were not recorded. The majority of the adult men were brought to Asunción during much earlier expeditions and therefore would have been made captives when they were young boys. Few adult males were taken as captives because Guaicurú martial culture encouraged warriors to die in battle. Of a second group counted (including "indios Tupíes" and "unknown naciónes"), most had been captured during expeditions against bandeirantes. There were 38 individuals: 7 adult women, 14 adult men, 9 boys, and 8 girls. Totaling the two groups together, there were 211 indios of non-Guaraní origin living in Asuncion. Many of the adult captives who had resided in Asunción before 1688 had spouses (some of whom were black slaves) and could recite Catholic prayers. The register does not indicate what language these people used but, given the large number of individuals married to Guaraní yanaconas, many had surely acquired Guaraní.[41]

The fact that these indios were counted in a separate padrón suggests a different legal status than yanaconas, but one that shared many of its characteristics. If Marcela's case is any indication, Spanish soldiers used most captives—Guaicurú, Tupí, or otherwise—as personal servants, but Marcela's claim that she enjoyed "liberty" demonstrates that the legal status of former Guaicurú captives was not always clear cut. Nonetheless, it appears that most captives were incorporated into encomienda units and lived like other yanacona. The presence of Guaicurú, Tupí, or other ethnicities in Asunción contributed to a cultural diversity in Asunción and adds another layer of complexity to an understanding of ethnogenesis in Paraguay.

A Social Portrait of *Yanaconas/Originarios*

By the mid-seventeenth century, the number of yanaconas in Asunción was declining (see Table 5). Because there is no way to calculate vital rates for the yanacona population, it is difficult to explain why the population declined from generation to generation over two centuries. Even so, the documentation points to the social organization of yanaconas, out-migration through flight, the changing status of indios to españoles, disease, and crown policies. Historians have mainly studied originarios from an economic perspective, with a focus on their onerous labor activities.[42] The labor demands on yanacona deserve attention, but equally important is a sense of yanaconas' communities.

Unlike mitayos, who served a Spaniard for a fixed period of time, yanaconas were expected to serve their encomenderos year-round. Not surprisingly, one of the greatest complaints yanaconas had about their encomenderos was not allowing them enough time to cultivate their own fields, celebrate religious festivals, or attend mass. At the same time, originarios were not regularly asked to labor under the state-run mandamiento or the yerba beneficio. Local law dictated that yanaconas serve five days of the week, reserving Saturday for the cultivation of their own fields and Sunday for worship, but most Guaraní reported working for their masters every day. Moreover, according

TABLE 6. *Originario* Population of Asunción, 17th and 18th Centuries

YEAR	1651	1690	1694	1726	1754
TOTAL POPULATION	2,183	1,364	1,476	805	553
NUMBER OF ENCOMIENDAS	167	96	91	66	45
ABSENTEE PERCENTAGE	11	7.8	12.2	14.8	—

Source: Garavaglia, *Mercado interno*, 271. Data for the year 1694 is from the Originario visita, vol. 185, no. 3, NE, ANA.

TABLE 7. *Originario Visita* Data, 1694

	TRIBUTARIES	MARRIED WOMEN	SINGLE WOMEN	CHILDREN	ABSENTEES	RETIRED	DECLARED MESTIZO	MARRIED TO BLACK
TOTAL	401	301	88	616	130	58	28	14
AVERAGE PER ENCOMIENDA	4.4	3.3	.96	6.74	1.4	.63	NA	NA

Source: 1694, vol. 185, no. 3, NE, ANA.

to Alfaro's reforms, encomenderos were obligated to give yanaconas five yards of cloth each year; many reported not receiving a single yard of cloth.[43]

Akin to urban slavery and Indian personal service in other Ibero-American cities, yanaconas in Asunción were sometimes employed in skilled tasks and regulated by the cabildo as official artisans.[44] These included tailors, carpenters, blacksmiths, cart makers, and weavers.[45] For example, three yanaconas of doña Francisca Ricardo's encomienda—named Pedro, Juan, and Mateo— served as official blacksmiths in the city. But most other yanacona labored on their encomenderos' chacras. The gendered divisions of labor seem to have been similar to those in the pueblos: women worked as domestics, labored in the fields, and wove textiles, while men managed fields and livestock. The high labor demands on yanaconas, as well as the frequent opportunities for work in regional trade or yerba maté, contributed to a high rate of absenteeism. The number of male tributaries counted in the 1694 census totaled 531, and 130 (24.4 percent) of these were absentees.[46]

Another contributing factor to yanacona flight were the abuses they experienced at the hands of their encomenderos. The 1651 visita conducted by the audiencia judge, Garabito de León, is an important source for understanding yanacona labor conditions as well as social dynamics within encomiendas (see chapter 2). Garabito de León recorded statements from yanaconas who experienced beatings, illegal renting of their labor, and arranged marriages, among other abuses at the hands of their encomenderos.[47] An indio named Gonzalo of Antonio González Freyre's encomienda reported that his encomendero had treated him badly, verbally abusing him and forcing him to work on festival days. María, of the same encomienda, explained that González Freyre had demanded she spin an amount of cotton too large for one day and berated her for not completing the task. She added that he gave her no cloth to make clothing for herself and her children.

Ironically, alongside testimonies of severe abuses, Garabito de León documented indios' expressions of satisfaction with or even love for their encomenderos. Guaraní and encomenderos invoked ideas of reciprocity, friendship, and love to describe their responsibility toward each other, not taxation or contracts. When Garabito de León conducted interviews with yanaconas, he typically asked them if they were aware that Alfaro's reforms required payment for Indian tribute and put limitations on the number of days for service. During the inspection of Diego de Olibarri's encomienda, the indios responded that they were present during Alfaro's visita, were aware of the law, but preferred to serve year-round (as yanaconas) of their own will (*por su voluntad*). In another unit, two indias identified as mestizas explained that their encomendero and his wife treated them like "they were their daughters."[48] Another india named Sebastiana (also identified as mestiza) explained that she "serves [her encomendero] with good will and in gratitude for having raised her and healed her when she is sick" and therefore she did not think it necessary that he pay her.[49] When the three blacksmith yanaconas discussed above were asked what they did with their earnings, they explained that they supported their families as well as their encomendera, who apparently was very poor. Between the three of them, they had a few children who remained with doña Francisca to care for her. The visitador asked if their encomendera paid them for their children's service, and they responded that when their encomendera had tried to pay they refused. They seemed to have had pity on the woman because of her poverty.[50] Cuñadasgo continued to inform yanaconas' perceptions of their encomenderos by keeping alive the notion of reciprocity and kinship. While some Guaraní spoke of their encomendero as kin, their strongest relationships were with those indios with whom they hoed fields, spun cotton, and shared kitchen hearths. The chacra was a community where individuals shared resources and cooperated in labor tasks. Generally, yanaconas of the same encomienda remained loyal to each other and defended their encomenderos' property.[51]

Labor in Paraguay was understood and framed through paradigms of reciprocity that did not correlate with the payments and quotas prescribed by crown law. Even though the labor that yanaconas performed was onerous and the treatment they received was frequently demeaning, their experiences were further informed by their legal position within the Spanish system of corporate identities.

The *Indio República* in Asunción

Throughout Spanish America, urban indios generated community and shared identity through a variety of institutions. These institutions were a result of indios' own initiatives, as well as the Spanish crown's vision of maintaining two segregated populations of españoles and indios. Spaniards referred to the distinct corporate identities of españoles and indios with the concept of separate republics or sociopolitical spheres: *república de los españoles* and *república de los indios*.[52] The concept of separate republics allowed for indigenous institutions to continue, albeit in modified forms, in colonial spaces and to shape colonial institutions. The concept of separate repúblicas led Spanish officials to try to separate populations in cities and keep españoles out of reducciones. These efforts largely failed, and mixture became normative. Even so, in places like Lima and Mexico City, many indios resided in neighborhoods and worshiped in parishes assigned to their corporate identity. Indios of higher status organized *cofradías* (religious sodalities) to venerate particular saints, organize religious festivals, and elevate members' statuses. Spanish American cities also hosted indigenous cabildos and guilds of indigenous artisans. Some indigenous communities also organized militias, like the Ciudad Vieja community in Guatemala, which represented its illustrious status as a conquistador community in Santiago de Guatemala's Fiesta de Volcán, a celebration of the Spanish victory over local Natives.[53] Throughout the Americas, indios maintained an important institutional and corporate presence in cities.

While the indigenous institutions of Asunción are almost completely absent in the documentary record, evidentiary fragments suggest an outline.

While it is unclear if an indio cabildo existed in Asunción, the city did have indigenous administrators. These were minor officers who served the city's indio populations. During the 1651 visita of Geronimo de Guillermo's encomienda, a yanacona named Sebastián explained that just that year he had become "alcalde de los yndios" and was therefore less frequently in the fields working. He said he spent lots of time in the "house of the lord governor."[54] An alcalde was a justice of the peace, and so we can imagine that Sebastián was involved in disputes or legal matters involving yanaconas or other indios in the city. Sebastián does not say why he was selected to be the alcalde de indios, but it may have been that he was proficient in Spanish, a rarity among yanaconas. Some indios who had originated from the reducciones brought their leadership mantles to Asunción. In a 1608 criminal investigation, indigenous witnesses as well as a Spanish witness identified the defendant, Alonso, a mitayo-turned-yanacona, as a "cacique of Asunción."[55] The fact that caciques were not recorded or counted in the padrones of yanacona populations suggests that officials did not formally recognize caciques in Asunción and that Alonso had brought his office with him as a kind of contraband authority. In the reducciones, the caciques and other officials were crucial for organizing everyday activities and mita service, but in Asunción the presence of the encomendero made the position of cacique obsolete.

Indios in Asunción also participated in ecclesiastical institutions. At an unknown date, officials in Asunción created a parish for the Indians and blacks of the city and selected San Blas (Saint Blaise, a physician) as the patron of the church.[56] Indians gathered at the San Blas parish for worship, festivals, and other events specific to their own república. For example, when officials requested that the indios of the city accept Alfaro's reforms in 1613, the meeting was held in San Blas parish.[57] Priests noted that Guaraní worshiped in their parish in the Guaraní language, not in Spanish.[58] This is an important detail, especially considering that blacks also attended the parish, and speaks to the role that San Blas played in the process of guaranization at work in the city. Associated with the Indian parish was a cofradía. In the year 1688, the two clerics assigned to San Blas, Domingo Cerím and Joseph Domíngue, noted that the yanaconas were fervent devotees of the cofradía.[59] It is unclear how this cofradía was funded, but its existence provides evidence of social differentiation among the yanacona population.[60]

One final aspect of indio life in the city is justice. Spanish law provided indios with legal protections that encouraged litigiousness. For example, indios had access to free legal representation in the form of an official called the protector de indios or *protector de naturales*.[61] Guaraní in Asunción did not develop a strong legal culture when compared to many Andean and Nahua communities, but some Guaraní did use the Spanish legal system to adjudicate conflicts. For example, in 1610 Francisco Pané, a yanacona in the service of Juan Cantero, went directly to the protector's house after an altercation with an encomendero named Tomás Rolón. According to Pané, while he and another yanacona were tending to their encomendero's crops, they noticed that Rolón's cattle had wandered into the field and destroyed some plants. As the two yanacona chased the cattle off the land, Rolón approached atop his horse, accused them of robbery, and physically punished Pané. During the investigation that ensued, Rolón claimed that the indios had sought to steal his cattle and that he had been compelled to defend his property. The judge was not convinced and fined him two pesos for the royal treasury, five pesos to cover court costs, a new cotton shirt for Francisco Pané, plus the two months of jail time he had served during the course of the investigation.[62] This kind of sentence for Spaniards was typical for nonmortal wounds against indios.[63] Pané's use of the protector de indios suggests that that Guaraní in the city were aware of the system of justice available to them. But ultimately indios' most ardent defenders were their own encomenderos, who frequently initiated suits against other Spaniards, slaves, or yanaconas on behalf of their indios. Similar to slave masters defending their human property, encomenderos sought to protect their personal servants, who provided key financial support to the household and, as we have already seen, were sometimes described as part of the family unit.[64]

Indios in Asunción had opportunities furnished by the ideal of the two repúblicas. Historians assume that yanaconas were slaves except in name. They reach this conclusion by emphasizing the severe abuses and the reality of personal service. Indeed, yanaconas were subject to their encomenderos' every beck and call and were at times traded among Spaniards. Yanaconas' conditions do approximate those of slaves, but the juridical reality of their status as indios within a legal framework of decentralization generated alternative positions for them in society. John Leddy Phelan argues that the

Spanish bureaucracy was not a hierarchical monolith with authority central-ized in one body but instead was marked by overlapping jurisdictions and competing mandates that served to eliminate the need for a centralized power.[65] Other historians note that decentralization defined relations within political and social institutions in Spanish America, thereby "promoting asymmetry, disequilibrium, and difference, while at the same time ensuring authority and flexibility and, ultimately, social stability."[66] This system of decentralization provided Guaraní in Asunción with legal identities and privileges specific to their corporate status. The social positions available to people in Spanish American society were not binaries (español/indio, slave/free, male/female); they were continuums "along which individuals sought to place themselves to maximize their interests."[67]

"Privileges of Mestizos"

Yanaconas experienced a mix of coercion, violence, community, and care. The ambiguities of yanacona life are further reflected in the diverse mean-ings associated with the socioracial categories applied to them. In Asunción, biological mixture was common, allowing individuals to move or be moved between different socioracial categories. A 1688 civil investigation into the status of an individual who hoped to demonstrate his descent from mestizos is a good place to start. Domingo Flores was born to María, who several wit-nesses identified as mestiza. María belonged to don Francisco Flores's enco-mienda, and the latter also happened to be Domingo Flores's father. But typical of encomenderos who sired children with their servants or slaves, don Flores never publicly recognized his son, making him an illegitimate child or "hijo natural." However, this did not mean that don Flores com-pletely abandoned young Domingo, for he sent him to live with his sister on another farmstead in Asunción. The removal of Domingo was prompted by don Flores's wife, doña Isabel, who had become irritated by the sexual rela-tionship between her husband and his mestiza encomendada. To further assuage the disgruntled doña Isabel, don Flores married María to an indio of his encomienda. The depositions suggest that don Flores hoped to raise Domingo as an español, for he was nursed by an española and raised by his paternal grandmother. After Domingo Flores came of age, he married a woman identified as a mestiza, had two sons, and lived on a chacra that provided most of the family's provisions.[68] This pattern of concubinage and the relocation of *hijos naturales* to the homes of relatives was typical in Spanish America, but what matters here is that Domingo's status was challenged.[69] A Spanish fiscal, or crown attorney, claimed that Domingo Flores and his family were part of an encomienda. This encomienda had recently become vacant (the encomendero died) and was set to be reassigned to another encomendero. Ironically, Domingo Flores got a protector de indios to represent him—if anyone saw the irony in a self-professed mestizo using a legal representative assigned to protect indios, it did not register in the written record. The depositions that make up Domingo Flores's defense sought to demonstrate that he was raised by españolas/mestizas and raised as an español/mestizo. The point of all this was to show that Domingo enjoyed, in the words of one of the deponents, the "privilege of mestizos," or nontributary status.[70] The depositions suggested that Domingo Flores was mestizo through descent and through his cultural upbringing, although descent was the primary factor. In a region where the Guaraní language was spoken widely and people shared a material culture, it was difficult to draw hard boundaries between españoles and indios. As an illegitimate mestizo, Domingo's legal status in society was ambiguous. The file ends with no resolution, but it reflects the avaricious nature of the encomendero class and the precarious position of mestizos.

Domingo Flores's case is demonstrative of a common legal strategy that revolved around proving mestizo status. Other legal conflicts where the stakes were not so high reveal a lack of consensus about individuals. For example, in 1669, a woman seeking to reclaim her eleven-year-old daughter from an apprenticeship was identified by officials as a vecina while a second witness labeled her an india.[71] This categorical ambiguity was common throughout the Americas.[72] In the legal contexts discussed here, Spaniards used the term *indio* as a corporate and fiscal category that could imply connection to an encomienda. Thus, when the encomienda was in question, to be an indio was to belong to an encomienda.[73] When officials described an individual as an "indio mestizo" among the yanacona population, they suggested that the person paid tribute but was of mixed ancestry. Similarly, there were individuals who could be described as "españoles mestizos," or individuals free of tribute status and outside the indio corporate status but also of mixed descent. Descent and physiognomy interacted with ascribed categories to generate an individual's status as tributary or nontributary. This status was indexed through categories that we might call racial but were much more than lineage. Race involved a variety of different categories of difference, including socioeconomics, physiognomy, clothing, locale, and, importantly, the position of the individual assigning the racial category. As Joanne Rappaport argues, individuals were not assigned a specific "racial identity" through a "caste system." Instead, classification "constituted a series of disparate procedures that were relational in nature, generated out of the interaction of specific people through particular speech-acts."[74]

In Paraguay, taxonomical acts varied, but language, dress, and physiognomy mattered a great deal. Most individuals of plebeian rank spoke only Guaraní and no Spanish, including many mestizos not raised as Spaniards. So being fluent in Spanish ("ladino en lengua castellano") was a way of distinguishing oneself, although there were many mestizos who spoke only Guaraní. Dress was also an important sign of racial difference. A mestizo named Andres Benítez, whose case went all the way to the crown, argued that he was not encomendado, but witnesses who disagreed claimed that even though he wore Spanish clothing, he was only feigning.[75]

The cases just reviewed show how Spaniards hoped to impose a new status on an individual to benefit from their labor, but not all Spaniards hoped to create indios. During visitas, Spanish governors moved indios to the español sphere, legally liberating them from tribute. These were official legal acts called *declaraciones de mestizo* or mestizo declarations. Almost like writs of manumission, the *declaraciones* were delivered to the subject and potentially gave him or her the legal right to leave the encomienda or reducción and live a life as an español. Alexia Ibarra Dávila identifies 350 declaración de mestizo petitions from the Province of Quito for the years 1689 and 1815. All petitions were initiated by or for males who disputed claims by officials or priests that they were tribute-paying Indians.[76] The Paraguayan declaraciones analyzed here are significantly different. First, there are many declaraciones for female indias in the Paraguayan corpus. Because women were recorded in the padrones, female indias benefited just as much as male indios from being declared mestiza/o.[77] The second major difference between the

Quito and Paraguay declaraciones has to do with how they were initiated. The Quito petitions were always brought by the individual or his or her family member and the processes could take weeks, months, or years to conclude. The burden of proof fell on the petitioner and his family, which involved acquiring a legal representative or hiring a notary, providing witness depositions, and even presenting themselves before the magistrate as physiognomic evidence of mestizaje. In Paraguay, the procedure occurred as part of the governor's visita, recorded in the padrón, and was therefore concluded immediately. Moreover, while Guaraní might petition the governor for a writ, the governor just as frequently initiated the investigation.

A declaración de mestizo initiated in Altos in the year 1677 exemplifies the ambiguities associated with indio status. The investigation was initiated by María on behalf of her daughter, Paula, who, at the time of the padrón, had been serving in the house of her encomendero in Asunción:

> María, wife of Domingo, declared under oath that when she was single she had a daughter named Paula, daughter of a Spaniard, and Maria and her aforementioned husband declare [Paula] to be mestiza. . . . His Honor the Governor . . . declared [Paula] as mestiza, daughter of a Spaniard, so that she enjoy every liberty and use Spanish garb (*traje español*) and that she be removed from the power of Francisco Delgado de Vera in whose house she presently was found and that she be handed over to her mother so that she be raised under maternal protection (*abrigo*) until she reaches the appropriate age.[78]

It may seem ironic that the governor ordered that Paula be returned from Asunción to her Indian pueblo so that she could be raised by her Guaraní mother as a mestiza. But the governor's edict changing Paula's official status from india to mestiza was designed to lift her out of tributary obligations. In her study of mestizos in Nueva Granada (modern-day Colombia), Joanne Rappaport describes a process of "deindianization" whereby individuals shed their indio status but continued to maintain indigenous lifeways.[79] This is precisely the path the governor laid in place for Paula by declaring her mestiza.

Declaraciones de mestizos were relatively rare in the reducción visitas but unsurprisingly frequent among yanaconas in Asunción, where biological mixture was more common. In the 1694 visita of originarios, 28 indios/as were declared mestizo/a out of a total population of 1,476 indios. Paula's case was similar to other declaraciones, except that Paula was not physically present for the governor to behold her. When a suspected mestizo was present, the governor typically noted a variety of proofs. These included witness testimony that spoke to the individual's lineage but the governor also observed an individual's physical appearance. In fact, physical features were apparently what caused governors to issue impromptu declaraciones. In those cases, the notary would normally record the following: "by his/her appearance, I declare him/her mestizo/a" ("y por su aspecto lo declaró por mestizo"). Because governors did not include descriptions of the individuals they declared mestizos, it is unclear what informed their "physiognomical eye."[80]

When investigations were launched by indios, parents were most commonly the petitioners; however, indigenous leaders might also present mestizos. During the visita at Arecayá and Altos, a cacique addressed the governor and explained that an india in his cacicazgo had given birth to a son named Juan whose father was Spanish. His mother had recently died, so the cacique had sent Juan to live with his Spanish relatives in Asunción. The governor declared Juan mestizo. That a cacique would initiate a declaración de mestizo suggests he was not interested in increasing the size of his cacicazgo.[81]

It is a reasonable assumption that most individuals would hope to enjoy the "privilege of mestizos," but this was not the case. Not all mestizos claimed the freedom that their mixed descent could provide them. One yanacona named Pascual had been declared mestizo by the governor during a previous visita, but he chose to remain a tribute-paying indio. Pascual was married to an india who was also a member of the same encomienda, and they had a child. When asked why he chose to remain, Pascual stated that because of the "love that [Pascual] had for his encomendero and because [his encomendero] treated and paid him well" he chose to remain an indio in the encomienda.[82] Since most indios were connected to a Spaniard and were therefore supplied with land to meet their basic necessities, few indios owned land or property they legally bequeathed to their children. Most indios died intestate, underscoring the lack of a strong legal culture among the Guaraní, as well as the poverty of the region.[83]

Analyzing the mestizo category sheds new light on what it meant to be Guaraní and indio in Asunción. The networks of friends and family in Asunción expanded and gave individuals options. The work of empire was at once broad and interconnected, disaggregated and contingent. As colonial practice was enacted in specific moments, categories of difference were constructed in order to maintained boundaries between free and semifree tributary populations. In Paraguay, the lack of material markers, like elaborate indigenous sumptuary aesthetics, created a context where physiognomy became more pronounced and therefore served as a marker of difference.

Guaranization of *Españoles*: Paraguay's Lingua Franca

Individuals who sought the "privilege of mestizos" hoped to demonstrate a degree of Spanishness, but these attempts were difficult given the weakness of distinctive markers separating corporate groups. The records featuring the movement between categories point to an ongoing process whereby indigenous culture, especially Guaraní culture, imprinted itself on español culture and vice versa. This process of cultural give and take in a colonial context has been described as creolization. Creolization included much more than a simple two-way exchange between ostensibly opposing cultures but encompassed the swirl of interactions between diverse ethnic and political bodies, environmental forces, and changing power relations. Scholars emphasize that, unlike concepts like "accommodation" or "assimilation," which suggest either coercion or choice, creolization was a complex of mix of involuntary and voluntary processes. Creolization therefore can be a useful concept because it breaks down the conqueror-conquered paradigm to describe cultural change while still allowing for historical agency. The analysis that follows draws attention to the ways that Guaraní forced the hand of cultural change by virtue of their numerical and political power.[84]

The most relevant example of cultural mixing partially driven by Guaraní is the spread of the Guaraní language. Unless they were priests assigned to serve in reducciones, most Spaniards did not learn Guaraní in schools or with tutors but instead absorbed it from close interaction with indio associates, fellow laborers, domestics, midwives, and kin, both Guaraní and español. Guaraní was as much "their" local language as it was the language of

Guaraní. By at least the second generation of creoles in Paraguay, Spanish fathers and mothers could have restricted the spread of Guaraní by forcing servants to learn Spanish or perhaps sending their children to elite schools— which some may have done—but the poverty of Spaniards, the demographic dominance of Guaraní, and the political realities of cuñadasgo would have made such actions difficult.

Glimpses into everyday interethnic exchanges show that in Paraguay most españoles learned Guaraní and few indios learned Spanish. While Spanish remained the language of state and a marker of elite status among españoles, Guaraní became the "unofficial lingua franca" just as Tupí, or Brasílica, was for parts of Portuguese Brazil.[85] Evidence of the ubiquity of Guaraní could literally be heard from Asunción's streets, houses, and chacras. Recall the investigation cited above from the year 1610 when the encomendero Tomás Rolón physically assaulted Francisco Pané, a yanacona from a neighboring chacra, after assuming Pané had stolen Rolón's livestock.[86] As an example of español-indio violence, this is a typical case: a Spaniard first berates then physically abuses an indio over an issue of property. But what is noteworthy about this encounter is that the exchange between the español Rolón and the indio Pané was conducted entirely in Guaraní.[87]

The Guaraní language proliferated in colonial Paraguay for a number of reasons, the most important being that it was already a language of wide usage when Europeans arrived. Kittiya Lee argues that in Brazil Tupí became the dominant colonial indigenous language because at the time of contact, Tupí-Guaraní groups were engaged in a process of conquest and expansion.[88] Priests recognized that it was widely spoken across the lowland Atlantic basin, making it the language of choice for priests conducing evangelical missions. Bartomeu Melià's classic study of the colonial Guaraní language shows that in the Jesuit reducciones of Tapé there were many dialects of Guaraní and the Jesuits promoted a "classic Guaraní" among indigenous residents. This Guaraní contrasted with "Paraguayan Guaraní," or that spoken by creoles, which over the years experienced significant changes as it combined with Spanish forms, syntax, and pronunciations.[89] Outside observers noted that the Paraguayan Guaraní was altogether vulgar and unlike the "classic Guaraní" spoken in the reducciones. Jesuit José Cardiel, who was in Paraguay in the mid-eighteenth century, called Paraguayan Guaraní "gobbledygook."[90] Just as with the mixing of peoples, Cardiel looked down upon linguistic mixture, a strong feature of Paraguayan Guaraní. While the topic of how much Guaraní changed is significant, the question of who pioneered bilingualism in the colonial period also merits attention.

The scholarship promotes a notion that the proliferation of Guaraní among creoles was largely due to miscegenation and the uneven influence that Guaraní mothers had over their mixed descent children.[91] In this reading, biological mixing results in transculturation as mestizos adopt an indigenous language.[92] The late eighteenth-century naturalist and crown-appointed emissary Félix Manuel de Azara provided a description of the prominence of the Guaraní language in Paraguay that belies his anxieties about cultural exchange:

> The Spaniards of Paraguay always speak Guaraní, and only the most refined speak Spanish. . . . The Spanish founders of [Asunción and Villa Rica] took indias as their women and their children naturally learned the language of their mothers . . . and they did not retain the Spanish language, except as a statement of honor and to prove that their race (*raza*) was more noble. But the Spaniards of the rest of this province did not think the same way, for they have forgotten their language and substituted it with another taken from the Guaraní. . . . I deduce that the mothers, not the fathers, teach and perpetuate the languages.[93]

Azara attributes the perpetuation of the Guaraní language among the creole population to women. Azara's belief that Guaraní mothers were the sole promoters of the Guaraní language among Spanish society was part of a broader European pattern to see women inhabiting privileged positions as mediators along the paths of cultural transformation. Spaniards throughout the Americas noted that if indigenous mothers raised mestizo children, those children would become Indians.[94] In the minds of early moderns, cultural change was both physical and social. For example, some Spaniards believed that indigenous or African wet nurses could pass physical and moral traits on to their elite creole children and therefore only a Spanish woman should have breastfed Spanish children.[95] While women and mothers certainly played a major role in Guaraní language transmission, to single them out as the sole agents of cultural and linguist guaranization ignores a whole host of other activities that included men. Mark Lentz explores a similar historical problem for the late colonial Yucatán and argues that language transmission was not limited to the intimate relationships among creoles or mestizos and their wet nurses or indigenous mothers but occurred as Maya speakers and creoles labored together and increasingly intermingled in interethnic spaces.[96] Opportunities for interethnic labor abounded in Paraguay, as small farmers worked alongside Guaraní hired hands, interethnic gangs of laborers ferried yerba maté along rivers and roads, and mixed militias went to war.

One of the more obvious promoters of Guaraní were encomenderos. The encomienda began as an indigenous system of exchange framed around kinship but over time modulated into a colonial institution. As such, in order to participate in the system of cuñadasgo, encomenderos required Guaraní cultural capital. In fact, the system grew out of that cultural capital—there would have been no cuñadasgo had there not been Guaraní-speaking conquistadors and encomenderos. And since many encomenderos could not afford mayordomos, they relied on their own words to negotiate with Guaraní. As the encomienda was a family affair—usually possessed for two generations—it seems plausible that encomenderos promoted Guaraní language acquisition among their children or at least were unconcerned that their children learned the language from the Guaraní living on their chacras and in their homes.

The presence of nonindio interpreters provides further evidence of the social power of Guaraní in Asunción and shows that possessing fluency in an indigenous language did not necessarily damage a vecino's social standing. Government officials' practices for appointing interpreters in Paraguay differed from other Spanish American regions that enlisted official interpreters for specific periods of time. The colonial Yucatán shared with Paraguay a peripheral status, strong indigenous population, and a widespread bilingualism or Mayan monolingualism among its creole or non-Indian population and therefore provides an ideal comparative example. By the late eighteenth century, Maya had become the "interethnic lingua franca" of the Yucatán, the primary language for *castas*, or individuals of mixed descent, and commonplace for Spanish creoles.[97] The first "general interpreters" in the Yucatán were indigenous, but after 1600 all general interpreters were from the Spanish sphere. The reason for this transition from indio to español interpreters in the Yucatán is likely related to the fact that the position was paid and therefore highly coveted by creoles. The post was funded through a tax on Mayan communities known as the *medio real*, or *holpatán*.[98] The general interpreters not only translated oral testimony but also used their literacy to translate written documents such as petitions from Mayan officials, land documents, and public edicts. Moreover, interpreters served as ambassadors for the colonial government to autonomous or rebellious Mayan communities.

In sixteenth- and seventeenth-century Paraguay, municipal and crown officials did not appoint a regular, salaried interpreter but instead called upon individuals to fill the role on a case by case basis. The absence of a "general interpreter" position in Paraguay can be attributed to a dearth of resources. The colonial government in Asunción did not tax its Guaraní populations, except in the form of personal service, and therefore could not afford to support such an office. Moreover, the need for an official post was unnecessary given the high number of bilingual intermediaries. This pattern holds true for the Yucatán as well, where the decline in status of the general interpreter paralleled the rise of Maya language dominance among the non-indio population in the late eighteenth century.[99] In Paraguay, even though interpreters could not rely on regular salaried positions, many received modest compensations when they served.[100] The titles that these ad hoc interpreters bore shows that many were of relatively high status. A random sampling of thirty-five separate litigative records registers forty-three interpreters, and only one of these was indio.[101] Of the forty-two nonindio interpreters, twenty-eight were identified as vecinos. Some also carried positions on the municipal and royal governments, including scribe, lieutenant general, captain, Indian protector, ensign (*alférez*), and lieutenant bailiff mayor (*teniente de alguacil mayor*). Interpreters were generally called upon to translate oral testimony; therefore, it is impossible to determine if they were literate or not. When conducting legal proceedings at Guaraní pueblos, magistrates sometimes employed pobleros, suggesting that the position was filled pragmatically. This seemingly haphazard selection pattern suggests that officials mixed patronage with pragmatism when selecting interpreters.

The fact that Spaniards of such rank were willing to use their linguistic abilities in official capacities suggests that locals saw Guaraní fluency as a social stepping-stone, not a stumbling block. Since officials were uninterested in fostering unity, but instead sought to maintain distinctions among different types of people (indios, españoles, blacks, elites), it is unsurprising that officials did not promote one language over another. It seems plausible that Spaniards who sought to communicate their status as noble Spaniards spoke to their social peers in Spanish, not Guaraní, but there is no evidence to indicate that was the norm. As Azara's comments indicated above, many españoles of lower rank were not concerned that their primary language was Guaraní. These linguistic patterns run counter to core areas. For Mexico, James Lockhart notes "that many more Nahuas attempted Spanish than Spaniards Nahuatl. By the second and third postconquest generations, even the majority of the professional translators acting as intermediaries between the two languages were native speakers of Nahuatl."[102] Rolena Adorno suggests that similar patterns existed in the Andes.[103] The ubiquity of the Guaraní language was more than a product of miscegenation but was an outgrowth of the realities of cuñadasgo and a reflection of the impact of Guaraní peoples on colonial society.

Conclusion

At the end of his extensive report on the encomienda in Paraguay to crown officials, the scribe and secretary Alonso Fernández Ruano described the yanaconas of Asunción as a distinct population of indios in Paraguay: "[The yanaconas] are those that generally dress the most splendidly and because of their regular communication with españoles they and their families are the most politically Spanish and they speak and understand the Spanish language."[104] With their speech and dress, Ruano suggested, the yanacona reflected a positive cultural change. In the same breath, Ruano described how poor Spaniards are: "very few things from Peru (a symbol of wealth and commerce) ever arrive in Paraguay, they dress in the plain cotton shirts and jackets that their indios make for them, and instead of bread they eat mandioca or cassava root." Ruano exaggerated on two accounts. First, while yanaconas may have understood Spanish, the sociohistorical record suggests that most spoke only Guaraní. Second, Ruano does not go far enough in describing Spanish cultural change. Spaniards not only ate cassava root instead of wheat bread but spoke Guaraní instead of Spanish. What Ruano ultimately argued was that the yanacona population should continue as personal servants to españoles—otherwise, the latter would be sunk into economic oblivion. While politically charged, Ruano's report raises an issue at the heart of this chapter: creolization as an intertwined and contingent process but one not wholly bereft of agency. Españoles ate cassava instead of wheat bread out of economic necessity, but they also developed a taste for the starchy root. Yanaconas may have understood Spanish, but because of the political realities of cuñadasgo, Guaraní became the dominant language in Asunción. And finally, yanaconas were "politically Spanish" insofar as they worshiped in the San Blas parish, possessed their own cofradía, and were promoted to an unknown number of official posts, but these same institutions and practices provided space for yanaconas to resist unwanted policies.

From their physical layout down to their social networks, cities in Spanish America require an ethnohistorical understanding. The early relations of cuñadasgo and the subsequent assignment of small encomiendas—a result of the Guaraní social reality—drew Spaniards into a reliance on Guaraní servants. Instead of creating an urban center of contiguous households, Spaniards radiated out into the nearby hinterland where their handfuls of Guaraní personal servants grew crops, spun cotton, and tended to livestock. These farmsteads were places of profound ambiguity. Encomenderos and their families possessed yanaconas like chattel slaves, and yet indios inhabited a legal position that provided them with access to legal protections and freedom of movement. Indios sustained and created new social networks within the city and beyond in the reducciones. While some risked reprisal from their encomenderos, many indios moved freely throughout the city to visit, friends, neighbors, lovers, and kin. The mobility in the city was not only physical but categorical. As places of intimate and often abusive contact, sex between indios and españoles was common, resulting in a biologically mixed and phenotypically diverse population. Within one generation, the mestizo category opened up pathways of freedom for yanacona to leave the encomienda. Some struck out on their own, like Andrés Benítez, who had a family on his own plot of land. But the gravitational pull of the encomienda was strong, and it behooved mestizos to prove the privileges their "race" afforded them. Other mestizos chose to remain yanacona because they found community, family, and safety on their encomenderos' farmsteads. Yanaconas' reference to love and kinship between themselves and their encomenderos signal the lasting legacy of cuñadasgo on the society in Asunción.

This book defines *Guaraní* as an ethnonym imposed by conquistadors but also an ethnic identity in constant flux and change. Guaranization in the reducciones was certainly different than the guaranization occurring in Asunción, but there were also areas of overlap. In all of these spaces, Guaraní gradually lost a host of practices and cultural values: a social structure built on polygyny, shamans, the practice of cannibalism, etc. But one similarity is that in each of these colonial spaces, Guaraní actively mitigated their experiences with colonial power and colonial actors. Claiming that indios in Asunción were indeed Guaraní underscores the profound ambiguities of colonial life and maintains that what was indigenous was not the absence of Spanish things or traits. The documents give voice to an ongoing process of biological mixture but framed within the boundaries of corporate/fiscal identities. There were no mestizos in Paraguay except when an individual's corporate category was suspect or invoked. The lack of evidence that individuals evoked casta categories or racially framed insults reflects the areas of cultural convergence among the city's inhabitants. This chapter began with a portrait of Asunción's patchwork urban geography and its rural-urban character to illustrate the limits of colonialism on the landscape and the impact of Guaraní on Spaniards' occupation of space. Asunción is a microcosm of the contradictions at work in colonial Paraguay. The humility of the city—with its twisting ravines, uneven blocks, ladder entryways, and heavy wild vegetation—spoke just as much to the resilience of españoles as to its susceptibility to what was local.

CHAPTER 8

Beyond Mestizos

Afro-Guaraní Relations

AN UNDERSTANDING OF the Guaraní experience in the colonial period would be incomplete if it did not elaborate on African slaves and their descendants.[1] Guaraní and blacks labored together, soldiered together, fought with and robbed each other, married each other, and snubbed each other. The social closeness of blacks, enslaved or free, and Guaraní occurred in the cultural and legal contexts of cuñadasgo and encomienda, and these shaped the legal practice of slavery and blacks' social positions.

Demographic figures on Paraguay's slave and freedmen populations are thin, but by 1682, 15 percent of Asunción's population was slaves. By the late eighteenth century, there were 1,150 slave and 1,500 free blacks.[2] These were fairly modest populations compared to regions like northeastern Brazil. Even so, the African presence in Paraguay cannot be ignored. Generally, there is a dearth of sources on blacks, but ironically the lack of documentation is a result of the ubiquity of enslaved Africans in colonial societies. Matthew Restall explains: "Enslaved Africans were perceived as property, and thus no more worthy of mention than the horses and carriages of the Spanish elite, or the furniture in their houses. But, unlike horses and furniture, Africans were needed, they were ubiquitous—and they were taken for granted."[3]

In recent years, scholars have turned their attention to the African diaspora on the peripheries of Spanish America and demonstrated that slavery was a significant social variable. In terms of numbers, Kara Schultz shows that between 1587 and 1640, 34,224 slaves were disembarked at Buenos Aires through a variety of licit and illicit means.[4] Spanish owners and traders took a small portion of these individuals to Paraguay. Others have also examined slavery's impact on societies with comparably modest slave populations and demonstrated that defining societies as "slaves societies" and "societies with slaves" is a misleading characterization. According to the "slave society/ society with slaves paradigm," the ruling society is completely dependent upon large concentrations of slave populations, while in the latter slaves provide essential labor or capital to the ruling classes but are not the socioeconomic base. These are important distinctions but by emphasizing societies with majority slave populations, scholars ignored slavery's impact in places like Mexico City, monasteries, and colleges. Sherwin Bryant refuses the materialism the "slave society/society with slaves" dichotomy implies and argues that wherever slavery was practiced, slavery informed the creation of differences among a multiethnic population and was therefore fundamental to governance.[5] Rachel Sarah O'Toole, in her work on Africans and Indians in Peru, further shows that since the institutions of slavery and indigenous tribute were examples of race governance, they should be analyzed together.[6] These insights apply to Paraguay where the encomienda, with its history of cuñadasgo, was a culturally diffuse practice that informed español-indio relations throughout the colonial period. Given the misguided tendency in the scholarship to equate the Paraguayan encomienda with slavery, an analysis of the legal practice of slavery alongside the encomienda clarifies that the institutions remained legally distinct. Slaves experienced fewer rights and restricted access to freedoms than their indio tributary counterparts.

In the legal imagination of the Spanish imperial system, Africans occupied an ambiguous position in the "two republics" scheme. Awkwardly situated between españoles and indios, *negros* straddled two different corporate spheres and sometimes forged their own. Since slaves were legally associated with españoles as their auxiliaries, they were subject to Spanish laws that defined them as property but also ecclesiastical laws, which defined them as God's children. Scholars have scrutinized slaves' claims to rights and positions within the colonial system and demonstrated that, in practice, a few African communities represented themselves as a "republic of blacks" and that colonial officials recognized their status as such.[7] At the same time, slaves and free blacks associated closely with indios—sometimes as Spaniards' overseers, sometimes as friends and kin. From maroon communities to marriages, scholars have demonstrated that Africans and indigenous throughout the Americas forged relationships with each other and that their intermingling in families, communities, labor settings, and religious institutions resulted in multidirectional cultural change.[8] For example, Matthew Restall notes that in areas of Yucatán where African populations were pronounced, many Maya had become Afro-Maya, reflecting an intense intercultural exchange and African cultural resilience.[9] This chapter contributes to the scholarly discussion on Afro-Indio relations by highlighting ways that Africans experienced cultural change oriented toward a Guaranized culture. Moreover, it demonstrates that slavery was changed by the encomienda and cuñadasgo.

Studying Africans, their descendants, and their relationships with Guaraní further contributes to efforts to denationalize some of the historiography on race in Paraguay, which has purged the country's history of its African ancestry.[10] Since the War of the Triple Alliance (1864–1870)—which pitted Brazil, Argentina, and Uruguay against Paraguay—historians have sought to "de-Africanize" Paraguay. Wartime propaganda created for Paraguayan soldiers portrayed their Brazilian enemies as racially inferior because of their blackness. In 1911, during the nationalist hype of Paraguay's centenary, one of the country's foremost scholars wrote that "a perfect ethnic homogeneity exists among us; the black pigment does not darken our skin."[11] Until 2007, the Paraguayan state had not officially recognized black populations in the country, even as many Paraguayans embraced Afro-Paraguayan cultural expressions like those of the Kamba Cuá community's celebration of the purportedly black Saint Balthasar.[12] Asserting the significant demographic, social, and cultural impact of Africans in colonial Paraguay, this chapter argues that Afro-Guaraní relations are a fundamental element of an ethnohistory of Guaraní peoples and that cuñadasgo left its mark on local race governance. The following pages describe the earliest evidence for African populations in Paraguay and then turn to a discussion of Afro-Guaraní relations and, specifically, the impact of cuñadasgo on the practice of slavery.

Africans in Paraguay

Africans accompanied Spaniards in the earliest conquest ventures to the Río de la Plata. In his expedition to the region, the adelantado Álvar Núñez Cabeza de Vaca brought a slave named Juan Blanco who was later sold to a conquistador for six hundred gold pesos.[13] Besides the rare sale contract, conquistadors reported that during their dangerous expeditions to the Gran Chaco a few of their slaves attempted to flee and take up residence among Guaicurú bands. In the conquests of Peru and Mexico, some bondsmen leveraged their contributions and were rewarded with their freedom and an incredible amount of social mobility.[14] "Black conquistadors" acquired significant wealth and coveted homes in the center of the new Spanish American cities, and a small few were awarded encomiendas. By contrast, the conquest in Paraguay was disjointed, prolonged, and did not yield much wealth for its conquistadors. Cuñadasgo was the primary means to acquire status and wealth in early colonial Paraguay. While there are no extant records demonstrating that blacks possessed encomiendas in Paraguay, it is hard to imagine that free blacks in Paraguay did not engage in the networks of cuñadasgo to acquire Guaraní personal servants. But like voices in the wind, the experiences of blacks in the early conquest period are muffled at best.

David Wheat demonstrates that in most locales throughout the Spanish Caribbean in the early seventeenth century, African slaves were Spaniards' "surrogate colonists." Replacing Iberian and indigenous laborers, Africans did much of the heavy lifting when creating colonies.[15] Colonial officials in Paraguay hoped to use Africans as "surrogate colonists" to exploit the territories they claimed on paper.[16] For example, Governor Hernando Arias de Saavedra, writing in 1610, an era of uncertainty about the reliability of Guaraní mitayos, complained to the crown that 1,050 African slaves who had been shipped off to Peru via Buenos Aires could have better served the realm in Asunción.[17] The dean of the cathedral chapter in Asunción also chimed in, urging the governor in Buenos Aires to ship all slaves disembarked in Buenos Aires to Asunción. Reflecting on Alfaro's new restrictions on indio personal service, the dean argued that African slaves "were the solution to all the economic problems" of the region.[18] In Asunción, where encomenderos held tight grips on their encomendados, corporate groups clambered for labor (and living capital) and officials believed that African slaves were the best alternative to fill the need. For example, Governor Saavedra requested permission to purchase one hundred slaves from Angola to provide for Asunción's impoverished orphanage managed by Sister Bocanegra, as well as for other ecclesiastical institutions in the city. While grand visions of mass importations of Africans to Paraguay were never realized, a slow trickle of

African captives made their way to Paraguay via the Paraguay River and an unknown quantity of slaves came overland from São Paulo.

The biggest purchasers of slaves were the religious orders. These institutions were reliant on African slave labor because they did not possess encomiendas. They put slaves to work in their convents, ranches, haciendas, and other industries. In the mid-sixteenth century, a Spanish vecina named Isabel López donated a handful of Africans to the Mercedarian convent (founded in 1540). From that bequest (and probably others), the black population on the Mercedarian's rural hacienda, Areguá, grew to around five hundred by 1666.[19] The Jesuit college in Asunción and its ranches and factories possessed the largest number of slaves by the end of the colonial period. The Jesuit college served many purposes: a producer of consumer goods, a school for the region's elite, a training center for novitiate priests, and a church. On its rural ranches just outside of Asunción, the college produced wheat, sugar, roof tiles, and many other goods. The earliest extant record of the college's purchase of slaves is from the year 1614; in that year, the Jesuits purchased (on credit) a sugar mill, a wheat mill, and seven black slaves to service them.[20] Through similar investments and consistent growth, the Jesuits became the largest slaveholders in the Río de la Plata. At the time of the Jesuit expulsion in 1767, the college owned 1,002 slaves: 388 in the college in Asunción, 84 in its San Lorenzo ranch, and 530 in Paraguarí ranch.[21] In the seventeenth century, large concentrations of Africans were limited to the monasteries and their rural holdings, but in the eighteenth century blacks became connected to frontier defenses. Free black communities emerged around presidios, or fort towns. The community of Emboscada (also known as Camba Reta) was founded in 1741 by the local governor to serve as a barrier to Native enemies and housed nearly 1,500 free *pardos*.[22]

Besides Asunción's monasteries and frontier towns, African slaves were common on Spanish farmsteads, where they worked alongside Guaraní personal servants. Testaments and sales from the early seventeenth century provide a faint outline of the networks that moved African slaves between purchasers, as well as the shape of small slaveholding in Asunción. In 1600, doña María de Guzmán willed thirteen slaves to her daughter María de Irala and two slaves to her second husband, Francisco de Alva.[23] María de Guzmán descended from the illustrious Vergara and Guzmán families and was one of the wealthiest vecinas in Asunción, with connections to traders in Buenos Aires. Her possession of at least fifteen slaves was unusual. Most slaveholders only possessed one or two slaves who supplemented their yanacona populations.

Notarial records and sale contracts speak to the circuits of transactions and provide brief glimpses into slaves' lives. In the year 1618, Gaspar Fernández, a *morador* and mostly likely a yerba maté trader, was in Asunción and asked a notary to record that he had deposited one of his slaves, Ana, with trusted vecinos in the city. Fernández had recently concluded the sale of Ana in Corrientes and was not preparing to have her transported to her new master in Corrientes. Fernández also sold another slave, named Antón, but upon hearing of the sale the latter fled to Tucumán. That Antón fled to Tucumán suggests that he was familiar with the trade routes in Paraguay and was likely involved in the transport industry. Traders frequently used slaves on the barge and cart caravans that moved yerba maté and other goods throughout the trade networks of the Río de la Plata and Tucumán.[24] Fernández claimed that his slaves were "Guinee" and listed their many "defects." Ana was apparently in poor health and her owner used the chilling phrase "costal de huesos, alma en boca" (bag of bones, soul in mouth) to describe her condition. Fernández was eager to rid himself of these two slaves, considering them "drunkards" and "thieves." They sold for four hundred pesos each.[25]

What few sale contracts exist suggest a strong commercial network between the Jesuit college and individual slave owners. In a sale contract from the year 1621, doña Úrsula de Rojas Aranda sold her mulatta slave, Rufina, and the slave's young daughter, Petrona, to the Jesuit college for 550 *patacones de plata* because Rufina had married a slave owned by the Jesuits. Doña Úrsula stated that she intended to sell Rufina and her daughter to keep the slave family united, something most slave owners did not consider.[26]

In Asunción and its hinterlands, African slaves were concentrated in the religious establishments' ranches and farms, while encomenderos, yerba maté traders, and vecinos owned a few slaves to work their ranches, farms, warehouses, and transport operations. Indios performed the bulk of the labor for the region, while Africans supplemented. Moreover, Spaniards used slaves as liquid assets or collateral. This economic portrait sets the stage for an analysis of the relationship between tribute and slavery.

Continuums of Servitude: Slavery, Tribute, and *Cuñadasgo*

Indios experienced more rights under colonial law than blacks even if some black communities asserted their status as "republics" and acquired special status in the local as well as imperial contexts.[27] The varied articulation of slave and free blacks' statuses in Spanish America suggests the need for local analyses. And while the basic legal frameworks governing slaves were defined by crown law, the institution was adapted to the local context.

In Paraguay, one of the more obvious ways that tribute and slavery interacted was in indio-negro unions and their children's legal status. In a 1598 suit filed in Asunción, the local practice in Paraguay of categorizing women as tributaries impinged on the right of a slave to possess his mulatto children. An encomendero from Santa Fe named Captain Antonio Tomás (acting through a power of attorney named Martín de Insauralde) sued a black bondman and widower named Antón. Antón had two "mulatillo" sons and Tomás claimed they were his yanaconas. Six years earlier, Antón had married one of Tomás's india yanacona servants, named Teresa, while accompanying his master, lieutenant governor Felipe de Cáceres, on business in Santa Fe. After their marriage, Antón's master returned to Asunción, taking Antón and Teresa with him. Tomás argued that Cáceres had encouraged his slave to marry Teresa in a ploy to take her back to Asunción as his own yanacona and that he had planned to use the couple's children as slaves.

A few days after this civil suit was initiated, Felipe de Cáceres had still not submitted a defense on behalf of his slave and the governor ruled in favor of Tomás, ordering that Antón's boys, Antón and Domingo, be returned to Santa Fe and delivered to their encomendero to serve him as indio yanaconas.[28] Upon receiving news of the sentence, Antón quickly submitted an appeal. Calling himself "Antón de Cáceres de color moreno," he explained that it was on his own account that he had married Teresa and it was under the auspices of both the law and tradition (*costumbre*) that he had taken his wife to live with him in Asunción.[29] Antón explained that when he had attempted to leave Santa Fe with Teresa, Tomás had sued him, but the magistrate had sided with Antón and allowed him to take his wife to his home. In July of the same year, the governor issued the final sentence, which seemed to find a middle ground between the two litigants' logics of possession of these children. He definitively declared the legal categories of the two boys: "children of an Indian and not slaves" ("hijos de yndia y no como esclavos, pues no lo son"). Defining them as indios, the governor concluded that the boys were still required to provide personal service to their encomendero in Santa Fe but that they were to remain with their father until he died. Antón must have had mixed feelings about this sentence: perhaps a sense of relief that he could retain his children but tinged with the bitter possibility that at a future date they might be forced to return to an encomendero as his personal servants.

This suit highlights the entangled categories of servitude and tribute. Following the Roman legal principle of *partus sequitur ventrem*, the judge reasoned that the mulatillo sons did not inherit their father's servitude since that condition could only be inherited from a slave mother. However, what the two boys did inherit from their mother were the categories "indio" and, more specifically, "yanacona." As a legal category, "yanacona" was closer to slave than mitayo because local custom dictated that yanaconas pay tribute in perpetual personal service to an encomendero. It is notable that the magistrate did not order the boys to return to their encomendero, as he might have done had the boys been described as slaves. Instead, he allowed them to remain with their father and potentially escape yanacona service altogether. Had the sentence favored the encomendero, Antón would have found few opportunities for "forum shopping" or finding a court that would be most likely to hear and adjudicate a grievance.[30] In places like Lima or Mexico City, slaves could use ecclesiastical courts to pursue a variety of rights provisioned under Spanish law: the right to live with a spouse, the right to marry, and the right to pursue manumission. Even so, blacks like Antón found that the courts provided a degree of protection from owners' and encomenderos' claims on his family.[31]

The social ambiguities and legal questions generated from Afro-indio unions also arose during visitas of Guaraní reducciones. When conducting a census, if governors identified unions between indios and black slaves, they sometimes adjudicated on where these couples should reside, revealing colonial constructions of subjugated legal identities. Some indios' black partners lived with them in the pueblos, but most indios were absent from their encomiendas, living with their black partners on separate encomienda estates or perhaps as tenants. The governor typically commanded that an indio return with his black or mulatto partner to live in the pueblo, but only if the black partner was free. For example, during the visita of an encomienda in Arecayá, the governor learned that an indio named Baltazar was living with a mulatta from the Mercedarian convent. Because this mulatta was free, the governor ordered that the couple return to live in the pueblo, thus allowing Baltazar to remain in his reducción and pay the mita.[32] Contrarily, when a governor discovered that a tributary was married to an enslaved black, he did not order the tributary to leave his or her black spouse and return to the pueblo, underscoring the bitter irony that an india/o's official freedom from tribute obligations was contingent on their black partners' servitude.[33] Gubernatorial orders on Afro-indio residence reflected colonial logics about tribute, property, and marriage. The Church required that married couples live together so that they could realize vida maridable or domestic coresidence and sexual relations. Also known as the "matrimonial debt," sex was framed as a responsibility and duty within marriage because it provided an important protection against illicit relations.[34] The canonical priorities were bound to colonial-economic priorities that advocated for a discrete and prolific population of indio-tributaries.[35] The rights of the slaveholder took precedence over the rights of the encomendero; the rights of property trumped the rights of conquest.

This book has demonstrated that the dominant mode of colonial governance in Paraguay was the encomienda and its cultural modality of cuñadasgo. Local colonials applied cuñadasgo to the practice of African slavery and the treatment of free blacks and defined some blacks as encomendados. For example, the Mercedarian convent possessed a population of "freed" blacks that were described in an official report as an "encomienda of blacks." The ambivalent definition of the Mercedarian's blacks is rooted in the mendicants' official attitudes toward captives. The Mercedarians, or Order of Our Lady of Mercy for the Ransom of Captives, was born in Iberian Reconquista history. Founded in the year 1218 in Barcelona, the order's principal mission was to ransom or redeem captives who had been captured by Muslims in Iberia and in North Africa.[36] Applying this philosophy to its practice of colonialism in Paraguay, the Mercedarians apparently freed African slaves from official servitude but did not liberate them from labor obligations to the convent.[37] The notary and secretary Alonso Fernández Ruano's 1674 report on the encomienda provides the bulk of the documentation on this population and it recorded information about the Mercedarian's black population as if it had been an encomienda. Ruano recounted that the Mercedarians' families of "mulattos" and "zambaigos" were descendants of blacks originally donated to the convent by a vecina named Isabél López in 1597. The documentation does not clarify the nature of this transaction, but the governor, Juan Ramírez de Velasco, became embroiled in this donation and transferred the slaves to the Mercedarians as a "merced real" or royal donation. Since the crown theoretically adjudicated slave ownership—as physically manifested in the royal brands that scarred Africans' faces and bodies—crown authorities in this case were compelled to accept the vecina's donation and then officially transfer the lease to the Mercedarians.[38] At a later date, the governor Hernando Arias de Saavedra transferred (encomendar) the slaves from the convent to a vecino named Jeronimo de Ovelar for an unnamed reason. Unsurprisingly, upon Ovelar's death the convent sued at the provincial and audiencia levels, ultimately resulting in the transfer of the black population to the Mercedarians by 1606. While the blacks donated to the Mercedarians were not an encomienda, Ruano's report treats them as such, even noting how many of the black men were of tributary age.[39]

Finally claiming a legal right over the blacks, the Mercedarians organized them as if they were reducción. By at least 1666, the black families were living on the Mercedarians' farm, Areguá, and totaled ninety-nine souls. Areguá possessed a church and a priest remained permanently there to attend to the population's spiritual needs. Ruano noted that the families were engaged in subsistence living, raising livestock, and maintaining the Mercedarians' convent. Ruano noted that besides these tasks, the blacks of Areguá were otherwise not submitted to other kinds of "servitude."[40] In her study of Areguá, Margarita Durán Estragó claims that the population of blacks at Areguá were endogamous, but the sources do not support this.[41] In the first place, Ruano refers to the population as "mulattos" and "zambaigos," terms used to describe individuals of mixed African, Spanish, and Indian descent. Evidence from padrones further shows that Areguá inhabitants were in frequent contact with neighboring pueblos.[42] Areguá seems to have functioned like other reducciones in the area, albeit with a much smaller population and less

formal leadership. Institutionally, Areguá supported a church and a Mercedarian priest. The community also maintained its own fields and livestock.

The application of the encomienda and reducción to black populations
reflects their importance as the primary modes of local governance. Similar
to the ways Sherwin Bryant demonstrates that slavery was a form of governance in Quito, in Paraguay slavery was reshaped into encomienda as a way
of organizing colonized peoples. In this case, the mulattos of Areguá were
"redeemed" from servitude by the Mercedarians, and the price they paid was
allegiance to the "reducción" of Areguá. Whereas Portuguese in Brazil used
slavery as the dominant mode of governance—colonials called Natives
"blacks of the land"—in Paraguay colonials applied the legal framework of
indios to blacks, turning slaves into encomendados.

Of course, blacks were not universally incorporated into encomienda
units, however some were de facto tributaries because of their marriages with
Guaraní yanaconas. During the 1694 visita of yanaconas in Asunción, the
notary recorded the following family: "Domingo, free *pardo*, married to
Dominga, with two children." Domingo was only recorded in this visita
because of his marriage to an india; nonetheless, because he was counted it
is likely that he resided on the encomendero's land and was therefore
expected to labor for the encomendero.[43]

Even when free, most people of color in Paraguay did not enjoy complete
freedom. The *amparo* (also called *taza*) system in Paraguay suggests that
institutional sinews existed between slavery and indigenous service. Amparo
was based on a royal ordinance issued in 1574, allowing Spanish officials to
tax all free blacks and mulattos.[44] This tax was not practiced systematically
in Spanish America but appears to have been important in colonial Paraguay
because it was melded with indio personal service.[45] Registers of the amparo
indicate that most free colored men and women paid the tax in personal
service to an español appointed by the governor. The creation of the amparo
system can probably be attributed to don Francisco de Alfaro, who may have
instituted the system sometime after he had arrived in Paraguay in 1611.
Apparently, Alfaro ordered all blacks eighteen to fifty years old to pay a tribute of three pesos annually, but because there was no currency in the region
they were ordered to pay in personal service to Spaniards or convents.[46] The
earliest extant record of the amparo is a 1650s register of 222 free blacks and

mulattos, of whom 38, or 17 percent, were "de taza."[47] The register's form is similar to that of a padrón of an Indian pueblo: an español "master" is listed as "appearing with" one or more "mulattos," "pardos," or "negros," who were assigned as amparados. Two of these mulattos were not connected to a master but paid their tax in fruits of the land, probably yerba maté. Thus, the tax on free blacks was enforced in Paraguay and paid in personal service. Each master functioned like an encomendero who received free blacks as personal servants on their estates. Only a few paid their tax in local currencies. In this way, the vast majority of blacks were connected to a Spaniard through the official ties of the tax. The amparo system continued into the eighteenth century. In 1722, there were one thousand amparados, and thirty-eight of these paid the tax in the common Paraguayan currency, either yerba maté or tobacco, rather than in personal service.[48] The amparo tax practically disappeared by the end of the eighteenth century, probably because the amparo turned into forced conscription of blacks into military service. For example, in 1740, the governor of Paraguay relocated hundreds of free blacks to the presidio of Emboscada.[49] The systematic application of the tax on freedmen in Paraguay resembles the logic of encomienda and cuñadasgo. Since most free blacks in the Asunción region paid the amparo tax in personal service, few lived independently of Spaniards; instead, they were incorporated into extended households as tenant farmers or servants.

Spaniards occasionally describe blacks in their households as kin. An español vecino and alférez named Ignacio Azurza described his relationship with a free black man named Francisco Palomares as an "agregación" or "addition" to his family ("agregación en mi familia"). Palomares resided on Azurza's chacra in Lambaré, just southeast of Asunción, where we can assume he managed the farm in exchange for a place to live and a portion of the crops—perhaps Palomares was Azurza's assigned amparo. A 1716 criminal investigation reveals that Azurza extended his family's honor to include Palomares. One evening, Palomares was traveling on the highway to visit one of his married daughters when he passed a contingent of officials and soldiers. Assuming he was a thief, the officers tried to detain Palomares. The surprised and desperate Francisco attempted to flee from his would-be captors, but the soldiers caught him, tied him to a tree, and gave him sixteen lashes for resisting arrest. In the aftermath, Azurza sued the official, claiming that by whipping a "free black man in my family," the official had dishonored Azurza. He demanded the official pay him and thereby "restore my ancient honor and credits, which I am publicly reputed."[50] Azurza's framing of honor as a family affair was typical, but it is striking that his honor was extended to a free black "agregado."

Free and enslaved Africans were situated along a continuum of service and servitude, and enslaved blacks experienced considerably less freedom than their yanacona or mitayo counterparts. When free, people of color were not altogether liberated from the context of personal service and were drawn into relationships like that of Francisco Palomares or other amparados who paid a race tax in the form of personal service.

Africans, *Indios*, and Social Closeness

Africans and indio personal servants were in frequent contact with each other, especially on Spanish chacras. While less frequent, blacks and indios also connected in the reducciones and the religious orders' haciendas. Finally, blacks and indios interacted outside the bounds of Spanish law, cooperating in small bands of maroons or bandits who preyed on travelers coming in and out of Asunción.

Census data from the tributary populations demonstrates that Guaraní-African unions occurred but were not an overwhelming demographic feature.[51] Table 8 includes reports of Afro-indio unions during visitas at pueblos in Paraguay, as well as among the yanacona population in Asunción. There are no records of Afro-indio unions in the padrones prior to 1670; however, this may have been a result of officials' lack of interest in such unions or the ad hoc nature of early padrones. Afro-indio relationships began during periods of labor service: yerba maté harvests or transports, public works projects in Asunción, or field and ranch work on encomenderos' farmsteads. Most Afro-indio married couples resided outside of the pueblos, but some blacks resided with the reducción community.

Aside from the sanctioned spaces within colonial society, blacks and indios associated in small groups of bandits. As early as 1625 in Asunción, officials noted that a group of blacks and Indians robbed unsuspecting travelers as they moved in and out of the city and also stole livestock, clothing,

TABLE 8. Afro-Indian Unions

YEAR	PUEBLO	MALE INDIO UNITED WITH BLACK OR MULATTA
1672	Atira	1
1673	Altos	6
1673	Arecayá	7
1694	Altos	3
1694	Originarios of Asunción	14
1694	Yaguarón	3
1694	Ypane	4
1699	Yuty	4
1714	Guarambaré	3
1714	Yaguaron	6
1714	Yuty	5
1724	Altos	3

Sources: Visita, Altos and Arecayá, 1673, vol. 177, no. 1, NE, ANA; 1694, Visita, Yaguarón, vol. 212, no. 1, NE, ANA; 1694, Visita, Ypane, vol. 212, no. 2, NE, ANA; 1694, Visita, Altos, vol. 212, no. 3, NE, ANA; 1699, Visita, Yuty, vol. 209, no. 1, NE, ANA; 1714, Visita, Yaguarón, vol. 350, no. 1, NE, ANA; 1714, Visita, Guarambare, vol. 350, no. 2, NE, ANA; 1714, Visita, Yuty, vol. 350, no. 3, NE, ANA; 1724, Visita, Altos, vol. 28, no. 4, NE, ANA; and 1672, Visita, Atira, vol. 212, no. 7, NE, ANA.

and weapons from Spanish chacras in Asunción.[52] Led by a runaway mulatto named Antón, the group was composed of three slaves (two from the same Spanish master) and two indios. An example of petit marronage, the group worked together to steal from Spaniards and received help from their families who resided in Lambaré, just on the outskirts of Asunción.[53] In one encounter in September of 1625, two español victims of the bandits' theft went out looking for them in the nearby forests. When the two vecinos found the bandits, a chase on horseback ensued through paths in the thick forests that only the bandits knew. During the chase, Antón, the group's leader, fell from his horse to the ground and the pursuers and pursued came to a standstill with each side threatening the other with arrow shots, sword thrusts, and angry words. Unmoved by these threats, one of the bandits yelled out to his companions: "let's kill these *putos.*" When Antón asked the españoles what they wanted, they asked for their stolen property and demanded that the bandits turn themselves in. Antón hostilely retorted that "by Jesus Christ" they would not turn themselves in to the justices, for surely they would be hanged. To break the stalemate, the bandits returned a few of the stolen items to the vecinos, in exchange for a peaceful separation.

After this dramatic chase and standoff, Antón, an indio named Lope, and a young Spanish-speaking black named Jerónimo all fled the Asunción region with the horses they had stolen and headed north, where they took refuge in a pueblo called Perico (later abandoned and absorbed by Guarambaré). From Perico they moved on to a second pueblo, named Jejuy.[54] These reducciones were fairly young and did not have priests permanently residing in them. If members of these communities had been opposed to these runaways visiting their pueblo, the records do not mention it. The bandits could have arrived under many pretenses, including claiming that they were selling their livestock at the behest of their masters. After what was likely a short stay in the pueblos, Antón and Lope announced that they were going to continue north to trade their horses in Atyrá pueblo (on the northern side of the Jejuy River) where Guaraní were "in rebellion."

Young Jerónimo did not accompany his companions to Jejuy pueblo; somewhere in their journeys he came into contact with an español who knew his master and who convinced him to return to Asunción in his transport barge. Once he arrived in Asunción, Jerónimo went straight to the Mercedarian convent, which hosted a sizeable black population, where he thought he might find safety from the Spanish justices. He was wrong, and on November 7, the sheriff took Jerónimo into custody. Jerónimo's testimony provided ample evidence for the alcalde to put out warrants for the bandits' arrests, but only for the two blacks in the group, not the indios. The Spanish magistrate who issued the warrants defined Antón and his black companion as the architects of this criminal activity and the others, including Jerónimo and the several indios, as pawns or dupes. This was the strategy of Jerónimo's defensor and master, who claimed that Jerónimo was too young, naïve, and immature to be conscientiously associated with Antón and his companions.[55]

Jerónimo's statement revealed that the group was rather fluid, with individuals coming and going as their circumstances changed or as the threat of capture waxed or waned. Jerónimo identified two indios who ran with the bandits for a short time: Hernando, who belonged to Espinoza (supposedly an encomendero), and Mateo, who "used to serve" Juan Bautista Valle. The blacks in the group appear to have been closer as associates and they relied heavily on networks with other blacks. Jerónimo noted that their ringleader, Antón, had often lived with a black slave named Manuel and that on a few occasions the group had interacted with slaves in the "Valle of Balpurunga," who gave them food and information about what was happening in Asunción. Antón's mother, presumably a slave, resided in the Valle de Lambaré and gave the group food and warned them of officials' movements. The documentary trail ends with no resolution. The 1620s were a dangerous time for colonials, who were occupied with major shamanic movements as well as potential Guaraní rebellions and flight, not to mention Guaicurú attacks, so officials may not have had the time or resources to pursue Antón and his band of thieves.

Another band of at least five Afro-indio robbers who preyed on mitayos as they traveled from their pueblos on the camino real to Asunción were active around the year 1669.[56] Several of the black members of the group shared the same Spanish owner, and it is probable that some of the Natives shared the same encomendero. A few of the bandits had formerly been locked up for their crimes, but an india woman and partner to one of the band's Native members had sprung them from jail. Just as in the former case, black bandits' families aided the group. Officials revived their efforts to capture the group after they had kidnapped a mitaya woman in 1669 while she was bathing in the Paraguay River and had stolen the mitaya's belongings, including livestock and a few bows and arrows.

Blacks and indios who found themselves outside the law sought out safety and markets on the Guaraní mission frontier. That Antón and his companion chose to sell their loot in an Indian pueblo rather than Asunción suggests that Asunción was too dangerous a market. Apparently in Atyrá the bandits found privy buyers who were unconcerned by or unaware of how the goods were acquired. Atyrá maintained a reputation as a reliable market for stolen goods; in 1695 a black slave named José was found selling contraband there.[57] A 1623 investigation into the purported murder of an español at the hands of a mulatto slave named Antón from Corrientes suggests that some slaves saw the reducciones as places of refuge from the law. Antón's owner in Corrientes sent an español named Juan Domínguez to recapture Antón for the price of a rifle. Domínguez located Antón and transported him from the Jesuit reducción to the Franciscan reducción of Itatín. It was there that Antón escaped, and when Domínguez attempted to bring him back Antón lassoed him from atop a horse and dragged him behind his horse until he died. Antón was eventually caught and tried, though the record is incomplete.[58] Blacks' and bandits' use of reducciones as places to escape the law and hawk their stolen goods and livestock reflects their far-reaching social networks. Evidence from inquiries into quasi-maroon bands reveals that they developed social bonds while serving together on Spanish chacras and that despite their status as slaves and tributaries they were also able to maintain ties with their kin. Yanacona and black slaves alike possessed a remarkable mobility.

As neighbors on Spanish chacras scattered throughout Asunción and its environs, conflict inevitably arose between slaves and indios. In 1609, a black slave named Antón and two of his fellow slaves attacked an indio from a nearby chacra. Antón explained that the indio Domingo had stolen a horse from his master's property and that when he had attempted to stop him, Domingo hit him in the face with a stick. Incensed at this physical affront and the loss of his master's property, Antón was ready to "avenge" himself (and perhaps his master). Antón asked his two slave companions to help him track Domingo down and punish him. When they found Domingo, they beat him severely, took his clothing, and left him naked and bruised. The magistrate did not look kindly on the slave Antón's retributive justice and punished him with fifty lashes and all the court costs.[59] The nature of the interactions between Antón and Domingo appear similar to those between a Spaniard and indio. Antón was a proficient Spanish speaker but he likely spoke in Guaraní to Domingo. Antón's actions suggest that he was defending his honor. Although Antón may have acted like a Spaniard, or perhaps out of sensibilities of honor that overlapped with español creole culture, the magistrate meted out a punishment he perceived appropriate to Antón's status as a slave: fifty lashes was a grave punishment, one reserved for individuals of the lowest status.

Afro-indio relations ran the gamut, but as subjugated groups blacks and indios had more reasons to create friendships and cooperation. Laboring together in chacras, on yerba maté beneficios, and on public works projects, indios and blacks found community in their common plight. But perhaps indicative of the uneven weight of their respective servitude, it was a black who led each of the two bandit groups discussed above, not an indio. The stakes were higher for a runaway slave than they were for a yanacona, who were often found in places other than their assigned encomienda.

Conclusion

Africans and their descendants were a common feature in colonial Paraguayan society. They mixed with yanaconas on Spanish farmsteads, found partners in the pueblos, labored on the religious ranches and workshops, worked on yerba maté transport gangs, and pestered royal authorities as bandits. As blacks were integrated into the encomienda yanacona, the logic of encomienda, personal service, and relatedness were applied to inform how they experienced community. In his analysis of colonial Yucatán, Matthew Restall identifies six potential "bases of community" for people of color: culture and religion of native African origin, Christian identity, ethnic or racial classifications, occupation, kinship and family life, and location.[60] Applying these categories to Paraguay, the first three are very difficult to analyze given the lack of ecclesiastical records. While there is evidence that blacks participated in the parish of San Blas with other indios, there are no extant records that tell us about their participation in religious sodalities or other religious activities. When it comes to racial and ethnic categories, the data is likewise very thin, but future research based in documentation from the eighteenth and nineteenth centuries will certainly shed new light on the topic.[61] Regarding the last three categories, this chapter has demonstrated that blacks were employed in an array of sectors alongside indios. Kinship and the locations of blacks were linked: Afro-Guaraní unions were frequent because of their constant interaction with yanaconas and mitayos.

The social closeness of Africans and Guaraní, especially in Asunción, led to cultural exchange, but this exchange was uneven depending on the locale. For example, in the Jesuit college in Asunción, African cultural continuity was the norm where at least one priest spoke "Angolan" in order to communicate with the slave population.[62] Of course, cultural continuity here is relative, as creolization and ethnic disruption and reformulation occurred when individuals were taken from their home communities or sold from one master to another. Nonetheless, since the Jesuit college created large, conglomerated populations of African slaves, these populations largely maintained African languages. Imagining African languages mixing with the various Tupí-Guaraní dialects, Guaicuruan languages, and Spanish certainly expands our understanding of colonial Asunción.

While African languages may have predominated on the Jesuits' haciendas and ranches, Africans throughout the rest of Paraguay quickly adopted the Guaraní language. Many blacks who appeared in litigation proceedings could only speak the Guaraní language.[63] In the course of a criminal investigation, the magistrate had asked a bondman named Fernando to testify and even though he had some familiarity with Spanish, as a "black creole" he "knows [Guaraní] better."[64] Fernando gave his testimony in Guaraní and it was translated into Spanish. Somewhere between bilingual Spaniards and the vast majority of monolingual Guaraní-speaking indios on the linguistic continuum, blacks possessed more Spanish than their indio counterparts but less Spanish than poor españoles.

The cultural changes blacks experienced because of their close association with Guaraní ran alongside a degree of community cohesion. For example, black slaves and yanacona servants could be found standing together to defend their masters' property from thieves. Blacks and indios worked closely together and because of their circumstances formed bonds of friendship and allegiance.[65] It is not surprising, therefore, that blacks and Guaraní drank and celebrated together and the presence of Africans in communal gatherings raises questions about the intermingling of African and Guaraní practices in the realm of religion and cosmology.[66] While the population of Africans in Paraguay was modest compared to other regions, it was substantial, especially in Asunción. Further research will surely reveal the myriad manifestations of African cultural influence on Paraguayan colonial and postcolonial society. This chapter has shown that the practice of encomienda overlapped with the practice of slavery. This does not mean that servitude was softer; rather, it points to the impact of Guaraní-informed modes of tribute on colonial practice.

Conclusion

IN FEBRUARY 1707, a middle-aged Guaraní named Nandu (short for Fernando) appeared before one of Asunción's magistrates to defend himself and his family from don Joseph de Abendaño, who claimed that Nandu pertained to his encomienda.[1] To prove that he was not part of a tribute population, Nandu provided a brief narrative of his personal background. As a boy, he belonged to the pueblo of Terecañy, originally founded by Spaniards and Franciscans sometime between 1580 and 1600 in Itatín, a frontier region to the northeast of Asunción. Terecañy was in the heart of the tumultuous yerba maté region and was under constant threat from Guaicurú and Brazilian bandeirantes. In 1676, a massive bandeira destroyed Terecañy, capturing hundreds of Guaraní who were then sold into slavery in São Paulo. Among those who escaped was twelve-year-old Nandu. After arriving in Asunción, he was placed in the care of the Jesuit college. Many of Nandu's townspeople and kin from Terecañy were in Asunción for a brief time before pushing southeast to join one of the Guaraní-Jesuit reducciones.[2] Nandu explained that he "entered into the service of the Jesuits," working on one of their haciendas and farms in and around Asunción. By the 1730s, the Jesuit college in Asunción was an economic powerhouse, possessing 345 African slaves who worked the many properties and industries of the Jesuits. It may have been from among this large African population that Nandu met Manuela, a free mulatta who he married and with whom he had several children.[3]

Nandu claimed that he had never been subject to an encomendero and had always enjoyed his freedom. He added that he was prepared to assemble witnesses to defend his position and keep himself and his children out of "slavery." Nandu's conflation of tribute service and slavery was a common trope among his Jesuit patrons. Nandu made his case through the legal logic of residence, citing a royal provision from 1634 stipulating that a person who had been in one place for ten years or longer could be considered a natural-born inhabitant. Since Nandu had been in the service of the Jesuits for more than ten years, he claimed that he was not subject to Abendaño's encomienda, which originated from a different locale.[4] Unfortunately for Nandu, the governor of the province, don Baltazar García Ros, sided with Abendaño, ordering Nandu to pay tribute. Much was at stake for Nandu. If the sentence were upheld, Nandu and his children would be subject to pay tribute in the form of personal service to their would-be encomendero, a frightening possibility for one who had enjoyed freedom from this system. Nandu appealed and requested that the governor consult the archives to verify that he and his family had not appeared in the most recent padrón of Abendaño's encomienda. The governor found no record of Nandu in the encomienda.

For his part, don Abendaño decried Nandu's "treacheries" and appealed to his own virtuous character, describing himself as a man who sustained his wife and dependents by his own labor. Abendaño further explained that as the crown's royal vassal, he had spent his own resources in defending the king's territories in Paraguay from "frontier enemies." Ultimately, Nandu's tactic paid off. In July of the same year, the governor offered his final sentence and declared Nandu "free from Abendaño's encomienda and any other encomienda."

Nandu's life and the events discussed in his dispute provide a final anecdote to summarize the central findings of this book. First, Nandu's experiences were recovered from a civil trial held in the Civil y Judicial section of the Asunción National Archives and represent a set of sources that have been neglected by historians. This book has used these records to access the lives of Guaraní and construct new narratives about their ethnogenesis and the impact they had on cultural change for españoles and blacks. Nandu's suit unveils his background to suggest that he was an individual who experienced terror and hope, frustration and calm. From a refugee fleeing bandeirantes to a father and husband escaping the grasp of an encomendero, Nandu's narrative allows us to confront his humanity. For decades historians have relied on institutional sources to tell the Guaraní's stories, and these have and will continue to reveal compelling narratives. But, for this historian, there is something moving about being able to access the voices of indigenous men and women and recount their stories of triumph, misery, or mundaneness.

Perhaps the most disruptive period of Nandu's life followed the 1676 bandeira invasion of his reducción. As a frontier and borderland region, Paraguay could be a tumultuous place. Guaicurú attacks and bandeirante raids contributed to a great deal of human suffering, violence, and migration. These frontier dynamics produced unexpected consequences. Guaraní militia activities fostered an interdependence between Spaniards and indios as they both sought to defend themselves and their communities from raids. While Spaniards surely coerced Guaraní to participate in these defensive activities—especially when it came to constructing and maintaining a defensive apparatus—these martial activities also produced an alliance and interdependence. Initial Guaraní-conquistador relations began with creating a common enemy, and throughout the colonial period, the heightened threats that Guaicurú and bandeirantes represented strengthened a sense of colonial community. The numerical importance of Guaraní militias when compared to español militias underscores a truth about the periphery: the colony would not have survived without Guaraní soldiers.

That Nandu's wife, Manuela, was a free mulatta is no surprise given the significant population of Africans in Paraguay generally and the Jesuit college specifically. It may seem odd that there were so many African slaves in Paraguay, given Spaniards' relative poverty, but it only affirms other scholars' findings that African slavery was a fundamental aspect of life in Spanish America and a crucial component of governance.[5] Beyond numerical or economic significance, this book has analyzed the relationship between black and indio social and legal categories. Because most labor relations were understood within the framework of personal service and informed by cuñadasgo, there were few spaces in between the Spanish and Indian (e.g., tributary) socioracial spheres. The 1598 legal dispute over Antón's two mulatto children (reviewed in the previous chapter) underscores encomenderos' dependence on Native personal service and their attempts to expand the category of indio to as many individuals as possible.[6] That freedmen serving under the amparo system were considered an encomienda indicates that indigenous tribute shaped the casta category of "negro" and the practice of slavery. At the level of African cultural changes, it is clear that African ethnogenesis was heavily influenced by Guaraní culture, especially in Africans' use of the Guaraní language. These insights contribute to an expanding patchwork constituting the histories of the African diaspora in Ibero-America and reinforce the need for historians to analyze the construction of "indio" and "negro" corporate-racial categories as imbricated processes.

Nandu's legal troubles stemmed from an entrenched class of encomenderos dependent on indio personal servants. Nandu's predicament was experienced by many other Guaraní who tried to escape the grasp of encomenderos, but his experience was not universal. In fact, as an indio attached to the Jesuit college, Nandu was somewhat of a rarity. This study has disaggregated the Guaraní experience and demonstrates that many Guaraní chose to remain among encomenderos because they found security on Spanish chacras. Those Guaraní who claimed the various farmsteads of Asunción as their "pueblo and reducción" reflected an adoption of the colonial project of reducción, but perhaps their reasons for doing so go beyond hegemony.[7] Cuñadasgo was a deeply rooted paradigm of colonial interrelation and provides an ethnohistorical framework for understanding the actions and behaviors of Guaraní and españoles alike. Spaniards envisioned families as expansive networks and, given the importance of the brother-in-law relationship among Guaraní, Spanish families came to include their encomendados. Personal service included terror, violence, and coercion, but it also could include intimacies. Many españoles of indigenous descent who learned Guaraní from their wet nurses or indigenous mothers and grew up in close social contact with Guaraní servants registered sentiments of relatedness when describing their encomendados. Calling each other "tovajá" or other Guaraní terms of affinal kinship suggests that universal colonial categories are insufficient to describe the local sociality that emerged in Paraguay's encomienda community.

Traditionally, the fringes have been considered spaces of either indigenous desolation or indigenous autonomy; historians have left little room for the overlay of colonial institutions with indigenous sociopolitical organization. In Paraguay, the overlay produced melding and transformation. Spaniards applied tribute obligations to the Guaraní practice of affinal integration and the result was cuñadasgo. In the process, Spaniards and Guaraní both experienced ethnogenesis. Kinship paradigms from distinct cultures, close social contact, violent encounters on the frontiers and borderlands, minimal European immigration, and the vitality of Indian communities in reducciones were the key components of colonial cultural transformation.

NOTES

Introduction

1. Visita, Capt. Juan de Ibarra de Velasco, Villa Rica del Espíritu Santo, 11 March 1652, no. 20, f. 25, Expedientes Coloniales (EC), Archivo y Biblioteca Nacional de Bolivia (ABNB).

2. Brooks, *Captives & Cousins*.

3. I elaborate on relatedness below. See Carsten, *Cultures of Relatedness*.

4. Lockhart, *Of Things of the Indies*, 99.

5. Visita, Capt. Juan de Ibarra Velasco, Villa Rica del Espíritu Santo, 11 March 1652, no. 20, f. 25, EC, ABNB.

6. De Guzmán, *La Argentina*, chap. 18.

7. "Anonymous Jesuit report, 1620 December," in Cortesão and Angelis, *Jesuítas e bandeirantes no Guairá*, 163.

8. For French North America, see Sleeper-Smith, *Indian Women and French Men*. For Peru, see Mangan, *Transatlantic Obligations*; and O'Toole, "Bonds of Kinship."

9. Lambert, "Sentiment and Substance in North Indian Forms of Relatedness," 74–75.

10. Bodenhorn, "'He Used to Be My Relative.'"

11. Mangan, *Transatlantic Obligations*, 4.

12. On the emotional and familial dynamics of master-servant relationships, see van Deusen, "Intimacies of Bondage"; and Stoler, "Tense and Tender Ties."

13. Hanks, *Converting Words*, 2–4.

14. Illustrative of the connections priests drew between reducciones and utopias, the Jesuit José Manuel Peramás (1732–1793) wrote a book that compared the Guaraní reducciones to Plato's *Republic*. Hosne, "Jesuit Reflections on Their Overseas Missions."

15. Sarreal, *Guaraní and Their Missions*, 48. For a demographic portrait of the missions, see Jackson, *Demographic Change and Ethnic Survival*. Numbers for the encomienda pueblos extrapolated from Garavaglia's count of around 6,800 tributaries. If each tributary had three other family members then the population total equals around twenty thousand. Garavaglia, *Mercado interno y economía colonial*, 270.

16. On "tunnel vision," see Lockhart, *Letters and People of the Spanish Indies*, chap. 2.

17. Mörner, *Political and Economic Activities*. See also Hernández, *Misiones del Paraguay*; Furlong, *Misiones y sus pueblos de guaraníes*; and Maeder, *Misiones del Paraguay*. Romanticized portraits of the missions include Cunninghame, *Vanished Arcadia*; and Caraman, *Lost Paradise*.

18. Ganson, *Guaraní under Spanish Rule*; and Wilde, *Religión y poder*. For an analysis of Guaraní religion, see Chamorro, "La buena palabra"; Chamorro, *Teología Guaraní*; and Shapiro, "From Tupã to the Land without Evil." See also the essays in the 2014 special edition of the journal *Revista de Indias*. Several scholars have approached this topic using archaeology: Soares, *Guaraní*; Schiavetto, *A arqueologia guarani*; and Barcelos, *Espaço e arqueologia nas missões jesuíticas*.

19. Fausto, "If God Were a Jaguar"; Tuer, "Old Bones and Beautiful Words"; and Wilde, *Religión y poder*.

20. Ganson, *Guaraní under Spanish Rule*, appendices; Neumann, "'Mientras volaban correos por los pueblos'"; Neumann, "A lança e as cartas"; and Wilde, *Religión y poder*. A great pioneer in Guaraní historical linguistics is Bartomeu Melià, *La lengua guaraní*. Another important linguist of the Guaraní language today is Capucine Boidin, who is the lead scholar on the LANGAS Project or General Languages of South America. Boidin, *Mots guarani du pouvoir*; and Boidin and Melgarejo, "Toward a Guarani Semantic History." See also Brignon, *Mba'e mÿmba pype*; Cerno and Obermeier, "Nuevos aportes de la lingüística para la investigación de documentos en guaraní de la época colonial"; and Melgarejo, *Práctica y semántica en la evangelización de los Guaraníes del Paraguay*.

21. Sarreal, *Guaraní and Their Missions*; Sarreal, "Revisiting Cultivated Agriculture"; and Neumann, *O trabalho guarani missioneiro no Rio da Prata colonial*.

22. Wilde, "Prestigio indígena"; Sarreal, "Caciques as Placeholders"; Avellaneda and Quarleri, "Las milicias guaraníes"; Avellaneda, "La alianza defensiva jesuita-guaraní"; and Avellaneda, "Orígenes de la alianza jesuit-guaraní."

23. Sarreal, *Guaraní and Their Missions*.

24. See Millé, *Crónica de la Orden Franciscana*; and Molina, "La obra franciscana en el Paraguay." For a survey of the Franciscans in Paraguay, see Durán Estragó, *Presencia franciscana en el Paraguay*. Durán Estragó also treats the individual pueblo of Caazapá in *San José de Caazapá*. Meléndez, *Levantamientos indígenas ante los abusos de la encomienda en Paraguay*. Writing in a hagiographic vein, Fray José Luis Salas describes Franciscan activities in Guairá in "Villa Rica y los Franciscanos."

25. It is a Spanish translation of his 1979 French-language monograph. Necker, *Indiens Guarani et chamanes franciscains*. See also Necker, "La reacción de los guaraníes"; and Necker, *Indios Guaraníes y chamanes franciscanos*.

26. Salinas, "Vida y trabajo en la misión"; Salinas, *Dominación colonial y trabajo indígena*; and Garavaglia, *Mercado interno y economía colonial*.

27. Franciscans were the first to admit this. Lamenting the loss of crucial depositions about the alleged killing of a priest at the hands of rebellious Guaraní, one

Franciscan noted in 1627 that "this carelessness with our past . . . is worthy of crying tears of blood." "Investigación del martirio del hermano fray Juan Bernardo," Fray Gregorio de Osuna, 1627, in Salas, *Selección de documentos Franciscanos*, 401.

28. Branislava Susnik's ethnohistories of the Guaraní are foundational. Susnik moves between civil, Franciscan, and Jesuit records to construct a narrative of indigenous cultural decline. Her close attention to ethnographic detail in the sources yields a wealth of insights into colonial Guaraní culture, but the prose is often confusing, the narrative overreaching, and the use of sources uncritical. Susnik, *Los aborígenes del Paraguay; El rol de los indígenas; Una visión socio-antropológica del Paraguay del siglo XVIII; Una visión socio-antropológica del Paraguay, XVI–1/2 XVII;* "Ni indio, ni española"; and *El indio colonial del Paraguay.*

29. A staple in the field of the study of Tupí-Guaraní peoples, or Tupinology, is Eduardo Batalha Viveiros de Castro, *From the Enemy's Point of View.* Hélène Clastres's influential *The-Land-without-Evil: Tupí Prophetism* argues that Tupian prophetism was a destructive social force, but it relies too heavily and without sufficient scrutiny on modern anthropological accounts. See also H. Clastres, *La terre sans mal.* Earlier ethnographies explore Guaraní religion's supposed syncretism or purity. Curt Nimuendajú argues that colonial Guaraní adopted Christianity only to mask inward Guaraní cosmologies. Nimuendajú, *Eastern Timbira;* and Nimuendajú, *Los mitos de creación y de destrucción.* Egon Schaden's *Aspectos fundamentais da cultura guaraní* argues that Guaraní were profoundly changed by Christianization but that these external elements were incorporated into primitive frameworks. Schaden draws on León Cadogan's work, *Ayvu rapyta.* See also Pierre Clastres, *Chronicle of the Guayaki Indians.* Carlos Fausto's brilliant analysis challenges historians to avoid the trap of using modern anthologies as "ground zero" for analyzing change across time (Fausto, "If God Were a Jaguar").

30. Garavaglia, *Mercado interno y economía colonial.*

31. Roulet, *La resistencia de los guaraní;* and Tuer, "Tigers and Crosses."

32. Restall, *Seven Myths of the Spanish Conquest,* 57.

33. Hassig, *Polygamy and the Rise and Demise of the Aztec Empire,* 7. There are few studies of Guaraní women, but an important exception is Potthast-Jutkeit, "*Paraíso de Mahoma.*"

34. See Ruíz de Montoya, *Conquista espiritual,* chap. 21 and his discussion of celibacy.

35. Barabara Ganson briefly treats women with an analysis of the *coty guazy,* a kind of *recogimiento* for single, widowed, or orphaned women and girls. Ganson, *Guaraní under Spanish Rule,* 72–76.

36. Melià, *La lengua guaraní,* 124, 129.

37. Paraguay is more like Brazil in this regard. On the importance of Portuguese or mestizo go-betweens in Brazil, see Metcalf, *Go-Betweens and the Colonization of Brazil;* and Tuer, "Tigers and Crosses." Paraguay can be contrasted with Mexico, where

indigenous notaries and translators had a profound impact on state practice. Lockhart, *Nahuas after the Conquest*; Terraciano, *Mixtecs of Colonial Oaxaca*; and Yannakakis, *Art of Being In-Between*.

38. Boidin, "Mots guarani du pouvoir, pouvoir de mots guarani."

39. Garavaglia, *Mercado interno y economía colonial*, 206–10.

40. Powers, *Andean Journeys*, 7.

41. Dean and Leibsohn, "Hybridity and Its Discontents," 5; and Salomon, "Indian Women of Early Colonial Quito."

42. While his primary subjects are the Amazonian Araweté, Viveiros de Castro makes arguments about the larger Tupian cultural community, both past and present. Viveiros de Castro, *From the Enemy's Point of View*, 3–4.

43. Wilde, *Religión y poder*, 113.

44. Viveiros de Castro, *From the Enemy's Point of View*, 25.

45. Lee, "European Promise of Militant Christianity." On "centrifugal dynamism," see Viveiros de Castro, *Inconstancy of the Indian Soul*, 31.

46. Burkhart, *Slippery Earth*.

47. Karen Powers defines *ethnogenesis* as "the process by which distinct ethnic cultures are continually recreated over time, especially cultures that have experienced colonization." Powers, *Andean Journeys*, 183n1. Jonathan Hill's definition of *ethnogenesis* highlights the severities of colonialism: "a creative adaptation to a general history of violent changes—including demographic collapse, forced relocations, enslavement, ethnic soldiering, ethnocide, and genocide—imposed during the historical expansion of colonial and national states in the Americas." Hill, "Introduction," 1, 2.

48. Voss, *Archaeology of Ethnogenesis*, 3.

49. Ortiz, *Cuban Counterpoint*.

50. Service, "Encomienda in Paraguay"; and *Spanish-Guaraní Relations*, 7. See also Foster, *Culture and Conquest*.

51. Alberro, *Del gachupín al criollo*.

52. Calloway, *New Worlds for All*; and Merrell, *Indians' New World*.

53. Earle, "'If You Eat Their Food'"; and Earle, *Body of the Conquistador*. See also Memmi, *Colonizer and the Colonized*.

54. Voss uses the term *Californios* to refer to colonial settlers in Alta California, but she is also dealing with a much later period. Voss, *Archaeology of Ethnogenesis*.

55. The literature on race is vast. A few notables that have influenced my framing are Cope, *Limits of Racial Domination*; Fisher and O'Hara, *Imperial Subjects*; Rappaport, *Disappearing Mestizo*; Seed, "Social Dimensions of Race"; and R. Schwaller, *Géneros De Gente in Early Colonial Mexico*.

56. Voss, *Archaeology of Ethnogenesis*, 2.

57. Telesca, *Tras los expulsos*, 132.

58. Bryant, *Rivers of Gold*, 5.

59. Pla, *Hermano negro*. Pla focuses on eighteenth-century sources and highlights Blacks' roles as domestic servants. See also de Granda, "Origen, función y estructura";

Argüello Martínez, *El rol de los esclavos negros*; and Boccia Romañach, *Esclavitud en el Paraguay*. Argentine historian Ignacio Telesca shows in his important *Tras los expulsos* that the Paraguayan slave population was crucial to the regional economy.

60. See, especially, the works of Cecilio Báez (1862–1941), Manuel Domínguez (1868–1935), Fulgencio R. Moreno (1872–1933), Blas Garay (1873–1899), and Juan O'Leary (1879–1969).

61. On this generation of historians, see Telesca's excellent essay "Paraguay en el centenario."

62. Restall, *Beyond Black and Red*; and Restall, *Black Middle*.

63. See O'Toole, *Bound Lives*.

Chapter 1

1. Male and female Guaraní served Spaniards, but the majority of the servant population in the early years were women. In the following suit, witnesses mentioned that indios were engaged in building an adobe wall while india *criadas* or servants labored on hammocks. Juan Rodríguez sues Cristobal Bravo, 1552, vol. 5, f. 19–69, Sección Copias (SC), Archivo Nacional de Asunción (ANA).

2. "Presbítero Francisco González Paniagua, Carta al cardinal Juan de Tavira," 3 March 1545, in Torre Revello, *Documentos históricos y geográficos*, 449.

3. Steve Stern makes the following observation about the conquest in Paraguay: "Not only did treasure dreams become anachronistic. So did conventional Christian morality: the Paraguayan conquistadors discarded the fusion of formal monogamy and informal concubinage tolerated by the Church, and turned toward the Guarani practice of open polygamy." I agree with Stern's sentiment that something new was going on in Paraguay, that cuñadasgo was not simply concubinage. However, this did not demand a radical break from the Spaniards' regular practice of concubinage. Stern, "Paradigms of Conquest," 13–14.

4. "1620 December, Anonymous Jesuit report," in Cortesão and Angelis, *Jesuítas e bandeirantes no Guairá*, 163. This account was likely written by Marciel de Lorenzana. See Melià, *La lengua guaraní*, 117n57.

5. Lévi-Strauss, "Social Use of Kinship Terms," 398.

6. Ruíz de Montoya, *Tesoro de la lengua Guaraní* (2011), 121.

7. See "Inquiry into the discovery of a dead Indian," 1545, vol. 3, f. 128, SC, ANA.

8. For documented references to male captives, see Testament of Pedro Arias, 1549, vol. 4, f. 153–60, SC, ANA.

9. This functioned in Guaraní society as valiant warriors redirected bride debts toward themselves by distributing female captives taken in war. See Roulet, *La Resistencia de los guaraní*, 80–87.

10. This narrative summary is distilled from authors who have painstakingly reviewed a large corpus of sources to elucidate aspects of the early settler experience. Roulet, *La resistencia de los guaraní*; Tuer, "Tigers and Crosses"; Susnik, *El indio*

colonial del Paraguay; and Rubio, *Exploración y conquista del Río de la Plata*. For a synthesis, see Kleinpenning, *Paraguay*.

11. Schmidl, *Viaje al Río de la Plata* (1997), 43.

12. Ruíz de Montoya, *Spiritual Conquest*, chap. 10.

13. Soares, *Guaraní*, 122.

14. Catafasto de Souza, "O sistema econômico," 224.

15. See Ruíz de Montoya, *Tesoro de la lengua Guaraní* (2011), 16.

16. Susnik, *El indio colonial del Paraguay*; Susnik, *Los aborígnes del Paraguay*; Susnik, *Una visión socio-antropológica del Paraguay, XVI-1/2 XVII*; and Roulet, *La resistencia de los guaraní*.

17. Wilde, "Prestigio indígena"; Wilde, *Religión y poder*, 110; and Santos, "Clastres e Susnik," 210–13.

18. "Father Francisco de Andrada to Council of the Indies," 1 March 1545, in Torre Revello, *Documentos históricos y geográficos*, 415. See also de Barros Laraia, "Kinship Studies in Brazil"; Lévi-Strauss, "Social Use of Kinship Terms." For a concise summary of social organization among the Tupinambá, see Fausto, "Fragmentos de história e cultura tupinambá."

19. Roulet, *La resistencia de los guaraní*, 80–90.

20. Ruíz de Montoya, *Spiritual Conquest*, chap. 10.

21. Roulet, *La resistencia de los guaraní*, 85. Turner describes bride service among the Kayapó, a Gê group of the southern Amazon, and the basic principles and patterns may approximate the Guaraní practice. Turner, "Kayapo of Central Brazil," 258.

22. Ruíz de Montoya, *Spiritual Conquest*, chap. 10.

23. Ruíz de Montoya, chap. 10.

24. Ruíz de Montoya, *Tesoro de la lengua Guaraní* (2011), 236, 90.

25. A special thanks to Brian Owensby for his suggestions on this topic.

26. Thomaz de Almeida and Mura, "Historia y territorio entre los Guarani"; and Lévi-Strauss, "Social Use of Kinship Terms."

27. Metcalf, *Go-Betweens and the Colonization of Brazil*, 24; and Coates, *Convicts and Orphans*.

28. Tuer, "Tigers and Crosses," 124n15.

29. "Carta de Hernando Ribera al Emperador," 25 February 1545, in Torre Revello, *Documentos históricos y geográficos*, 410.

30. For a discussion of conquistador cannibalism at Buenos Aires, see Tuer, "Tigers and Crosses," 92–97.

31. Tuer, 101.

32. Metcalf, *Go-Betweens and the Colonization of Brazil*, 10.

33. Schmidl, *Viaje al Río de la Plata* (1997), chap. 18; and "Carta de Francisco de Villalta," 22 June 1556, in Schmidl, *Viaje al Río de la Plata* (1903), app. A.

34. Pagden, *Fall of Natural Man*, 91; and Earle, *Body of the Conquistador*, 78–83.

35. This was a common practice among conquistadors. See Schwaller and Nader, *First Letter from New Spain*.

36. Schmidl, *Viaje al Río de la Plata* (1997), chap. 21.

37. Barco de Centenera, *La Argentina*, canto tercero.

38. This nationalist history is described in Telesca, "Paraguay en el centenario," 185.

39. Roulet, *La resistencia de los guaraní*, 116–18.

40. "Carta dirigida al Consejo de Indias," fray Francisco de Andrada, 1 March 1545, in Torre Revello, *Documentos históricos y geográficos*, 416; Tuer, "Tigers and Crosses," 115–16; and Roulet, *La resistencia de los guaraní*, 119.

41. Tuer, "Tigers and Crosses," 116; and Roulet, *La resistencia de los guaraní*, 135.

42. Roulet, *La resistencia de los guaraní*, 123.

43. "Relación sobre lo ocurrido en el Rio de la Plata," Pero Hernández, 28 January 1545, in Torre Revello, *Documentos históricos y geográficos*, 397.

44. "Carta dirigida al Consejo Real de las Indias," Gerónimo Ochoa de Eizaguirre, 8 March 1545, in Torre Revello, *Documentos históricos y geográficos*, 451–52. For comments on the social inequality in the conquest, see Tuer, "Tigers and Crosses," 119.

45. "La relación que dejo Domingo Martínez de Irala en Buenos Aires al tiempo que la despobló," ca. 1541, in Torre Revello, *Documentos históricos y geográficos*, 299.

46. Tuer, "Tigers and Crosses," 119.

47. Owensby, "'As Currency in These Realms.'"

48. Tuer, "Tigers and Crosses," 117.

49. "Relación sobre lo ocurrido en el Rio de la Plata," Pero Hernández, 28 January 1545, in Torre Revello, *Documentos históricos y geográficos*, 397. See also Rubio, *Exploración y conquista del Río de la Plata*, 190. Tuer notes that "by issuing this injunction against ritual cannibalism, Cabeza de Vaca had intervened in a more serious matter of an indigenous warrior norm. Before his arrival, the conquistadors' tolerance of ritual cannibalism had been an important aspect of their identification by the Carios as *avá* and the ability of Irala as a *mburuvichá* to attract warriors and undertake raids. With its prohibition, a distinction was being drawn between the Spanish command and the Cario war chiefs that threatened the social cohesion of their alliance and the unity of tekó-ás in the region, which was affirmed by eating enemy warriors taken in raids." Tuer, "Tigers and Crosses," 156.

50. "Instrucciones dadas por el adelantado Álvar Núñez Cabeza de Vaca al teniente de gobernador, capitán Juan de Salazar de Espinosa," September 1543, in Torre Revello, *Documentos históricos y geográficos*.

51. "Relación sobre lo ocurrido en el Rio de la Plata," Pero Hernández, 28 January 1545, in Torre Revello, *Documentos históricos y geográficos*, 397.

52. "Decretos del adelantado Álvar Núñez Cabeza de Vaca," 5 and 16 April 1542, in Fitte Ernesto, *Hambre y desnudeces*, 294–95.

53. "Carta dirigida al Consejo de Indias," Presbítero Francisco de Andrada, 1 March 1545, in Torre Revello, *Documentos históricos y geográficos*, 416–17. Andrada noted that a Guaraní chieftain named Pedro de Mendoza was the one and only chieftain to receive Catholic marriage. Andrada's main concern was that he not be married to a relative and therefore break canon laws related to incest.

54.   "Hallsmos señor en esta trra una maldita costumbre q las mugeres son las q siembran y cojen el bastimento y como quiera q no nos podrimas aqui sostentar con la pobreza de la trra contentando sus parientes con rescates para q les hiziesen de comer." "Carta dirigida al Consejo de Indias," Presbítero Francisco de Andrada, 1 March 1545, in Torre Revello, *Documentos históricos y geográficos,* 417.

55.   Roulet, *La resistencia de los guaraní,* 179.

56.   Lockhart, *Of Things of the Indies,* 99.

57.   Potthast-Jutkeit, *"Paraíso de Mahoma,"* 34.

58.   De Guzmán, *La Argentina,* chap. 18; and Trelles, *Revista del archivo general,* 50–65. Jesuit priests observed that Spaniards referred to Guaraní caciques as *cherutí* or "maternal uncle," though it is unclear how this term functioned socially. It may have been to designate nonmarriageable kinship units. Children of maternal uncles did not marry. Uncles were called fathers. Wilde, *Religión y poder,* 142. See also Lafone Quevedo, "Guaraní Kinship Terms."

59.   "El guaraní se huelga en gran manera / De verse emparentar con los cristianos: / A cada cual le dan su compañera / Los padres, y parientes mas cercanos. / ¡O lástima de ver muy lastimera, / Que de aquestas mancebas los hermanos, / A todos los que están amancebados, / Les llaman hoy en dia sus cuñados." Barco de Centenera, *La Argentina,* canto cuarto. I thank Violeta Lorenzo for her assistance with the translation of these stanzas.

60.   "India mujer; hembra; parienta; mujer verdadera." Ruíz de Montoya, *Tesoro de la lengua Guaraní* (2011), 119.

61.   For *kuña* as wife, see Lafone Quevedo, "Guaraní Kinship Terms," 429.

62.   Orozco, *Tesoro de la lengua castellana,* 551v.

63.   Patterson, *Slavery and Social Death.*

64.   See, Carta anua, Claudio Ruyer, 9 November 1627, in Trelles, *Revista del archivo general,* 171; Ruíz de Montoya, *Spiritual Conquest,* chap. 10; and Soares, *Guaraní,* 109.

65.   See the following case of rape, which will be discussed in the next chapter: 1577, vol. 11, no. 7, f. 110, SH, ANA, SH.

66.   Stoler, "Tense and Tender Ties," 4.

67.   Van Deusen focuses on indigenous slaves who experienced deracination through forced migrations over vast distances. Van Deusen, "Intimacies of Bondage," 15–16. See also van Deusen, *Global Indios;* and van Deusen, "Diasporas, Bondage, and Intimacy in Lima." For more on violence and sexuality in early colonial society in Spanish America, see Burket, "Indian Women and White Society"; and Powers, *Women in the Crucible of Conquest.*

68.   Van Deusen, "Intimacies of Bondage," 26.

69.   "Tiene muchas mugeres de la dha generación hermanas e primas hermanas e otras parientes teniendo açeso carnal con ellas çelandolas como si fueran sus mugeres." "Relación," escribano Pero Hernández, 28 January 1545, in Torre Revello, *Documentos históricos y geográficos,* 396.

70.   "Testamento," Domingo Martínez de Irala, 13 March 1556, in de Lafuente

Machaín, *El gobernador Domingo Martínez de Irala*, 239. See Burns, "Gender and the Politics of Mestizaje."

71. The analysis that follows is drawn from a sampling of seventy-six testaments from the 1540s to 1700, fourteen from the sixteenth century. See also Susnik's analysis of last wills and testaments in Susnik, *El indio colonial del Paraguay*, 13–14.

72. "Se de a María niña hija de María my criada e a Petrolyna niña hija de Francisca my criada a cada una de las dhas niñas mil pesos de oro a su justo peso...si dios fuere servido de las llegr a tpo q se puedan casar o tomar otro estado e orden de vivir lo cual yo les mando." 1547, vol. 4, f. 78, SC, ANA.

73. In 1612, the cabildo begged that the crown endow Bocanegra's casa de recogidas and orphanage (consisting of one hundred "orphan daughters of the nobles"), claiming that it was in utter ruin. 1612, vol. 14, no. 3, SH, ANA, SH.

74. Burns, "Gender and the Politics of Mestizaje," 9. See also Burns, *Colonial Habits*.

75. 1543, vol. 1, f. 151, SC, ANA.

76. 1549, vol. 4, f. 153–60, SC, ANA.

77. Emphasis added. A Special thanks to Luis Fernando Restrepo for reviewing my translation and Carlos Fausto for providing insights on this passage. "Hera la costumbre de los yndios de la tierra servir a los xpianos y de darles sus hijas o hermanas y venir a sus casas por via de parentesco y amystad y ansi heran servidos los xpianos porque tenian los xpianos muchos hijos en la gente natural de aquella tierra y a esta causa venian los yndios a servir como a casa de parientes y sobrinos." "Relación de las cosas que han pasado desde que prendieron don Álvar Núñez Cabeza de Vaca," Diego Tellez de Escobar, 1556, in Garay, *Colección de documentos*, 270.

78. *Sobrinos* could be read as including both genders.

79. I thank Suzanne Oakdale for helping me think through this idea. Tuer also argues that conquistadors' mestizo children were part of Guaraní social networks. She contends that as fathers-in-law to the conquistadors, Guaraní tuvichá could call on mestizo children to fight in their raids; therefore, numerous mestizo children increased a conquistador's social importance. See Tuer, "Tigers and Crosses," 112.

80. In the following suit, witnesses mentioned that male indios were engaged in building an adobe wall while criadas labored on hammocks. "Juan Rodriguéz against Cristóbal Bravo for breaking and entering and kidnapping," 1552, vol. 5, f. 19–69, SC, ANA.

81. For an account of enslavement among the Mbayas and Tomacosis, see "Deposition of Juan Redondo vecino," 1564, in Garay, *Colección de documentos*, items 7 and 9.

82. Zavala, *Origenes de la colonización*, 162; C. Pastore, *La lucha por la tierra*, 344; Saeger, "Survival and Abolition," 63; Necker, *Indios Guaraníes y chamanes franciscanos*, 64–66; and Susnik, *Una visión socio-antropológica del Paraguay, XVI-1/2 XVII*, 85. By the end of the sixteenth century, governors worked to eradicate trading of Guaraní servants. See "Governor Hernando Arias de Saavedra on the bad treatment of indios," 1591, vol. 1, no. 52, SH, ANA.

83.   On the sale of indias, see also Roulet, *La resistencia de los guaraní*, 178.

84.   See Candela, "Las mujeres indígenas," 11.

85.   "Fray Martín González to emperor don Carlos, Asunción," 25 June 1556, in *Cartas de Indias*, 609.

86.   "Relación sobre lo ocurrido en el Río de la Plata," Pero Hernández, 28 January 1545, in Torre Revello, *Documentos históricos y geográficos*, 395.

87.   For his part, Irala blamed unnamed conquistadors for having sold Carío to traders from Brazil and accused Portuguese authorities for their complicity. Candela, "Las mujeres indígenas," 11–12; and Tuer, "Tigers and Crosses," 274–75. One the sale of indias, see also Roulet, *La resistencia de los guaraní*, 178.

88.   "Carta dirigida al Consejo Real de las Indias," Gerónimo Ochoa de Eizaguirre, 8 March 1545, in Torre Revello, *Documentos históricos y geográficos*, 454.

89.   See Brooks, *Captives & Cousins*.

90.   "Carta dirigida al Consejo Real de las Indias," Gerónimo Ochoa de Eizaguirre, 8 March 1545, in Torre Revello, *Documentos históricos y geográficos*, 454.

91.   "Relación sobre lo ocurrido en el Río de la Plata," Pero Hernández, 28 January 1545, in Torre Revello, *Documentos históricos y geográficos*, 395.

92.   "Para que fuese a llorar." 1545, vol. 3, f. 128, SC, ANA.

93.   Schmidl, *Viaje al Río de la Plata* (1997), chap. 20.

94.   See Schmidl, chap. 20; "Against Juan Gallego for disturbing Indian villages," [1540s], vol. 1, f. 60, SC, ANA; and "Decretos del adelantado Álvar Núñez Cabeza de Vaca," in Fitte Ernesto, *Hambre y desnudeces*, 293–95.

95.   Roulet, *La resistencia de los guaraní*, 165–65. See also Susnik, *El indio colonial del Paraguay*.

96.   Tuer, "Tigers and Crosses," chap. 6.

97.   Other documents featuring officials who specifically marked individual yanacona as captives are litigation records. See, for example, the dispute over the possession of a yanacona named Juana who was taken as a captive in 1605. Vol. 2185, no. 1, Civil y Judicial (CJ), ANA. The majority of the suits reveal, however, that yanacona were acquired through kinship networks.

98.   [Ca. 1595], vol. 162, f. 103, Nueva Encuadernación (NE), ANA.

99.   [Ca. 1595], vol. 162, f. 112, NE, ANA.

100.   [Ca. 1595], vol. 162, f. 105, NE, ANA.

101.   "Relación sobre lo ocurrido en el Rio de la Plata," Pero Hernández, 28 January 1545, in Torre Revello, *Documentos históricos y geográficos*, 399.

102.   Rousseau, *Discourse on Inequality*, 35.

103.   Crosby, *Ecological Imperialism*.

104.   See "Decretos del adelantado Álvar Núñez Cabeza de Vaca," in Fitte Ernesto, *Hambre y desnudeces*, 293–95.

105.   "Domingo Martínez to Council of the Indies," 2 July 1556, in *Cartas de Indias*, 623.

106.   Fray Diego Gonzalez, Carta anua, 1611, in Ravignani and Leonhardt, *Iglesia*,

128–29. For Guaireño observations about the centrality of iron, see Romero Jensen, *El Guairá*, 55.

107.   1544, vol. 11, no. 4, f. 34, SH, ANA.

108.   1577, vol. 11, no. 7, SH, ANA.

109.   Murray, *Indian Giving*, 1, 6, 21.

110.   Gregory, *Gifts and Commodities*, 19.

111.   Compare to the North American context where colonists recognized that some Indians used metal objects as prestige items. Richter, *Before the Revolution*, 133–41.

112.   "Y vengo con los míos a hacer el trueque (que en su lengua quiere decir venganza) de la muerte de los batates que vos otros matasteis." Cabeza de Vaca, *Naufragios y comentarios*, chap. 25.

113.   A special thanks to Mickaël Orantin for making me aware of this concept. Orantin, "Remarques sur le verbe 'vendre.'"

114.   Ruíz de Montoya, *Tesoro de la lengua Guaraní* (2011), 255.

115.   Staden, *Hans Staden's True History*, app. See also Ruíz de Montoya's account of two neophyte evangelizers who approached a Guaraní village to invite them to join the reducción. They were both offered a wife. One refused, one accepted, both were cannibalized. Ruíz de Montoya, *Spiritual Conquest*, chap. 20.

116.   See Fausto, *Warfare and Shamanism*, 182, 231.

117.   Fausto, 231.

118.   Staden, *Hans Staden's True History*, app.

119.   Mathieu and Meyer, "Comparing Axe Heads." See also Mann, *1491*, 335–36.

120.   William M. Denevan and William E. Doolittle, respectively, are proponents of this idea. See Mann, *1491*, 337.

121.   "Anonymous Jesuit report, 1620," in Cortesão and Angelis, *Jesuítas e bandeirantes no Guairá*, 167.

122.   "Antonio de la Trinidad to the Council of the Indies," 2 July 1556, in Garay, *Colección de documentos*, 227.

123.   Fausto, *Warfare and Shamanism*, 37. Compare Fausto's observations with the case studies in Métraux, "Revolution of the Ax," 30.

124.   Viveiros de Castro, *Inconstancy of the Indian Soul*, 50.

125.   See "Rodrigo Ortiz Melgarejo to Governor Céspedes Jeria," 1629, cited in Romero Jensen, *El Guairá*, 163–65.

126.   "Carta dirigida al Consejo Real de las Indias," Gerónimo Ochoa de Eizaguirre, 8 March 1545, in Torre Revello, *Documentos históricos y geográficos*, 453.

127.   See Surah 4 in the Koran.

128.   "Carta dirigida al Consejo Real de las Indias," Gerónimo Ochoa de Eizaguirre, 8 March 1545, in Torre Revello, *Documentos históricos y geográficos*, 451.

129.   "Carta de Juan de Salazar," 20 March 1556, in *Cartas de Indias*, 581.

130.   "Paniagua to Cardenal Juan de Tavira," 3 March 1545, in Torre Revello, *Documentos históricos y geográficos*. See also, "Father Francisco de Andrada to Council of the Indies," 1 March 1545, in Torre Revello, *Documentos históricos y geográficos*, 417.

131. Service, "Encomienda in Paraguay," 232. See Lockhart, *Nahuas after the Conquest*; and Gibson, *Aztecs under Spanish Rule*.

132. See Roulet, *La resistencia de los guaraní*, 118.

Chapter 2

1. "Martin de Orué to the Crown," 4 April 1573, in Garay, *Colección de documentos relativos*, 165.

2. See also Vargas Machuca, *Indian Militia*.

3. In 1552, Juan Rodriguez Barbero described himself as an *estante* (temporary inhabitant) "in this conquest of the Río de la Plata." 1552, vol. 5, f. 19, SC, ANA.

4. Susnik, *Una visión socio-antropológica del Paraguay, XVI-1/2 XVII*, 26; Susnik, *El indio colonial del Paraguay*; Zavala, *Orígenes de la colonización*, 176–96; and Necker, *Indios Guaraníes y chamanes franciscanos*, 57. With slight variations, these authors argue that the introduction of the encomienda abruptly ended networks of kinship and inaugurated a form of colonial slavery. Others discern a gradual waning of Guaraní cultural influence on the encomienda and an ambiguous Spanish colonial dominance. Service notes that around 1600 kinship entirely disappeared from the encomienda. Service, "Encomienda in Paraguay," 234; and Service, *Spanish-Guaraní Relations*. Roulet's conclusions are more nuanced, for she argues that kinship was entirely excluded from the encomienda but that by the seventeenth century Guaraní were somehow able to reinsert elements of kinship into the encomienda. Roulet, *La resistencia de los guaraní*, 18, 248–68. Tuer finds a waning influence of Guaraní kinship reflected in the diminishing power of the mburuvichá and mestizo go-betweens. Tuer, "Tigers and Crosses," chap. 8.

5. Necker, *Indios Guaraníes y chamanes franciscanos*, 57.

6. Roulet, *La resistencia de los guaraní*; and Tuer, "Tigers and Crosses," 309–10. Both Roulet and Tuer note that Guaraní rebellions in the 1550s, 1560s, and 1580s reflected the profound transformations introduced by the encomienda. I do not disagree but add that other sources simultaneously demonstrate that Guaraní actively used networks of cuñadasgo.

7. For the Nahuatl, see Gibson, *Aztecs under Spanish Rule*; and Lockhart, *Nahuas after the Conquest*. For Peru, see Spalding, *Huarochiri*; Stern, *Peru's Indian Peoples*; and Puente Brunke, *Encomienda y encomenderos*.

8. Silvio Zavala's classic works on Indian personal service in New Spain, Peru, and the Río de la Plata argue that the institution was a thinly veiled form of slavery. Zavala, *Orígenes de la colonización*, 162; Zavala, *El servicio personal de los indios en el Perú*; Zavala, *El servicio personal de los indios en la Nueva España*; and M. Pastore, "Taxation, Coercion, Trade and Development," 344.

9. See Rushforth, *Bonds of Alliance*; Brooks, *Captives & Cousins*; and Miller, *Problem of Slavery as History*.

10. After the crown issued the New Laws (1542), Spanish enslavement of Natives

waned, especially with legal enforcement in the 1550s. Simpson, *Encomienda in New Spain*, chap. 10; van Deusen, "Diasporas, Bondage, and Intimacy"; van Deusen, "Intimacies of Bondage"; and van Deusen, *Global Indios*.

11. 1595, vol. 12, ff. 130r–145r, SC, ANA.

12. Saeger, "Survival and Abolition."

13. Tuer, "Tigers and Crosses," 278.

14. Roulet, *La resistencia de los guaraní*, 247.

15. Susnik, *Una visión socio-antropológica del Paraguay, XVI-1/2 XVII*, 31.

16. On early campaigns to maintain discrete populations in the Americas, see Simpson, *Encomienda in New Spain*, chaps. 9 and 10. On reducciones in Peru, see Mumford, *Vertical Empire*.

17. "Juan Pavón to Council of the Indies," 15 June 1556, in *Cartas de Indias*, 595.

18. Governor Irala's response to crown officials regarding repartimientos, cited in de Lafuente Machaín, *El gobernador Domingo Martínez de Irala*, 485–86.

19. Tuer, "Tigers and Crosses," 315.

20. "Juan Salmerón de Heredia to the crown," 1556, in Garay, *Colección de documentos*, 235. Irala did create larger encomiendas but these were apparently rare. One early encomienda grant, given to Francisco de Escobar in 1558, included the teyÿ or perhaps teko'a of a tuvichá named Icoca and contained some forty-four men, totaling two hundred souls. Susnik, *El indio colonial del Paraguay*, 171.

21. "Bartolomé García to the crown," 24 June 1556, in *Cartas de Indias*, 601–3.

22. See "Antonio de la Trinidad to Council of Indies," ca. 1556, in Garay, *Colección de documentos*.

23. "Juan Pavón to Council of the Indies," 15 June 1556, in *Cartas de Indias*, 595.

24. "Woman as Conqueror," Letter of doña Isabel Guevara, 1556, Paraguay, in Lockhart and Otte, *Letters and People of the Spanish Indies*, 15–17.

25. Zavala, *Orígenes de la colonización*, 168.

26. I follow Tuer's average estimates here. Tuer, "Tigers and Crosses," 313.

27. "Relación de las cosas que han pasado desde que prendieron don Álvar Núñez Cabeza de Vaca," Diego Tellez de Escobar, 1556, in Garay, *Colección de documentos*, 270. I thank Tuer for bringing this passage to my attention. Tuer, "Tigers and Crosses," 319.

28. Accounts of the 1560 uprising are brief. See "Provanzas de los méritos y servicios de Francisco Ortiz de Vergara," in Garay, *Colección de documentos*, 473; de Guzmán, *La Argentina*, chap. 8; and Schmidl, *Viaje al Río de la Plata* (1997).

29. "Martín González to the Council of the Indies," 5 July 1556, in *Cartas de Indias*, 632; and "Domingo Martínez to don Carlos," 2 July 1556, in *Cartas de Indias*, 625.

30. "Ordenanzas sobre repartimientos y encomiendas," Gov. Irala, 14 May 1556, in de Lafuente Machaín, *El gobernador Domingo Martínez de Irala*, 512.

31. Tuer suggests that the encomienda removed women's political power. Her argument hinges on the idea that before the encomienda mestizo *lenguas*—the product of Spanish-criada unions—served as the link between Spaniards and tuvichá, thereby strengthening the power of Guaraní mothers. After 1556, mestizos were swept aside,

leaving their mothers with no formal power. Tuer, "Tigers and Crosses," 321. I do not dispute that mestizo lenguas had important political power; however, I argue that their mothers' political significance did not derive solely from their mestizo sons' political activities but also from their brothers, uncles, or fathers who gave them out as brides.

32.   1577, vol. 11, no. 7, f. 110, SH, ANA.

33.   1577, vol. 11, no. 7, f. 112v, SH, ANA.

34.   The problem with analyzing specific sociopolitical units and levels of leadership (besides the extended family or teyÿ) is that the documents do not use this terminology. Instead, one tends to find references to homogenizing terms like *casa, pueblo, cacique,* etc. The only exception I have identified is found in 1595, vol. 12, f. 186, SC, ANA, in which an indigenous witness noted that a daughter pertained to "tequa" of a powerful cacique. *Tequa* might refer to *teko'a.* The only reason the scribe recorded the Guaraní word was because the translator could not identify a Spanish equivalent, suggesting that this translator was not fully aware of the nuances of Guaraní political organization.

35.   Lafone Quevedo, "Guaraní Kinship Terms," 423; Lévi-Strauss, "Social Use of Kinship Terms"; and Wagley and Galvão, "O parentesco tupí-guaraní."

36.   Lévi-Strauss, "Social Use of Kinship Terms," 404; Trelles, "Ad maiorem gloriam Dei"; Wagley and Galvão, "O parentesco tupí-guaraní," 4; and Wilde, *Religión y poder,* 142.

37.   Lavrin, "Sexuality in Colonial Mexico." See also Powers, *Women in the Crucible of Conquest.*

38.   Assuming that Maçaru allowed the marriage to take place, what did he have in mind? Perhaps Maçaru desired a marriage between two baptized Guaraní under the auspices of the church in the hopes that it would provide some kind of material, political, or spiritual benefit. Moreover, after Arbildo's abusive behavior, perhaps Maçaru saw the Catholic marriage as a form of protection against other encomenderos who sought to remove María. The other alternative is that Captain Melgarejo took María and Alonso to Villa Rica to be wed without Maçaru's prior approval in an attempt to preempt Maçaru's wrath at Arbildo's rape.

39.   On rebellions or "alzamientos" as relocation/flight, see Roulet, *La resistencia de los guaraní,* 125–26.

40.   On the fragility of these moments, see H. Clastres, *Land-without-Evil,* 57–68.

41.   Necker, *Indios Guaraníes y chamanes franciscanos,* 219–21.

42.   Governor Saavedra was one of the driving forces behind the support of both Franciscan and Jesuit reducciones. Hernandarias, *Hernandarias.* On the Peruvian origins of the reducciones in Paraguay, see Morales, "Los comienzos de la reducciones."

43.   Necker, *Indios Guaraníes y chamanes franciscanos,* 93.

44.   Necker, 66, 134; and Salas, "Villa Rica y los Franciscanos," 113.

45.   This figure is imprecise because priests often founded a reducción that then quickly dissolved or merged into another reducción.

46.   Necker, *Indios Guaraníes y chamanes franciscanos,* 196. For other, albeit

hagiographic, portraits of the Franciscans, see Durán Estragó, *Presencia franciscana en el Paraguay, 1538–1824*; Durán Estragó, *San José de Caazapá*; and Salas, "Villa Rica y los Franciscanos."

47. H. Clastres, *Land-without-Evil*, 34–42; and Susnik, *El indio colonial del Paraguay*, 232–35.

48. Necker, *Indios Guaraníes y chamanes franciscanos*, 57.

49. Cited in Molina, "La obra franciscana en el Paraguay," 491.

50. Hanks, *Converting Words*, 1; and *Diccionario de autoridades*.

51. Necker, *Indios Guaraníes y chamanes franciscanos*, 89.

52. 1603, vol. 144, 2, NE, ANA.

53. See Wilde, *Religión y poder*, 94–95.

54. Kleinpenning, *Paraguay*, 222.

55. As was the norm in Spanish scribal practice, the notary changed the voice from first to second person; I have rendered the passage in the first person to augment the cacique's perspective. "Visita of Tobatí by Oidor don Andrés Garabito de León," 1652, no. 8, EC, ABNB.

56. Like the previous quote, I have rendered it in the first person. "Decrees pursued by don Francisco Núñez de Avalos with don Alonso Ruiz de Rojas about cacique Cururu's encomienda and his Indians in the Paraná, deposition of Capt. Francisco de Vallejo, protector de indios," 1653, no. 34, f. 10r-v, EC, ABNB.

57. For example, see the statement by don Felipe Franco, archdeacon of the Asunción cathedral, 1618, cited in Molina, "La obra franciscana en el Paraguay," 488.

58. Molina, "La obra franciscana en el Paraguay," 490.

59. "Ordenanzas de Domingo Martínez de Irala," 1556, in de Lafuente Macháin, *El gobernador Domingo Martínez de Irala*, 516.

60. Valderrama, who could not represent himself in court, was represented by Diego González de Santa Cruz, but to avoid confusion, I will refer to Valderrama. 1595, vol. 12, f. 177–251, SC, ANA.

61. 1597, "Encomienda de indios nas vizinhanças da cidade da cidade de Xerez, Asunción," in Cortesão and Angelis, *Jesuítas e bandeirantes no Itatím*, 11.

62. "Son hermanas de padre segun su costumbre q llama a las primas hermanas quanto son hijos o hijas de los hermanos o hermanas." Cortesão and Angelis, *Jesuítas e bandeirantes no Itatím*, f. 210.

63. Schaden, *Aspectos fundamentais da cultura guaraní*; Catafasto de Souza, "O sistema econômico," 226; Lévi-Strauss, "Social Use of Kinship Terms," 398–99; and Wagley and Galvão, "O parentesco tupí-guaraní," 3.

64. 1595, vol. 12, f. 250, SC, ANA.

65. 1596, vol. 13, f. 26–96, SC, ANA.

66. See "Martín de Negrón to the Crown," 1619, 1239, Manuel E. Gondra Manuscript Collectin, Benson Latin American Library, University of Texas at Austin (hereafter MG).

67. "Que algunas personas vecinos y moradores de la ciudad maliciosamente

persuaden e yncitan a sus yndios se casen con yndias agenas por que las traygan a sus casas y tener quien les sirva." 1596, vol. 13, no. 2, f. 21, SH, ANA.

68.   See Mora Mérida, *Historia social de Paraguay*, 180–85.

69.   "Que estando yo en los pueblos de mi encomienda en precencia de mucha gente española queriendo tener una yndia de ella a mi casa me dixo un yndio del dicho Pedro de Lugo que no trajese yo aquella yndia sino a la dicha Malgarida y que aunque entrambas eran mias que les dexase la otra y asi lo hice." 1596, vol. 13, f. 37, SC, ANA.

70.   There are no extant accounts of epidemics before 1600. Tuer suggests that if indeed epidemics did not ravage Guaraní before 1600, this helps explain the integrity of Guaraní sociopolitical units. Tuer, "Tigers and Crosses," 289–90. One of the first references to an epidemic I have identified is from the year 1607. Vol. 1477, MG; and 1607, vol. 1690, no. 13, AGI. For an analysis of disease in the Jesuit missions, see Jackson, *Demographic Change and Ethnic Survival*.

71.   "Ordenanzas de Saavedra," ord. 21–22, in García Santillán, *Legislación sobre indíos*, 385.

72.   Emphasis added. "Ordenanzas de Juan Ramírez de Velasco," ord. 40, in García Santillán, *Legislación sobre indíos*, 371.

73.   Recent scholarship demonstrates the ambiguous results of viceroy Francisco Toledo's reforms in Peru. See, especially, Stern, *Peru's Indian Peoples*, chap. 4; and Spalding, *Huarochiri*. Mumford examines the "colonial ethnographies" and colonial logic that informed Toledo's reforms and shows that what actually occurred "on the ground" was ambiguous. Mumford, *Vertical Empire*. Susnik, Mora Mérida, and Garavaglia portray Alfaro's reforms as effective and as a critical historical juncture. Susnik, *El indio* (1965), 35–39; Mora Mérida, *Historia social de Paraguay*, 174–76; and Garavaglia, *Mercado interno y economía colonial*, 273–74.

74.   Alfaro also addressed the legal status of the Jesuit missions and granted the majority of them exemption from the encomienda, incensing encomenderos in the region. The missions formed in areas already under Spanish control remained subject to encomenderos in Asunción. These included San Ignacio del Paraná, San Ignacio de Ipaumbuzú, Loreto de Pirapo, Itapúa, Corpus, San Ignacio de Caaguazú, and Nuestra Señora de Fe. Maeder, "Las encomiendas en la misiones jesuíticas," 120–21.

75.   "Ordenanzas de Francisco de Alfaro," 1612, ord. 1, in Gandía, *Francisco de Alfaro*.

76.   Ord. 9, ord. 10, respectively, in Gandía, *Francisco de Alfaro*.

77.   "Francisco de Alfaro to the Crown," 1613, in Gandía, doc. XX.

78.   "Ordenanzas de Francisco de Alfaro," in Gandía, 221.

79.   Ord. 57, Gandía, doc. XX.

80.   Gandía, 453.

81.   "Biven con ellos con tanto amor como si todos fueran de un natural en tanta manera que los llaman parientes a los españoles." Gandía, 453.

82.   See Twinam, *Purchasing Whiteness*; and Rappaport, *Disappearing Mestizo*.

83.   "Father Jerónimo Luján de Medina to the crown," 19 March 1612, in Gandía, *Francisco de Alfaro*, 453.

84.   A statistical schema of encomenderos' bequests is difficult since testaments do not state if a Spaniard was an encomendero. Problems with analyzing last wills and testaments for colonial Paraguay are rooted in the disorganized state of the Asunción National Archive. Testaments are not organized by the notaries that produced them; they are instead spread almost randomly throughout a section of the archive called Nueva Encuadernación.

85.   1593, vol. 12, f. 46–50, SC, ANA.

86.   See Lane, "Captivity and Redemption."

87.   "Father Jerónimo Luján de Medina to crown," 19 March 1612, in Gandía, *Francisco de Alfaro*, 453.

88.   Simpson, *Encomienda in New Spain*, chap. 10.

89.   Consider, for example, the following account from Lieutenant Governor Pedro Sánchez Valderrama, who noted in May 1612 that when Alfaro's ordenanzas were announced in the Pueblo de Pitu, eighty Indians interpreted the news as a renunciation of Spanish labor demands on them. So they fled back to the forests where they were "free to celebrate their ancient rites" and idolatries. With no other supporting records, the account is dubious. Cited in Gandía, *Francisco de Alfaro*, 520. Martín Morales analyzes the Guaraní responses to Alfaro's reforms and believes that they are authentic. Morales, "Los comienzos de la reducciones," 121–22.

90.   1613, Charcas, 33, AGI. It is unclear what *ladino* meant in this context. It could have implied Spanish-speaking or more culturally español than Guaraní.

91.   1613, Charcas, 33, f. 6, AGI.

92.   If a Guaraní had been to Peru, he most likely would have been a porter as part of a mule train taking goods to Potosí from Tucumán. See Mangan, *Trading Roles*, 41.

93.   "Amor q ay de ambas partes y parentesco que ay de por medio." 1614, Charcas, 33, f. 2, AGI.

94.   Hernandarias, *Hernandarias*, 137.

95.   On the Garabito de León visita, see Salinas, "Reclamos y multas en pueblos de indios."

96.   See Lockhart, *Spanish Peru*, chap. 10.

97.   "Visita to the originarios of Asunción," Garabito de Leon, 1651, no. 29, folder 1, f. 32r-v, EC, ABNB.

98.   "Visita to the originarios of Asunción," Garabito de Leon, 1651, no. 29, folder 1, f. 212v, EC, ABNB.

99.   "Visita, Villa Rica," 1652, no. 20, folder 1, f. 15r, EC, ABNB.

100.   "Visita, Villa Rica," 1652, no. 20, folder 1, f. 15v, EC, ABNB.

101.   "Garabito de Leon's visita of the originarios of Asunción," 1651, no. 29, first folder, f. 102r, EC, ABNB.

102.   In Ruíz de Montoya, *Arte, bocabulario, tesoro y catecismo*, 162. *Amor* is translated as "mboraihú" or "poraihû."

103.   Cited in Fausto, "If God Were a Jaguar," 99n25.

104.   Fausto, 92.

105. "Visita to the originarios of Asunción," Garabito de Leon, 1651, no. 29, folder 1, f. 212v, EC, ABNB.

106. "Visita to the originarios of Asunción," Garabito de Leon, 1651, no. 29, folder 2, f. 6v, EC, ABNB.

107. Freyre, *Masters and Slaves*.

108. 1688, vol. 7, SH, ANA. On decentralized authority, see Phelan, "Authority and Flexibility."

109. 1694, vol. 185, f. 3, NE, ANA. More on "declaraciones de mestizo" in chapter 7.

110. "Se declaro de ser y gosar del privilegio de mestizo y que solo por el amor que tubo a su encomendero El Mre de Campo Juan de Ensinas por el buen trato y pago no desamparo la encomienda." 1694, vol. 185, f. 3, NE, ANA.

Chapter 3

1. Furlong, *Misiones y sus pueblos de guaraníes*; Monteiro, *Negros da terra*; Mörner, *Political and Economic Activities*; Wilde, *Religión y poder*; Tuer, "Old Bones and Beautiful Words"; Alencastro, *O trato dos viventes*; Romero Jensen, *El Guairá*; and Salas, "Villa Rica y los Franciscanos."

2. Adelman and Aron, "From Borderlands to Borders."

3. Sahlins, *Boundaries*.

4. John Leddy Phelan's decentralization thesis helps to explain how these multiple interests could coexist. Phelan, "Authority and Flexibility."

5. Herzog, *Frontiers of Possession*.

6. L. Benton, *Search for Sovereignty*.

7. Alencastro, *O trato dos viventes*, 194. For examinations of Indian slavery, see van Deusen, *Global Indios*, 2. For Central America, see Sherman, *Forced Native Labor*, 82.

8. The estimates range widely; I have used a conservative estimate. For discussion of these numbers, see Monteiro, *Negros da terra*, 74; and Alencastro, *O trato dos viventes*, 192.

9. See also Alencastro, *O trato dos viventes*; and Metcalf, *Go-Betweens and the Colonization of Brazil*.

10. See Mörner, *Political and Economic Activities*, 74, 90; Garavaglia, *Mercado interno y economía colonial*, 126; and Susnik, *Una visión socio-antropológica del Paraguay, XVI-1/2 XVII*.

11. For Paraguay, see Romero Jensen, *El Guairá*; and Cardozo, *El Paraguay colonial*. For a hagiographic portrait of the Franciscans, see Salas, "Villa Rica y los Franciscanos." Recent ethnohistorical research has helped to elucidate Guaraní attitudes toward Jesuit evangelization. Wilde, *Religión y poder*, chap. 2.

12. Ruy Díaz de Guzman notes that Governor Irala took count of the population of Guairá in the 1550s and found 40,000 *fuegos*, a term denoting the smallest kin units in a Guaraní longhouse. If each "fire" represented a unit of four, the total population

was around 160,000. De Guzmán, *La Argentina*, chap. 3. See also Garavaglia, *Mercado interno y economía colonial*, 161–66.

13. "Relación de Gov. Céspedes Jeria's," 23 June 1629, in *Anais do museu paulista*, 209–11; *Carta anua*, Claudio Ruyer, 9 November 1627, in Trelles, *Revista del archivo general*, 178; and Monteiro, "Dos campos de Piritininga," 27.

14. Nacuzzi, *Identidades impuestas*; and Erbig, "Borderline Offerings."

15. Wilde, *Religión y poder*, 100.

16. "Ruy Diaz Melgarejo to Crown," 4 July 1556, in *Cartas de Indias*, 630–31. In his history of Paraguay, Ruy Díaz de Guzmán claims that Guairá was settled after a Guaraní cacique from the region requested Spanish military assistance against Tupí enemies. De Guzmán, *La Argentina*, chaps. 13–14.

17. Lockhart and Schwartz, *Early Latin America*, 78; and Restall, *Seven Myths of the Spanish Conquest*, 33.

18. Juan Perez Cartar was given an encomienda of forty-three Indians that was previously held by the Portuguese Juan Gz [*sic*] (perhaps González or Gonzalo). Encomienda titles in Cortesão and Angelis, *Jesuítas e bandeirantes no Guairá*, 131.

19. The Jesuit Antonio Ruíz de Montoya states that by 1620, nine Guaraní villages were subject to encomenderos in Villa Rica with varying degrees of Spanish-mediated leadership structure. If each village had 200 souls, then the total encomienda population would have been 1,800. The sources do not say how many villages were subject to Ciudad Real. Ruíz de Montoya, *Conquista espiritual*, chap. 37. But this is only Villa Rica, and similar estimates are unavailable for Ciudad Real and Jérez.

20. Cortesão and Angelis, *Jesuítas e bandeirantes no Guairá*, 122–35.

21. Cortesão and Angelis, 124.

22. 1582, vol. 1593, no. 5, fol. 109r, CJ, ANA.

23. "Juan de Salazar to Council of Indies," 20 March 1556, in *Cartas de Indias*, 580–82.

24. Rodrigo Ortiz Melgarejo to Governor Céspedes Jeria, 1629, cited in Romero Jensen, *El Guairá*, 163–65. In his poem about Paraguay, the priest Martín Barco de Centenera mentioned the mine in Guairá. "Poblada está tambien otra ciudad, / Cuarenta leguas mas arriba de esta. / En ella hay de metales cantidad, / Empero, aunque los haya ¿de que presta?—/ Hablando como es justo la verdad, / Que el hombre es lo que solo allá les resta, / Pues vemos plomo saca Melgarejo, / Y hierro, con tener poco aparejo." Barco de Centenera, *La Argentina*.

25. See "Información hecho por el Capt. Tomás Martín de Yante," 18 November 1628, cited in Romero Jensen, *El Guairá*, 105.

26. Ruíz de Montoya, *Tesoro de la lengua guaraní* (1876), 77.

27. Ruíz de Montoya, 329.

28. I thank Leonardo Cera and Brian Owensby for their help in analyzing this Guaraní name. Several of these insights are theirs.

29. "Procurador General Bartolomé Garcia on rebellion and cannibalism," September 1612, vol. 14, f. 211v–212r, SC, ANA.

30.   "Rodrigo Ortiz Melgarejo's report on the Jesuit reducciones," 1629, cited in Romero Jensen, *El Guairá*, 163–65; and 1577, vol. 11, no. 7, SH, ANA.

31.   See, for example, "Testimonio de varios caciques," 30 November 1628, cited in Romero Jensen, *El Guairá*, 109.

32.   "Anonymous Jesuit report," 1620, in Cortesão and Angelis, *Jesuítas e bandeirantes no Guairá*, 167–68.

33.   "Declaration of Captain Francisco de Vallejos," 25 October 1630, cited in Romero Jensen, *El Guairá*, 33.

34.   Romero Jensen, 55.

35.   "Céspedes Jeria to crown," 1628, cited in Romero Jensen, *El Guairá*, 89–90.

36.   "Nicolás Durán, Carta anua," 12 November 1628, in Cortesão and Angelis, *Jesuítas e bandeirantes no Guairá*, 212.

37.   Earle, *Body of the Conquistador*.

38.   Astrain, *Jesuitas, guaraníes y encomenderos*, 123.

39.   De Guzmán, *La Argentina*, chap. 13.

40.   1582, vol. 5, ff. 99–117, CJ, ANA.

41.   1582, vol. 5, fol. 100 r, CJ, ANA.

42.   Staden, *Hans Staden's True History*, 124–26.

43.   See also Léry, *History of a Voyage*, 61–62, 140–45.

44.   Viveiros de Castro, *From the Enemy's Point of View*, 221–23. A special thanks to Suzanne Oakdale for her thoughts on the maracá.

45.   Cabeza de Vaca, *Naufragios y comentarios*, chap. 21.

46.   Léry, *History of a Voyage*, 142.

47.   1582, vol. 5, f. 100r, CJ, ANA.

48.   Metcalf, *Go-Betweens and the Colonization of Brazil*, 110–12; Monteiro, "From Indian to Slave"; Monteiro, *Negros da terra*; Mesgravis, "De bandeirante a fazendeiro"; and Monteiro, "Dos campos de Piratininga."

49.   Monteiro, "Dos campos de Piritininga," 34.

50.   The literature on bandeirantes is extensive. Some of the more noteworthy works are Monteiro, *Negros da terra*, and Alencastro, *O trato dos viventes*. See also Morse, *Bandeirantes*; and Hemming, *Red Gold*. Morse attempts to bring the Brazilian "pathfinder" into the realm of frontier heroes familiar to North America. Hemming's *Red Gold* seeks to center on indigenous peoples in Brazil's history, but it consistently reifies Natives as either docile or bellicose. When discussing the bandeiras in Paraguay, Hemming relies almost entirely on Jesuit sources.

51.   "Fray Diego de Torres," 1614, in Ravignani and Leonhardt, *Iglesia*, 302.

52.   Alencastro, *O trato dos viventes*, 191.

53.   Monteiro, *Negros da terra*, 77.

54.   Alencastro, *O trato dos viventes*, 194, 362–63.

55.   Alencastro, 198.

56.   Romero Jensen, *El Guairá*, 53–54; and Monteiro, *Negros da terra*, 69.

57.   Romero Jensen, *El Guairá*, 54.

58. Alencastro, *O trato dos viventes*; and Monteiro, *Negros da terra*, 69.

59. Lieutenant Governor Diego de Teba's official inspection of Guairá, 1607, Contaduria, vol. 1690, no. 13, AGI.

60. "Lieutenant Gov. Diego de Teba's inspection of the Royal Hacienda in Guairá," September 1607, Contaduría, vol. 1690, no. 13, AGI.

61. Mörner, *Political and Economic Activities*, 89; and Garavaglia, *Mercado interno y economía colonial*, 67.

62. "Bishop Andres Cornejo to Audiencia," 1662, vol. 138 B, Charcas, AGI.

63. Garavaglia, *Mercado interno y economía colonial*, 325.

64. Cabildo of Mbaracayú to Asunción, 10 March 1612, vol. 1599, no. 6, CJ, ANA.

65. *Anais do museu paulista*, 2:183–87.

66. Garavaglia, *Mercado interno y economía colonial*, 124.

67. "Information taken under the direction of Gov. Céspedes Jeria on Mbaracayu," 27 February 1629, in *Anais do museu paulista*, 2:183–87.

68. Alencastro, *O trato dos viventes*, 203.

69. See Salas, "Villa Rica y los Franciscanos."

70. On Jesuit activities in Guairá, see especially Mörner, *Political and Economic Activities*; Kern, *Missões*; and Wilde, *Religión y poder*.

71. See Cortesão and Angelis, *Jesuítas e bandeirantes no Guairá*, 117–22.

72. "Father Nicolás Durán," 12 November 1628, in Ravignani and Leonhardt, *Iglesia*, in 256–57.

73. Morales, "Los comienzos de la reducciones," 33, 49–68.

74. "Letter from Lieutenant Gov. don Antonio de Añasco," November 1609, in Cortesão and Angelis, *Jesuítas e bandeirantes no Guairá*, 137.

75. Mörner, *Political and Economic Activities*, 72, 74.

76. Tuer, "Old Bones and Beautiful Words"; and Wilde, *Religión y poder*.

77. "Carta anua, Father Nicolas Mastrillo Durán," 12 November 1627, in Cortesão and Angelis, *Jesuítas e bandeirantes no Guairá*, 242.

78. Susnik, *El indio colonial del Paraguay*, 169.

79. Santos, "Clastres e Susnik," 210–13.

80. The witness noted that "alliance" or "kinship" was not regarded during a festival.

81. "Procurador General Bartolomé Garcia on rebellion and cannibalism," September 1612, vol. 14, f. 202r-25v, SC, ANA.

82. Wilde, *Religión y poder*, 111. See also Roulet, *La resistencia de los guaraní*, 73–77.

83. Ruíz de Montoya referred to the "Province of Tayaoba." Ruíz de Montoya, *Spiritual Conquest*, chap. 30.

84. Whitehead, *Dark Shamans*, 192.

85. See Melià, *La lengua guaraní*, 129. Examples of the use of *guarîni* can be found in Guaraní-language sources, especially caciques' letters to Spanish officials during the Guaraní War, 1754–1756. See Lenguas generales de América del Sur, www.langas.cnrs.fr.

86. Fausto, *Warfare and Shamanism*, 5–6.

87. "Carta Anua, Claudio Ruyer," 9 November 1627, in Trelles, *Revista del archivo general*, 178–79.

88. "Deposition of Capt. Rodrigo Ortíz Melgarejo," November 1628, cited in Romero Jensen, *El Guairá*, 105.

89. "Carta anua, Antonio Ruíz de Montoya," 1627, in Cortesão and Angelis, *Jesuítas e bandeirantes no Guairá*, 243–44.

90. "Carta anua, Antonio Ruíz de Montoya," 12 November 1628, in Cortesão and Angelis, *Jesuítas e bandeirantes no Guairá*, 242–44.

91. "Carta anua, Antonio Ruíz de Montoya," 12 November 1628, in Cortesão and Angelis, *Jesuítas e bandeirantes no Guairá*, 235–39.

92. Avellaneda, "Orígenes de la alianza jesuit-guaraní," 181–82.

93. "Carta anua, Claudio Ruyer," 9 November 1627, in Trelles, *Revista del archivo general*, 170.

94. On the acquisition of arms, see Avellaneda, "Orígenes de la alianza jesuit-guaraní," 181. The number of Indian allies that Ruíz de Montoya had access to is unclear, but in his own 1639 account, he puts it at fifty. He does not mention the firearms. Ruíz de Montoya, *Conquista espiritual*, chap. 30.

95. Ruíz de Montoya, *Spiritual Conquest*, 95.

96. "Depositions of various caciques," 20 November 1628, cited in Romero Jensen, *El Guairá*, 109–11.

97. Wilde, *Religión y poder*, 94–97; and Ruíz de Montoya, *Conquista espiritual*, chap. 45.

98. Ravignani and Leonhardt, *Iglesia*, 128–29.

99. Ruíz de Montoya, *Spiritual Conquest*, chap. 30.

100. "Captain Felipe Romero's inspection of San Pablo reducción," 13 November 1628, cited in Romero Jensen, *El Guairá*, 116.

101. In 1653, a shipment of "iron for tools" from Buenos Aires destined for reducciones in the Paraná was apprehended by a Spanish authority in Corrientes who cited the governor's order that no firearms, other weapons, or iron be transported in the province without a license. "Sargento Mayor don Pedro de Orrego y Mendoza investigates Jesuit shipment of iron," 1653, Asunción, no. 15, fol. 4–7, EC, ABNB. On the importance of iron trading in the Atlantic world, see Evans and Rydén, "'Voyage Iron.'"

102. "Cabildo to Governor," March 1618, in Cortesão and Angelis, *Jesuítas e bandeirantes no Guairá*, 160; and Avellaneda, "Orígenes de la alianza jesuit-guaraní," 181. See also Romero Jensen, *El Guairá*, 91, 95, 237; and Mörner, *Political and Economic Activities*, 74.

103. Pueblo Indians in New Mexico wielded firearms. Jones, *Pueblo Warriors & Spanish Conquest*, 88.

104. Governor Luis de Céspedes Jeria, account of travels to Guairá and initial petitions, 1628, vol. 30, no. 1, f. 17v, Charcas, AGI; and "Relación de Procurador Capt. Juan de Zuñiga," 25 September 1628, cited in Romero Jensen, *El Guairá*, 90–91. On the racial dimensions of the right to bear arms, see R. Schwaller, "'For Honor and Defence.'"

105. "Father Antonio Astrain," 1626, in Cortesão and Angelis, *Jesuítas e bandeirantes no Guairá*, 272n1.

106. "Antonio Ruíz de Montoya," 2 July 1628, in Ravignani and Leonhardt, *Iglesia*, 272.

107. "Declaration by Capt. Luis Álverez Martínez," [ca. 1628], cited in Romero Jensen, *El Guairá*, 133–34.

108. Azara, *Viajes por la America del sur*, 290; and Furlong, *Misiones y sus pueblos de guaraníes*, 115.

109. "Deposition of various caciques," 20 November 1628, cited in Romero Jensen, *El Guairá*, 109–12.

110. "Deposition of various caciques," 20 November 1628, cited in Romero Jensen, *El Guairá*, 109, 111.

111. "Deposition of various caciques," 20 November 1628, cited in Romero Jensen, *El Guairá*, 110.

112. The image was painted by a Jesuit artisan named Louis Berger. Ruíz de Montoya, *Spiritual Conquest*, chap. 33.

113. It was not unusual in Brazil for maize wine and cassava cakes to be used in communion, but in Ruíz de Montoya's account the use of such substances heightened Artiguaye's distortions. Ruíz de Montoya, *Conquista espiritual*, chap. 11.

114. See 1625, vol. 1533, no. 4, ff. 1–19, CJ, ANA, which I will review in greater detail in chapter 4.

115. Ruíz de Montoya, *Spiritual Conquest*, chap. 10.

116. For an interesting analysis of the meaning of the eucharist among Tupian groups in Brazil, see Lee, "Cannibal Theologies."

117. "We keep silent in public on the sixth commandment so as not to wither these tender plants . . . ," Ruíz de Montoya, *Spiritual Conquest*, chap. 11.

118. On Guaraní's persistent resistance to adopting surplus and trade economies in the eighteenth-century missions, see Sarreal, "Revisiting Cultivated Agriculture."

119. "Carta anua, Claudio Ruyer," 9 November 1627, in Trelles, *Revista del archivo general*, 170. For Jesuit perceptions of the relationship between political organization and religiosity among the Tupinambá, see Viveiros de Castro, *A inconstância da alma selvagem*, 216.

120. H. Clastres, *Land-without-Evil*, 63.

121. "Carta anua, Antonio Ruíz de Montoya," 2 July 1628, in Astrain, *Jesuitas, guaraníes y encomenderos*, 271.

122. Similar to how a shaman would be asked to prophecy before a battle and inspire the warriors to take up arms, Guaraní requested that Jesuits apply their supernatural powers to capture the jaguar. See Staden, *Hans Staden's True History*, chap. 24; and H. Clastres, *Land-without-Evil*, 38.

123. "Carta Anua, Claudio Ruyer," 9 November 1627, in Trelles, *Revista del archivo general*, 183–84. On jaguars as part of Jesuit evangelization, see Vélez, "'By Means of Tigers.'"

124. Ruíz de Montoya, *Conquista espiritual*, chap. 10.

125. Viveiros de Castro, *From the Enemy's Point of View*, 370n23.

126. "Carta Anua, Claudio Ruyer," 9 November 1627, in Trelles, *Revista del archivo general*, 174.

127. "Relación de lo sucedido en las reducciones de la sierra y en special en la de Jesús María," 29 January 1655, in Vianna, *Jesuitas e bandeirantes no Uruguai*, 278. Ruíz de Montoya, *Spiritual Conquest*, chap. 70.

128. Fausto, "If God Were a Jaguar." On Jesuit spirituality, see Worcester, *Cambridge Companion to the Jesuits*.

129. See Neumann, "Fronteira e identidade"; Avellaneda and Quarleri, "Las milicias Guaraníes"; Quarleri, *Rebelión y guerra*; Garcia, *As diversas formas de ser índio*; and Erbig, "Borderline Offerings."

130. "Deposition of Captain Francisco Vallejos," 25 October 1630, cited in Romero Jensen, *El Guairá*, 33.

131. "Capt. Francisco Romern's *visita* of San Francisco Javier," 28 November 1628, cited in Romero Jensen, *El Guairá*, 123.

132. Monteiro, "From Indian to Slave," 105; and Monteiro, *Negros da terra*, 8.

133. Monteiro, "From Indian to Slave," 114.

134. Monteiro, "From Indian to Slave."

135. Monteiro, "Dos campos de Piritininga," 34.

136. However, many local crown officials, especially the city council, encouraged or even invested in the bandeiras. The social organization of the bandeiras is detailed in Monteiro, *Negros da terra*. On crown support for bandeiras, see Alencastro, *O trato dos viventes*, 192.

137. Ferguson and Whitehead, "Violent Edge of Empire," 18–22. Ethnic soldiering emphasizes state power of coercion, but recent scholarship on the conquest emphasizes the cultural meanings of violence for native participants, raising several questions for the case of the Tupí. For example, what did it mean for a Tupí to take a Guaraní captive in the bandeira raids when the captive was destined to return to São Paulo rather than to a Tupí village? Or were Tupí allowed to take captives to their own villages? A borderlands framework reveals a lacuna in the historiography: Native perspectives on their experiences as "ethnic soldiers." See Matthew and Oudijk, *Indian Conquistadors*.

138. Monteiro, *Negros da terra*, 89. On ethnic soldiering, see Ferguson and White-head, "Violent Edge of Empire," 21.

139. Monteiro, *Negros da terra*, 91.

140. Mörner, *Political and Economic Activities*, 66; and "Lt. Governor don Antonio de Añasco to Governor of Paraguay," 14 November 1611, cited in Romero Jensen, *El Guairá*, 188.

141. "Father Nicolás Mastrillo Durán," letter, 12 November 1628, in Cortesão and Angelis, *Jesuítas e bandeirantes no Guairá*, 278.

142. Bailey, *Art on the Jesuit Missions*, 154–55, 172.

143. See Matthew and Oudijk, *Indian Conquistadors*.

144.   "Relación de Bartolomé Torales," 19 December 1612, cited in Romero Jensen, *El Guairá*, 189–91; and "Cabildo of Ciudad Real to Governor of Paraguay," 20 December 1612, cited in Romero Jensen, *El Guairá*, 191–92.

145.   "Antonio Ruíz de Montoya, Carta anua," 2 July 1628, in Astrain, *Jesuitas, guaraníes y encomenderos*, 271.

146.   "Proclamations made by Capt. Felipe Romero for the Jesuit reducciones of Guairá," November 1628, cited in Romero Jensen, *El Guairá*, 123. See also 27 February 1631, 7, fol. 1v-2r, Charcas, AGI, in which Céspedes Jeria commands that any Indians "with the name Tupí" belonged to the Portuguese Andrés Fernández.

147.   11 December 1619, vol. 2183, no. 6, fol. 112r, CJ, ANA. This unusual document contains Preto's petitions written by his hand in Portuguese. I thank Jeffrey Erbig for helping me transcribe and translate the text.

148.   Carlos Ernesto Romero Jensen argues that the bandeiras' nonviolent approach in the 1610s was typical, but once the Jesuits acquired a more aggressive posture toward taking in Indians from São Paulo, the Paulistas turned to more violent methods. Romero Jensen sees the Preto expedition of 1619 as a turning point toward increased violence. Romero Jensen, *El Guairá*, 192, 197.

149.   Romero Jensen, *El Guairá*, 43.

150.   "Declaration of Capt. Felipe Romero," 22 December 1628, cited in Romero Jensen, *El Guairá*, 149–53.

151.   Monteiro, *Negros da terra*, 72.

152.   "Céspedes Jeria to the lieutenant governor," 1629, cited in Romero Jensen, *El Guairá*, 180–81.

153.   Monteiro, Alencastro, and Herzog all reach similar conclusions. Romero Jensen demonstrates that while there were Guaireños who supported Paulistas, many defended encomendados and mission Indian populations. Romero Jensen, *El Guairá*, 221–31.

154.   Romero Jensen, 221–22.

155.   Romero Jensen, 221–22; and Mörner, *Political and Economic Activities*, 91.

156.   "Jesuit relación of the grievances committed by the Portuguese . . . ," 1629, in *Anais do museu paulista*, 247–70.

157.   Campos, "La frontera del Paraguay en el siglo XVIII."

158.   Fr. Justo Mancilla and Fr. Simón Manceta, relación, Baía de Todos os Santos, 10 October 1629, in *Anais do museo paulista*, 258.

159.   Guaireños made the same observation. "*Relacíon* by various vecinos of Ciudad Real," 29 October 1631, cited in Romero Jensen, *El Guairá*, 236.

160.   Coming to the defense of Guaireño vecinos, who have long been blamed in the Jesuit literature for colluding with the Paulistas, Romero Jensen concludes that the Guaireño militias did everything they could to defend the Indians of Guairá and that they are the "true heroes of Guairá." Writing from a Paraguayan nationalist position, Romero Jensen ignores the colonial position of Guaireños and the fact that their pueblos were also targets for Paulistas. Romero Jensen, *El Guairá*, 247.

161.   "Visita de los Pueblos de Caasapá," 1652, no. 16, fol. 40r, EC, ABNB.

Chapter 4

1. Scott, *Weapons of the Weak*.

2. Informing my thought on Guaraní religion is the concept of "Christianities" as described in Tavárez, *Words & Worlds Turned Around*.

3. Roulet, *La resistencia de los guaraní*, 77–80. See also Fausto, "If God Were a Jaguar."

4. Viveiros de Castro, *From the Enemy's Point of View*, 269.

5. On the destruction of Christian symbols and European animals during the Pueblo Revolt, see Gutiérrez, *When Jesus Came*, 135–36.

6. Ruíz de Montoya made this claim in his *Apología* (1651), cited in Chamorro, "La buena palabra," 127. See also Léry, *History of a Voyage*, 135.

7. Just how rich this cosmography could be did not become clear until the twentieth century. See H. Clastres, *La terre sans mal*; H. Clastres, *Land-without-Evil*; P. Clastres, *Chronicle of the Guayaki Indians*; and Viveiros de Castro, *From the Enemy's Point of View*.

8. Antonio Vieira, "Sermon of the Holy Spirit," 1657, cited in Viveiros de Castro, *Inconstancy of the Indian Soul*, 2.

9. Viveiros de Castro, *Inconstancy of the Indian Soul*, 47.

10. Chamorro, "La buena palabra," 122.

11. Chamorro, 117, 119.

12. Rípodas Ardanaz, "Movimientos shamánicos." Rípodas Ardanaz analyzed twenty-four of these movements and determined that a little over half were "messianic," which she defined as being led by a shaman or shamans who claimed to be divine and were culturally conservative. By contrast, in *Land-without-Evil*, Hélène Clastres argues that Tupí-Guaraní "prophetism" was exactly the opposite of messianism and promoted a self-destructive program: the interminable dancing and migrations to find the "land-without-evil," a kind of Guaraní utopia. Guaraní migrations, Clastres suggests, did not originate from the destruction brought about by colonialism but instead by a political evolution predating contact that saw the rise of karaí or itinerant prophets at odds with purely political authority. While the "political" tuvichá sought to create and expand society, the "religious" karaí (wandering prophets) sought to disperse society to the Land-without-Evil. There are many holes in this theory, especially the idea that political and religious authority were mutually exclusive. See Wilde, "Prestigio indígena"; and Wilde, *Religión y poder*. Pompa and Santos show that Clastres's claims were often built on modern ethnographies, not colonial sources. Pompa, *Religião como tradução*; and Santos, "Clastres e Susnik." Pompa shows, for example, that only one documented migration (1609 in Maranhão) was religiously motivated. Pompa notes that it was in Curt Nimuendajú's ethnography (1914) that we find, as she puts it, the "original sin" of Tupniology (101). For a similar warning about "upstreaming," see Fausto, "If God Were a Jaguar," 75. My analysis of Cuaraçí contributes to this question and demonstrates that political and religious authority were deeply intertwined for the shaman.

13. Importantly, the information about Cuaraçí was recorded in two very different sources: a priestly narrative designed for broad consumption and a criminal trial produced for officials' eyes only. The first is Nicolás del Techo, *Historia de la provincia del Paraguay de la Compañia de Jesús*. The section on Juan Cuará, as del Techo calls him, is brief, only one page. The second is 1625, vol. 1533, no. 4, ff. 1–19, CJ, ANA. Much of the information about Guaraní religion and shamanic activities is derived from priestly accounts. These sources are ethnographically rich and rhetorically complex. While several of these priests personally encountered Guaraní shamans, others only rehearsed reports. Compare, for example, del Techo, *Historia de la provincia*; Ruíz de Montoya, *Conquista espiritual*; and Lozano, *Historia de la conquista del Paraguay*, 1873–75. While Ruíz de Montoya provided many firsthand accounts, del Techo and Lozano typically recounted stories they had read or heard about pajés. See, for example, Lozano's treatment of Oberá, a shaman who led a rebellion in the 1570s, which relies almost entirely on Martín Barco de Centenera's poem about early Paraguay. Regardless of their proximity to the pajé, priests' accounts often emplot Guaraní shamanic activities within a narrative that ends in their demise. The result is that these narratives construct Guaraní shamans as either tricksters or the servants of the devil, and in nearly every case they reveal them as charlatans. Once exposed, they either convert and become faithful, humble Christians, are destroyed by God's power, or disappear into the oblivion of the jungle. Although the criminal trial I draw on is highly structured, it is not confined by any of these plots. The multiple voices present in the document freely shaped narratives about their present and past. In the twenty folio pages that make up the criminal investigation into Juan Cuaraçí, there are statements from a Jesuit priest, the Spanish magistrate, six Guaraní men, and Cuaraçí himself. Moreover, the notary recorded a handful of Cuaraçí's words in the original Guaraní, an extremely rare occurrence in the colonial sources from Paraguay. Thanks to Kevin Terraciano for his thoughts on this.

14. The notary added "tabay" to the placename, which may have been a transliteration of "táva" or "pueblo."

15. 1625, vol. 1533, no. 4, f. 125v, CJ, ANA.

16. Juan Jiménez appears in a 1622 census cited in Romero Jensen, *El Guairá*, 309.

17. 1625, vol. 1533, no. 4, f. 125v, CJ, ANA.

18. H. Clastres, *Land-without-Evil* (chapter two), provides a succinct analysis of Tupí-Guaraní spiritual specialists. For a critical primary source on the topic, see Léry, *History of a Voyage*.

19. Wilde, *Religión y poder*, chap. 2.

20. While Cuaraçí claimed that local Spaniards had urged officials to free him from jail to avoid disturbances, the Jesuit Nicolás del Techo, in his brief account of Cuaraçí, believed that Cuaraçí had escaped. 1625, vol. 1533, no. 4, f. 125v, CJ, ANA; and del Techo, *Historia de la provincia*, 179.

21. 1625, vol. 1533, no. 4, f. 125v, CJ, ANA.

22. 1625, vol. 1533, no. 4, f. 119r, 126v–127r, CJ, ANA.

23. For this and the other Guaraní translations in this chapter, I am heavily indebted

to Bartolomeu Melià, Carlos Fausto, Leonardo Cerno, Michael Huner, Mickaël Orantín, and Capucine Boidin, who all graciously took the pains to examine these passages and provide their expert opinions. These scholars have worked extensively with Guaraní-language sources from a variety of periods and contexts. While their approaches to translating varied slightly, depending on their experience with modern Guaraní, a common trend was to consult the oldest sources for the Guaraní language, especially Antonio Ruíz de Montoya's *Tesoro de la lengua guaraní* (1639) and *Arte y vocabulario de la lengua guaraní* (1640). With legal documents in which the translators were not trained in Guaraní, a very liberal approach to the translation is necessary; the reason these phrases were recorded in the first place is thanks to the translators' knowledge gaps. As to this phrase, Cerno and Melià thought that *colomi* could be *co rami*, "in this manner." Fausto translated *yubete* as *yube + ete*, which has been translated as "to be awake while lying down." Another possibility is "in this manner, be calm." Cerno agrees and suggests that the imperative (*pe*) could have been lost in the transliteration and so it could have been *pejuvõte*, or "be calm." Given the context, I have leaned toward Huner's suggestion that perhaps *colomi* was transliterated from *côgôi*: "the yerba that is commonly consumed" (Ruíz de Montoya, *Tesoro de la lengua Guaraní* [2011]).

24. Viveiros de Castro, *From the Enemy's Point of View*, 119–20.

25. *Tacua* is found in Ruíz de Montoya, *Tesoro de la lengua Guaraní* (2011). *Vera* is found in a modern dictionary.

26. We do not know if Cuaraçí used the Spanish *indio*, but that is the word the translator and notary used.

27. On art in the reducciones, see Bailey, *Art on the Jesuit Missions*.

28. Chamorro, "La buena palabra," 125. It is fitting that the homemade cannons Jesuits taught the Guaraní to fashioned were constructed of bamboo.

29. I follow Leonardo Cerno here who suggests that *ybatinbire* is actually *ibaîtíba* or *arboleda fructífera* and the verb *apaikyé* indicates that the fruit withers. Ruíz de Montoya, *Tesoro de la lengua Guaraní* (2011), 479, 261. The final word, *cheiañandua*, could be read as *che* (i) *ñanduba*.

30. Ruíz de Montoya, *Tesoro de la lengua Guaraní*, 479, 261.

31. Ruíz de Montoya, *Arte y vocabulario*, 196.

32. Cabeza de Vaca documented richly adorned Guaraní in feathers bearing shimmering shields. Cabeza de Vaca, *Naufragios y comentarios*, chap. 20. This emphasis on brilliance interacted with Catholic worship, for among modern Apapocuva and Chiripá there are beliefs akin to the Catholic cult of the "sacred heart." See Fausto, "If God Were a Jaguar," 90.

33. Testimony of Father Juan Pastor, rector of the Jesuit college in Asunción, 1625, vol. 1533, no. 4, f. 115r, CJ, ANA.

34. Viveiros de Castro, *From the Enemy's Point of View*, 72, 154, 185, 206, 239, 245, 273–91.

35. See Ruíz de Montoya on the deaths of three fathers. Ruíz de Montoya, *Conquista espiritual*, chap. 57; and Fausto, "If God Were a Jaguar," 83–84.

36. Ruíz de Montoya, *Conquista espiritual*, chap. 20.

37. See Ruíz de Montoya, chaps. 10, 29.

38. H. Clastres, *Land-without-Evil*.

39. Buenos Aires cabildo to crown, 1606, 1531–1920, 1477, MG; and Diego de Teba visita, Guairá, 1607, Contaduria, vol. 1690, no. 13, AGI.

40. Antonio Ruíz de Montoya provides this account, cited in Fausto, "If God Were a Jaguar," 82–83.

41. I have interpreted *piojos* as "maggots" instead of "lice" because the context suggests that Cuaraçí was speaking of decaying flesh.

42. Viveiros de Castro, *A inconstância da alma selvagem*, 231.

43. Even in the later period of the Jesuit reducciones, polygyny returned. In the 1730s, hundreds of Guaraní fled their reducciones to establish a fugitive community in the Iberá wetlands, presumably with some cooperation from Charrúa. A secondhand account of the Iberá community notes that Guaraní rejuvenated polygyny. Maeder, "Un desconocido pueblo de desertores Guaraníes."

44. "Que no multiplicasen y acabasen." 1625, vol. 1533, no. 4, f. 122v, CJ, ANA.

45. 1625, vol. 1533, no. 4, f. 122v, CJ, ANA.

46. 1625, vol. 1533, no. 4, f. 117r, CJ, ANA.

47. Deposition of Miguel indio from Caazapá reducción, 1625, vol. 1533, no. 4, f. 119v, CJ, ANA.

48. Ruíz de Montoya, *Conquista espiritual*, chap. 20.

49. Wilde, "Prestigio indígena," 135.

50. Fausto, "If God Were a Jaguar," 98–99.

51. 1625, vol. 1533, no. 4, f. 127v, CJ, ANA.

52. Deposition of fray Juan Pastor, 1625, vol. 1533, no. 4, f. 115v, CJ, ANA. On disaggregating "shamanism," see Whitehead, *Dark Shamans*.

53. This undisclosed location might have been a place Jesuit Nicolás del Techo called Maracanaín, "a place for perverse men." Del Techo, *Historia de la provincia*, 179.

54. While the criminal record does not mention it, del Techo reported that the shaman was betrayed by one of his concubines. This idea of female Indian betrayal is a common trope in the colonial literature and functions to reinforce the idea that colonials were winning the battle for the hearts and minds of Guaraní. Del Techo, *Historia de la provincia*, 180.

55. Prosecution of Indian idolatry in the Andes is described in Griffiths, *Cross and the Serpent*; and Mills, *Idolatry and Its Enemies*. For Mexico, see Tavárez, *The Invisible War*.

56. Juan Pastor attempted to organize an Abipón reducción in the Chaco frontier, near Santiago del Estero, but the project failed. See Saeger, *Chaco Mission Frontier*, 149–50.

57. Ruíz de Montoya, *Conquista espiritual*, chap. 50.

58. On the fragility of the missions, see Wilde, *Religión y poder*, 111.

59. Fausto, "If God Were a Jaguar," 83.

60. Viveiros de Castro, *From the Enemy's Point of View*, 87.

61. On the creation of new Christianities, see Burkhart, *Slippery Earth*; and Tavárez, *Words & Worlds Turned Around*.

62. The classic treatment is Velázquez, *La rebelión de los indios de Arecaya*. See also Garavaglia, *Mercado interno y economía colonial*, 345–46. For a recent and fresh perspective on the rebellion, see Svriz Wucherer, *Un levantamiento indígena*.

63. Several scholars have noticed the shamanic elements of the uprising, but they have analyzed them in isolation without considering the larger context of the rebellion. Chamorro, *Teología Guaraní*, 97; and Rípodas Ardanaz, "Movimientos shamánicos."

64. 1660, no. 33, Charcas, AGI. Demographic information about the pueblo is thin. The only clear number provided is 160 families. I have calculated the total population by multiplying the number of families by the average family size (4) in the Jesuit missions. Sarreal, *Guarani and Their Missions*, 50.

65. Azara, *Viajes por la America del sur*, 251. It is possible that the pueblo was only formally recognized in this year but existed ad hoc for several years prior. A place called Arecayá is mentioned in a document from 1627. Visita de Balsa, Valley of Tapua, vol. 212, no. 6, NE, ANA.

66. Visita by Capt. Juan de Ybarra Velasco for don Andrés Garabito de León, 10 March 1651, no. 17, EC, ABNB. The numerical analysis is drawn from Svriz Wucherer, *Un levantamiento indígena*, 39–41.

67. "Testimony of General Francisco Sánchez de Vera," 1660, Escribanía de Cámara de Justicia, no. 882, f. 38, AGI.

68. "Visita del Pueblo San Miguel de Arecaya por Capitan Juan de Ybarra Velasco por Garabito de Leon," 1651, no. 17, EC, ABNB.

69. 1651, no. 17, EC, ABNB.

70. Lozano, *Historia de la conquista del Paraguay*, 335.

71. 5 November 1660, Escribanía de Cámara de Justicia, no. 882, AGI.

72. Lozano, *Historia de la conquista del Paraguay*, 335.

73. Lozano S. J. Testimonies of Fray Alonso de Arce of the Franciscan Order and vecino Geronimo Méndez, 1665, Escribanía de Cámara de Justicia, no. 882, AGI.

74. Svriz Wucherer, *Un levantamiento indígena*, 45.

75. Testimony of Capt. Diego de Yegros, 19 January 1665, Escribanía de Cámara de Justicia, 882, f. 17, AGI, cited in Svriz Wucherer, 46.

76. Deposition of General Pedro de Gamarra y Mendoza, 5 November 1660, Escribanía de Cámara de Justicia, no. 882, AGI. This figure was likely inflated but is the best estimation available. Other analyses use the higher figure of eight hundred to a thousand, citing a cabildo record. See Svriz Wucherer, *Un levantamiento indígena*, 49. The cabildo record is found in 1660, no. 33, Charcas, AGI. But the political context of the cabildo's account is important. At the time, the governor had been under attack for his harsh punishment of Arecayá. As an ally of the governor, the cabildo's representative hoped to vindicate the Figueroa and so composed an account of the rebellion in

the bleakest of terms. Ostensibly relying on the cabildo's figure, Jesuit Pedro Lozano, writing in the early eighteenth century, inflated the eight hundred warriors to one thousand. Lozano, *Historia de la conquista del Paraguay*, 343.

Two Spanish witnesses also claimed that Arecayá formed an alliance with the nonsedentary Payaguá (see chapter 5). These claims do not hold water for a variety of reasons. First, no Arecayense or other captured rebels mentioned this. It is hard to imagine a Guaraní-Payaguá alliance since Payaguá frequently raided and killed Guaraní. Tobatí, a pueblo that contributed rebels, was frequently a target of Payaguá attacks. Finally, it was in the interest of Spaniards to create a connection between a Guaraní rebellion and Payaguá in order to justify their harsh punishment of the pueblo. Payaguá were nonsedentary and part of a broader group of Chaco Indians Spaniards deemed perpetual enemies. If Arecayá could be linked to the Chaco enemies, then their harsh treatment of the pueblo would be further justified.

77.   Testimony of don Ambrosio Taupi, 4 February 1665, Escribanía de Cámara de Justicia, no. 882, f. 47, AGI.

78.   Testimony of Pascual de Oviedo, 5 November 1665, Escribanía de Cámara de Justicia, no. 882, fol. 139v, AGI, cited in Svriz Wucherer, *Un levantamiento indígena*, 50.

79.   Cabeza de Vaca, *Naufragios y comentarios*, chap. 6.

80.   See especially Combès, *La tragédie cannibale*; Whitehead, "Hans Staden and the Cultural Politics of Cannibalism"; and Viveiros de Castro, *From the Enemy's Point of View*, 154–55, 240–41.

81.   Fausto, "If God Were a Jaguar."

82.   Svriz Wucherer, *Un levantamiento indígena*, 60.

83.   Svriz Wucherer, 60. *Mameluco* in Brazil implied "mestizo" or mixed raced.

84.   Recognizing their free status, the governor gave Arecayense the choice of remaining as yanacona in Asunción or of moving to the reconstituted merged pueblos of Arecayá/Los Altos. A total of twelve adults and twenty-five orphans chose to stay in Asunción.

85.   1669, vol. 160, NE, ANA.

86.   1669, vol. 160, NE, ANA.

87.   Fausto, "If God Were a Jaguar," 83.

Chapter 5

1.   McEnroe, "Sleeping Army," 110. On the state monopolization of violence, see Weber, *Politics as a Vocation*.

2.   Takeda, "Las milicias Guaraníes," 55.

3.   Jesuits' efforts to create indio militias armed with firearms did not go unanswered by local españoles, but they were ultimately unsuccessful in hindering the development of these reducción fighting units.

4.   See especially Quarleri, *Rebelión y guerra*. Ferguson and Whitehead argue that when states expand, Native groups often militarize. *Tribalization* is another term for

ethnogenesis as it relates to the sociocultural transformations of indigenous groups who respond to the new alliances and threats put in motion by an expanding state. Ferguson and Whitehead, "Violent Edge of Empire."

5. Svriz Wucherer, "Jesuitas, guaraníes y armas," 282. On the Guaraní-Jesuit militias, see Takeda, "Las milicias Guaraníes"; Svriz Wucherer, "Jesuitas, guaraníes y armas"; Avellaneda, "Orígenes de la alianza jesuit-guaraní"; Avellaneda, "La alianza defensiva jesuita-guaraní"; Avellaneda and Quarleri, "Las milicias guaraníes"; Quarleri, *Rebelión y guerra*; Neumann, "Fronteira e identidade"; and Salinas and Svriz Wucherer, "Liderazgo Guaraní." Velázquez and Garavaglia discuss the role of militias in Paraguay but do not analyze Indian soldiers in any detail. Velázquez, "Organización militar de la governación"; and Garavaglia, "Soldados y campesinos."

6. Restall, "New Conquest History."

7. Lamana, *Domination without Dominance*.

8. See Schroeder, "Introduction."

9. Matthew, *Memories of Conquest*, chap. 5.

10. While blacks served mainly as auxiliaries, there were occasions when they were enlisted in large companies, as in the conflict between Gonzalo Pizarro and Viceroy Núñez Vela in 1546. Bryant, *Rivers of Gold*, 25–26; and Restall, "Black Conquistadors." For Andean militias, see Spalding, *Huarochiri*, 231. A definitive study of black militia is Vinson, *Bearing Arms for His Majesty*. On black and Indian militias in comparative context, see Vinson and Restall, "Black Solders, Native Soldiers" in Restall, *Beyond*. On Indian militias in northern New Spain, see Bustos, "Ethnic Militias and Insurgency"; Mirafuentes Galván, "Las tropas de indios auxiliares"; Powell, *Soldiers, Indians, & Silver*; and McEnroe, "Sleeping Army." For New Mexico see Jones, *Pueblo Warriors & Spanish Conquest*.

11. For overviews of the Guaicurú in the colonial era, see Saeger, "Warfare, Reorganization, and Readaptation"; Saeger, *Chaco Mission Frontier*; and Nacuzzi, Lucaioli, and Nesis, *Pueblos nómades en un estado colonial*.

12. Santos-Granero, *Vital Enemies*; and Saeger, "Warfare, Reorganization, and Readaptation."

13. Cabildo requests munitions, 19 March 1676, vol. 33, Charcas, AGI.

14. Santos-Granero, *Vital Enemies*, 120, 127. Guaicurú power might be compared to Comanche power in the American Southwest. For a provocative argument along those lines, see Hämäläinen, *Comanche Empire*.

15. For Guaicurú as "bellicose" and possessing a strong "warrior ethos," see Saeger, *Chaco Mission Frontier*; and Susnik, *Los aborígnes del Paraguay*. Some have challenged the use of these labels. Nacuzzi, Lucaioli, and Nesis, *Pueblos nómades en un estado colonial*, 21. See also Ganson, "Evueví of Paraguay."

16. Martin Dobrizhoffer, *Historia de los abipones*, vol. 1 (Resistencia, Argentina: Universidad Nacional del Nordeste, 1968), 116, cited in Nacuzzi, Lucaioli, and Nesis, *Pueblos nómades en un estado colonial*, 68.

17. Martin Dobrizhoffer, *Historia de los abipones*, vol. 3 (Resistencia, Argentina:

Universidad Nacional del Nordeste, 1970), 14–15, cited in Svriz Wucherer, "Jesuitas, guaraníes y armas," 292.

18. See Ganson, "Evueví of Paraguay."

19. Saeger, *Chaco Mission Frontier*, 60–62, 189.

20. Nacuzzi, *Identidades impuestas*; and Nacuzzi, Lucaioli, and Nesis, *Pueblos nómades en un estado colonial*, 64–67.

21. There is a need to investigate the trade in bronze and other exotic items in the Gran Chaco and Pantanal. Two interesting studies that point in that direction are Julien, "Kandire in Real Time and Space"; and Candela, "Corpus indígenas en la conquista."

22. Tuer, "Tigers and Crosses," 238–39, 241. On the "mala entrada," see "Governor Diego de Góngora on Payaguás," 1622, 1668, MG. Roulet, *La resistencia de los guaraní*, 135.

23. One of the earliest accounts by a Spanish governor in the postrepartimiento period of a Guaicurú raid is March 1594, vol. 13, no. 2, f. 20v, SH, ANA.

24. Saeger, *Chaco Mission Frontier*, 7; and Lt. Governor Francisco González de Santa Cruz, edict regarding Guaicurú, 1613, vol. 14, f. 195r, SC, ANA.

25. Governor on defenses, 7 October 1675, vol. 11, f. 539r, Actas Capitulares (AC), ANA; and Governor Mendiola, various edicts, 1694, vol. 38, no. 11, f. 171r–174r, SH, ANA.

26. Governor Díaz de Andino and the Asunción cabildo on Guaicurú, 18 December 1668, vol. 33, no. 2, f. 200r, SH, ANA.

27. "Mas suaves." Asunción cabildo on "indios fronterizos" trading in the city, 28 December 1668, vol. 10, f. 36r, AC, ANA.

28. Cabildo on Guaicurú, 1613, vol. 14118, MG.

29. Eagle, "Beard-Pulling and Furniture-Rearranging."

30. Juan Bautista Corona on defenses, 4 April 1614, 1415 B, MG.

31. Santos-Granero, *Vital Enemies*, 92.

32. Cabildo on potential Guaicurú attack, 2 April 1613, 14118, MG.

33. Fray Luís de Bolaños, deposition in an *información*, 4 April 1614, cited in Molina, "La obra franciscana en el Paraguay," 517–18.

34. Santos-Granero, *Vital Enemies*, 95.

35. Socolow, "Spanish Captives in Indian Societies." At some presidios on the Texas borderlands in the eighteenth century, Spanish captains ransomed Apache women from Caddos in order to restore them to their Apache communities and promote peace. Barr, *Peace Came*, 176–77. On the relationship between property, wealth, and redemption as it relates to African slavery, see Lane, "Captivity and Redemption."

36. Governor Felipe Reje Gorvalán on Indian militias, 22 January 1672, vol. 35, no. 2, f. 68r, SH, ANA.

37. Other documents state that captive exchanges included both Spanish and Guaraní Christians. See Governor Díaz de Andino on Payaguá, 18 December 1668, vol. 33, no. 2, f. 200r, SH, ANA.

38.　Cabildo on Guaicurú in Asunción, 15 September 1675, vol. 11, f. 535r, AC, ANA. On Atirá's destruction, see Durán Estragó, *Presencia Franciscana en el Paraguay, 1538–1824*, 111.

39.　Durán Estragó, *Presencia Franciscana en el Paraguay, 1538–1824*, 111.

40.　Diego de Góngora to Crown, Buenos Aires, 2 March 1620, vol. 1668, MG.

41.　1675, vol. 11, f. 508–14, AC, ANA.

42.　Asunción Cabildo on Guaicurú, 7 January 1630, f. 162r, AC, ANA; and Tuer, "Tigers and Crosses," 159–63.

43.　Visita, Atira Pueblo, 4 November 1614, vol. 160, f. 158r, NE, ANA.

44.　Cabildo on Guaicurú attack, 8 February 1628, vol. 5, f. 20r, AC, ANA.

45.　Sargento Mayor don Juan Díaz de Andino on Arecayá Pueblo donations, March 1669, vol. 160, f. 21r, NE, ANA.

46.　Azara, *Geografía física y esférica*, 55. Cabildo on Guaicurú attack, 1675, vol. 11, f. 480r–507r, AC, ANA.

47.　A total of two thousand Guaraní from the Jesuit reducciones resettled in the Paraná. Nicolás del Techo to the Crown, Asunción, March 1681, Sección Jesuítica, IX 6-9-4, doc. 45, Archivo General de la Nación, Buenos Aires (hereafter AGN). See also Mörner, *Political and Economic Activities*, 147–48.

48.　The raid that devastated Atirá was five hundred strong. Governor Reje Corvalán on enemy Indians, 1674, Carpetas Sueltas (CS), ANA.

49.　"Governor organizes an expedition *río arriba*," 1 December 1670, vol. 10, f. 98r, Actas Capitulares (AC), ANA; and Governor calls a war council, October 1688, vol. 37, no. 3, f. 20v, SH, AHA.

50.　Saeger, "Survival and Abolition," 8; and Santos-Granero, *Vital Enemies*, 93.

51.　Saeger, *Chaco Mission Frontier*, 27.

52.　Saeger, *Chaco Mission Frontier*, 27–33.

53.　Fray Luís de Bolaños, deposition, *información*, 4 April 1614, in Molina, "La obra franciscana en el Paraguay," 517–18.

54.　4 July 1675, vol. 11, f. 514, AC, ANA.

55.　The number of soldiers in a company was never fixed. By the mid-eighteenth century some military manuals prescribed sixty-eight soldiers to an infantry company. Velázquez, "Organización militar de la governación," 49. For an overview of military matters in the Americas, see Fernández, *Oficiales y soldados*; and Fernández, *Ejército y milicias*.

56.　Velázquez, "Organización militar de la governación"; and 1676, vol. 17, f. 109, SC, ANA.

57.　Asunción procurador Sargento Mayor Juan Ortíz de Zarate to Crown, 1688, vol. 7, SH, ANA.

58.　Velázquez, "Organización militar de la gobernación," 44.

59.　Ganson, "Evueví of Paraguay," 461.

60.　In 1677, the governor ordered the repair of the San Ildefonso fort, because it had burned, along with its watchtower. February 1677, vol. 11, f. 659r, AC, ANA.

61. See Velázquez, "Organización militar de la gobernación," 36. My own count is slightly lower at twenty-eight, which may be due to discounting ambiguous references in years where expeditions were already noted.

62. Hernández, *Misiones del Paraguay*, 524–43; and Svriz Wucherer, "Jesuitas, guaraníes y armas," 134–35.

63. Svriz Wucherer, "Jesuitas, guaraníes y armas," 286.

64. 3 March 1662, vol. 2, no. 27, SH, ANA.

65. See Alonso Fernández Ruano's report on the encomienda, 1674, 30, r. 7, no. 19, Charcas, AGI.

66. 1689, vol. 37, no. 3, f. 51r, SH, ANA.

67. Takeda, "Las milicias Guaraníes," 53; Svriz Wucherer, "Jesuitas, guaraníes y armas," 283; and Furlong, *Misiones y sus pueblos de guaraníes*, 384.

68. See 1669, vol. 1679, no. 2, f. 35v, CJ, ANA.

69. Governor Francisco de Monforte Cavallero's account of an expedition to the Chaco, 1689, vol. 37, no. 3, f. 115r, SH, ANA.

70. Governor Francisco de Monforte Cavallero's account of an expedition to the Chaco, 1689, vol. 37, no. 3, f. 127r, SH, ANA.

71. Governor Francisco de Monforte Cavallero's account of an expedition to the Chaco, 1689, vol. 37, no. 3, f. 129v, SH, ANA.

72. Governor Francisco de Monforte Cavallero's account of an expedition to the Chaco, 1689, vol. 37, no. 3, f. 130v, SH, ANA.

73. Cabildo on defenses, 31 May 1680, vol. 48, no. 10, f. 1–9, CS, ANA.

74. Garabito de León, visita, Pueblo San Benito, 7 May 1652, no. 10, f. 17r, EC, ABNB.

75. Manuel Frías on Payaguá, 8 May 1624, CACh, vol. 810, f. 1v, ABNB; and Deposition, Diego Núñez de Añasco, visita, Pueblo Tobatí, 28 April 1652, no. 8, f. 3v, EC, ABNB.

76. 20 June 1672, vol. 11, f. 236r, AC, ANA.

77. "Relación compendioso de los servicio . . . desde 1637–1735," 1735, Sección Jesuítica, f. 44–46, AGN; and Quarleri, *Rebelión y guerra*.

78. López, *Colonial History of Paraguay*; Telesca, *Tras los expulsos*; Telesca, *La provincia del Paraguay*; and Avellaneda, *Guaraníes, criollos y jesuitas*.

79. Mörner, *Political and Economic Activities*, chap. 3; and López, *Colonial History of Paraguay*.

80. López, *Colonial History of Paraguay*, 61.

81. Avellaneda, *Guaraníes, criollos y jesuitas*, 84.

82. Adalberto and Mörner do not mention Indian soldiers in Cárdenas's force, and this is likely because they are not mentioned in most sources, both on the Jesuit side and Cárdenas's side. Avellaneda notes that there were "indios amigos" present in the battle and that six died. Avellaneda, *Guaraníes, criollos y jesuitas*, 86. The source detailing the numbers of "indios amigos" present in Cárdenas's force is "Memorial y defensorio al rey nuestro señor por el credito y opinion y derechos episcopales de la persona

y dignidad del ilustrisimo y reverendisimo Don Fray Bernardino de Cárdenas," 1652, MS 1300.5, p. 2, S 19, f. 86r, Edward E. Ayer Collection, Newberry Library, Chicago.

83. "Memorial," 1652, MS 1300.5, p. 2, S 19, f. 50v, Edward E. Ayer Collection, Newberry Library, Chicago.

84. "Memorial," 1652, MS 1300.5, p. 2, S 19, f. 50v, Edward E. Ayer Collection, Newberry Library, Chicago.

85. "Y si los Indios no se huvieran entretendio en desnudar a los Españoles muertos, los huvieran muerto a todos. Pero tassadamente veian muerto al Español, quando avia mas de veinte Indios en litigio sobre quen le avia de llevar el vestido." "Memorial," 1652, MS 1300.5, p. 2, S 19, f. 50v, Edward E. Ayer Collection, Newberry Library, Chicago.

86. Avellaneda also mentions that Guaraní fought to acquire war booty, something that several observers of the conflict noted. Avellaneda, *Guaraníes, criollos y jesuitas*, 85.

87. This 1735 expedition was the most recent military activity the Guaraní militias had experienced. The governor of Buenos Aires had employed the Guaraní in an assault on Colônia do Sacramento in 1680 and 1705. Avellaneda and Quarleri, "Las milicias guaraníes," 119. "Carta de indios de San Juan Bautista" translated into English by Barbara Ganson, in Ganson, *Guaraní under Spanish Rule*, app. 2.

88. Ypané Indians demand payment for canoes, 1671, Escribanía, vol. 894A, f. 5r, AGI.

89. See, for example, the list of donations in the 1689 expedition: vol. 37, no. 3, f.124r–125v, SH, ANA.

90. Oakah Jones argues that unpaid Pueblo participated so readily in these expeditions because they saw their alliance with the Spaniards as giving them an edge against their Indian enemies and because each violent encounter resulted in an opportunity to take booty and trophies to enhance their status. For a time, many Pueblo warriors decorated their bodies in paint while participating in military expeditions. All of these behaviors suggest that their own traditions and understanding of violence informed their ideas about martial activity. In other words, Pueblos did not narrowly perceive of their service in colonial militia as an opportunity to get paid or to demonstrate their loyalty to God and King. Jones, *Pueblo Warriors & Spanish Conquest*, 93.

91. The exact description of the payment is: "Two hundred *cuñas*, two hundred *hachas*, and one thousand *cuerdas*." The difference between *hachas* and *cuñas* is not clear. Vol. 37, no. 3, f. 23r, SH, ANA.

92. 30 August 1655, vol. 9, f. 353r, AC, ANA.

93. Governor orders donations to Tobatí, 9 April 1668, vol. 10, f. 18r, AC, ANA.

94. Governor Juan Díaz de Andino on defense, 1668, vol. 2, SH, ANA. See also "Jesuits seek recompense for Indians military service," 28 April 1676, vol. 11, f. 661r, AC, ANA.

95. 1677, vol. 30, no. 9, SH, ANA. Another example of exemption from the

beneficio is Governor Francisco Monforte Caballero on military expedition, 4 November 1688, vol. 37, no. 3, f. 23r, SH, ANA.

96.   1671, Escribanía, 894A, AGI.

Chapter 6

1.   This chapter concurs with Ernesto Maeder that when comparing economies and organizational structures across reducciones of different jurisdictions, there were more similarities than differences. Ernesto Maeder, "Asimetría demográfica," 76.

2.   See especially Garavaglia, *Mercado interno y economía colonial*; and Mora Mérida, *Historia social de Paraguay*. By contrast, Julia Sarreal's *The Guaraní and Their Missions* emphasizes Guaraní agents in shaping their communities.

3.   The foundational study of Paraguay's political economy is Garavaglia, *Mercado interno y economía colonial*. See also Garavaglia, "La demografía paraguaya"; and Garavaglia, "Soldados y campesinos." For a portrait of the Paraguayan economy in the later colonial period, see Whigham, *Politics of River Trade*; and Whigham, *La yerba mate del Paraguay*.

4.   Garavaglia, *Mercado interno y economía colonial*; and Mora Mérida, *Historia social de Paraguay*.

5.   Sarreal, "Yerba Mate," chap. 1.

6.   Garavaglia, *Mercado interno y economía colonial*, 68–73.

7.   López, "Economics of Yerba Mate," 493.

8.   Mora Mérida, *Historia social de Paraguay*, chap. 9; Garavaglia, *Mercado interno y economía colonial*; and Salinas, *Dominación colonial y trabajo indígena*.

9.   Garavaglia, *Mercado interno y economía colonial*, 311.

10.   "Pregón y remate de la coca o hierva," 1 January 1603, f. 44r, AC, ANA.

11.   Sarreal, "Yerba Mate," 18.

12.   Mörner, *Political and Economic Activities*, 89; and Garavaglia, *Mercado interno y economía colonial*, 67.

13.   "Bishop Andres Cornejo to Audiencia," 1662, vol. 138 B, Charcas, AGI.

14.   Garavaglia, *Mercado interno y economía colonial*, 323–26.

15.   In one year, the governor required half. 20 December 1692, vol. 38, no. 11, SH, ANA.

16.   Garavaglia, *Mercado interno y economía colonial*, 327. See Whigham, *La yerba mate del Paraguay*, for a description of the beneficio in the eighteenth century.

17.   Garavaglia, *Mercado interno y economía colonial*, 314–15.

18.   22 October 1675, vol. 11, f. 541r, AC, ANA.

19.   See, for example, the governor's comments, 20 December 1692, vol. 38, no. 11, SH, ANA.

20.   Garavaglia, *Mercado interno y economía colonial*, 315–19.

21.   Due to the dearth of sources, there is little understanding of the process of secularization. Durán Estragó painstakingly provides dates for secularization of individual

reducciones but little analysis of the process. Much of the scholarship focuses on the Jesuits' ability to retain their independence of the encomendero class. Durán Estragó, *Presencia franciscana en el Paraguay, 1538–1824*. See especially Morales, "Los comienzos de la reducciones." For a discussion of secularization in Mexico, see J. Schwaller, *Church and Clergy*, 82–83. For Peru, see Griffiths, *Cross and the Serpent*.

22. "Asunción vecinos on appointing a priest in Yaguarón," 12 December 1622, CACh, vol. 755, ABNB.

23. "Yaguarón cabildo requests Franciscans priests," 4 November 1622, CS, ANA.

24. See Governor on Indians, 1677, vol. 30, no. 9, f. 119, SH, ANA.

25. Garavaglia, *Mercado interno y economía colonial*, 335.

26. 11 August 1655, CS, ANA.

27. Cited in Salinas, "Liderazgos indígenas," 267.

28. Sarreal, "Caciques as Placeholders," 230.

29. Ruíz de Montoya, *Tesoro de la lengua Guaraní*, 169v; Wilde, "Prestigio indígena," 137. To this date, there has been no systematic study of indigenous leadership in the non-Jesuit Guaraní reducciones.

30. For example, see Garabito de Leon visita de Pueblo de Yuty, 1652, no. 17, EC, ABNB.

31. For a comparison of leadership in Franciscan and Jesuit reducciones, see Salinas and Svriz Wucherer, "Liderazgo Guaraní."

32. See the Ordenanzas of Governor Saavedra, 29 December 1603, in García Santillán, *Legislación sobre indíos*, 376–79.

33. Meliá, *El primer sínodo del Paraguay*, 8th constitution. On the crucial roles of fiscales in New Spain, see Yannakakis, *Art of Being In-Between*, 66–70.

34. 26 February 1693, vol. 1682, no. 3, CJ, ANA.

35. See Yaguarón cabildo records, CS, ANA. These copies contain a handful of entries from the eighteenth century as well as one from 1622.

36. See the request for a priest for young children, 4 September 1673, vol. 11, f. 346r, AC, ANA.

37. H. Clastres, *Land-without-Evil*, argues that the power exercised by karaí (shaman) and mburuvichá (chiefs) was mutually exclusive. Wilde suggests that the division between spiritual and political power among precontact Guaraní was never so neat and that such a division was a product of Jesuits' explicit separation of spiritual and political power in the missions. Wilde, *Religión y poder*, 88. Within the missions, Wilde shows that Jesuits struggled to construct political authority as an institution of primogeniture in contrast to traditional Guaraní political authority, which was built through charisma, eloquence, and generosity. Wilde, "Prestigio indígena." Whereas Wilde underscores the persistence of a Guaraní political authority that was fluid and contingent, Sarreal, in "Caciques as Placeholders," reveals the care with which Jesuits maintained primogeniture. Among Chaco groups, scholars are exploring the ways that Natives used diplomacy and political savvy to negotiate colonial power. See Lucaioli, "Negociación and diplomacía."

38. Wilde, "Prestigio indígena."

39. Sarreal, "Caciques as Placeholders."

40. Visita, Tobatí, Oidor Garabito de León, 28 April 1652, no. 8, f. 22r, EC, ABNB.

41. Paz, *Labyrinth of Solitude*. See the skilled revisionist treatment of Malintzín in Townsend, *Malintzin's Choices*.

42. Stern, *Peru's Indian Peoples*. See also Spalding, *Huarochiri*.

43. Metcalf, *Go-Betweens and the Colonization of Brazil*; Garrett, *Shadows of Empire*; Karttunen, *Between Worlds*; and Yannakakis, *Art of Being In-Between*.

44. "Dueño absoluto de la familia." Investigation of abuse alleged by Pedro Quattí, Governor don Cristobál Garay y Saavedra, 18 April 1654, no. 6, f. 9r–12r, EC, ABNB.

45. Don Juan Tucuray's defense during the visita of Altos, Oidor Garabito de León, 2 May 1652, no. 11, f. 3v, EC, ABNB.

46. Petition by corregidor and cacique Alonso of Tobatí, 26 June 1602, vol. 45, no. 2, f. 16r, SH, ANA. The typical "don" is not used in connection with Alonso's name.

47. Susnik, *Los aborígenes del Paraguay*, 133–34. See also the sixth constitution of the 1603 synod in Meliá, *El primer sínodo del Paraguay*.

48. Governor don Antonio de Añasco, edicts, 16 January 1605, vol. 14, f. 107r, SC, ANA.

49. Petition from corregidor and cacique Alonso of Tobatí Pueblo, 26 June 1602, vol. 45, no. 2, f. 16r, SH, ANA. Alonso was not alone in his frustration with Guaraní unwilling to labor in community tasks, for Jesuits recorded a similar disregard for producing surplus or careful management of community resources. Sarreal, "Revisiting Cultivated Agriculture"; and Sarreal, "Globalization and the Guaraní," 71.

50. Doña María inherited her encomienda from her father. "Alonso Jiménez files a claim against Juan Vernal over an encomienda Indian," 1610, vol. 2010, no. 3, CJ, ANA.

51. 1608, vol. 1549, no. 5, CJ, ANA.

52. Necker, *Indios Guaraníes y chamanes franciscanos*, 155, 196. For a discussion of Guaraní mission production and tupambaé/abambaé, see Sarreal, *Guaraní and Their Missions*, 68; and Ganson, *Guaraní under Spanish Rule*, 68. The tupambaé/abambaé categories of labor were used frequently by the Jesuits, but it is unclear how important these categories were outside the Jesuit reducciones, considering the considerable time mitayos served outside the reducción. The existence of separate cultivation plots on encomendero estates likely reinforced notions of private land and led them to rely less on resources in the reducción.

53. On the Jesuit ideal to keep Guaraní occupied, see Wilde, *Religión y poder*, 69–73. Sarreal and Ganson discuss the discrepancy between prescription and practice. Sarreal, *Guaraní and Their Missions*; and Ganson, *Guaraní under Spanish Rule*, 61–68.

54. Visita, Yaguarón, 6 July 1673, vol. 28, no. 5, f. 150v, NE, ANA.

55. Yaguarón Cabildo, 19 February 1790, CS, ANA.

56. Labor contract with Altos Pueblo, 28 July 1659, vol. 163, f. 3v–4r, NE, ANA.

57. Asunción Cabildo orders a *beneficio*, 11 November 1675, vol. 11, f. 539r, AC, ANA. See also Asunción cabildo, 23 July 1646, CS, ANA.

58. See, for example, Cabildo on preparations for a *jornada*, 2 July 1646, vol. 7, f. 460r, AC, ANA.

59. "Protector de Indios Isidro de Hermosa petitions the governor on behalf of Itapé and Caazapá," 12 June 1698, vol. 2015, no. 9, CJ, ANA.

60. Ordenanzas, Gov. Saavedra, 29 December 1603, in García Santillán, *Legislación sobre indíos*, 381. Ordenanza 12 stipulated that no encomendero could take a female Indian for mita service and if females accompanied male tributaries on the mita, encomenderos may not ask them to perform service.

61. Graubart, *With Our Labor and Sweat*, 31–35.

62. Ganson, *Guaraní under Spanish Rule*, 18.

63. Juan Ramírez de Velasco, Ordenanzas, ord. 40, in García Santillán, *Legislación sobre indíos*, 363.

64. Garavaglia, *Mercado interno y economía colonial*, 279.

65. 1693, vol. 1682, no. 3, CJ, ANA. Ganson, *Guaraní under Spanish Rule*, 73, briefly treats hilanderas in the Jesuit reducciones. I have not found any labor contracts for hilanderas, suggesting that most of this work was performed through the encomienda.

66. For abusing her mitayos by extending their service periods, the visitador charged the encomendera 20 pesos. He charged her another 120 pesos for not appearing at the visita or sending an "escudero" or page. The physical presence of the encomendero during the visita, as a representation of the physical protection for and perhaps dominance over tributaries, was important for this royal official. Visita, Yaguarón, Oidor Garabito de León, 16 May 1652, no. 14, f. 20v–21r, EC, ABNB.

67. Visita, Yaguarón, Oidor Garabito de León, 16 May 1652, no. 14, f. 27r–29r, EC, ABNB.

68. Visita, Itatí, Oidor Garabito de León, 1653, no. 7, f. 4r, EC, ABNB.

69. Visita, Tobatí, Oidor Garabito de León, 28 April 1652, no. 8, f. 20r–v, EC, ABNB.

70. Typical transport gangs included a dozen or more laborers. During an "inspection" of a river barge, a lieutenant governor found sixteen indios from a secular reducción accompanied by their cacique working for a yerba maté agent. They were each contracted to earn five varas of cloth. 1669, vol. 165, NE, ANA. On the transport industry, see Garavaglia, *Mercado interno y economía colonial*, 309–10.

71. Powers, *Andean Journeys*. See also Roller, *Amazonian Routes*. Contrary to Western assumptions about social development, Roller demonstrates that mobility and community formation were complementary processes.

72. Alonso Fernández Ruano, report on the encomienda, 1674, vol. 30, R7, no. 19, Cartas de Gobernadores, Charcas, AGI. For a demographic picture derived from Ruano's report, see Velázquez, "Carácteres de la encomienda paraguaya."

73. Officials' methods for recording absenteeism varied, but they generally did not distinguish between different kinds of absences as in "ausente en mita," "ausente," "fugitivo," and "huido"—the 1714 Yuty visita being an exception. The official who conducted the Yuty census systematically used two different categories: "ausente en mita" and "ausente en Paraguay," suggesting licit and illicit absenteeism.

74. 1671, vol. 160, NE, ANA.

75. Comparing the differences between Franciscan and Jesuit reducciones, Maeder suggests that distance from Asunción provided liberty for a reducción. Maeder, "Asimetría demográfica," 75.

76. 1697, vol. 8, no. 13, NE, ANA.

77. "Fray Gonzalo Murillo and Fray Joseph (ill.) on the reducciones," 1694, 1151, MG.

78. Maeder, "Asimetría demográfica"; and Jackson, *Demographic Change and Ethnic Survival*, 86.

79. Garavaglia, *Mercado interno y economía colonial*, 271.

80. Garavaglia, 288.

81. Emphasis mine. Investigation of abuse alleged by Pedro Quattí, Governor don Cristobál Garay y Saavedra, 18 April 1654, no. 6, f. 11v, 9r, EC, ABNB.

82. Visita, Caazapá, Oidor Garabito de León, 25 May 1652, no. 16, f. 76r, EC, ABNB.

83. Visita, Caazapá, Oidor Garabito de León, 25 May 1652, no. 16, f. 69v, EC, ABNB.

84. Governor evaluates a group of monteses, 9 April 1688, vol. 38, no. 1, SH, ANA.

85. Wilde, "Estrategias indigenas y límites étnicos," 217. Sarreal's "Caciques as Placeholders" demonstrates that foreign groups like Guayanás entered reducciones in small numbers and often as a result of concerted efforts to incorporate them.

86. Wilde, "Estrategias indigenas y límites étnicos," 219.

87. Sarreal, *Guaraní and Their Missions*, 48. See also Wilde, *Religión y poder*.

88. On the presence of Spaniards in Indian towns, see Rappaport, *Disappearing Mestizo*, 216–17.

89. Pobleros or *sayapayas* in the Tucumán province were more numerous than in Paraguay and played a more important role in a variety of economic ventures. Mayo, "Los pobleros del Tucuman colonial." For a few brief comments, see Garavaglia, "Crises and Transformations of Invaded Societies," 42–43.

90. Garavaglia, *Mercado interno y economía colonial*, 287.

91. Tuer, "Tigers and Crosses," 121, 190–92, 234, 237. See also Necker, *Indios Guaraníes y chamanes franciscanos*, 91, who argues that pobleros would not have existed before 1575 and the several rebellions because the Guaraní would not have allowed them to reside near their villages. In Tucumán ladino Indians, perhaps from Peru, sometimes were called pobleros and resided among Indian pueblos. Garavaglia, "Crises and Transformations of Invaded Societies," 39.

92. For more regulations and comments on pobleros, see Oidor Francisco de Alfaro, letters to the crown, 15 February 1613, in Gandía, *Francisco de Alfaro*, 483. Meliá, *El primer sínodo del Paraguay*, Article 3.

93. Governor Saavedra, Ordenanzas, 23 December 1603, in García Santillán, *Legislación sobre indíos*, Article 16.

94. 1608, vol. 1811, no. 8, CJ, ANA.

95. The ideal—as per Alfaro's reforms—was that pobleros live at a distance of at least three leagues from the reducción, but this appears not to have been the norm.

According to one priest, a poblero family actually lived inside the Itá and Itapé mission towns. Fray Diego Gonzalo Murillo, 1694, 1151, MG.

96. 1608, vol. 1532, no. 4, CJ, ANA.

97. Hanks, *Converting Words*, 2–5.

98. Hanks, 5. Griffiths in *Spiritual Encounters* makes a similar point by highlighting the difference between Christianization (external) and evangelization (internal).

Chapter 7

1. On the power of architecture, see Fraser, *Architecture of Conquest*. On Spanish-colonial cities, see Martínez Lemoine, *El modelo clásico*; Kinsbruner, *Colonial Spanish-American City*; and Osorio, *Inventing Lima*.

2. Murillo, Lentz, and Ochoa, *City Indians in Spain's American Empire*; Murillo, *Urban Indians in a Silver City*; Dean, *Inka Bodies*; Burns, *Colonial Habits*; and Nair, *At Home with the Sapa Inca*.

3. 1668, no 6, ff. 9r, 12v, EC, ABNB.

4. *Recopilación de leyes de los reynos*, vol. 2, book 6, title 3, law 12.

5. Carta anua to Diego de Torres, 17 May 1609, in Ravignani and Leonhardt, *Iglesia*, 9.

6. Garavaglia, "La demografía paraguaya," 40.

7. Garavaglia, *Mercado interno y economía colonial*; Susnik, *Una visión socio-antropológica del Paraguay del siglo XVIII*; and Telesca, *Tras los expulsos*. Telesca's treatment of indios in Asunción is the most nuanced, arguing that those considered indios successfully "passed" as españoles to escape tribute demands.

8. Murillo, *Urban Indians in a Silver City*, 9–10.

9. Rappaport, *Disappearing Mestizo*, 4.

10. Stern, *Peru's Indian Peoples*.

11. Azara was sent to the Río de la Plata in 1777 as part of a delegation to negotiate the territorial terms of the Treaty of San Ildefonso between Portugal and Spain.

12. Duarte de Vargas, *Cartografía colonial asuncena*, 24.

13. Asunción cabildo, 23 July 1673, vol. 11, f. 335r, AC, ANA. See also Asunción cabildo, 23 July 1673, vol. 11, f. 335r, AC, ANA; 14 March 1655, vol. 9, f. 321, AC, ANA; 1597, vol. 13, ff. 116–26, SC, ANA; and 1675, vol. 11, f. 539, AC, ANA.

14. The Spanish crown in 1573 had established the "Ordinances for the Discovery, New Settlement and Pacification of the Indies," which required cities to be on a grid. Kinsbruner, *Colonial Spanish-American City*, 24.

15. Garavaglia, *Mercado interno y economía colonial*, 213.

16. 1694, vol. 38, no. 11, SH, ANA.

17. Garavaglia reviewed governors' residencias and found that there was no mention of any market regulation until the late eighteenth century. Garavaglia, "Soldados y campesinos," 66. On the royal tobacco monopoly, see Whigham, *Politics of River Trade*.

18. Mora Mérida, *Historia social de Paraguay*. For Corrientes, see Salinas,

Dominación colonial y trabajo indígena; and Salinas, "Reclamos y multas en pueblos de indios."

19.   See Juan López de Velasco, *Geografía* (1574), cited in Service, "Encomienda in Paraguay," 26–27. The documentation on this trading system is very thin.

20.   An illustrative source on the kinds of social arrangements that existed in the valley under the Asunción jurisdiction is "Visita of Valle de la Cordillera by the Alcalde de la Santa Hermandad," 7 November 1716, vol. 361, NE, ANA.

21.   On the importance of urban plots around the central city square or *solares*, see Graubart, "Creolization of the New World," 478.

22.   Kinsbruner, *Colonial Spanish-American City*, 2.

23.   Quevedo, "La Asunción de mil seiscientos."

24.   This is similar to Corrientes. Salinas, *Dominación colonial y trabajo indígena*, 135.

25.   Mora Mérida, *Historia social de Paraguay*.

26.   Mora Mérida, 198.

27.   1652, Visita, Tobatí, no. 8, f. 22v, EC, ABNB.

28.   Telesca, *Tras los expulsos*, 165. See also Service, "Encomienda in Paraguay."

29.   Cahill, "Ethnogenesis in the City," 33.

30.   Garavaglia, *Mercado interno y economía colonial*, 269.

31.   1545, 1545, vol. 3, f. 128, SC, ANA.

32.   1608, vol. 1811, no. 8, CJ, ANA.

33.   Fahrenkrog, "Los indígenas músicos," 54–57.

34.   Investigation into purported sorcery, 6 January 1665, vol. 1535, no. 6, CJ, ANA.

35.   Few, *Women Who Live Evil Lives*; and Silverblatt, *Moon, Sun, and Witches*.

36.   There were also Charrúa, Abipón, Andean, and other ethnicities from the Tucumán region. See the following barge registry, which notes a number of indios from disparate provinces as well as a number of black slaves. Visita de barco, 10 April 1652, vol. 178, NE, ANA.

37.   Cabildo on Guaicurú damage to the province, [c. 1676], vol. 33, Charcas, AGI.

38.   Santos-Granero, *Vital Enemies*, 122–23.

39.   26 June 1664, vol. 543, f. 85r, NE, ANA.

40.   These included groups taken from the most recent expedition (most likely the January 1686 expedition following a Guaicurú attack on cattle herds), as well as individuals taken from earlier expeditions.

41.   Visita of Guaicurú and Tupíes in Asunción, 25 January 1688, vol. 212, no. 4, NE, ANA. For another example of Guaicurú-Guaraní unions, see 1594, vol. 12, f. 76–78, SC, ANA.

42.   Garavaglia, *Mercado interno y economía colonial*; Susnik, *Una visión socio-antropológica del Paraguay del siglo XVIII*; Susnik, *Una visión socio-antropológica del Paraguay, XVI-1/2 XVII*; and Susnik, *El indio colonial del Paraguay*.

43.   Visita of originarios in Asunción, Garabito de León, 1651, no. 29, primer and segundo cuadernos, EC, ABNB. Garabito de León's visita provides the most detailed

portrait of the labor demands on originarios and was thoroughly studied in Garava-glia, *Mercado interno y economía colonial.*

44. Lockhart, *Spanish Peru*, chap. 11; Graubart, *With Our Labor and Sweat*; Furtado, *Chica Da Silva*; and O'Toole, "Bonds of Kinship."

45. Garavaglia, *Mercado interno y economía colonial*, 276n67.

46. Alonso Ruíz Fernando report on the encomienda in Paraguay, 1674, Charcas 30, R7, no. 19, Cartas de Gobernadores, AGI.

47. Cases of sexual abuse were apparently rarely reported, both at the level of crim-inal justice and during visitas. Even in the 1577 case reviewed in chapter 2 involving Ortuño Arbildo and María, the indigenous petitioner did not make Arbildo's sexual abuse the central issue but rather that he took her without permission.

48. Visita of Francisco de Espinola's originarios, Asunción, Garabito de León, 1651, no. 29, segundo cuaderno, EC, ABNB.

49. Visita of Francisco Sánchez de Cabrera's originarios, Asunción, Garabito de León, 1651, no. 29, primer cuaderno, EC, ABNB. See similar statements from the origi-narios of Francisco Rolón's encomienda, f. 212v.

50. 1651, no. 29, f. 32, EC, ABNB.

51. Most disputes involving physical violence between originarios were between indios of distinct encomiendas. See, for example, 1684, vol. 1594, no. 3, CJ, ANA.

52. See Owensby, *Empire of Law*, chap. 7.

53. Matthew, *Memories of Conquest.* For a sampling of works on city Indians, see Murillo, Lentz, and Ochoa, *City Indians in Spain's American Empire*; B. Benton, *Lords of Tetzcoco*; Mundy, *Death of Aztec Tenochtitlan*; and Osowski, *Indigenous Miracles.*

54. 1651, no. 29, primer cuaderno, EC, ABNB.

55. There was no consensus about Alonso's cacique status, for Indians from Yaguarón identified Alonso as a cacique while a Spanish witness did not. 1608, vol. 1811, no. 8, f. 139r, CJ, ANA.

56. San Blas was a Christian physician and bishop who, according to the Church's tradition, was martyred with an iron comb, a tool used for wool production.

57. "Teniente General Francisco González de Santa Cruz requests that originarios inhabit a pueblo," August 1613, no. 33, Charcas, AGI.

58. 1688, vol. 7, SH, ANA.

59. 1688, vol. 7, SH, ANA.

60. On cofradías in the reducciones, see Wilde, "Les modalités indigènes de la dévotion."

61. Owensby, *Empire of Law.*

62. 1610, vol. 1600, no. 2, CJ, ANA.

63. For example, see 1617, vol. 1605, no. 1, CJ, ANA.

64. For example, see 1604, vol. 1774, no. 4, CJ, ANA.

65. Phelan, "Authority and Flexibility."

66. Gauderman, *Women's Lives in Colonial Quito*, 7.

67. Black, *Limits of Gender Domination*, 14. See also Thurner, *From Two Republics.*

68.   1688, vol. 1362, no. 3, f. 51v, CJ, ANA.

69.   Twinam, *Public Lives, Private Secrets.*

70.   1688, vol. 1362, no. 3, f. 50r, CJ, ANA.

71.   17 October 1669, vol. 1776, no. 3, f. 30v, CJ, ANA.

72.   See especially Cope, *Limits of Racial Domination.*

73.   This is the position of Juan Carlos Garavaglia in Garavaglia, *Mercado interno y economía colonial,* 206.

74.   Rappaport, *Disappearing Mestizo,* 5.

75.   1665, Escribanía, 876B, AGI. See also Garavaglia's analysis of this source and other examples of dress marking caste in Garavaglia, *Mercado interno y economía colonial,* 206–10.

76.   Ibarra Dávila, *Estrategias del mestizaje.*

77.   Salinas notes the inherent contradiction in the fact that while Indian women were not counted as tributaries by law, their inclusion in the visitas belied the reality of their tributary status. Salinas, *Dominación colonial y trabajo indígena,* 140. Graubart notes that in many visitas from early colonial Peru, only male heads of households were counted, even though it was assumed that their families would participate in labor tasks. Graubart, *With Our Labor and Sweat,* 31. In Paraguay, men, wives, and children were regularly counted.

78.   Visita, Altos, Governor don Felipe Reje Corbalán, 1677, vol. 177, no. 1, f. 7r, NE, ANA.

79.   Rappaport, *Disappearing Mestizo,* 217.

80.   The phrase is Martin Porter's, cited in Rappaport, 185.

81.   Visita, Arecayá and Altos, 1677, vol. 177, ff. 15v–16r, NE, ANA.

82.   Visita of originarios, Asunción, 1694, vol. 185, no. 3, f. 105r, NE, ANA.

83.   One exception is Diego de Espinoza, who in 1594 declared himself "indio ladino" as part of his last will and testament. Espinoza explained that he was "criado" or servant of a Franciscan father named Luís de Espinoza. Similar to slaves and other Indian personal servants, Diego acquired his master's last name. It is unclear how long Diego de Espinoza served his Franciscan master, but he had a wife, children, a two-acre plot of land in Tacumbú, and a variety of possessions reflecting a modest but typical livelihood in Asunción. Espinoza's is the only last will and testament for an indio I have identified in the sixteenth- and seventeenth-century Asunción documentation. Testamento, Diego de Espinoza, June 1594, vol. 3417, no. 144, NE, ANA.

84.   Buisseret and Reinhardt, *Creolization in the Americas,* 4–8.

85.   See Lee, "Language and Conquest," 143.

86.   Against Tomás Rolón for injury of Francisco Pané, 30 March 1610, vol. 1600, no. 2, CJ, ANA.

87.   During the investigation, a translator was appointed for the indio witnesses, including for Pané, therefore indicating that Rolón was at least conversant in Guaraní.

88.   Lee, "Language and Conquest."

89.   Melià, *La lengua guaraní.*

90. "Jerigonza." Melià, 124.

91. Service, "Encomienda in Paraguay," 251; and Potthast-Jutkeit, *"Paraíso de Mahoma,"* 40–44.

92. Nickson, "Governance and the Revitalization of the Guaraní Language," 5.

93. Azara, *Viajes por la America del sur*, 210.

94. Burns, "Gender and the Politics of Mestizaje," 16.

95. Earle, *Body of the Conquistador*, 51–53. Of course, most chose to disregard this advice or were not aware of it.

96. Lentz, "Castas, Creoles," 45.

97. Lentz, 33.

98. "Additional tax." Lentz, "Los intérpretes generales de Yucatán," 146.

99. Lentz, "Castas, Creoles," 42.

100. For example, in the 1577 case against Ortuño Arbildo, who had kidnapped and raped María, the translator was awarded fifty cuñas for his services. This amount paled in comparison to the scribe's payment of 324 cuñas, not including his compensation for the paper. This case is one of the few in which the *arancel* or list of fees was recorded in the trial records. 1577, vol. 11, no. 7, f. 124r, SH, ANA.

101. In fact, I have only identified one indio interpreter, Juan de Acosta, labeled "indio ladino, native of Asunción." 1625, vol. 1533, no. 4, f. 116v, CJ, ANA.

102. Lockhart, *Nahuas after the Conquest*, 302.

103. Adorno, *Polemics of Possession*, 25.

104. Alonso Fernández Ruano's report on the encomienda, 1674, Charcas 30, r. 7, no. 19, AGI.

Chapter 8

1. Works on Africans in Paraguay during the early to mature colonial periods include Pla, *Hermano negro*; de Granda, "Origen, función y estructura"; Argüello Martínez, *El rol de los esclavos negros*; Boccia Romañach, *Esclavitud en el Paraguay*; and Telesca, "Esclavitud en Paraguay."

2. Telesca, "Esclavitud en Paraguay," 154, 158.

3. Restall, *Black Middle*, 206.

4. Schultz, "'Kingdom of Angola,'" 427.

5. Bryant, *Rivers of Gold*, introduction. Bryant is not suggesting that the "slave society/society with slaves" model is useless but instead that it privileges economic questions without considering other implications of slavery. For an effective use of this framework, see Restall and Lane, *Latin America in Colonial Times*, 154. Bryant draws on the work of Bennett, *Africans in Colonial Mexico*, 14. Bennett is critical of historians' fixations on plantation-style slavery and argues that Mexico was also a "slave society" not simply a "society with slaves."

6. O'Toole, *Bound Lives*; Bryant, *Rivers of Gold*; and Restall, *Black Middle*.

7. Landers, "Cimarrón and Citizen"; Díaz, *Virgin, the King, and the Royal Slaves*; and Lane, *Quito 1599*, chap. 1.

8. Restall, *Black Middle*; Restall, *Beyond Black and Red*; and O'Toole, "Bonds of Kinship."

9. Restall, *Black Middle*, 5. See also Sweet, *Recreating Africa*; and Lohse, *Africans into Creoles*.

10. Lipski, "Afro-Paraguayan Spanish."

11. Arsenio López Decoud, "La reconstruction de l'identité paraguayenne au début du 20e siècle, fut fondée sur un imaginaire de la race guerrière et du métissage," cited in Telesca, "Paraguay en el centenario," 187.

12. Lipski, "Afro-Paraguayan Spanish."

13. Blanco's name appears in the register of goods confiscated from Cabeza de Vaca after Domingo Martínez de Irala had imprisoned him. 1544, vol. 3, f. 29r, SC, ANA.

14. Restall, "Black Conquistadors," 171–205.

15. Wheat, *Atlantic Africa*, 12, 14, 280.

16. See Francisco Aucibay's 1592 proposal for Popayán in the Audiencia of Quito in Bryant, *Rivers of Gold*, 1–3.

17. Hernando Arias de Saavedra to the crown, 4 May 1610, 4 April 1604, in Hernandarias, *Hernandarias*, 138, 80–90. See also Mora Mérida, *Historia social de Paraguay*, 113.

18. "Fontana de Zárate to Saavedra," 22 June 1615, 112, Charcas, AGI, cited in Mora Mérida, *Historia social de Paraguay*, 113.

19. Mora Mérida, 199; and Durán Estragó, *Areguá*.

20. Fray Diego de Torres, 1614, in Ravignani and Leonhardt, *Iglesia*, 284.

21. Telesca, "Esclavitud en Paraguay," 153. Many slaves destined for the Jesuit college in Asunción came from Buenos Aires through individual agents. 12 January 1624, Seccion Jesuitica, IX 6–9-3, doc. 43, AGN.

22. De Granda, "Origen, función y estructura"; and Telesca, "Esclavitud en Paraguay," 156. For an analysis of blacks and militias in Uruguay, see Borucki, *From Shipmates to Soldiers*.

23. 1600, vol. 125, ff. 137–40, NE, ANA.

24. Garavaglia, *Mercado interno y economía colonial*, 256–59.

25. 1618, vol. 363, f. 141, NE, ANA. On slave sales and slaves in testaments, see Lane, "Captivity and Redemption."

26. 1621, vol. 17, f. 193, SC, ANA. On slaves' rights to marriage, see McKinley, "Fractional Freedoms."

27. Restall, *Beyond Black and Red*; Restall, *Black Middle*; O'Toole, *Bound Lives*; Díaz, *Virgin, the King, and the Royal Slaves*; and Landers, "Cimarrón and Citizen."

28. Captain Antonio Tomás sues the slave Antón de Cáceres for his two children, 1598, vol. 1941, no. 3, CJ, ANA.

29. "Es costumbre y se guarda que cualquera yndia q se casare libremente la puede llevar su marido a donde el quisiere . . . de mas de ser ley es costumbre . . . en la ciudad de Santa Fe." Captain Antonio Tomás sues the slave Antón de Cáceres for his two children, 1598, vol. 1941, no. 3, CJ, ANA.

30. On "forum shopping," see McKinley, "Fractional Freedoms," 769.

31. See Bennett, *Africans in Colonial Mexico*.

32. "Baltasar casado con una mulata del combento de nuestra señora de las Mercedes y por ser la dha mulata libre, se mando siguise el pueblo del marido y desde el paque tributo a su encomendero." There is no evidence that these orders to return were ever enforced. Visita, Arecayá, 1673, vol. 177, f. 38v, NE, ANA.

33. Visita, Arecayá, 1673, vol. 177, f. 42v, NE, ANA.

34. Lavrin, "Introduction"; and Lavrin, "Sexuality in Colonial Mexico," 73.

35. On the rights of slaves to maintain vida maridable, see Barrantes, "Slavery, Writing, and Female Resistance."

36. J. Schwaller, "Mercedarians"; and Brodman, *Ransoming Captives in Crusader Spain*.

37. The Mercedarians were one of the earliest orders in Paraguay. Margarita Durán Estragó argues that the Mercedarians applied their unique mission of redemption to enslaved blacks who fell into the hands of unfriendly Natives, although there is no evidence to support this claim. Durán Estragó, *Areguá*.

38. Bryant, *Rivers of Gold*, 80–82.

39. I thank Alex Borucki for reading portions of this document and helping me to interpret the nature of the transaction.

40. Report on the encomienda, Alonso Fernández Ruano, 1674m, vol. 30, r.7, no. 19, f. 40v–40r, Charcas, AGI.

41. Durán Estragó, *Areguá*, 62.

42. See Visita, Arecayá, 1673, vol. 177, f. 38v, NE, ANA.

43. 1694, vol. 185, no. 3, f. 165r, NE, ANA.

44. See appendix F in Pla, *Hermano Negro*.

45. For a thorough treatment of taxes on free blacks, see Gharala, *Taxing Blackness*.

46. Argüello Martínez, *El rol de los esclavos negros*, 45, relies on the eighteenth-century source Azara, *Viajes por la America del sur*, 271.

47. Ca. 1650, vol. 1, f. 9–13, AC, ANA. The precise date is illegible.

48. Pla, *Hermano negro*, 120.

49. Telesca, "Esclavitud en Paraguay," 156.

50. "Negro libre en mi familia" and "restitución de mi antigua honor y creditos en que publicamente estoy reputado." 1716, vol. 1431, no. 5, CJ, ANA. The comments on honor appear in folio 46r.

51. Although rare, there were also blacks present in the Guaraní-Jesuit reducciones. Sarreal, *Guarani and Their Missions*, 47.

52. 1625, vol. 1678, no. 2, CJ, ANA.

53. Dos Santos Gomes, "Africans and Petit Marronage in Rio De Janeiro."

54. Azara, *Geografía física y esférica*, 14, 17, 56.

55. 1625, vol. 1678, no. 2., f. 60r, CJ, ANA.

56. 1669, vol. 1679, no. 2, CJ, ANA.

57. 1695, vol. 1682, no. 6, CJ, ANA.

58. 1623, vol. 1533, no. 3, CJ, ANA.

59. 1609, vol. 1532, no. 5, CJ, ANA.

60. Restall, *Black Middle*, 204.

61. Telesca, "Esclavitud en Paraguay" is a good start.

62. Telesca, *Tras los expulsos*, 134.

63. For example, see 1600, vol. 1810, no. 10, f. 129, CJ, ANA; and 1669, vol. 1679, no. 2, f. 43, CJ, ANA. In 1609, vol. 1532, no. 5, CJ, ANA, the notary took depositions from a black man charged with theft and noted that the deponent did not require a translator, suggesting that many blacks required translators.

64. 1669, vol. 1679, no. 2, f. 43v, CJ, ANA.

65. 1694, vol. 1682, no. 2, CJ, ANA.

66. Asunción cabildo, 19 November 1629, vol. 5, f. 150, AC, ANA.

Conclusion

1. 1707, vol. 71, ff. 130–39, NE, ANA. It is possible that the name Nandu was a "guaranization" of "Nando," short for Fernando or Hernando. A special thanks to Carla Rahn Phillips and Ignacio Telesca for their insights.

2. See 1676, vol. 17, SC, ANA; and Garavaglia, *Mercado interno y economía colonial*, 284. Other transmigrants remained in the Indian pueblos near Asunción. See Susnik, *El indio colonial del Paraguay* (2011), 1:200–1.

3. On the Jesuit college, see Telesca, *Tras los expulsos*, 133–34.

4. The royal provision is cited in full in another suit involving litigants from Tucumán. See 1643, vol. 2, no. 24, SH, ANA.

5. Bryant, *Rivers of Gold*.

6. 1598, vol. 1941, no. 3, CJ, ANA.

7. Investigation of abuse alleged by Pedro Quattí, Governor don Cristobál Garay y Saavedra, 18 April 1654, no. 6, f. 9r, EC, ABNB. On hegemony, see Gramsci, *Prison Notebooks*.

BIBLIOGRAPHY

Archives

ARCHIVO GENERAL DE INDIAS (AGI)

Buenos Aires
Cartas de Governadores
Charcas

ARCHIVO GENERAL DE LA NACIÓN, BUENOS AIRES (AGN)

ARCHIVO NACIONAL DE ASUNCIÓN (ANA)

Actas Capitulares (AC)
Carpetas Sueltas (CS)
Civil y Judicial (CJ)
Nueva Encuadernación (NE)
Sección Copias (SC)
Sección Historia (SH)

ARCHIVO Y BIBLIOTECA NACIONAL DE BOLIVIA (ABNB)

Expedientes Coloniales (EC)
Manuel E. Gondra Manuscript Collection, Benson Latin American Library, University
    of Texas at Austin (MG)
Edward E. Ayer Collection, Newberry Library, Chicago, Illinois

Published Primary Sources

Anais do museu paulista: historia e cultura material. 2 vols. São Paulo: Universidade de
    São Paulo, 1922.

Azara, Felix de. *Geografía física y esférica de las provincias del Paraguay, y misiones guaraníes*. Montevideo: Talleres A. Barreiro y ramos, 1904.

———. *Viajes por la America del sur*. 1809. Reprint, Montevideo: Universidad de la República, Facultdad de Humanidades y Ciencias, Instituto de Investigaciónes Históricas, 1982.

Barco de Centenera, Martín. *La Argentina, conquista del Río de la Plata con otros acontecimientos de los reynos del Perú, Tucumán, y estado del Brasil*. 1602. Reprint, Buenos Aires: Imprenta del Estado, 1836.

Cabeza de Vaca, Álvar Núñez. *Naufragios y comentarios*. Madrid: Historia 16, 1984.

Cartas de Indias. Madrid: Ministerio de Fomento, Imprenta de Manuel G. Hernández, 1877.

Cortesão, Jaime, and Pedro de Angelis, eds. *Jesuítas e bandeirantes no Guairá (1549–1640)*. Vol. 1. Rio de Janeiro: Biblioteca Nacional, Divisão de Obras Raras e Publicações, 1951.

de Guzmán, Ruy Díaz. *La Argentina, historia del descubrimiento, conquista, y población del Río de la Plata*. 1612. Reprint, Madrid: Historia 16, 1986.

del Techo, Nicolás. *Historia de la provincia del Paraguay de la Compañia de Jesús*. Asunción: Librería y Casa Editorial A. de Uribe y Compañía, 1897.

Garay, Blas, ed. *Colección de documentos relativos a la historia de América y particularmente a la historia del Paraguay*. Asunción: Talleres Kraus, 1899.

García Santillán, Juan Carlos. *Legislación sobre indios del Rio de la Plata en el siglo XVI*. Madrid: Imp. del Asilo de Huérfanos del S. C. de Jesús, 1928.

Hernandarias, Walter Rela, ed. *Hernandarias, criollo asunceño: estudio preliminar, cronología anotada y ordenamiento de cartas y memoriales al rey Felipe III y al Consejo de Indias, 1600–1625*. Montevideo: Embajada de la República del Paraguay, 2001.

Léry, Jean de. *History of a Voyage to the Land of Brazil, Otherwise Called America*. Translated by Janet Whatley. 1578. Reprint, Berkeley: University of California Press, 1990.

Ravignani, Emilio, and Carlos Leonhardt, eds. *Iglesia; cartas anuas de la provincia del Paraguay, Chile y Tucumán, de la Compañía de Jesús*. Buenos Aires: Talleres S. A. Casa Jacobo Peuser, 1927.

Recopilación de leyes de los reynos de las Indias. 4 vols. Madrid: por la viuda de Joaquín Ibarra, 1791.

Ruíz de Montoya, Antonio. *Arte y vocabulario de la lengua Guaraní*. Madrid: Juan Sanchez, 1640.

———. *Conquista espiritual hecha por los religiosos de la compañía de Iesus, en las Provincias del Paraguay, Parana, Uruguay, y Tape*. Madrid: Imprenta del Reyno, 1639.

———. *The Spiritual Conquest Accomplished by the Religious of the Society of Jesus in the Provinces of Paraguay, Paraná, Uruguay, and Tape*. St. Louis, MO: Institute of Jesuit Sources, 1993.

———. *Tesoro de la lengua guaraní*. 1639. Reprint, Leipzig, Germany: B. G. Teubner, 1876.

———. *Tesoro de la lengua Guaraní*. Translated by Friedl Grünberg. 1639. Reprint, Asunción: CEPAG, 2011.

Salas, Fr. José Luis, ed. *Selección de documentos Franciscanos, Siglos XVI-XVII*. Asunción: Ediciones y Arte SRL, 2006.

Schmidl, Ulrich. *Viaje al Río de la Plata*. 1567. Reprint, Buenos Aires: Cabaut y Cía, 1903.

———. *Viaje al Río de la Plata*. 1567. Reprint, Buenos Aires: Emecé Editores, 1997.

Staden, Hans. *Hans Staden's True History: An Account of Cannibal Captivity in Brazil*. Edited and translated by Neil Whitehead and Michael Harbsmeier. Durham, NC: Duke University Press, 2008.

Torre Revello, Jose, ed. *Documentos históricos y geográficos relativos a la conquista y colonización rioplatense*. Buenos Aires: Talleres S. A., 1941.

Trelles, Manuel Ricardo. "Ad maiorem gloriam Dei, Demostración clara y evidente." In *Revista de la biblioteca de Buenos Aires Archivo general de Buenos Aires*, edited by Manuel Ricardo Trelles. Buenos Aires: Imprenta Europea, 1882.

———, ed. *Revista del archivo general de Buenos Aires*. Buenos Aires: Imprenta del "Porvenir," 1869.

Vargas Machuca, Bernardo de. *The Indian Militia and Description of the Indies*. Edited by Kris Lane. Durham, NC: Duke University Press, 2008.

Secondary Sources

Adelman, Jeremy, and Stephen Aron. "From Borderlands to Borders: Empires, Nation-States, and the Peoples in between in North American History." *American Historical Review* 104 (1999): 814–41.

Adorno, Rolena. *The Polemics of Possession in Spanish American Narrative*. New Haven, CT: Yale University Press, 2007.

Alberro, Solange. *Del gachupín al criollo: o de cómo los españoles de México dejaron de serlo*. Mexico City: Colegio de México, Centro de Estudios Históricos, 1992.

Alencastro, Luiz Felipe de. *O trato dos viventes: formação do Brasil no Atlântico Sul, séculos XVI e XVII*. São Paulo: Companhia das Letras, 2000.

Argüello Martínez, Ana María. *El rol de los esclavos negros en el Paraguay*. Asunción: Centro Editorial Paraguayo, 1999.

Astrain, Antonio. *Jesuitas, guaraníes y encomenderos: historia de la compañía de Jesús en el Paraguay*. Asunción: Centro de Estudios Paraguayos "Antonio Guasch," 1996.

Avellaneda, Mercedes. *Guaraníes, criollos y jesuitas: luchas de poder en las revoluciones comuneras del Paraguay, Siglos XVII y XVIII*. Asunción: Editorial Tiempo de Historia, 2014.

———. "La alianza defensiva jesuita-guaraní y los conflictos suscitados en la primera parte de la revolución de los comuneros." *Historia Paraguaya* 44 (2004): 337–404.

———. "Orígenes de la alianza jesuita-guaraní y su consolidación en el siglo XVII." *Memoria Americana* 8 (1999): 173–200.

Avellaneda, Mercedes, and Lía Quarleri. "Las milicias guaraníes en el Paraguay y Río de la Plata: alcances y limitaciones (1649–1756)." *Estudos Ibero-Americanos* 33, no. 1 (2007): 109–32.

Bailey, Gauvin A. *Art on the Jesuit Missions in Asia and Latin America, 1542–1773*. Toronto: University of Toronto Press, 1999.

Barcelos, Artur H. F. *Espaço e arqueologia nas missões jesuíticas: o caso de São João Batista*. Porto Alegre, Brazil: Pontífica Universidade Católica do Rio Grande do Sul, 2000.

Barr, Juliana. *Peace Came in the Form of a Woman: Indians and Spaniards in the Texas Borderlands*. Chapel Hill: University of North Carolina Press, 2007.

Barrantes, Maribel Arrelucea. "Slavery, Writing, and Female Resistance: Black Women Litigants in Lima's Tribunals of the 1780s." In *Afro-Latino Voices: Narratives from the Early Modern Ibero-Atlantic World, 1550–1812*, edited by Kathryn Joy McKnight and Leo J. Garofalo, 285–301. Indianapolis: Hackett Publishing Co., 2009.

Bennett, Herman L. *Africans in Colonial Mexico: Absolutism, Christianity, and Afro-Creole Consciousness, 1570–1640*. Bloomington: Indiana University Press, 2003.

Benton, Bradley. *The Lords of Tetzcoco: The Transformation of Indigenous Rule in Post-conquest Central Mexico*. Cambridge: Cambridge University Press, 2017.

Benton, Lauren. *A Search for Sovereignty: Law and Geography in European Empires, 1400–1900*. Cambridge: Cambridge University Press, 2009.

Black, Chad Thomas. *The Limits of Gender Domination: Women, the Law, and Political Crisis in Quito, 1765–1830*. Albuquerque: University of New Mexico Press, 2011.

Boccia Romañach, Alfredo. *Esclavitud en el Paraguay: vida cotidiana del esclavo en las Indias Meridionales*. Asunción: Servilibro, 2004.

Bodenhorn, Barbara. "'He Used to Be My Relative': Exploring the Bases of Relatedness Among Iñupiat of Northern Alaska." In *Cultures of Relatedness: New Approaches to the Study of Kinship*. Cambridge: Cambridge University Press, 2000.

Boidin, Capucine. "Mots guarani du pouvoir, pouvoir de mots guarani. Essai d'anthrpologie historique et linguistique (XIX–XVI et XVI–XIX)." Thèse de habilitation, Université Sorbonne Nouvelle, 2017.

Boidin, Capucine, and Angélica Otazú Melgarejo. "Toward a Guarani Semantic History: Political Vocabulary in Guarani (Sixteenth to Nineteenth Centuries)." In *Indigenous Languages, Politics, and Authority in Latin America: Historical and Ethnographic Perspectives*, edited by Alan Durston and Bruce Mannheim. Notre Dame, IN: University of Notre Dame, 2018.

Borucki, Alex. *From Shipmates to Soldiers: Emerging Black Identities in the Río de la Plata*. Albuquerque: University of New Mexico Press, 2015.

Brignon, Thomas. *Mba'e mỹmba pype: "par le biais des animaux."* La traduction en *guarani d'un bestiaire salutaire : l'édition missionnaire de la Diferencia entre lo temporal y eterno de Juan Eusebio Nieremberg (Loreto, 1705)*. Paris: Institut des Hautes Études de l'Amérique Latine (IHEAL), Université Paris III Sorbonne Nouvelle, 2016.

Brodman, James. *Ransoming Captives in Crusader Spain: The Order of Merced on the Christian-Islamic Frontier*. Philadelphia: University of Pennsylvania Press, 1986.

Brooks, James. *Captives & Cousins: Slavery, Kinship, and Community in the Southwest Borderlands*. Chapel Hill: University of North Carolina Press, 2002.

Bryant, Sherwin K. *Rivers of Gold, Lives of Bondage: Governing through Slavery in Colonial Quito*. Chapel Hill: University of North Carolina Press, 2014.

Buisseret, David, and Steven G. Reinhardt. *Creolization in the Americas*. College Station: Texas A & M University, 2000.

Burket, Elinor. "Indian Women and White Society: The Case of Sixteenth-Century Peru." In *Latin American Women: Historical Perspectives*, edited by Asunción Lavrin, 101–28. Westport, CT: Greenwood Press, 1978.

Burkhart, Louise M. *The Slippery Earth: Nahua-Christian Moral Dialogue in Sixteenth-Century Mexico*. Tucson: University of Arizona Press, 1989.

Burns, Kathryn. *Colonial Habits: Convents and the Spiritual Economy of Cuzco, Peru*. Durham, NC: Duke University Press, 1999.

———. "Gender and the Politics of Mestizaje: The Convent of Santa Clara in Cuzco, Peru." *Hispanic American Historical Review* 78 (1998): 5–44.

Bustos, José Marcos Medina. "Ethnic Militias and Insurgency in the Arizpe Intendancy." *Journal of the Southwest* 56, no. 1 (2014): 53–81.

Cadogan, León. *Ayvu rapyta; textos míticos de los mbyá-guaraní del Guairá*. São Paulo: Universidade de São Paulo, 1959.

Cahill, David. "Ethnogenesis in the City: A Native Andean Etnia in a Colonial City." In *City Indians in Spain's American Empire: Urban Indigenous Society in Mesoamerica and Andean South America, 1530–1810*, edited by Dana Velasco Murillo, Mark Lentz, and Margarita R. Ochoa. Portland: Sussex Academic Press, 2013.

Calloway, Colin G. *New Worlds for All: Indians, Europeans, and the Remaking of Early America*. Baltimore, MD: Johns Hopkins University Press, 1997.

Campos, Herib Caballero. "La frontera del Paraguay en el siglo XVIII: Relaciónes y disputas entre Curuguaty e Igatemi." Paper presented at the Río de la Plata Workshop, College of William and Mary, Williamsburg, VA, February 22, 2014.

Candela, Guillaume. "Corpus indígenas en la conquista del Paraguay (siglo XVI)." *Corpus* 4, no. 1 (2014): 2–17.

———. "Las mujeres indígenas en la conquista del Paraguay entre 1541 y 1575." *Nuevo Mundo Mundos Nuevos* (2014): 2–17.

Caraman, Philip. *The Lost Paradise: The Jesuit Republic in South America*. New York: Seabury Press, 1976.

Cardozo, Efraím. *El Paraguay colonial: Las raíces de la nacionalidad*. Buenos Aires: Ediciones Nizza, 1959.

Carsten, Janet, ed. *Cultures of Relatedness: New Approaches to the Study of Kinship*. Cambridge: Cambridge University Press, 2000.

Catafasto de Souza, José Otávio. "O sistema econômico nas sociedades indígenas guarani pré-coloniais." *Horizontes Antropológicos* 8, no. 18 (2012): 211–53.

Cerno, Leonardo, and F. Obermeier. "Nuevos aportes de la lingüística para la investigación de documentos en guaraní de la época colonial (Siglo XVIII)." *Folia Histórica del Nordeste* 21 (2013): 33–56.

Chamorro, Graciela. "La buena palabra: experiencias y reflexiones religiosas de los grupos guaraníes." *Revista de Indias* 65 (2004): 117–40.

———. *Teología Guaraní*. Quito: Abya-Yala, 2004.

Clastres, Hélène. *The Land-without-Evil: Tupí Prophetism*. Translated by Jacqueline Grenez Brovender. Urbana-Champagne: University of Illinois Press, 1995.

———. *La terre sans mal: le prophétisme Tupi-Guarani*. Paris: Editions du Seuil, 1975.

Clastres, Pierre. *Chronicle of the Guayaki Indians*. New York: Zone Books, 1998.

Coates, Timothy J. *Convicts and Orphans: Forced and State-Sponsored Colonizers in the Portuguese Empire, 1550–1755*. Stanford, CA: Stanford University Press, 2001.

Combès, Isabelle. *La tragédie cannibale chez les anciens Tupi-Guarani*. Paris: Presses Universitaires de France, 1992.

Cope, R. Douglas. *The Limits of Racial Domination: Plebeian Society in Colonial Mexico City, 1660–1720*. Madison: University of Wisconsin Press, 1994.

Crosby, Alfred W. *Ecological Imperialism: The Biological Expansion of Europe, 900–1900*. Cambridge: Cambridge University Press, 2004.

Cunninghame, Graham. *A Vanished Arcadia: Being Some Account of the Jesuits in Paraguay, 1607 to 1767*. London: W. Heinemann, 1901.

de Barros Laraia, Roque. "Kinship Studies in Brazil." *Vibrant* 8, no. 2 (2011): 427–49.

de Granda, German. "Origen, función y estructura de un pueblo de negros y mulatos libres en el Paraguay del siglo XVIII (San Agustín de la Emboscada)." In *Pasado y presente de la realidad social Paraguay*. Asunción: Centro Paraguayo de Estudios Sociológicos, 1983.

de Lafuente Machaín, Ricardo. *El gobernador Domingo Martínez de Irala*. Buenos Aires: Librería y Editorial La Facultad, 1939.

Dean, Carolyn. *Inka Bodies and the Body of Christ: Corpus Christi in Colonial Cuzco, Peru*. Durham, NC: Duke University Press, 1999.

Dean, Carolyn, and Dana Leibsohn. "Hybridity and Its Discontents: Considering Visual Culture in Colonial Spanish America." *Colonial Latin American Review* 12, no. 1 (2003): 5–35.

Díaz, María Elena. *The Virgin, the King, and the Royal Slaves of El Cobre: Negotiating Freedom in Colonial Cuba, 1670–1780*. Stanford, CA: Stanford University Press, 2000.

Diccionario de autoridades. Vol. 5. Madrid: Real Academia, 1735. http://web.frl.es/DA.html.

dos Santos Gomes, Flávio. "Africans and Petit Marronage in Rio De Janeiro, ca. 1800–1840." *Luso-Brazilian Review* 47, no. 2 (2010): 74–99.

Duarte de Vargas, Alberto. *Cartografía colonial asuncena*. Asunción: Academia Para-guaya de la Historia: Municipalidad de Asunción, 2001.

Durán Estragó, Margarita. *Areguá: rescate histórico, 1576–1870*. Asunción: Fondo Nacional de la Cultura y las Artes, 2005.

———. *Presencia franciscana en el Paraguay*. Asunción: Universidad Católica, 1987.

———. *Presencia franciscana en el Paraguay, 1538–1824*. Asunción: Ediciones y Arte, 2005.

———. *San José de Caazapá: un modelo de reducción franciscana*. Asunción: Editorial Don Bosco, 1992.

Eagle, Marc. "Beard-Pulling and Furniture-Rearranging: Conflict within the Sev-enteenth-Century Audiencia of Santo Domingo." *Americas* 68, no. 4 (2012): 467–93.

Earle, Rebecca. *The Body of the Conquistador: Food, Race, and the Colonial Experience in Spanish America, 1492–1700*. Cambridge: Cambridge University Press, 2012.

———. "'If You Eat Their Food': Diets and Bodies in Early Colonial Spanish America." *American Historical Review* 115, no. 3 (2010): 688–713.

Erbig, Jeffrey A., Jr. "Borderline Offerings: Tolderías and Mapmakers in the Eigh-teenth-Century Río de la Plata." *Hispanic American Historical Review* 96, no. 3 (2016): 445–80.

Evans, Chris, and Göran Rydén. "'Voyage Iron': An Atlantic Slave Trade Currency, Its European Origins, and West African Impact." *Past & Present* 239, no. 1 (2018): 41–70.

Fahrenkrog, Laura. "Los indígenas músicos en el Paraguay colonial: consideraciones desde la movilidad espacial." *Resonancias* 20, no. 39 (2016): 43–62.

Fausto, Carlos. "Fragmentos de história e cultura tupinambá: da etnologia como instrumento crítito de conhecimento etno-histórico." In *História Dos Índios No Brasil*, edited by Manuela et al. Carneiro da Cunha, 381–96. São Paulo: Editora Schwarcz, 1992.

———. "If God Were a Jaguar: Cannibalism and Christianity among the Guarani (16th–20th Centuries)." In *Time and Memory in Indigenous Amazonia: Anthropological Perspectives*, edited by Carlos Fausto and Michael Heckenberger, 74–105. Gaines-ville: University Press of Florida, 2007.

———. *Warfare and Shamanism in Amazonia*. Cambridge: Cambridge University Press, 2012.

Ferguson, R. Brian, and Neil L. Whitehead. "The Violent Edge of Empire." In *War in the Tribal Zone: Expanding States and Indigenous Warfare*, edited by R. Brian Ferguson and Neil L. Whitehead. Santa Fe: School of American Research Press, 2002.

Fernández, Juan Marchena. *Ejército y milicias en el mundo colonial americano*. Madrid: Editorial MAPFRE, 1992.

———. *Oficiales y soldados en el ejército de América*. Seville, Spain: Escuela de Estudios Hispano-Americanos, 1983.

Few, Martha. *Women Who Live Evil Lives: Gender, Religion, and the Politics of Power in Colonial Guatemala.* Austin: University of Texas Press, 2002.

Fisher, Andrew B., and Matthew D. O'Hara, eds. *Imperial Subjects: Race and Identity in Colonial Latin America.* Durham, NC: Duke University Press, 2009.

Fitte, Ernesto, J. *Hambre y desnudeces en la conquista del Rio de la Plata.* Buenos Aires: Emecé Editores, 1963.

Foster, George M. *Culture and Conquest: America's Spanish Heritage.* New York: Wenner-Gren Foundation for Anthropological Research, 1960.

Fraser, Valerie. *The Architecture of Conquest: Building in the Viceroyalty of Peru, 1535–1635.* Cambridge: Cambridge University Press, 1990.

Freyre, Gilberto. *Masters and Slaves: A Study in the Development of Brazilian Civilization.* New York: Alfred Knopf, 1946.

Furlong, Guillermo. *Misiones y sus pueblos de guaraníes.* Buenos Aires: Ediciones Theoría, 1962.

Furtado, Júnia Ferreira. *Chica Da Silva: A Brazilian Slave of the Eighteenth Century.* Cambridge: Cambridge University Press, 2009.

Gandía, Enrique de. *Francisco de Alfaro y la condición social de los indios; Río de la Plata, Paraguay, Tucumán y Perú, siglos XVI y XVII.* Buenos Aires: Libreria y editorial "El Ateneo," 1939.

Ganson, Barbara. "The Evueví of Paraguay: Adaptive Strategies and Responses to Colonialism, 1528–1811." *Americas* 45 (1989): 461–88.

———. *The Guaraní under Spanish Rule in the Río De La Plata.* Stanford, CA: Stanford University Press, 2003.

Garavaglia, Juan Carlos. "The Crises and Transformations of Invaded Societies: The La Plata Basin (1535–1650)." In *The Cambridge History of the Native Peoples of the Americas,* 1–58. Cambridge: Cambridge University Press, 1999.

———. "La demografía paraguaya; aspectos sociales y cuantitativas (siglos XVI a XVIII)." *Suplemento Antropológico* 19, no. 2 (1984): 19–87.

———. *Mercado interno y economía colonial.* México: Grijalbo, 1983.

———. "Soldados y campesinos: dos siglos en la historia rural del Paraguay." *Suplemento Antropológico* 21, no. 1 (1986): 7–71.

Garcia, Elisa Frühauf. *As diversas formas de ser índio: Políticas indígenas e políticas indigenistas no extremo sul da América Portuguesa.* Rio de Janeiro: Arquivo Nacional, 2009.

Garrett, David T. *Shadows of Empire: The Indian Nobility of Cusco, 1750–1825.* Cambridge: Cambridge University Press, 2005.

Gauderman, Kimberly. *Women's Lives in Colonial Quito: Gender, Law, and Economy in Spanish America.* Austin: University of Texas Press, 2003.

Gharala, Norah L. A. *Taxing Blackness: Free Afromexican Tribute in Bourbon New Spain.* Tuscaloosa: University of Alabama Press, 2019.

Gibson, Charles. *The Aztecs under Spanish Rule: A History of the Indians of the Valley of Mexico, 1519–1810.* Stanford, CA: Stanford University Press, 1964.

Gramsci, Antonio. *Prison Notebooks*. Translated by Joseph A. Buttigieg. New York: Columbia University Press, 1992.

Graubart, Karen B. "The Creolization of the New World: Local Forms of Identification in Urban Colonial Peru, 1560–1640." *Hispanic American Historical Review* 89, no. 3 (2009): 478.

———. *With Our Labor and Sweat: Indigenous Women and the Formation of Colonial Society in Peru, 1550–1700*. Stanford, CA: Stanford University Press, 2007.

Gregory, C. A. *Gifts and Commodities*. London: Academic Press, 1982.

Griffiths, Nicholas. *The Cross and the Serpent: Religious Repression and Resurgence in Colonial Peru*. Norman: University of Oklahoma Press, 1996.

Griffiths, Nicholas, and Fernando Cervantes, eds. *Spiritual Encounters: Interactions between Christianity and Native Religions in Colonial America*. Lincoln: University of Nebraska Press, 1999.

Gutiérrez, Ramón A. *When Jesus Came, the Corn Mothers Went Away: Marriage, Sexuality, and Power in New Mexico, 1500–1846*. Stanford, CA: Stanford University Press, 1991.

Hämäläinen, Pekka. *The Comanche Empire*. New Haven, CT: Yale University Press, 2008.

Hanks, William F. *Converting Words: Maya in the Age of the Cross*. Berkeley: University of California Press, 2010.

Hassig, Ross. *Polygamy and the Rise and Demise of the Aztec Empire*. Albuquerque: University of New Mexico Press, 2016.

Hemming, John. *Red Gold: The Conquest of the Brazilian Indians*. London: Macmillan, 1978.

Hernández, Pablo. *Misiones del Paraguay*. Barcelona, Spain: G. Gili, 1913.

Herzog, Tamar. *Frontiers of Possession: Spain and Portugal in Europe and the Americas*. Cambridge, MA: Harvard University Press, 2015.

Hill, Jonathan David. "Introduction: Ethnogenesis in the Americas, 1492–1992." In *History, Power, and Identity: Ethnogenesis in the Americas, 1492–1992*. Iowa City: University of Iowa Press, 1996.

Hosne, Ana Carolina. "Jesuit Reflections on Their Overseas Missions." *ReVista* 14, no. 3 (2015): 56–57.

Ibarra Dávila, Alexia. *Estrategias del mestizaje: Quito a finales de la época colonial*. Quito: Ediciones Abya-Yala: Embajada de España, Agencia Española de Cooperación Internacional: Dirección del Departamento de Ciencias Históricas, Pontificia Universidad Católica del Ecuador, 2002.

Jackson, Robert H. *Demographic Change and Ethnic Survival among the Sedentary Populations on the Jesuit Mission Frontiers of Spanish South America, 1609–1803: The Formation and Persistence of Mission Communities in a Comparative Context*. Leiden, Netherlands: Brill, 2015.

Jones, Oakah L. *Pueblo Warriors & Spanish Conquest*. Norman: University of Oklahoma Press, 1966.

Julien, Catherine. "Kandire in Real Time and Space: Sixteenth-Century Expeditions from the Pantanal to the Andes." *Ethnohistory* 54, no. 2 (2007): 245–72.

Karttunen, Frances. *Between Worlds: Interpreters, Guides, and Survivors*. New Brunswick, NJ: Rutgers University Press, 2004.

Kern, Arno Alvarez. *Missões: Uma utopia política*. Porto Alegre, Brazil: Mercado Aberto, 1982.

Kinsbruner, Jay. *The Colonial Spanish-American City: Urban Life in the Age of Atlantic Capitalism*. Austin: University of Texas Press, 2005.

Kleinpenning, J. M. G. *Paraguay, 1515–1870: A Thematic Geography of Its Development*. Frankfurt, Germany: Iberoamericana Vervuert, 2003.

Lafone Quevedo, Samual A. "Guaraní Kinship Terms as Index of Social Organization." *American Anthropologist* 21, no. 4 (1919): 421–40.

Lamana, Gonzalo. *Domination without Dominance: Inca-Spanish Encounters in Early Colonial Peru*. Durham, NC: Duke University Press, 2008.

Lambert, Helen. "Sentiment and Substance in North Indian Forms of Relatedness." In *Cultures of Relatedness: New Approaches to the Study of Kinship*, edited by Janet Carsten. Cambridge: Cambridge University Press, 2000.

Landers, Jane G. "Cimarrón and Citizen: African Ethnicity, Corporate Identity, and the Evolution of Free Black Towns in Spanish Circum-Caribbean." In *Slaves, Subjects, and Subversives: Blacks in Colonial Latin America*, edited by Jane G. Landers and Barry M. Robinson, 111–46. Albuquerque: University of New Mexico, 206.

Lane, Kris E. "Captivity and Redemption: Aspects of Slave Life in Early Colonial Quito and Popayán." *Americas* 57, no. 2 (2000): 225–46.

——. *Quito 1599: City and Colony in Transition*. Albuquerque: University of New Mexico Press, 2002.

Lavrin, Asunción. "Introduction: The Scenario, the Actors, and the Issues." In *Sexuality and Marriage in Colonial Latin America*, edited by Asunción Lavrin. Lincoln: University of Nebraska Press, 1989.

——. "Sexuality in Colonial Mexico: A Church Dilemma." In *Sexuality and Marriage in Colonial Latin America*, edited by Asunción Lavrin, 47–95. Lincoln: University of Nebraska Press, 1989.

Lee, Kittiya. "Cannibal Theologies in Colonial Portuguese America (1549–1759)." *Journal of Early Modern History* 21, no. 1–2 (2017): 64–90.

——. "The European Promise of Militant Christianity for the Tupinambá of Portuguese America, 1550s–1612." In *Words & Worlds Turned Around: Indigenous Christianities in Colonial Latin America*, edited by David Tavárez, 127–49. Boulder: University of Colorado Press, 2017.

——. "Language and Conquest: Tupi-Guarani Expansion in the European Colonization of Brazil and Amazonia." In *Iberian Imperialism and Language Evolution in Latin America*, edited by Salikoko S. Mufwene, 143–67. Chicago: University of Chicago Press, 2014.

Lentz, Mark. "Castas, Creoles, and the Rise of a Maya Lingua Franca in Eighteenth-Century Yucatan." *Hispanic American Historical Review* 97, no. 1 (2017): 29–61.

———. "Los intérpretes generales de Yucatán: hombres entre dos mundos." *Estudios de Cultura Maya* 33 (2009): 135–58.

Lévi-Strauss, Claude. "The Social Use of Kinship Terms among Brazilian Indians." *American Anthropologist* 43, no. 3 (1943): 398–409.

Lipski, John M. "Afro-Paraguayan Spanish: The Negation of Non-existence." *Journal of Pan African Studies* 2, no. 7 (2008): 1–37.

Lockhart, James. *Letters and People of the Spanish Indies, Sixteenth Century.* Cambridge: Cambridge University Press, 1976.

———. *The Nahuas after the Conquest: A Social and Cultural History of the Indians of Central Mexico, Sixteenth through Eighteenth Centuries.* Stanford, CA: Stanford University Press, 1994.

———. *Of Things of the Indies: Essays Old and New in Early Latin American History.* Stanford, CA: Stanford University Press, 2000.

———. *Spanish Peru, 1532–1560: A Social History.* Madison: University of Wisconsin Press, 1994.

Lockhart, James, and Enrique Otte, eds. *Letters and People of the Spanish Indies, Sixteenth Century.* Cambridge: Cambridge University Press, 1976.

Lockhart, James, and Stuart B. Schwartz. *Early Latin America: A History of Colonial Spanish America and Brazil.* New York: Cambridge University Press, 1983.

Lohse, Russell. *Africans into Creoles: Slavery, Ethnicity, and Identity in Colonial Costa Rica.* Albuquerque: University of New Mexico Press, 2014.

López, Adalberto. *The Colonial History of Paraguay: The Revolt of the Comuneros, 1721–1735.* New Brunswick, NJ: Transaction Publishers, 2007.

———. "The Economics of Yerba Mate in Seventeenth-Century South America." *Agricultural History* 48, no. 4 (1974): 493–509.

Lozano, Pedro, S. J. *Historia de la conquista del Paraguay, Río de la Plata y Tucumán.* Buenos Aires: Imprenta Popular, 1873.

Lucaioli, Carina Paula. "Negociación and diplomacía en las fronteras del Chaco: Nuestra Señora de la Concepción de Abipones." *Revista, Historia y Cultura* 3, no. 2 (2014): 380–405.

Maeder, Ernesto. "Asimetría demográfica entres las reducciones franciscanas y jesuíticas de guaraníes." *Revista Complutense de Historia de América* 21 (1995): 71–83.

———. "Las encomiendas en la misiones jesuíticas." *Folia Histórica del Nordeste* 6 (1984): 119–37.

———. *Misiones del Paraguay: conflictos y disolución de la sociedad guarani (1768–1850).* Madrid: Editorial MAPFRE, 1992.

———. "Un desconocido pueblo de desertores Guaraníes en el Iberá (1736)." *Folia histórica del nordeste* 1, no. 1 (1974): 101–7.

Mangan, Jane E. *Trading Roles: Gender, Ethnicity, and the Urban Economy in Colonial Potosí.* Durham, NC: Duke University Press, 2005.

———. *Transatlantic Obligations: Creating the Bonds of Family in Conquest-Era Peru and Spain*. New York: Oxford University Press, 2016.

Mann, Charles C. *1491: New Revelations of the Americas before Columbus*. New York: Knopf, 2005.

Martínez Lemoine, René. *El modelo clásico de ciudad colonial hispanoamericana: ensayo sobre los orígenes del urbanismo en América*. Santiago: Universidad de Chile, 1977.

Mathieu, James R., and Daniel A. Meyer. "Comparing Axe Heads of Stone, Bronze, and Steel: Studies in Experimental Archaeology." *Journal of Field Archaeology* 24, no. 3 (1997): 333–51.

Matthew, Laura E. *Memories of Conquest: Becoming Mexicano in Colonial Guatemala*. Chapel Hill: University of North Carolina Press, 2012.

Matthew, Laura E., and Michel R. Oudijk, eds. *Indian Conquistadors: Indigenous Allies in the Conquest of Mesoamerica*. Norman: University of Oklahoma Press, 2007.

Mayo, Carlos A. "Los pobleros del Tucuman colonial: contribución al estudio de los mayordomos y administradores de encomienda en América." *Revista de Historia de América* 85 (1978): 27–57.

McEnroe, Sean F. "A Sleeping Army: The Military Origins of Interethnic Civic Structures on Mexico's Colonial Frontier." *Ethnohistory* 59, no. 1 (2012): 109–39.

McKinley, Michelle. "Fractional Freedoms: Slavery, Legal Activism, and Ecclesiastical Courts in Colonial Lima, 1593–1689." *Law and History Review* 28, no. 3 (2010): 749–90.

Meléndez, Guillermo, ed. *Levantamientos indígenas ante los abusos de la encomienda en Paraguay*. San Jose: Editorial Departamento Ecuménico de Investigaciones, 1992.

Melgarejo, Angélica Otazú. *Práctica y semántica en la evangelización de los Guaraníes del Paraguay (S. XVI-XVIII)*. Asunción: Centro de Estudios Paraguayos "Antonio Guasch," 2006.

Melià, Bartomeu, ed. *El primer sínodo del Paraguay y Río de la Plata en Asunción en el año de 1603*. Asunción: Centro de Estudios Paraguayos "Antonio Guasch": Missionsprokur Nürnberg, 2003.

———. *La lengua guaraní en el Paraguay colonial: que contiene la creación de un lenguaje cristiano en las reducciones de los guaraníes en el Paraguay*. Asunción: CEPAG: Distribuidora Montoya, 2003.

Memmi, Albert. *The Colonizer and the Colonized*. Boston: Beacon Press, 1991.

Merrell, James H. *The Indians' New World: Catawbas and Their Neighbors from European Contact through the Era of Removal*. New York: Norton, 1991.

Mesgravis, Laima. "De bandeirante a fazendeiro: Aspectos da vida social e econômica em São Paulo colonial." In *História da cidade de São Paulo: A cidade colonial*, edited by Paula Porta. São Paulo: Editora Paz e Terra, 2004.

Metcalf, Alida C. *Go-Betweens and the Colonization of Brazil, 1500–1600*. Austin: University of Texas Press, 2005.

Métraux, Alfred. "The Revolution of the Ax." *Diogenes* 25 (1959): 28–40.

Millé, Andrés. *Crónica de la Orden Franciscana en la conquista del Perú, Paraguay y el Tucumán y su Convento del antiguo Buenos Aires, 1612–1800.* Buenos Aires: Emecé Editores, 1961.

Miller, Joseph C. *The Problem of Slavery as History: A Global Approach.* New Haven, CT: Yale University Press, 2012.

Mills, Kenneth. *Idolatry and Its Enemies: Colonial Andean Religion and Extirpation, 1640–1750.* Princeton, NJ: Princeton University Press, 1997.

Mirafuentes Galván, José Luis. "Las tropas de indios auxiliares: conquista, contrainsurgencia y rebelión en Sonora." *Estudios de Historia Novohispana* 13 (1993): 93–114.

Molina, Raul. "La obra franciscana en el Paraguay." *Missionalia Hispanica* 11, no. 33 (1954): 485–521.

Monteiro, John M. "Dos campos de Piritininga ao Morro da Saudade: a presença indígena na história de São Paulo." In *História da cidade de São Paulo: a cidade colonial,* edited by Paula Porta. São Paulo: Editora Paz e Terra, 2004.

———. "From Indian to Slave: Forced Native Labour and Colonial Society in Sao Paulo during the Seventeenth Century." *Slavery and Abolition* 9, no. 2 (1988): 105–27.

———. *Negros da terra: índios e bandeirantes nas origens de São Paulo.* São Paulo: Companhia das Letras, 1994.

Mora Mérida, José Luis. *Historia social de Paraguay, 1600–1650.* Seville, Spain: Escuela de Estudios Hispano-Americanos, 1973.

Morales, Martín M. "Los comienzos de la reducciones de la Provincia del Paraguay en relación con el derecho indiano y el Instituto de la Companía de Jesús, evolución y conflictos." *Archivum Historicum Societatis* 67 (1998): 3–129.

Mörner, Magnus. *The Political and Economic Activities of the Jesuits in the La Plata Region: The Hapsburg Era.* Stockholm: Victor Pettersons Bokindustri Aktiebolag, 1953.

Morse, Richard M., ed. *The Bandeirantes: The Historical Role of the Brazilian Pathfinders.* New York: Knopf, 1965.

Mumford, Jeremy Ravi. *Vertical Empire: The General Resettlement of Indians in the Colonial Andes.* Durham, NC: Duke University Press, 2012.

Mundy, Barbara E. *The Death of Aztec Tenochtitlan, the Life of Mexico City.* Austin: University of Texas Press, 2015.

Murillo, Dana Velasco. *Urban Indians in a Silver City: Zacatecas, Mexico, 1546–1810.* Stanford, CA: Stanford University Press, 2016.

Murillo, Dana Velasco, Mark Lentz, Margarita R. Ochoa, eds. *City Indians in Spain's American Empire: Urban Indigenous Society in Colonial Mesoamerica and Andean South America, 1530–1810.* Portland: Sussex Academic Press, 2012.

Murray, David. *Indian Giving: Economies of Power in Indian-White Exchanges.* Amherst: University of Massachusetts Press, 2000.

Nacuzzi, Lidia Rosa. *Identidades impuestas: tehuelches, aucas y pampas en el norte de la Patagonia.* Buenos Aires: Sociedad Argentina de Antropologia, 1998.

Nacuzzi, Lidia Rosa, Carina Paula Lucaioli, and Florencia Sol Nesis. *Pueblos nómades en un estado colonial: Chaco, Pampa, Patagonia, siglo XVIII*. Buenos Aires: Editorial Antropofagia, 2008.

Nair, Stella. *At Home with the Sapa Inca: Architecture, Space, and Legacy at Chinchero*. Austin: University of Texas Press, 2015.

Necker, Louis. *Indiens Guarani et chamanes franciscains: les premières réductions du Paraguay 1580–1800*. Paris: Anthropos, 1979.

———. *Indios Guaraníes y chamanes franciscanos: las primeras reducciones del Paraguay, 1580–1800*. Asunción: Centro de Estudios Antropológicos, Universidad Católica, 1990.

———. "La reacción de los guaraníes frente a la conquista española del Paraguay; movimientos de resistencia indigena (siglo XVI)." *Suplemento Antropológico* 18, no. 1 (1983): 7–30.

Neumann, Eduardo. "A lança e as cartas: escrita indígena e conflito nas reduções do Paraguai, século XVIII." *História Unisinos* 2, no. 2 (2007): 160–72.

———. "Fronteira e identidade: confrontos luso-guarani na Banda Oriental, 1680–1757." *Revista complutense de Historia de America* 26 (2000): 67–92.

———. "'Mientras volaban correos por los pueblos': autogoverno e práticas letradas nas missões guaraní, século XVIII." *Horizontes Antropológicos* 10, no. 22 (2004): 93–119.

———. *O trabalho guarani missioneiro no Rio da Prata colonial, 1640/1750*. Porto Alegre, Brazil: Martins Livreiro, 1996.

Nickson, Andrew. "Governance and the Revitalization of the Guaraní Language in Paraguay." *Latin American Research Review* 44, no. 3 (2009): 3–26.

Nimuendajú, Curt Unkel. *The Eastern Timbira*. Los Angeles: University of California Press, 1946.

———. *Los mitos de creación y de destrucción del mundo como fundamentos de la religión de los Apapokuva-Guaraní*. Lima: Centro Amazónico de Antropología y Aplicación Práctica, 1978.

Orantin, Mickaël. "Remarques sur le verbe 'vendre': dire l'échange marchand en guarani dans les missions jésuites du Paraguay (XVIIe-XVIIIe siècle)." *L'homme* 233 (2020): 75–104.

Orozco, Sebastián de Covarrubias. *Tesoro de la lengua castellana, o española*. Madrid: Luís Sánchez, 1611.

Ortiz, Fernando. *Cuban Counterpoint: Tobacco and Sugar*. 1940. Reprint, Durham, NC: Duke University Press, 1995.

Osorio, Alejandra B. *Inventing Lima : Baroque Modernity in Peru's South Sea Metropolis*. New York: Palgrave Macmillan, 2008.

Osowski, Edward W. *Indigenous Miracles: Nahua Authority in Colonial Mexico*. Tucson: University of Arizona Press, 2010.

O'Toole, Rachel Sarah. "The Bonds of Kinship, the Ties of Freedom in Colonial Peru." *Journal of Family History* 42, no. 1 (2017): 3–21.

———. *Bound Lives: Africans, Indians, and the Making of Race in Colonial Peru*. Pittsburgh: University of Pittsburgh Press, 2012.

Owensby, Brian Philip. "'As Currency in These Realms:' Women, Exchange, and Gain in Early-Colonial Paraguay." Paper presented at the annual Ethnohistory meeting, Oaxaca, Mexico, October 13, 2018.

———. *Empire of Law and Indian Justice in Colonial Mexico*. Stanford, CA: Stanford University Press, 2008.

Pagden, Anthony. *The Fall of Natural Man: The American Indian and the Origins of Comparative Ethnology*. Cambridge: Cambridge University Press, 1982.

Pastore, Carlos. *La lucha por la tierra en el Paraguay*. Montevideo: Editorial Antequera, 1972.

Pastore, Mario. "Taxation, Coercion, Trade and Development in a Frontier Economy: Early and Mid-colonial Paraguay." *Journal of Latin American Studies* 29 (1997): 329–54.

Patterson, Orlando. *Slavery and Social Death: A Comparative Study*. Cambridge, MA: Harvard University Press, 1982.

Paz, Octavio. *The Labyrinth of Solitude*. New York: Grove, 1961.

Phelan, John Leddy. "Authority and Flexibility in the Spanish Imperial Bureaucracy." *Administrative Science Quarterly* 5 (1960): 47–65.

Pla, Josefina. *Hermano negro: la esclavitud en el Paraguay*. Madrid: Paraninfo, 1972.

Pompa, Cristina. *Religião como tradução: missionários, Tupi e Tapuia no Brazil colonial*. São Paulo: EDUSC, 2002.

Potthast-Jutkeit, Barbara. *"Paraíso de Mahoma" o "país de las mujeres?": el rol de la familia en la sociedad paraguaya del siglo XIX*. Asunción: Instituto Cultural Paraguayo-Alemán, 1986.

Powell, Philip Wayne. *Soldiers, Indians, & Silver: the Northward Advance of New Spain, 1550–1600*. Berkeley: University of California Press, 1952.

Powers, Karen Vieira. *Andean Journeys: Migration, Ethnogenesis, and the State in Colonial Quito*. Albuquerque: University of New Mexico Press, 1995.

———. *Women in the Crucible of Conquest: The Gendered Genesis of Spanish American Society, 1500–1600*. Albuquerque: University of New Mexico Press, 2005.

Puente Brunke, José de la. *Encomienda y encomenderos en el Perú: estudio social y político de una institución colonial*. Seville, Spain: Excma. Diputación Provincial de Sevilla, 1992.

Quarleri, Lía. *Rebelión y guerra en las fronteras del Plata: guaraníes, jesuitas, e imperios coloniales*. Buenos Aires: Fondo de Cultura Económica, 2009.

Quevedo, Roberto. "La Asunción de mil seiscientos en dos padrones inéditos." *Historia paraguaya* 8 (1965): 96–127.

Rappaport, Joanne. *The Disappearing Mestizo: Configuring Difference in the Colonial New Kingdom of Granada*. Durham, NC: Duke University Press, 2014.

Restall, Matthew, ed. *Beyond Black and Red: African-Native Relations in Colonial Latin America*. Albuquerque: University of New Mexico Press, 2005.

————. "Black Conquistadors: Armed Africans in Early Spanish America." *Americas* 57, no. 2 (2000): 171–205.

————. *The Black Middle: Africans, Mayas, and Spaniards in Colonial Yucatan.* Stanford, CA: Stanford University Press, 2009.

————. "The New Conquest History." *History Compass* 10, no. 2 (2012): 151–60.

————. *Seven Myths of the Spanish Conquest.* New York: Oxford University Press, 2004.

Restall, Matthew, and Kris Lane. *Latin America in Colonial Times.* Cambridge: Cambridge University Press, 2011.

Richter, Daniel K. *Before the Revolution: America's Ancient Pasts.* Cambridge, MA: Harvard University Press, 2011.

Rípodas Ardanaz, Daisy. "Movimientos shamánicos de liberacíon entre los Guaraníes (1545–1660)." *Teología* 50 (1987): 245–75.

Roller, Heather F. *Amazonian Routes: Indigenous Mobility and Colonial Communities in Northern Brazil.* Stanford, CA: Stanford University Press, 2014.

Romero Jensen, Carlos Ernesto. *El Guairá, caída y éxodo.* Asunción: Academia Paraguaya de la Historia, 2009.

Roulet, Florencia. *La resistencia de los guaraní del Paraguay a la conquista española, 1537–1556.* Posadas: Editorial Universitaria, Universidad Nacional de Misiones, 1993.

Rousseau, Jean-Jacques. *A Discourse on Inequality.* 1755. Reprint, New York: Philosophical Library, 2016.

Rubio, Julián María. *Exploración y conquista del Río de la Plata, siglos XVI y XVII.* Barcelona: Salvat Editores, 1942.

Rushforth, Brett. *Bonds of Alliance: Indigenous and Atlantic Slaveries in New France.* Chapel Hill: University of North Carolina Press, published for the Omohundro Institute of Early American History and Culture, 2012.

Saeger, James Schofield. *The Chaco Mission Frontier: The Guaycuruan Experience.* Tucson: University of Arizona Press, 2000.

————. "Survival and Abolition: The Eighteenth Century Paraguayan Encomienda." *Americas* 38, no. 1 (1981): 59–85.

————. "Warfare, Reorganization, and Readaptation at the Margins of Spanish Rule: The Chaco and Paraguay (1573–1882)." In *The Cambridge History of the Native Peoples of the Americas.* Cambridge: Cambridge University Press, 1999.

Sahlins, Peter. *Boundaries: The Making of France and Spain in the Pyrenees.* Berkeley: University of California Press, 1991.

Salas, Fr. José Luis. "Villa Rica y los Franciscanos: memoria de cuatro siglos caminando juntos." *Historia Paraguaya* 42 (2002): 79–122.

Salinas, María Laura. *Dominación colonial y trabajo indígena: un estudio de la encomienda en Corrientes colonial.* Asunción: Universidad Católica Nuestra Señora de la Asunción, 2010.

————. "Liderazgos indígenas en las misiones jesuíticas. Títulos de capitanes concedidos a los caciques guaraníes en el siglo XVII." *Folia Histórica del Nordeste* 16 (2006): 267–75.

———. "Reclamos y multas en pueblos de indios: la visita de Garabito de León a Corrientes. Río de la Plata, 1649–1653." *Revista Historia y Justicia* 3 (2014): 195–227.

———. "Vida y trabajo en la misión. Jesuitas y franciscanos en perspectiva comparada, siglo XVII." *XIII Jornadas Internacionales sobre las Misiones Jesuíticas* (2010): 223–46.

Salinas, María Laura, and Pedro Miguel Omar Svriz Wucherer. "Liderazgo Guaraní en tiempos de paz y de guerra. Los caciques en las reducciones Franciscanas y Jesuíticas, siglos XVII y XVIII." *Revista de Historia Militar* 55, no. 110 (2011): 113–51.

Salomon, Frank. "Indian Women of Early Colonial Quito as Seen through Their Testaments." *Americas* 44 (1988): 325–41.

Santos, María Cristina. "Clastres e Susnik: uma traducão do 'Guaraní do papel.'" In *Missoes Guaraní: Impacto Na Sociedad Contemporanea*, edited by Regina A. F. Gadelha, 205–20. São Paulo: EDUC, 1999.

Santos-Granero, Fernando. *Vital Enemies: Slavery, Predation, and the Amerindian Political Economy of Life*. Austin: University of Texas Press, 2009.

Sarreal, Julia. "Caciques as Placeholders in the Guaraní Missions of Eighteenth Century Paraguay." *Colonial Latin American Review* 23, no. 2 (2014): 224–51.

———. "Globalization and the Guarani: From Missions to Modernization in the Eighteenth Century." PhD diss., Harvard University, 2009.

———. *The Guaraní and Their Missions: A Socioeconomic History*. Stanford, CA: Stanford University Press, 2014.

———. "Revisiting Cultivated Agriculture, Animal Husbandry, and Daily Life in the Guaraní Missions." *Ethnohistory* 60, no. 1 (2013): 101–24.

———. "Yerba Mate: From Indigenous Good to a Tool of Empire." Working paper, Río de la Plata Working Group, William and Mary College, March 2017.

Schaden, Egon. *Aspectos fundamentais da cultura guaraní*. São Paulo: Difusão Européia do Livro, 1962.

Schiavetto, Solange Nunes de Oliveira. *A arqueologia guarani: construção e desconstrução da identidade indígena*. São Paulo: FAPESP, 2003.

Schroeder, Susan. "Introduction: The Genre of Conquest Studies." In *Indian Conquistadors: Indigenous Allies in the Conquest of Mesoamerica*, edited by Laura E. Matthew and Michel R. Oudijk, 5–27. Norman: University of Oklahoma Press, 2007.

Schultz, Kara D. "'The Kingdom of Angola is Not Very Far from Here': The South Atlantic Slave Port of Buenos Aires, 1585–1640." *Slavery and Abolition* 36, no. 3 (2015): 424–44.

Schwaller, John Frederick. *The Church and Clergy in Sixteenth-Century Mexico*. Albuquerque: University of New Mexico Press, 1987.

———. "Mercedarians." In *Encyclopedia of Latin American History and Culture*, 485–86. New York: Charles Scribner's Sons, 2008.

Schwaller, John Frederick, and Helen Nader. *The First Letter from New Spain: The Lost Petition of Cortés and His Company, June 20, 1519*. Austin: University of Texas Press, 2014.

Schwaller, Robert C. "'For Honor and Defense': Race and the Right to Bear Arms in Early Colonial Mexico." *Colonial Latin American Review* 21, no. 2 (2012): 239–66.

——. *Géneros De Gente in Early Colonial Mexico: Defining Racial Difference.* Norman: University of Oklahoma Press, 2016.

Scott, James C. *Weapons of the Weak: Everyday Forms of Peasant Resistance.* New Haven, CT: Yale University Press, 1985.

Seed, Patricia. "Social Dimensions of Race: Mexico City, 1753." *Hispanic American Historical Review* 62, no. 4 (1982): 569–606.

Service, Elman R. "The Encomienda in Paraguay." *Hispanic American Historical Review* 31, no. 2 (1951): 230–52.

——. *Spanish-Guaraní Relations in Early Colonial Paraguay.* Ann Arbor: University of Michigan Press, 1954.

Shapiro, Judith. "From Tupã to the Land without Evil: The Christianization of Tupi-Guarani Cosmology." *American Ethnologist* 14 (1987): 126–39.

Sherman, William L. *Forced Native Labor in Sixteenth-Century Central America.* Lincoln: University of Nebraska Press, 1979.

Silverblatt, Irene Marsha. *Moon, Sun, and Witches: Gender Ideologies and Class in Inca and Colonial Peru.* Princeton, NJ: Princeton University Press, 1987.

Simpson, Lesley Byrd. *The Encomienda in New Spain: The Beginning of Spanish Mexico.* Berkeley: University of California Press, 1982.

Sleeper-Smith, Susan. *Indian Women and French Men: Rethinking Cultural Encounter in the Western Great Lakes.* Amherst: University of Massachusetts Press, 2001.

Soares, Andres Luís R. *Guaraní: organização social e arqueologia.* Porto Alegre, Brazil: EDIPUCRS, 1997.

Socolow, Susan Migden. "Spanish Captives in Indian Societies: Cultural Contact along the Argentine Frontier, 1600–1835." *Hispanic American Historical Review* 72, no. 1 (1992): 73–99.

Spalding, Karen. *Huarochiri: An Andean Society under Inca and Spanish Rule.* Stanford, CA: Stanford University Press, 1988.

Stern, Steve J. "Paradigms of Conquest: History, Historiography, and Politics." *Journal of Latin American Studies* 24 (1992): 1–34.

——. *Peru's Indian Peoples and the Challenge of Spanish Conquest: Huamanga to 1640.* Madison: University of Wisconsin Press, 1993.

Stoler, Ann Laura. "Tense and Tender Ties: The Politics of Comparison in North American History and (Post) Colonial Studies." *Journal of American History* 88, no. 3 (2001): 829–65.

Susnik, Branislava. *El indio colonial del Paraguay.* Asunción: Museo Etnográfico "Andrés Barbero, 1965.

——. *El indio colonial del Paraguay.* Asunción: Secretaría Nacional de Cultura, 2011.

——. *El rol de los indígenas en la formación y en la vivencia del Paraguay.* Asunción: Instituto Paraguayo de Estudios Nacionales, 1982.

——. *Los aborígenes del Paraguay.* Asunción: Museo Etnográfico Andrés Barbero, 1978.

———. "Ni indio, ni española. La identidad ambigua de la elite colonial paraguaya." In *Muchas hispanoamericas: antropologia, historia y enfoques culturales en los estudios latinoamericanistas*, edited by Thomas Kruggeler and Ulrich Mucke, 131–50. Madrid: Iberoamericana, 2001.

———. *Una visión socio-antropológica del Paraguay, XVI-1/2 XVII*. Asunción: Museo Etnográfico Andrés Barbero, 1993.

———. *Una visión socio-antropológica del Paraguay del siglo XVIII*. Asunción: Museo Etnográfico Andrés Barbero, 1991.

Svriz Wucherer, Pedro Miguel Omar. "Jesuitas, guaraníes y armas. Milicias Guaraníes frente a los indios del Gran Chaco." *História Unisinos* 15, no. 2 (2011): 281–93.

———. *Un levantamiento indígena en las fronteras imperiales. La rebelión de Arecayá (1660)*. Editorial Academica Española, 2017.

Sweet, James H. *Recreating Africa: Culture, Kinship, and Religion in the African-Portuguese World, 1441–1770*. Chapel Hill: University of North Carolina Press, 2003.

Takeda, Kazuhisa. "Las milicias Guaraníes en las misiones jesuíticas del Río de la Plata: un ejemplo de la transferencia organizativa y tácticas militares de España a su territorio de ultramar en la primera época moderna." *Revista de Historia Social y de las Mentalidades* 20, no. 2 (2016): 33–72.

Tavárez, David. *The Invisible War: Indigenous Devotions, Discipline, and Dissent in Colonial Mexico*. Stanford, CA: Stanford University Press, 2011.

———, ed. *Words & Worlds Turned Around: Indigenous Christianities in Colonial Latin America*. Boulder: University Press of Colorado, 2017.

Telesca, Ignacio. "Esclavitud en Paraguay: las estancias jesuíticas." In *La ruta del esclavo en el Río de la Plata: aportes para el diálogo intercultural*, edited by Marisa Pineau, 153–72. Argentina: Editorial de la Universidad Nacional de Tres de Febrero, 2011.

———. *La provincia del Paraguay, revolución y transformación, 1680–1780*. Asunción: El Lector, 2010.

———. "Paraguay en el centenario: la creación de la nación mestiza." *Historia Mexicana* 60, no. 1 (2010): 137–95.

———. *Tras los expulsos: cambios demográficos y territoriales en el Paraguay después de la expulsión de los jesuitas*. Asunción: Universidad Católica Nuestra Señora de la Asunción, 2009.

Terraciano, Kevin. *The Mixtecs of Colonial Oaxaca: Ñudzahui History, Sixteenth through Eighteenth Centuries*. Stanford, CA: Stanford University Press, 2001.

Thomaz de Almeida, Rubem Ferreira, and Fabio Mura. "Historia y territorio entre los Guarani de Matto Grosso do Sur, Brasil." *Revista de Indias* 64, no. 230 (2004): 55–66.

Thurner, Mark. *From Two Republics to One Divided: Contradictions of Postcolonial Nationmaking in Andean Peru*. Durham, NC: Duke University Press, 1997.

Townsend, Camilla. *Malintzin's Choices: An Indian Woman in the Conquest of Mexico*. Albuquerque: University of New Mexico Press, 2006.

Tuer, Dorothy Jane. "Old Bones and Beautiful Words: The Spiritual Contestation between Shaman and Jesuit in the Guaraní Missions." In *Colonial Saints: Discovering the Holy in the Americas, 1500–1800*, edited by Allan Greer and Jodi Bilinkoff, 77–98. New York: Routledge, 2002.

———. "Tigers and Crosses: The Transcultural Dynamics of Spanish-Guaraní Relations in the Río De La Plata: 1516–1580." PhD diss., University of Toronto, 2011.

Turner, Terence. "The Kayapo of Central Brazil." In *Face Values: Some Anthropological Themes*, edited by Anne Sutherland, 245–79. London: British Broadcasting Corporation, 1978.

Twinam, Ann. *Public Lives, Private Secrets: Gender, Honor, Sexuality, and Illegitimacy in Colonial Spanish America*. Stanford, CA: Stanford University Press, 1999.

———. *Purchasing Whiteness: Pardos, Mulattos, and the Quest for Social Mobility in the Spanish Indies*. Stanford, CA: Stanford University Press, 2015.

van Deusen, Nancy E. "Diasporas, Bondage, and Intimacy in Lima, 1535 to 1555." *Colonial Latin American Review* 19, no. 2 (2010): 247–77.

———. *Global Indios: The Indigenous Struggle for Justice in Sixteenth-Century Spain*. Durham, NC: Duke University Press, 2015.

———. "The Intimacies of Bondage: Female Indigenous Servants and Slaves and Their Spanish Masters, 1492–1555." *Journal of Women's History* 24, no. 1 (2013): 13–43.

Velázquez, Rafael Eladio. "Carácteres de la encomienda paraguaya en los siglos XVII y XVIII." *Historia paraguaya* 19 (1982): 113–63.

———. *La rebelión de los indios de Arecaya, en 1660*. Asunción: Centro Paraguayo de Estudios Sociológicos, 1965.

———. "Organización militar de la governación y capitanía general del Paraguay." *Estudios Paraguayos* 5, no. 1 (1977): 25–69.

Vélez, Karin. "'By Means of Tigers': Jaguars as Agents of Conversion in Jesuit Mission Records of Paraguay and the Moxos, 1600–1768." *Church History* 84, no. 4 (2015): 768–806.

Vianna, Helio, ed. *Jesuitas e bandeirantes no Uruguai (1611–1750)*. Rio de Janeiro: Biblioteca Nacional, 1970.

Vinson III, Ben. *Bearing Arms for His Majesty: The Free-Colored Militia in Colonial Mexico*. Stanford, CA: Stanford University Press, 2001.

Vinson III, Ben, and Matthew Restall. "Black Soldiers, Native Soldiers: Meanings of Military Service in the Spanish American Colonies." In *Beyond Black and Red: African-Native Relations in Colonial Latin America*, edited by Matthew Restall. Albuquerque: University of New Mexico Press, 2005.

Viveiros de Castro, Eduardo. *A inconstância da alma selvagem e outros ensaios de antropologia*. São Paulo: Cosac & Naify, 2002.

———. *From the Enemy's Point of View: Humanity and Divinity in an Amazonian Society*. Chicago: University of Chicago Press, 1992.

———. *The Inconstancy of the Indian Soul: The Encounter of Catholics and Cannibals in Sixteenth-Century Brazil*. Chicago: Prickly Paradigm Press, 2011.

Voss, Barbara L. *The Archaeology of Ethnogenesis: Race and Sexuality in Colonial San Francisco*. Berkeley: University of California Press, 2008.

Wagley, Charles, and Eduardo Galvão. "O parentesco tupí-guaraní." *Boletim do Museo Nacional, Nova Série* 6 (1946): 1–23.

Weber, Max. *Politics as a Vocation*. Philadelphia: Fortress Press, 1965.

Wheat, David. *Atlantic Africa and the Spanish Caribbean, 1570–1640*. Chapel Hill: University of North Carolina Press for Omohundro Institute of Early American History and Culture, 2016.

Whigham, Thomas. *La yerba mate del Paraguay, 1780–1870*. Asunción: Centro Paraguayo de Estudios Sociológicos, 1991.

———. *The Politics of River Trade: Tradition and Development in the Upper Plata, 1780–1870*. Albuquerque: University of New Mexico Press, 1991.

Whitehead, Neil L. *Dark Shamans: Kanaimà and the Poetics of Violent Death*. Durham, NC: Duke University Press, 2002.

———. "Hans Staden and the Cultural Politics of Cannibalism." *Hispanic American Historical Review* 80, no. 4 (2000): 721–51.

Wilde, Guillermo. "Estrategias indigenas y límites étnicos. Las reducciónes jesuiticas del Paraguay como espacios socioculturales permeables." *Anuar IEHS* 22 (2007): 213–40.

———. "Les modalités indigènes de la dévotion. Identié religieuse, subjectivité et mémoire dans les frontières coloniales d'Amérique de Sud." In *Les Laïcs dans la mission: europe et Amériques XVI-XVIII siècles*, edited by Aliocha Maldavsky, 135–80. Tours, France: Presses Universitaires François-Rabelais de Tours, 2017.

———. "Prestigio indígena y nobleza peninsular: La invención de linajes guaraníes en las misiones del Paraguay." *Jahrbuch fur Geschichte Lateinamerikas* 43 (2006): 119–45.

———. *Religión y poder en las misiones de Guaraníes*. Buenos Aires: Editorial SB, 2009.

Worcester, Thomas, ed. *The Cambridge Companion to the Jesuits*. Cambridge: Cambridge University Press, 2008.

Yannakakis, Yanna. *The Art of Being In-Between: Native Intermediaries, Indian Identity, and Local Rule in Colonial Oaxaca*. Durham, NC: Duke University Press, 2008.

Zavala, Silvio Arturo. *El servicio personal de los indios en el Perú*. México: El Colegio de México, 1978.

———. *El servicio personal de los indios en la Nueva España*. México City: Colegio de México, 1984.

———. *Orígenes de la colonización en el Río de la Plata*. Mexico City: Colegio Nacional, 1977.